CCIE/CCNP SECURITY

SECURING NETWORKS WITH CISCO FIREPOWER (SNCF) 300-710

Volume II

Todd Lammle

Donald Robb

Aref Alsouqi CCIE #62163

About the Authors

Todd Lammle is the authority on Cisco certification and internetworking. He is a world-renowned author, speaker, trainer, and consultant and is Cisco certified in most Cisco certification categories.

Todd has over three decades of experience working with LANs, WANs, and large enterprise licensed and unlicensed wireless networks. Lately, he's been implementing advanced security technologies in large data centers and organizations in the USA and abroad with technologies including Cisco ISE, StealthWatch, and Cisco Firepower/FTD.

Todd's many years of real-world experience is evident in his writing. He isn't just another author—he's an accomplished networking engineer, having cultivated extensive practical experience working on some of the world's largest networks at companies like Xerox, Hughes Aircraft, Texaco, AAA, Cisco, and Toshiba, among many others.

Todd has published over 100 books, including the uber-popular *CCNA: Cisco Certified Network Associate Study Guide*, *CCNA Wireless Study Guide*, *CCNA Data*

Center Study Guide, SSFIPS Firepower Study Guide, Firepower 6.x Study Guide, and this dual Cisco CCNP Security Mastering Firepower volume, as well as many more.

Todd runs an international consulting and training company based in Coeur d'Alene, Idaho. He spends his free time with family, friends, and his two golden retrievers playing in the mountains, rivers, and lakes that surround his home.

You can reach Todd through his website and find more Firepower/FTD material, videos, and classes at `www.lammle.com`

Donald Robb, also known as the-packet-thrower online, has been the industry for over 15 years doing everything from help desk to network architect. He has worked in most areas of IT to an expert level including networking, security, collaboration, data center, wireless, and service providers. Currently he is a Principal Consultant for a major Cisco Value Added Reseller (VAR) and focuses on complex projects that usually involve several different technologies. He also acts as the company's Subject Matter Expert (SME) for Automation/DevOps, SDN, and Security topics.

During his time, he has worked with most of the big vendors and some of the smaller ones too and have earned many advanced certifications and specializations. These include most of the cloud certifications such as the Azure Solutions Architect Expert, most of the Cisco certifications, and some random ones across vendors like Fortinet, Palo Alto, and HPE. He is also recognized as a Cisco FireJumper proving his proficiency with Cisco's security solutions, and worked with Todd Lammle on several books and courses.

You can reach Donald through www.lammle.com or check out his YouTube channel at: https://www.youtube.com/c/ThePacketThrower

Aref Alsouqi has been in the industry for over 20 years doing everything from being a typist to a security architect. He has worked in most areas of IT to an expert level including help desk, infrastructure, networking, and security. His most known technical strengths are VPN, ISE, Firepower, AnyConnect and troubleshooting.

Currently he is a Security Technical Architect for one of the most awarded Cisco Gold partners in EMEA. He is based in the UK and focuses on complex networking and security projects. He also acts as a Technical Authority for some complex projects that usually involve several different technologies and vendors.

During his career, he has worked with most of the big vendors and have earned many advanced certifications and specializations. These include CCNP R&S, CCNP Security, Security Networks with Cisco Firepower Threat Defense NGFW 2.0, CompTIA Network+, CompTIA Security+, Designated VIP, and CCIE Security. His CCIE # is 62163.

Due to his known advanced skills and proficiency with Cisco's network and security solutions, he is also recognized by Cisco Learning Network as a Designated

VIP since 2015. He worked with Todd Lammle on this book and is working closely on other new projects with Todd Lammle as well.

You can reach Aref through www.lammle.com or check out his blog at: https://bluenetsec.com/blog/

Introduction

Cisco Firepower is an integral part of the suite of Cisco security products. There are Firepower managers and the various Firepower devices that are configured, managed, and monitored from the managers.

The devices are further categorized into Firepower appliances like 7000/8000s, which are all EOL, but there's a legion of SourceFire appliances out there, so Cisco still covers them in this exam for now.

In the figure below, you can see how the manager—an FMC in this example—sends configuration and Snort security policy out to the devices. The devices then make decisions about the packets traveling through them based upon the Snort Security policy and finally sends the Snort verdict back to the manager:

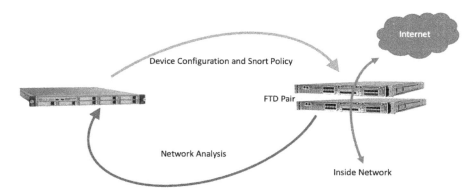

The new Adaptive Security Appliance (ASA), called Firepower Threat Defense (FTD), is definitely all the rage now! Even if you really just want to run plain, powerful ASA code, you'll want the new devices with their tremendous power and inspection throughput that can run either ASA or FTD code. So, the ASA code isn't going away anytime soon, although most people run FTD when they get the new devices.

I'm going to talk about the various Firepower managers in this introduction, but I'm only going to use one of them throughout the book—think exam objectives! The other Firepower devices will still be discussed thoroughly throughout this book though.

What Is This Book Really About?

Of course, we definitely penned this 2nd book with the additional CCNP Security SNCF objectives in mind, not covered in the 1st volume. Even so, we included a few chapters that go beyond the objectives and really dig deep into all my years of real-life Firepower experience, hence the new name Mastering Firepower!

The information in those is very valuable because it's based upon my real-world experience at hundreds of customers after installing well over 10,000 FTD devices in Fortune 50 and 500 companies all over the world.

We'll follow the Cisco FTD packet flow that took me quite a while to draw out because when I began working with this product, they didn't have FTD. Plus, when FTD finally made its appearance, it still took years for documentation worth reading to come out!

Whether you have a Firepower appliance (7000/8000), ASA with a FirePOWER module, or an FTD device, the Snort engine is basically the same for all models and configured mostly the same way through the FMC.

The figure below is based on FTD code, and you can tell because you can see the LINA engine, which is really the integrated base ASA code configured through the FMC. That's what makes the FTD different.

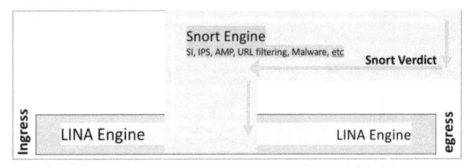

Based on packet traces and lots of network analysis, I was able to draw a really accurate packet flow for FTD that I'll use for reference throughout the book as we go through each policy.

I am well aware that the Cisco objectives also include the old, outdated Firepower appliances and they still follow the same flow, but only in the Snort process.

The appliances don't have a prefilter or LINA process at all, but that is the only difference.

You can see in the next drawing of the Ingress LINA process that the packets are delivered to the Snort process via a memory location. Then, after the packets traverse the Snort process, the Snort verdict is sent to the Lina egress for processing.

We'll be traveling through this drawing step-by-step in this book.

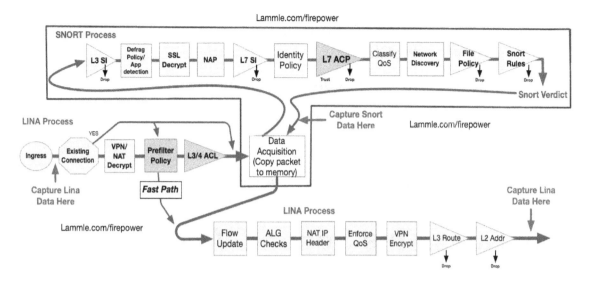

What Does the First Volume Cover?

You've learned, or should have learned, all of the following in the previous volume I book:

Introduction

Chapter 1: Firepower Management Center (FMC)

Chapter 2: Cisco Firepower Management Center (FMC) Configuration

Chapter 3: Firepower Management Center (FMC) Actions

Chapter 4: Licensing & Health Policy

Chapter 5: Chassis Manager

Chapter 6: Firepower Devices

Chapter 7: High Availability

Chapter 8: Objects

Chapter 9: Access Control Policy

Chapter 10: Malware and File Policy

Chapter 11: Firepower Network Discovery

Chapter 12: Intrusion Prevention System (IPS) Policy

Chapter 13: DNS Policy

Chapter 14: Prefilter

Chapter 15: Network Address Translation (NAT)

Chapter 16: Identity Policy

Chapter 17: User Management

Chapter 18: Advanced Network Analysis

What Does This Second Volume Cover?

Mastering Cisco Firepower: Securing Networks with Cisco Firepower (SNCF 300-710) Volume II Exam Objectives

So yes, of course this book is all about the objectives for the 300-710 exam. Still, I'm going to cover a lot more administration and troubleshooting than what's on the exam (Mastering Firepower!), so you can definitely use this book as a guide for your real-life network easily!

Here's the listing of objectives for Volume II, which is the foundation of the chapters in this book.

Exam Description

Securing Networks with Cisco Firepower v1.0 (SNCF 300-710) is a 90-minute exam associated with the CCNP Security and Cisco Certified Specialist - Network Security Firepower certifications.

In this CCNP Security SNCF series part II study guide, we will explore these important exam objectives and topics:

1.0 Deployment   **30%**

> **1.3.c Multi-instance**

2.0 Configuration   **30%**

> **2.2.f SSL**
>
> **2.3.b Application detectors (OpenAppID)**
>
> **2.3.c Correlation**
>
> **2.5.c VPN**
>
> **2.5.d QoS**
>
> **2.5.e Platform Settings**
>
> **2.5.f Certificates**

3.0 Management and Troubleshooting   **25%**

> **3.1 Troubleshoot with FMC CLI and GUI**
>
> **3.2 Configure dashboards and reporting in FMC**
>
> **3.3 Troubleshoot using packet capture procedures**

4.0 Integration   **15%**

> **4.3 Implement Threat Intelligence Director for third-party security intelligence feeds**
>
> **4.4 Describe using Cisco Threat Response for security investigations**
>
> **4.5 Describe Cisco FMC PxGrid Integration with Cisco Identify Services Engine (ISE)**
>
> **4.6 Describe Rapid Threat Containment (RTC) functionality within Firepower Management Center**

Chapter 19: Platform Settings

The CCNP Security SNCF exam objectives covered in this chapter are:

2.0 Configuration

> ***2.5 Configure devices using Firepower Management Center***

> ***2.5.e Platform Settings***

If you've used previous versions of Firepower, you're familiar with the System policy. Of course, few things tech remain the same for long and beginning in version 6, the System policy is no longer used for appliances. Now we have Platform Settings, with two different types of policies you can create: One for Firepower and one for Firepower Threat Defense (FTD).

You'd be partially right if you said that these policies replace the System policy because in previous versions, the System policy applied to FMC, formerly known as the Defense Center, as well as to the devices.

But today, Platform settings apply only to devices, so settings that applied only to the FMC have been removed. The FMC configuration is now only found under `System>Configuration`, which we covered already. The result is that the Platform settings policies are a bit smaller than the System policy used to be.

Firepower Platform Settings

So let's dive right in... From the FMC, navigate to `Devices>Platform Settings`. Since by default, there aren't any platform policies created, click the **New Policy** button in the upper right and select Firepower Settings to configure the settings for a 7000/8000 Appliance, ASA with Firepower, Meraki firewall, etc, basically anything but FTD.

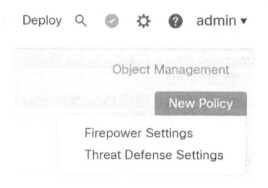

The default device settings will actually allow a managed device to function indefinitely with no changes, so as long as you don't care about things like the access list, external audit logging, the login banner, and so on, you really don't need to create this policy.

The thing is, most organizations will modify at least a few of the default settings to comply with security or audit standards. So let's check out the settings in the Firepower Platform policy now.

When you first create a policy, you'll be prompted for the name and the device targets. This is where the policy will be applied when you use the Deploy button in the main menu. After this you'll be presented with the list of settings shown here:

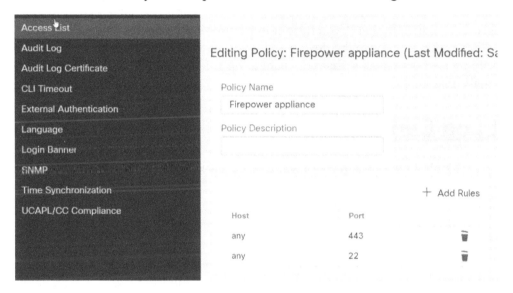

Access List

Same as with the Access List setting in the FMC System Configuration, this controls which IP addresses can access the management ports on the device. Keep in mind that even though port 443 is listed, if this policy is applied to a virtual device without a Web UI, it'll have no effect.

Audit Log

You need to complete this section if you want to send audit events to an external syslog or HTTP server. Audit events are generated for any logins/page views in the Web UI as well as any commands typed into the Cisco CLI via SSH or the console. One of these CLI commands is "`expert,`" which gives the user a Linux bash shell. Once the user arrives at this shell, commands won't be audited anymore.

Understand that in order to use the `expert` command, your users must have configuration access to the CLI because if you only set up users with basic CLI access, they won't be able to run configuration commands on the system or exit the CLI to a bash shell. You can configure the specific type of CLI access for a given user via the device's web interface or through the LDAP/RADIUS object if you're using external authentication.

If this is still worrying you, you can disable expert mode on a managed device to prevent any and all access to the bash command processor. Just disable expert mode from the device CLI with the command `system lockdown-sensor`.

Wait—*what*? Disable all access to bash? But if I disable expert mode on a device, I can't re-enable it, right? Well, true story that you can't re-enable expert mode, but Cisco TAC can help you if you need it to troubleshoot a device issue. Plus, you've got another option—reimage the device and revert to the original settings. The idea behind disabling access to bash is that you want to be able to audit all activity on the device and to make that happen you've got to eliminate the use of the non-auditable bash shell.

Audit Log Certificate

If your audit logging server supports Transport Layer Security (TLS), you can enable it here.

CLI Timeout

This setting has to do with the browser session and SSH shell timeouts. The defaults are shown in the next figure. If you need to modify these based on your organization's policies, do that here.

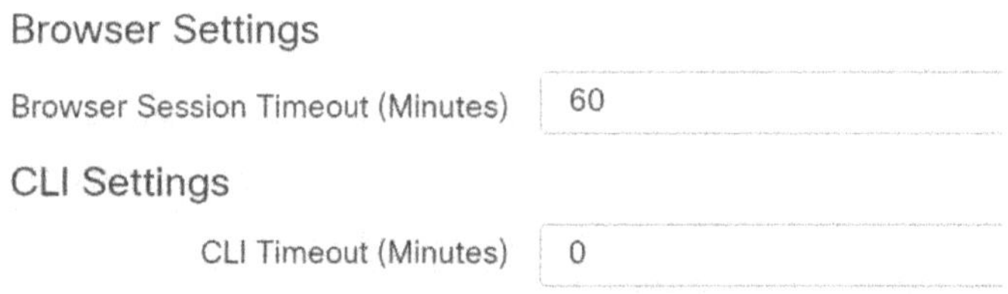

Browser Settings

Browser Session Timeout (Minutes)   60

CLI Settings

CLI Timeout (Minutes)   0

The Browser can be set up to 1440 minutes (24 hours), and the shell is set to infinity by default

External Authentication

Use these settings to enable authentication of users on the device from an external authentication source, (LDAP, RADIUS, etc.) To enable this feature, first set up an external authentication source under: `System>Users>External Authentication`. After this, you can return here and enable the external authentication method on your device(s).

Language

This is where you set the language—English, Japanese, two Chinese dialects and Korean.

Login Banner

We've already covered the login banner under the FMC System Configuration settings and it's the same thing here. This is text that'll display on the Web UI and the console prior to users logging in. Generally, it's a bunch of verbiage provided by your legal department that's standardized across the organization.

SNMP

An SNMP manager can be used to query the device for health status. Devices use a fairly standard Linux MIB (management information base) to define the types of information that can be queried. Remember, this is simply operating system/hardware data—we're not talking about event data here!

To enable, first select the SNMP version and then enter the appropriate community string or user information.

Time Synchronization

Keeping the time in sync across the devices and FMC is a pretty big deal because if the time is allowed to drift, events won't appear in the proper order on the FMC. This is because the event timestamp comes from the device's time where it was detected.

You have two options here. The device can get its time from the FMC or from an external NTP time source. The FMC is the default but pick the one that works best in your environment. Set your NTP on the FMC and leave this alone.

UCAPL/CC Compliance

These settings apply configurations to the device to make it compliant with the US Department of Defense Unified Capabilities Approved Products List (UCACL), or the ISO/IEC Common Criteria (CC). They're new in Version 6.

Changing them initially pops up a dialog warning you that they're nonreversible, If you continue to deploy the policy, the device will be rebooted.

You don't want to make these changes here unless you're absolutely positive you need to. Most of the time, these settings impose limitations to functionality, performance or both in the system that could ruin your whole day/week/month!

Threat Defense Platform Settings

If you're using FTD devices, there's a separate platform policy. Because the devices' ancestry includes the Cisco ASA, the settings are definitely different from the settings for Firepower devices.

A very important thing to understand here is that the security the ASA's had when you initially brought them up has completely vanished. Yep, you can now just merrily SSH to any interface, get SNMP info, even ping all interfaces by default and more! So, you definitely need to harden the device, which makes this policy the FTD's most important policy of all.

To get started, go to `System>Devices>Platform Settings`. By default, there are no platform policies created.

Click the **New Policy** button in the upper right and select Threat Defense Settings. You'll see the initial settings screen pictured here:

Let's go through each setting now.

ARP Inspection

This setting only applies to transparent mode FTD devices and the default setting for these devices is to allow Address Resolution Protocol (ARP) packets to pass through.

ARP Inspection
Banner
DNS
External Authentication
Fragment Settings
HTTP Access
ICMP Access
SSH Access
SMTP Server
SNMP
SSL
Syslog
Timeouts
Time Synchronization
Time Zone
UCAPL/CC Compliance

So basically, this setting allows you to control the flow of these packets. ARP Inspection comes in handy for preventing a notorious, malicious use of the ARP protocol known as ARP spoofing.

To enable ARP Inspection, click the Add button in the upper right to bring up the following dialog. (By the way, for this to work you must have Switched security zones on your device). Here's the ARP inspection dialog:

When you check the Inspect Enabled box and select the available switched zones, the device will filter ARP packets according the following criteria:

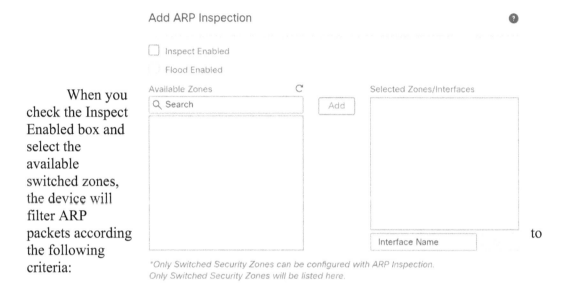

- If the IP address, MAC address and source interface match an ARP entry, the packet is passed through.
- If there's a mismatch between the MAC address, the IP address or the interface, then the Firepower Threat Defense device drops the packet.
- If the ARP packet doesn't match any entries in the static ARP table, you can set the Firepower Threat Defense device to either forward the packet out all interfaces (flood) or drop the packet.

Banner

This is a lot like the Login Banner setting on Firepower devices and the FMC, but it only applies to the CLI because there's no Web UI on an FTD device:

Something most people don't know is that you can use the variables **$(hostname)** or **$(domain)** to dynamically add the appropriate text to your device banner.

DNS

This is a new feature starting in v6.4 where your objects can resolve fully qualified domain names (FQDNs). The platform DNS settings here is only one part of the configuration for FQDNs:

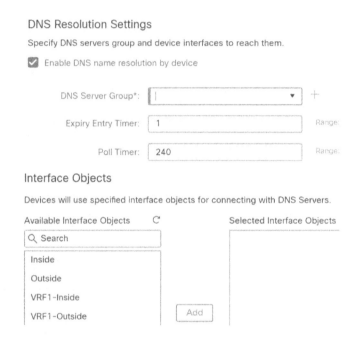

To start FQDN resolution, you've got to create a DNS Server Group in Objects. Once you've done that, the objects will show up in the DNS Server Group box.

External Authentication

Another sort of new feature is getting to enable external authentication when we SSH into our FTD devices. You don't configure anything here, you just enable what

you've created and are employing for external users of the FMC, which is configured in *System>Users*, and covered back in Chapter 17. Check it out:

So, once you create the external configuration, go to the FTD platform setting and enable the AD integration then redeploy.

Fragment Settings

This is where you control how fragmented IP packets are going to be handled. The default settings for Size, Chain and Timeout are shown below, and I recommend setting them all to one (1) because doing that disables all of them globally on all FTD interfaces the policy is applied to:

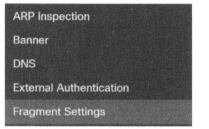

Here's a brief description list of the settings:

- Size (Block): The maximum number of fragments from all connections that can be waiting for reassembly.
- Chain (Fragment): The maximum number of packets into which a full IP packet can be fragmented. Set to 1 to disallow fragments.
- Timeout (Sec): The maximum number of seconds to wait for an entire fragmented datagram to arrive. If they're not received within this time, all fragments will be discarded.

The idea here is that FTD won't just allow any and all IP fragmentation to occur by default, which is actually a bad idea. Why? Just because there are legitimate reasons for packets to be fragmented, this process can be part of a denial of service (DoS) or even an attempt to evade detection, so it's really best to disable this on your Outside zone.

Here you can see all settings disabled globally for the FTD device:

Size (Block)	1	(1 - 30000)
Chain (Packet)	1	(1 - 8200)
Timeout (Sec)	1	(1 - 30)

I want to point out that the settings here become the defaults for all interfaces on the device, but they can still be overridden in the individual interface configuration.

Here, you can see the Inside interface and the global platform settings being overridden.

Typically, I will only allow only Inside zones or protected zones to perform fragment reassembly.

Edit Physical Interface

General   IPv4   IPv6   Advanced   Hardware Configuration

Information   ARP   Security Configuration

Enable Anti Spoofing: ☑

Allow Full Fragment Reassembly: ☑

Override Default Fragment Setting: ☑

Size:

200

(1 - 30000)

Chain:

24

(1 - 8200)

Time Out:

5

(1 - 30)

HTTP

The HTTP setting controls HTTPS access to interfaces on the FTD device. This doesn't mean the device actually has a web-based user interface because it doesn't when in an FMC. This connection is only for downloading PCAP files you've created by capturing traffic on the device.

The process you have to go through to make this happen is super long and involved and I'm just not going to get us lost in the weeds here. Just know that in summary, first you connect to the device CLI via SSH or some other way, then create a packet capture, and then connect using HTTPS to download the PCAP file.

Plus, there's just no reason to go through all that pain… If you've got an available TFTP, SCP or another supported server type, you can just copy the PCAP file from the device while you're still at the CLI! Downloading via HTTPS is another way to get this done and it doesn't require any other servers. You just painlessly browse to the device interface and grab the PCAP file—bam!

The configuration here is nice and minimal. First, you check the box to enable the HTTP server, confirm or change the port, then click the Add button.

In the IP Address field, select an existing network object to allow connections from that address. Then add the interfaces that you'd like to allow access for by selecting them from the Available Zones list—nice.

ICMP

This setting controls how the FTD device responds to Internet Control Message Protocol (ICMP) packets and the configuration is by all means an ICMP ACL for the FTD device. It's important to understand that ALL ICMP types are allowed by default on all FTD interfaces--something I've already mentioned. The issue here is that most companies wisely don't want their exposed interfaces responding to ping requests, but that's exactly what FTD interfaces do by default. So let's fix that!

By configuring rules here, you can limit ICMP to certain hosts, networks, or ICMP types. It's pretty straightforward: The main ICMP page allows us to set the rate limit for ICMPv4 unreachable messages from 1 to 100 per second. The default is 1 message per second and typically we'd go with that. Burst size isn't currently used by the system.

Okay, so you add ICMP rules by clicking the Add button. These rules are used to permit or deny specific ICMP services based on network, zone, ICMP type, and code.

Here's a sample configuration that I'll use to show you the ICMP ACL:

ICMP UnReachable

Rate Limit

| 1 |

(1 - 100)

Burst Size

| 1 |

(1 - 10)

Action	ICMP Service	Interface	Network
Deny	ICMP_Type_8	Outside	any-ipv4
Permit	ICMP_All_Types	Outside	any-ipv4

Now the way the rule set works is a lot like how any other access control list (ACL) works in that rules are evaluated from top to bottom. In the output above, you can see I left the ICMP UnReachable setting at the default, but added two rules.

The first is to deny any ICMP Type 8 packets on the Outside zone. Since this is an ICMP ACL, I'd probably want to add a permit rule or the default would be *deny icmp any any* on the interface, which is fine if that's what you want.

The second rule I added just allows all other ICMP packets. Even so, I just want to say that a lot of my clients just do what I pictured here, which effectively denies all ICMP packets on the Outside zone:

Secure Shell

As I've said again and again, the FTD devices have zero security on their interfaces by default, meaning anybody can attempt a SSH session on an interface so you definitely need to harden things. To do that, just choose your version, add the interface zones you want to be used and you're good!

Now, only someone from the Inside zone can SSH to the device:

Plus, you can now enable Secure Copy on the specified zone too—a really great new feature!

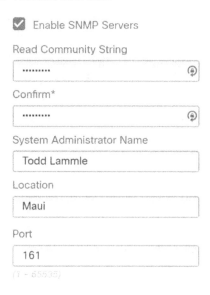

SMTP Server

This is a SMTP (Simple Network Management Protocol) server through which you can relay email messages configured for use only in the Syslog Platform configuration, so this should probably just be a subtab under Syslog.

SNMP

SNMP is provided to monitor the health and status of most of the FTD device's components. To configure access, just add the community string or user/password depending on the SNMP version like this:

Keep in mind that unlike Firepower appliances, which only provide read-only access, you can configure SNMP traps with FTD for things like SNMP authentication errors, link up/down, system restarts and so on:

Hosts	Users	SNMP Traps

Interface	Network	SNMP Version	Poll/Trap	Port
Inside	10.11.11.250	2c	Poll,Trap	162

Syslog

FTD offers hugely expanded syslog alerting capability compared to what Firepower used to offer, which was pretty weak. Previously, Firepower offered zero GUI configuration for remote syslog from the underlying operating system, meaning we had to hand edit the **/etc/syslog.conf** file. Thankfully, that's over and we can now configure detailed Syslog settings with FTD!

Here's a shot of the Syslog configuration page with some basic configuration. You'll need to add the settings for your network and syslog server configuration:

Logging Setup	Logging Destinations	Email Setup	Event Lists	Rate Limit	Syslog Settings	Syslog Servers

Basic Logging Settings

☐ Enable Logging

☐ Enable Logging on the failover standby unit

☐ Send syslogs in EMBLEM format

☐ Send debug messages as syslogs

Memory Size of the Internal Buffer

4096

(4096-52428800 Bytes)

Okay, from here you can configure a whole bunch of options like type of logging, destinations, email messages based upon severity, custom event lists, rate limits and more. Just remember you enable all the detailed Syslog ID's for your individual networks under the Syslog settings.

One important note is to take notice of the check box under Syslog Servers. It was unchecked until 6.4 code by default and can cause ALL sorts of havoc. The default configuration of Syslog servers is TCP 1470 instead of UDP 514, so PAY attention here.

Logging Setup	Logging Destinations	Email Setup	Event Lists	Rate Limit	Syslog Settings	Syslog Servers

☑ Allow user traffic to pass when TCP syslog server is down (Recommended to be enabled)

If your FTD device has stopped working and you just configured syslog and then deployed, check this setting first to make sure this box is checked!

Timeouts

This is where we implement the customization of timeout values for a list of common network conditions. Understand that I'm showing you a partial list but know that the defaults are pretty reasonable, and they're listed to the right of each setting. Also, keep in mind that if you didn't change these on your ASA's, you wouldn't change them here:

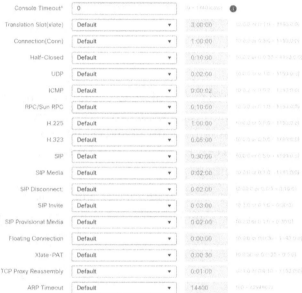

Time Synchronization

This is the same setting I mentioned earlier for Firepower devices. Keeping the time in sync across the devices and FMC is a pretty big deal because you don't want the time to drift. If it does, events won't appear in the right order because the event timestamp originates from the device's time where it was detected.

You have two options here: the device can get its time from the FMC or from an external NTP time source. The FMC is the default but pick the one that works best in your environment:

Set My Clock

⦿ Via NTP from Management Center

◯ Via NTP from

ⓘ This setting is unsupported on firepower 9300 and Firepower 4100 platforms.

The note in the previous figure is fairly self-explanatory... If you have a 9300 or 4100 device, the clock isn't set here and won't affect the FXOS Chassis Managers time because it has to be configured with its own NTP time source in the FXOS.

Time Zone

There's a Time Range object that can be configured in your ACP rules starting in code 6.5 for FTD devices. They've always had this Object, but it was only available for use in your Remote Access configurations. Now you can use them on a per-rule basis in your ACPs!

To make this work in a rule, you also need to add a global Time Range object. Configure this in your Platform settings for your FTD devices so all the devices are correctly sync'd:

UCAPL/CC Compliance

This is the same section and information as it was with Firepower. These settings apply configurations to the device to make it compliant with the US Department of Defense Unified Capabilities Approved Products List (UCACL) or the ISO/IEC Common Criteria (CC). These are new settings for version 6.

Changing them will first bring up a dialog warning you that they are nonreversible. If you continue, once you deploy the policy, the device will be rebooted.

Note that you should *not* make these changes unless you are *sure* you need to. Oftentimes these settings introduce limitations in functionality or performance in the system that could ruin your whole day/week or month!

Summary

In this chapter, we discussed the platform settings that are new for FTD. If you've used previous versions of Firepower, you're probably pretty familiar with the System policy that was used to configure both the FMC and appliances.

We covered two different types of policies you can create in this chapter: one for Firepower and one for Firepower Threat Defense (FTD).

Chapter 20: Firepower Domains

The CCNP Security SNCF exam objectives covered in this chapter are:

None, but very important exam information included!

I've got to tell you again that just because a subject isn't listed in the objectives, Cisco exams *can and will* ask you about any Firepower technology they feel like asking about! This is a "Mastering Firepower book", and that name is no accident. It covers everything you need to know to master this vital technology and Firepower Domains is no exception here!

Cisco Firepower Domains were created to allow multiple administrators to work on administrating their own environment. Cisco calls this "multitenancy", but it's important to understand that it still allows a Corporate Global domain to take precedence over anything the remote site domains have configured. This concept is called Leafs or Child.

To find exam study material like videos, downloadable supplemental material and practice questions, please head over to: www.lammle.com

---

Firepower Domains

So yes—the Firepower System allows for multitenancy, which means we get to implement multiple domains managed by multiple administrators. These domains segment user access to managed devices, configurations and events; they do NOT break up or segment your Cisco Firepower network in any way other than administratively. This is good! It gives us the flexibility to have many different administrators, which remain under the umbrella of the top global domain in your control. Keep in mind that your "tenant admins" do retain the ability to configure and manage their leaf and child devices.

When you log into the FMC, you log into a single domain called the current or Global domain and depending on your user account, you might be able to switch to other domains. In the past, you had to add a domain name to your user to login but not anymore.

In addition to any restrictions imposed by your user role, your current domain level can also limit your ability to modify various tasks like system software updates.

You must associate each managed device with a leaf domain and perform device management tasks from within the context of it. This means you'll be switching between domains a lot, especially when troubleshooting and doing network analysis.

Each leaf domain builds its own network map based upon the discovery data collected by its devices. Events reported by a managed device like connection, intrusion, malware and so on, are also associated with the device's leaf domain.

Domain Levels

You can create up to 100 subdomains under a top-level Global domain—up to two or three levels. But unless you want to make troubleshooting a huge challenge, you just won't configure so many domains.

One Domain Level: Global
If you don't configure domains (multitenancy), all devices, configurations and events belong to the Global domain, which in this scenario is also a leaf domain. Except for domain management, the system hides domain-specific configurations and analysis options until you add subdomains.

Two Domain Levels: Global and Second Level
In a two-level multidomain deployment, the Global domain has direct descendant domains only. This is the design people typically go with because it's straightforward, but still allows for one administrator per leaf domain without hassling with much.

This deployment is a good is a good way to go if you work for an ISP or someplace where you can log into as admin to the Global domain to manage all customers deployments.

Administrators for each customer can log into second level called subdomains and manage the devices, configurations and events applicable to their organizations *only*. These local administrators aren't allowed to view or affect any other customer's deployments on other domains or the global domain either.

Three Domain Levels: Global, Second Level, and Third Level
In a three-level multidomain deployment, the Global domain has subdomains plus an additional subdomain. Here again, if you work for an ISP or a good sized company, going with this approach lets you separately manage two classes of devices: devices placed on network edges and those placed internally. There are also two types of administrators:

- Administrators for the customer can log into a second-level subdomain to manage the customer's entire deployment.
- Administrators for the customer's edge network can log into a third level leaf domain to manage the devices deployed on the network edge only.

Another possibility here is to allow administrators for the customer's internal network to log into a different third-level domain for managing internal devices, configurations and events.

Domains Terminology

This is a great page to dog ear and refer back to whenever you need to moving through the rest of this chapter! Here are all the key terms describing domains and multidomain deployments:

Global Domain
In a multidomain deployment, this is the top-level and default domain. If you don't configure multitenancy, all devices, configurations and events belong to the Global domain. Administrators in the Global domain manage the entire Firepower System deployment.

Subdomain
A second or third-level domain.

Second-level domain
A child of the Global domain. Second-level domains can be leaf domains, or they can have subdomains.

Third-level domain
A child of a second-level domain. Third-level domains are always leaf domains.

Leaf domain
A domain with no subdomains. Each device must belong to a leaf domain.

Ancestor domain
A domain from which the current domain descends.

Descendant domain
A domain descending from the current domain in the hierarchy.

Child domain
A domain's direct descendant.

Parent domain
A domain's direct ancestor.

Sibling domain

A domain with the same parent.

Current domain
The domain you're logged into right now. The system displays the name of the current domain before your username at the top right of the web interface. Unless your user role is restricted, you can edit configurations in the current domain.

Creating Administrative Domains

So now that you've got the basic idea, let's create some domains, add leaf objects, and then create a hierarchical ACP to see how these domains behave.

1. To create domains, go to **System>Domains**.

2. Notice the user *admin* is listed with no domain at this time. This means it's in the Global domain, but you won't be able to see that until you create another domain.

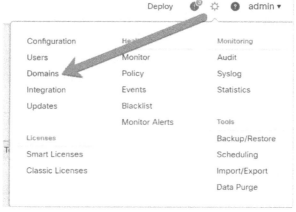

If you have an older code, then your screen would look like this:

3. Click on **Add Domain** to get it into the new domain.

4. Name your domain. The parent for the first domain would be Global, then add your device to the new domain, and click Save.

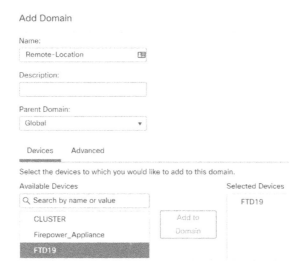

5. After you've added your domain and saved it, you'll get this message:

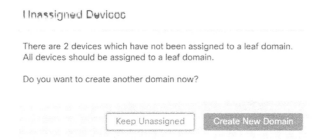

6. Now click on Create New Domain for as many leaf objects as you have. Know that you can't save the domains until all leaf objects have been assigned. You can put more than one leaf object into the same domain.

7. Your domains will look like this now, showing 3 devices in my example:

8. The next screen will ask if you want to inherit the current Firepower host/user database. Typically, you won't and if you don't want the current Firepower database of users and hosts on your new leaf domain, just click Save

For each parent domain, select a leaf domain to inherit the network map and events.
Select "None" to archive parent domain events and delete the old network map.

Parent Domain	Leaf Domain
Global	None ⌄

Save   Cancel

9. Before you can continue, you've got to redeploy your policies to your FTD devices.

Save Successful

 Domain configuration saved. You must deploy changes to affected devices. You may also want to apply an updated health policy.

OK

Creating Users for Leaf Domains

To have administrative domains, you need to create administrators for each leaf domain—the reason you created domains in the first place!

Look there in the upper right after deployment… you can see that I now have a *domain\name* listed. This way, you always know which domain you're in. Here it tells me I'm in *Global\admin*:

Deploy   Global \ admin ▾

Now, head over to **System>Users** and create all your administrators. Notice right there at the bottom, that you can create users for each of your domains now.

I created Bob as the administrator for the Remote Location domain:

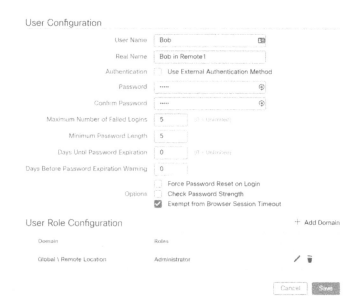

User Configuration

User Name	Bob
Real Name	Bob in Remote1
Authentication	☐ Use External Authentication Method
Password	·····
Confirm Password	·····
Maximum Number of Failed Logins	5 (0 = Unlimited)
Minimum Password Length	5
Days Until Password Expiration	0 (0 = Unlimited)
Days Before Password Expiration Warning	0
Options	☐ Force Password Reset on Login ☐ Check Password Strength ☑ Exempt from Browser Session Timeout

User Role Configuration   + Add Domain

Domain	Roles	
Global \ Remote Location	Administrator	✏ 🗑

Cancel Save

When I click on the *domain\name*, I can see all four domains, in the upper right, but once I login a user created in a domain, I'll see the same menu, but I'll only be able to choose and edit that specific domain:

User Role Configuration ❓

Domain

Global ▼
Global
Global \ Remote Location
Global \ Remote Location 2
Global \ Remote Location 3
External Database User (Read Only) ☐

Security Analyst ☐
Security Analyst (Read Only) ☐
Security Approver ☐
Intrusion Admin ☐
Access Admin ☐
Network Admin ☐
Maintenance User ☐
Discovery Admin ☐
Threat Intelligence Director (TID) User ☐

Cancel Save

Below, I can see that I've created new administrator users for each domain:

Username	Domains	Real Name	Roles	Authentication Method	Password Lifetime
admin				Internal	Unlimited
Aref	Aref in Remote3			Internal	Unlimited
Bob	Bob in Remote1			Internal	Unlimited
Sally	Sally in Remote2			Internal	Unlimited
todd				Internal	Unlimited

Switch Domains

You can configure a device only in its assigned domain.

Now I'm   Switch to domain **Global \ Remote**   going to login as each user to
create their ACP   **Location** .

37

Cancel Switch

because a global admin can't create or manage the other domains and the new admins can't manage anything but their own domain. But before I do that, check out this message I received as Admin of the global domain that I got when trying to go to FTD 19 that's assigned to Bob's domain:

I can do this, but I'll have to switch domains first before I can manage it. Just imagine having to do that with 50 domains while trying to troubleshoot and find the network analysis issues needed to fix things! Which domain is the problem at? And remember, Bob can't switch to any other domains because Bob is not Global Admin.

Create Leaf access control policies

So now I'm going to login and create ACP's for each domain. I'm going to start at Global to create the main Parent ACP:

1. Go to **Policies>Access Control**

2. I'm going to call my first Global ACP "**Parent_Corporate_ACP",** which will contain some simple rules that I want all domains to receive. I'll do this by putting them into my Mandatory category.

3. Next, I'm going to create a new ACP policy—one for each new leaf domain under the Parent ACP. There are three in my example. I'll use this new ACP as my Base policy.

4. To get this done, I'll have to login as my new users for each domain since they're the admins of those new domains.

5. After logging in as Bob here, notice the domain and the name. I can see the other Leaf domains, but they're not available for Bob to click on and manage:

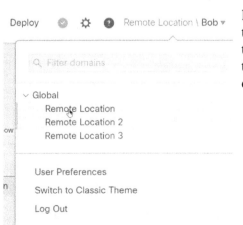

6. Now I'm going to create the first ACP and call it "Remote Location." I'll add the available FTD device into this policy that Bob will administrate:

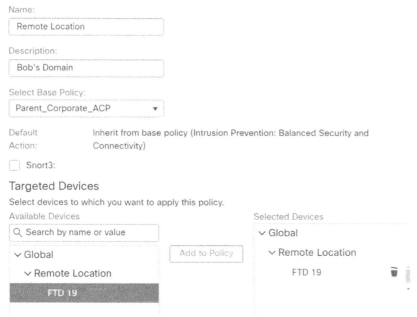

7. Notice the Base Policy now and also the fact that Bob can only add the Leaf object that's been assigned to his domain. The other devices aren't even available for him to see!

8. Now I am going to logout as Bob, login as Sally and then add a second policy named "Remote Location 2." After that, I'll add FTD into this policy. Check out the Base policy again:

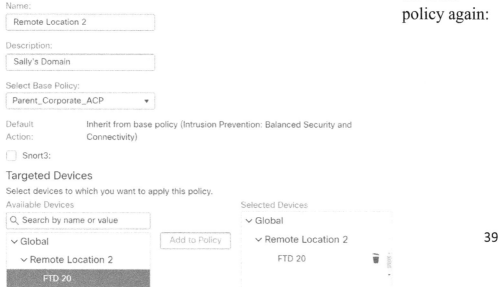

9. Next, I'm going to login as Aref and create a third ACP for the Aref domain named "Remote location 3."

10. Next, I'll logout as my domain users and log back in as admin. The only ACP I'll see from here is the Parent_Corporate_ACP. I can't see the Leaf ACP's even as admin, but as admin, I can switch to each domain in the upper right to view and manage each domain. It's really important to pay attention to which domain I'm in at this point in the configuration.

11. Look on the right-hand side where it shows that I'm in the Global domain. Remember as admin, I can switch to the other 3 locations and configure them, but those admins can't go into Global or any of the other domains listed other than their own domain:

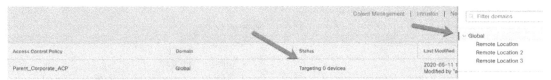

12. Now I'm going to create rules in the Parent ACP and then we'll take a look at a Leaf domain.

Here in the next screen shot, you can see that I created three rules in the Parent ACP under Mandatory, which happens to be the default Category that rules go into.

Also, at the bottom, notice that I added one rule in the Default Category.

For the Corporate ACP, there's really no difference in using either of these categories, but I added the last rule in the Default category so that the rule will show up under any child ACP as the last rule, a catch-all if you will. Let me demonstrate this now.

1. Let's create an ACP in another domain. First, I'll login as one of the other domain admins so I can create an ACP in that Leaf domain.

2. When creating a rule, only Bob's own categories, Mandatory and Default are available

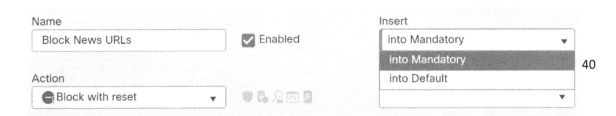

3. Focus on the rules that were inherited from the parent ACP in the Mandatory top rule set and the fact that Bob can't delete or edit those rules!

4. Bob can only create rules in his Mandatory and Default categories and what's more, the Parent ACP takes precedence over any of his rules.

5. The last rule I created in the Parent ACP Default category was Rule Number 5, which gets placed at the bottom of the Remote Location ACP, very nice.

It's really important to remember that Bob can't change, edit or delete this rule, and even though it's just sitting there doing nothing in this lab, it illustrates how to add something at the bottom of each leaf ACP when you need or want to. I also provided this rule so you can see the difference of using the Mandatory and Default categories.

How to Make Troubleshooting Domains Even Harder

Domains can make administration easier if you have a decent number of remote sites with a gaggle of Firepower administrators making changes constantly.

But when a problem rears it ugly head, troubleshooting becomes... well, cumbersome to say the least. Turns into a real pain in the rear because you have to keep changing domains to see any analysis when checking out multiple locations! This is why lots of people just stay completely away from this domain "feature".

But for the seriously bored who deeply yearn for a challenge, just make everything obnoxiously hard to troubleshoot by adding Objects with Allow Override enabled as pictured right here:

Once an object is enabled with Allow Overrides, then configure what the Object variable will be in another Domain.

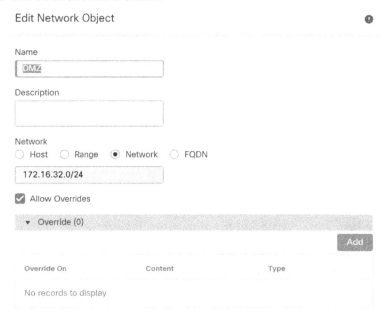

Now choose the target. Only the available FTD devices for that domain will be shown. Once you've chosen the target where the variable will be different, click on the Override tab there at the top:

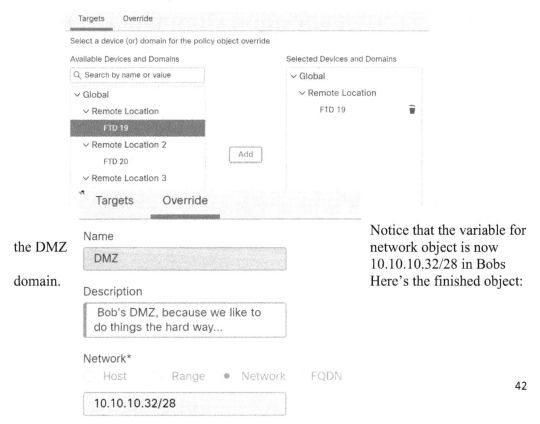

the DMZ

domain.

Notice that the variable for network object is now 10.10.10.32/28 in Bobs Here's the finished object:

So what this says is when the DMZ object is in the Global domain, the variable is 172.16.32.0/24, but when that same object is used in Bob's domain, the value is 10.10.10.32/28. Hmmm… Maybe you should just create multiple objects instead?

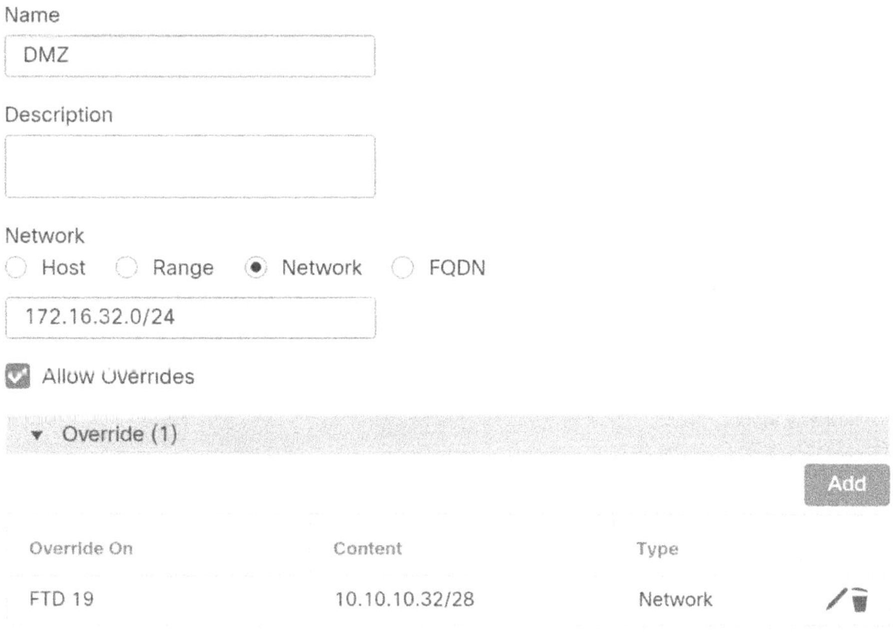

Name

DMZ

Description

Network

⭘ Host ⭘ Range ⦿ Network ⭘ FQDN

172.16.32.0/24

☑ Allow Overrides

▾ Override (1)

Add

Override On	Content	Type	
FTD 19	10.10.10.32/28	Network	✏️ 🗑️

In closing, I want to point out that you don't need to configure domains in order to use the Override "feature" for an object. Alternatively, just create hierarchical ACP's with multiple objects enabled with override. The thing is, I seriously don't recommend going with this configuration either! Climb K2 instead.

Summary

Just because Cisco Firepower Domains aren't listed in the objectives, you still really need to know and understand them for the exam. Also make sure you've got the terms used in domains down really well, like Parent/Child and Ancestor/Descendant.

Cisco Firepower Domains were created to allow multiple administrators to manage their own environment—something called "multitenancy"—yet still allow for a Corporate Global domain that takes precedence over anything on the remote site, known as Leafs or Child, domains have configured.

Chapter 21: Dashboards and Reporting

The CCNP Security SNCF exam objectives covered in this chapter are:

3.0: Management and Troubleshooting
3.2 Configure dashboards and reporting in FMC

Life in an operations role is not a day at the beach. Constantly chasing down issues, coordinating with other teams, etc. while sneaking in a bite of cold pizza at your desk gets old fast! It all makes having a army of sweet dashboards handy to help you make sense of what's going on in your Firepower environment a serious slice of heaven.

That's what we're going to cover in this chapter… You're going to learn all about Firepower's awesome dashboards and what they do. I'll also show you how to customize them and even guide you through making you're own so they work even better for you!

Since dashboards differ in a multi-domain environment, I'll touch on domains too. This means you might want to glance through chapter 20 before starting this chapter.

We're also going to dive into the spellbinding world of reports! Okay, so maybe the report universe isn't quite riveting, but management sure loves it when you can generate shiny reports for them to check out—especially in color! So, I'm going to tell you all about the built-in reports, plus how to make your own if you need more information than what you get out of the box.

Summary Dashboard

When you first log into Firepower you will be whisked to the **Summary Dashboard** by default. This dashboard gives you a ton of information spread out across six tabs that are focused on different areas like networking or active threats.

The default tabs are:

- Network
- Threats
- Intrusion Events
- Status
- Geolocation
- QoS

Here's a quick look at the Summary Dashboard tabs:

Let's go through each of the tabs in this section:

Network

This summary tab gives us a broad scope on all the activity seen in the Firepower environment including the types of applications, which operating systems are being used and how much traffic users are generating.

Since there's a bunch of different graphs to cover, we're going to look at each of them individually. You probably don't need to memorize all of them for any Cisco exam, but it's really good to know what's available to you out of the box for life in the real world.

The **Unique Applications over Time** graph shows you how many unique applications are being seen on your monitored networks over time. It's mostly just informational, but you'll definitely want to investigate if a bunch of new applications are suddenly discovered!

The Unique Applications over Time Graph:

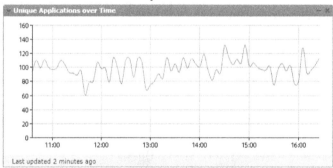

Top Web Applications Seen is a pretty self-explanatory. This graph reveals the web-based applications that Firepower has discovered and sorts the info by how much traffic the application has used. Clearly, this is useful for keeping tabs on which applications are being used in the network. In the example pictured in the next figure, it turns out that YouTube is the top application in use, followed by Google, which in most cases indicates your users are slackers:

The Top Web Applications Seen Graph:

Application	▼ Total Bytes (KB)
YouTube	44,385.57
Google	43,494.70
The Huffington Post	36,605.00
Google Play	35,133.86
Google APIs	30,181.23
BITS	22,654.97
BBC	15,266.55
JetBrains	14,527.41
+1 ⬆ Doubleclick	11,918.41
+1 ⬆ The New York Times	10,018.03
+1 ⬆ The Telegraph	9,783.20
+1 ⬆ Yahoo!	9,470.72
+1 ⬆ Akamai	8,282.10
+2 ⬆ Google Safebrowsing	7,767.28
-6 ⬇ Pathview	6,830.17

Last updated 2 minutes ago

"Tip"

NOTE: Back to chapter 20: Domains, you learned that Child domains can't view dashboards originating from an ancestor domain. In a multidomain deployment, even though you can't view dashboards from ancestor domains, you can create new dashboards, which are copies of the higher-level dashboards.

Next up is the **Top Client Applications Seen Graph.** It shows us all the non-web applications that Firepower has seen like email or other corporate apps, which have online connectivity. This is very cool because you can use it to help prevent Shadow IT since you can see unapproved cloud storage applications like Dropbox!

What's "Shadow IT"? It's when users try to create solutions without the IT department's knowledge and/or blessing. It's bad because it can lead to things like unexpected bills or data links due to employees sharing files they shouldn't be sharing to the cloud.

This graph can also provide handy information to web developers since you can let them know how many users are still using Internet Explorer when working on their applications.

The Top Client Applications Seen Graph:

Application	▼ Total Bytes (KB)
Chrome	334,525.79
Internet Explorer	113,641.12
YouTube	44,376.50
Firefox	26,095.16
BITS	22,654.97
JetBrains	14,527.41
Safari	11,569.14
Yahoo!	9,470.72
+1 ⬆ Google Update	6,777.61
-1 ⬇ Edge	5,943.60
Dropbox	4,436.12
Spotify	2,530.39
Java	1,689.63
Microsoft CryptoAPI	1,575.09
NetBIOS-ns	1,411.98

Last updated 3 minutes ago

The Top Server Applications Seen graph predictably shows the server-based applications on the network—things like apache or IIS. It's another useful graph for keeping an eye on Shadow IT because if you spot a server you don't recognize, you should definitely find out more about it. Worse, unexplained server traffic can also indicate a compromise because it could actually be an attacker that's trying to use SNMP traffic to map out your network and/or gain access to devices!

Top Operating Systems Seen… This graph displays the operating systems Firepower has discovered in your network. It's pretty much just informational as far as graphs go, but it's clearly a good idea to investigate if a new, surprise OS pops up in your network.

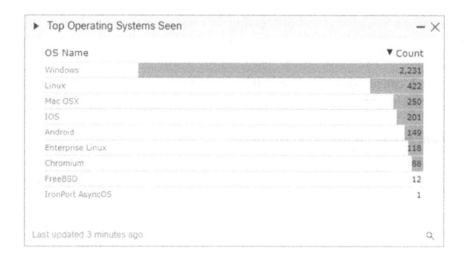

The Traffic by Application Risk Graph is super useful because it sorts the applications in your network by risk level. It's wise to keep a close eye on the higher risk applications so you can either remove them or do your best to reduce their associated risks.

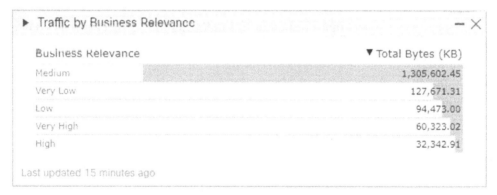

The Traffic by Business Relevance Graph sorts traffic by business relevance so something like email or DNS would be pretty relevant. On the other hand, BitTorrent would rank really low since it's often used for downloading things that shouldn't be downloaded rather than sharing Linux.

The Traffic by Business Relevance Graph

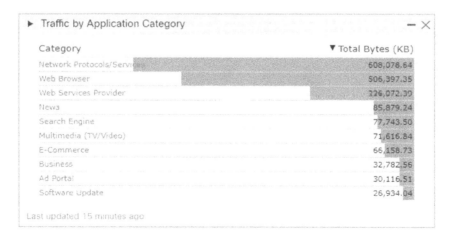

Traffic by Application Category This graph displays the applications in the network sorted nicely by their application category.

Traffic by Application Category graph:

Category	Total Bytes (KB)
Network Protocols/Services	608,078.64
Web Browser	506,397.35
Web Services Provider	226,072.30
News	85,879.24
Search Engine	77,743.50
Multimedia (TV/Video)	71,616.84
E-Commerce	66,158.73
Business	32,782.56
Ad Portal	30,116.51
Software Update	26,934.04

Last updated 15 minutes ago

The Risky Applications with Low Business Relevance Graph combines the info you get from the risky applications graph with the business relevance graph to deliver a list of applications considered high risk to your network as well as low value business-wise. This list of applications should be easily removed from your network—at least in theory.

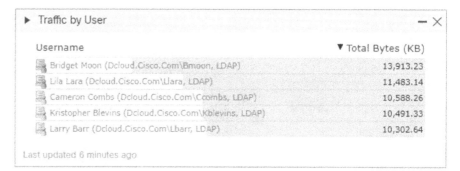

Traffic by User displays users that Firepower has identified on the network as well as how much traffic in KBs they're consuming. This graph comes in especially handy for keeping an eye on the heavy users in your network.

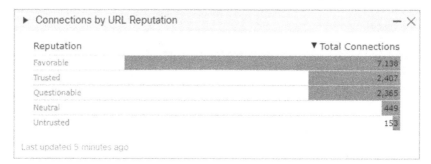

Connections by URL Reputation sorts the URLs that users are going into categories based upon the URL's reputation. URLs like advertisements or malware sites are good examples of the kind of high-risk things that would fall into the untrusted category.

Connections by URL Reputation — ×

Reputation	▼ Total Connections
Favorable	7,136
Trusted	2,407
Questionable	2,365
Neutral	449
Untrusted	153

Last updated 5 minutes ago

Connections by URL Category is the last graph in the network tab and it's a lot like the previous one except it sorts by a URL's category.

Connections by URL Category	─ ✕

Category	▼ Total Connections
Advertisements	4,693
Business And Industry	3,826
Search Engines And Portals	2,543
Uncategorized	2,311
Infrastructure And Content Delivery Networks	2,299
Computers And Internet	2,159
News	1,285
Social Networking	1,070
Online Storage And Backup	706
SaaS And B2B	621

Last updated 6 minutes ago

Threats

Always a great partner in keeping your network safe, these graphs found under the Threat Tab are vital to check in with regularly. We'll take a walk through them now.

Summary Dashboard (switch dashboard)

Provides a summary of activity on the appliance

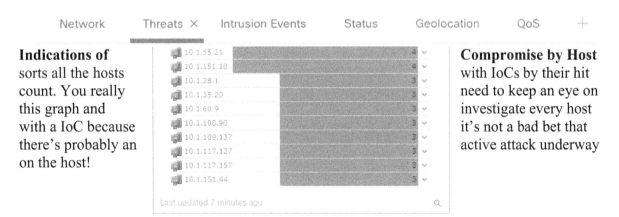

| Network | Threats ✕ | Intrusion Events | Status | Geolocation | QoS | + |

Indications of sorts all the hosts count. You really this graph and with a IoC because there's probably an on the host!

10.1.55.21	4 ⌄
10.1.151.18	4 ⌄
10.1.28.1	3 ⌄
10.1.35.20	3 ⌄
10.1.60.9	3 ⌄
10.1.108.90	3 ⌄
10.1.109.137	3 ⌄
10.1.117.127	3 ⌄
10.1.117.157	3 ⌄
10.1.151.44	3 ⌄

Last updated 7 minutes ago

Compromise by Host with IoCs by their hit need to keep an eye on investigate every host it's not a bad bet that active attack underway

Connections by Security Intelligence Category conveniently shows us matches within different security intelligence categories and sorts them by total connections.

Malware Threats is another is another great place to watch since it alerts us to the amount of malware threats that Firepower has detected in the network.

Indications of Compromise by User tells us how many IoC events have been mapped to a specific user in your network.

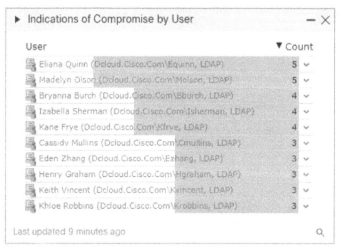

Traffic by Security Intelligence Category is the last graph in the threat tab and it displays the amount of traffic that matches up into the different Security Intelligence categories.

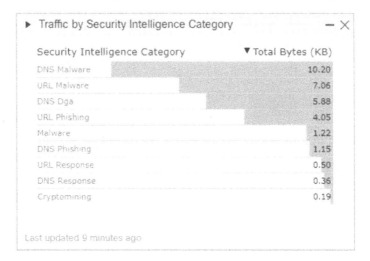

Intrusion Events

This tab is all about intrusion events. It reveals critical information to us like the top attackers and targets, as well as the severity of attacks.

Top Attackers displays the top malicious source IPs by how often they're associated with an attacker. If you notice a given IP starring frequently in this graph, it's a really good idea to consider blacklisting it or its network. If you happen to have a security scanning tool deployed in your network, don't forget to whitelist it so it doesn't show up in this list!

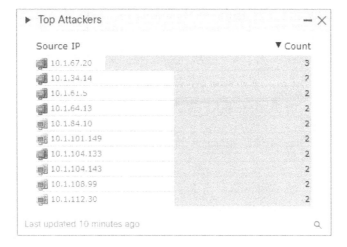

Top Targets highlights the most frequently attacked IPs in your network. If you see that a certain host is being attacked frequently, consider tightening the Access Control Policy entries so that host won't be as exposed.

All Intrusion Events tells us how many intrusion events have occurred.

Here's a look at the All Intrusion Events graph:

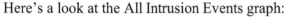

Intrusion Events reveals the intrusion events, which have occurred in the last 6 hours; it even sorts the events by severity and tells us the total number of events as well. It's mostly just showing how many events are occurring, but if you see a spike happen here, it can indicate that there's a larger scale attack happening.

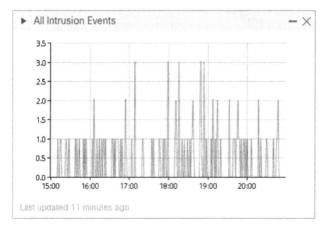

Dropped Intrusion Events tells us exactly what the Intrusion engine is actually dropping, plus what those packets have been classified as by the IPS. This is a sweet graph to check to find out about the type of attacks occurring on your network and it also helps us to make sure there aren't any false positives to correct.

Total Events by User predictably shows us the total intrusion events by specific users. If a certain user has a high number of events associated with it, you should check into exactly what that user is doing to cause this. They might be visiting sites that they shouldn't be, or maybe they're using some software that Firepower just doesn't like.

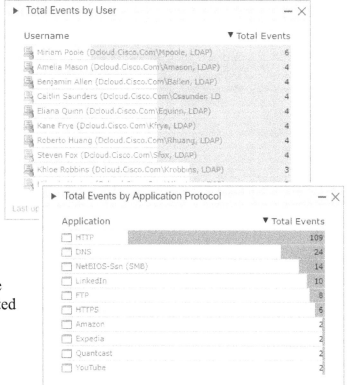

Total Events by Protocol reveals the intrusion events sorted protocol.

Application total number of by the application

Impact 1 Events by Application Protocols tells us about any Impact 1 events sorted by the application protocol that Firepower has seen:

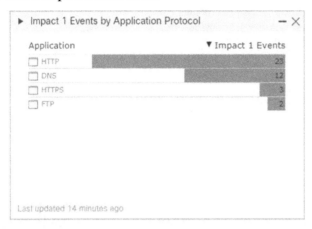

Impact 2 Events by Application shows us any Impact 2 events sorted by the application protocol that Firepower has seen.

Status

Okay yes—that's a huge amount of graphs we've covered and we're actually only halfway done with the summary dashboard!

The status tab is focused on the FMC appliance's health and it tells us about things like available product updates and the system load.

Application Status graphs the overall health of the FMC. Like most things, when you see green, everything is fine and when it's not, you've probably got a few problems to deal with.

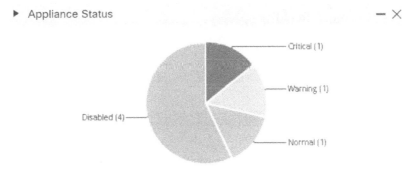

Application Information lists the appliance's IP address, model number and which version you're running. It's good info to be aware of, especially if you aren't logging into the FMC every day.

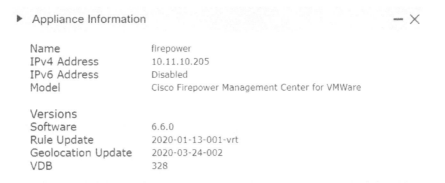

Product Updates

It's always a good idea to keep security solutions as up to date as possible to make sure you've got the latest vulnerability protection. This graph shows you any updates available and tells you if things are out of date.

Type	Current	Latest
Geolocation Update		
Local Geolocation Update	2020-03-24-002	2020-03-24-002
Rule Update		
Local Rule Update	2020-01-13-001-vrt	Unknown
Software		
1 Management Center	6.6.0	6.6.0
5 Devices	6.6.0	6.6.0
1 Device	6.5.0	6.5.0.4
VDB		
1 Management Center	328	Unknown

Disk Usage shows how much free disk space you've got on your FMC and if you're running out, you should adjust your logging configuration or delete some update images.

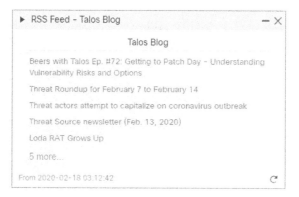

RSS Feed shows the RSS feed from the Talos blog, which provides solid security information on the latest threats.

Current Sessions tells us who's logged into the FMC and how long they've been in a session.

Username	Address	Accessed
admin	10.30.10.16	22:41:21

System Time shows the current time on the FMC, which is useful for making sure NTP is working. It also shows how long it's been since the FMC has been rebooted and when that boot time occurred.

System Load shows the load the FMC is under including CPU and Memory usage.

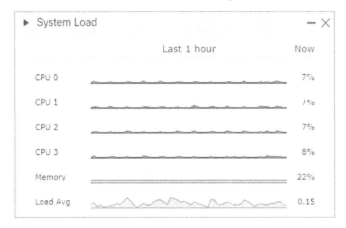

Geolocation

The geolocation tab focuses on showing intrusion events sorted by countries, so it can really help you shape your geolocation policy in the ACP.

Intrusion Events by Source Country graphs intrusions events sorted by the source country:

Intrusion Events by Source Country

Intrusion Events by Source Continent reveals intrusion events sorted by the source continents, which helps to identify high-risk regions you want to block as long as your company doesn't have any legit online business with that part of the world.

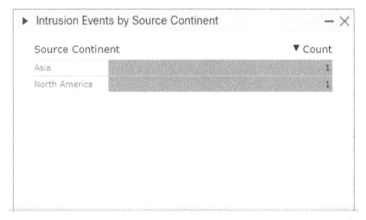

Intrusion Events by Destination Country specifies intrusion events by the destination countries, which helps in identifying unusual connections from your network that should be investigated.

Intrusion Events by Destination Continent pictures intrusions events sorted by the destination continents, which is useful for identifying unusual connections from your network that may need to be investigated.

QoS

We're going to dive into QoS in the next chapter, so I'm going to wait to cover this tab until we get there.

Custom Tab

Right there next to the QoS tab is a plus sign (+) that you can click and create a custom tab complete with custom widgets. I'm going to create a tab named Todd and add the widgets I want:

Built-in Dashboards

In addition to the Summary dashboard we just explored in detail, Firepower also comes with more dashboards, which allow us to dive even deeper because they provide very focused information. Since we already covered a good number of the graphs, I'll just give you a quick explanation of each dashboard.

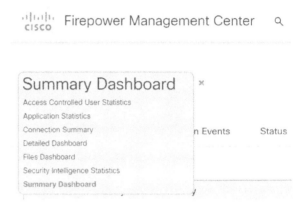

Access Controlled User Statistics

This dashboard focuses on providing traffic and intrusion event statistics by user:

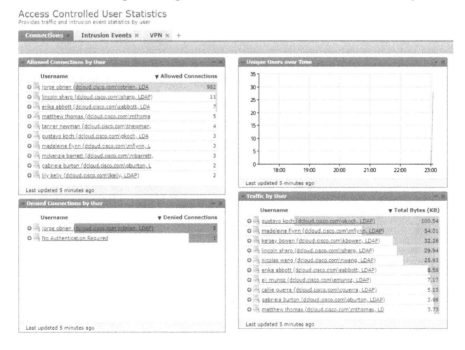

Application Statistics

This dashboard focuses on detailing traffic and intrusion event statistics by application:

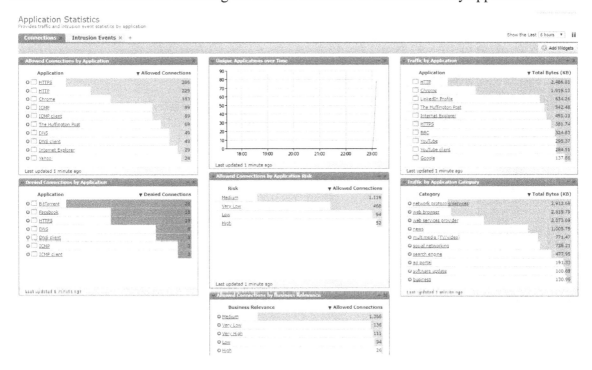

Connections Summary

This dashboard's focus is to provide tables and charts that pinpoint the activity on your monitored network segment.

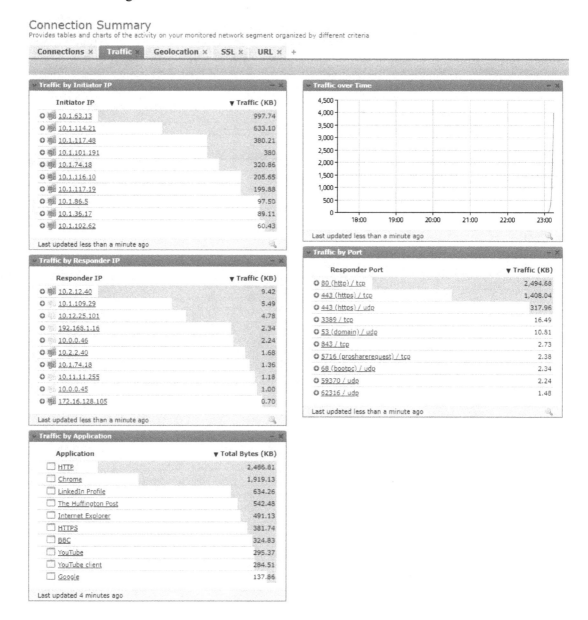

Connection Summary
Provides tables and charts of the activity on your monitored network segment organized by different criteria

Connections × | **Traffic** × | **Geolocation** × | **SSL** × | **URL** × | +

Traffic by Initiator IP

Initiator IP	▼ Traffic (KB)
10.1.63.13	997.74
10.1.114.21	633.10
10.1.117.48	380.21
10.1.101.191	380
10.1.74.18	320.86
10.1.116.10	205.65
10.1.117.19	199.88
10.1.86.5	97.50
10.1.36.17	89.11
10.1.102.62	60.43

Last updated less than a minute ago

Traffic by Responder IP

Responder IP	▼ Traffic (KB)
10.2.12.40	9.42
10.1.109.29	5.49
10.12.25.101	4.78
192.168.1.16	2.34
10.0.0.46	2.24
10.2.2.40	1.68
10.1.74.18	1.36
10.11.11.255	1.18
10.0.0.45	1.00
172.16.128.105	0.70

Last updated less than a minute ago

Traffic by Application

Application	▼ Total Bytes (KB)
HTTP	2,486.81
Chrome	1,919.13
LinkedIn Profile	634.26
The Huffington Post	542.48
Internet Explorer	491.13
HTTPS	381.74
BBC	324.83
YouTube	295.37
YouTube client	284.51
Google	137.86

Last updated 4 minutes ago

Traffic over Time

(Chart: traffic 0–4,500 over time 18:00 to 23:00)

Last updated less than a minute ago

Traffic by Port

Responder Port	▼ Traffic (KB)
80 (http) / tcp	2,494.68
443 (https) / tcp	1,408.04
443 (https) / udp	317.96
3389 / tcp	16.49
53 (domain) / udp	10.81
843 / tcp	2.73
5716 (prosharerequest) / tcp	2.38
68 (bootpc) / udp	2.34
59370 / udp	2.24
62316 / udp	1.48

Last updated less than a minute ago

Detailed Dashboard

This offers a detailed view of activity on the appliance:

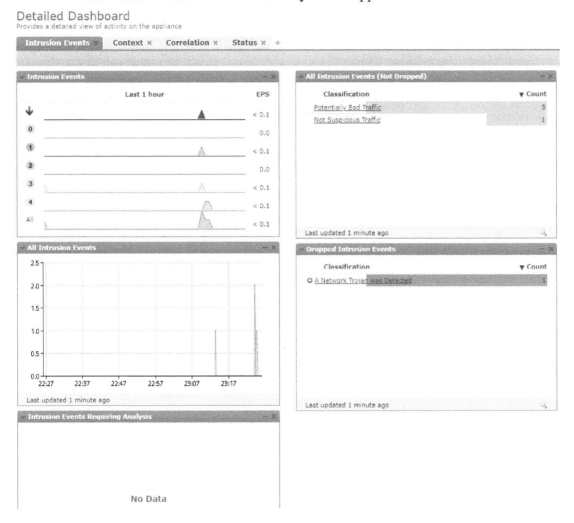

Dashboard

This dashboard serves up an overview of Malware and File Events:

Security Intelligence Dashboard

This dashboard equips you with Security Intelligence statistics:

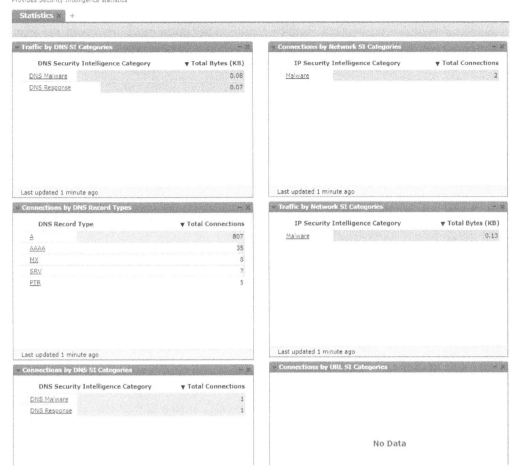

Firepower Reporting

Firepower seriously gears up our security capabilities with powerful tools like a flexible reporting system that lets us quickly generate multi-section reports with the event views or dashboards that appear on the FMC. You can even design your own custom reports from scratch, but make sure you're getting paid by the hour first!

Your reports can come in PDF, HTML or CSV with the content you choose. A template specifies the data searches and formats for the report and its sections. I'll level with you…The Firepower System's reporting templates can definitely be a bit unwieldy, but it does include a report designer that automates the design of report templates, which we'll explore more towards the end of the chapter.

The report designer allows you to replicate the content of any event view table or dashboard graphic displayed in the web interface and you can build as many report templates as your heart desires. Each template defines individual sections in the report and specifies the database search that creates the report's content, the presentation format (table, chart, detail view, and so on) and the time frame. Your template also specifies document attributes like the cover page and table of contents and if you want the document pages to have headers and footers. That header/footer option is only available for reports in PDF format. You can even export a report template in a file and import it on another FMC!

*Important Exam Objective Info here:

You can also include input parameters in a template to make it even more of a pain, but believe it or not, doing this can actually be useful if you want to get a report on a server for example.

So, if this is a cool feature, why am I griping about it? Well, when you generate a report with input parameters, the generation process prompts you to enter a value for each input parameter, meaning your FMC will stop and just sit there waiting for you to enter a variable. So, if you were to schedule this report to run, it could very well make you sit there all night!

Looking on the left of the figure below, you can see that it lists the Type of Input Parameters. On the right, you can see that I just wanted to get information from a particular host or server: 10.11.12.10. I will be prompted every time this report runs!

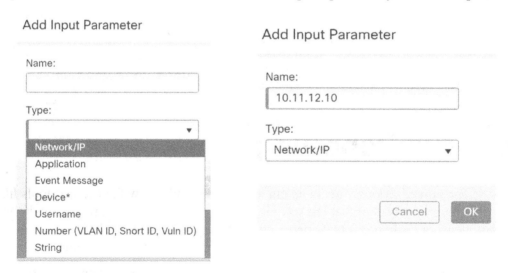

This is important to understand: You can create a report template to limit the report's results to the activity of a specific subnet on your network only by adding an Input Parameter in the advanced settings of the report template. Don't forget that!

Report Templates

So we use report templates to define the content and format of the data in each of the report's sections and in the document attributes of the report file, which includes the cover page, table of contents and page headers and footers. After you generate a report, the template stays available for reuse until you delete it.

Your reports contain one or more information sections. You choose the format (text, table or chart) for each section, individually. Understand that the format you select for a section might constrain the data that can be included. For instance, you just can't show time-based information in certain tables using a pie chart format. You can change the data criteria or format of a section at any time to optimize the presentation.

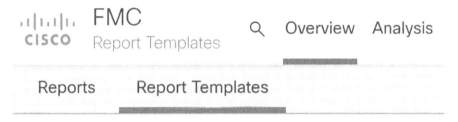

We can base a report's initial design on a predefined event view or you can start your design by importing content from any defined dashboard, workflow or summary. It's also possible to begin with an empty template, adding sections and defining their attributes one by one—time consuming, but possible.

So here's a shot of some of the default templates you can edit and use:

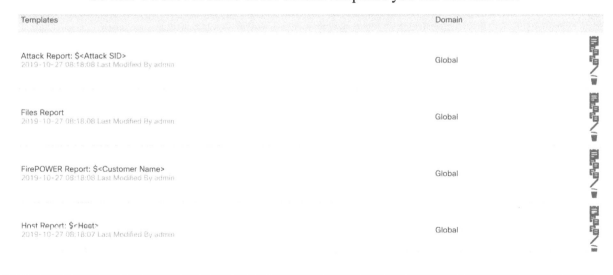

Templates	Domain
Attack Report: $<Attack SID> 2019-10-27 08:18:08 Last Modified By admin	Global
Files Report 2019-10-27 08:18:08 Last Modified By admin	Global
FirePOWER Report: $<Customer Name> 2019-10-27 08:18:08 Last Modified By admin	Global
Host Report: $<Host> 2019-10-27 08:18:07 Last Modified By admin	Global

I'm going to show you a much better way to create and use report templates right after the next section.

In a multidomain deployment, you can look but you can't touch report templates belonging to ancestor domains. No editing! So to generate reports from these templates, you've got to copy them to your current domain.

Risk Reporting

Risk reports are pre-created with high-level, easy-to-interpret information about risks found in your organization. These are really valuable so I highly recommend that you run these reports on your production networks! They're really great information packaged with lots of pretty pictures that your managers will just love.

Plus, you can use these reports to share information about areas of risk and recommendations for addressing these risks, which tees up the discussion into areas that are ripe for investing into the security of your network.

Risk Reports were born back in the 6.1 code and you can't edit them or add to them—you can't even add your logo! You can only run them, but they're still worthwhile.

The three reports are:

- Advanced Malware Risk Report
- Attacks Risk Report
- Attack Report

	Create Report Template

Risk Report Templates	Domain	
Advanced Malware Risk Report	Global	
Attacks Risk Report	Global	
Network Risk Report	Global	

Clicking the top icon on the right side of the report lets you run and generate the report, which will then allow you to schedule and email the report through the Task Management section of the FMC.

After clicking the top, right icon of the report you want to schedule and run, you get taken to some fields to fill out. The name is automatically added into the report and if you don't have an email relay configured in your System Configuration, just click the pencil to get to the page for configuring SMTP settings

Finally, add your Company name and your name, which is pretty irrelevant because it won't show up anywhere in the report.

Generate Report

Report Generation Information

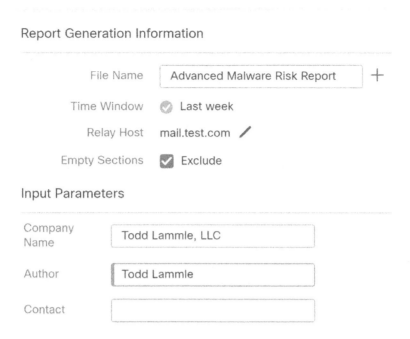

File Name   Advanced Malware Risk Report   +

Time Window   ✓ Last week

Relay Host   mail.test.com ✎

Empty Sections   ☑ Exclude

Input Parameters

Company Name   Todd Lammle, LLC

Author   Todd Lammle

Contact

If you want to schedule and email this report, add the email information next. It's actually mandatory for you to fill in the email list and subject, and you've got to put something there in the body of the text. Here's an example:

▼ Email

Email Options	◉ Send email ○ Do not send email
Recipient List	firepower@lammle.com
CC	
BCC	
Subject	Weekly Advanced Malware Risk Re ＋

B *I* U X₂ x² ▤ ▦ ▤ S̶ ▦ ≡ ≡ 🔗 Color ▼ Font ▼ Size

Weekly Advanced Malware Risk Report

You'll find the finished reports in the Reports tab and you can open them here if needed:

Reports   Report Templates

	Name	Time Requested	Time Completed	User	Location	Status
☐	Advanced_Malware_Risk_Report-20200517150713-24550.zip Reports	2020-05-17 11:07:13	2020-05-17 11:07:16	admin	Local	Successfully Processed

Report Designer (Reporting)

Now here's where we get to the easy way to make custom report templates:

First, pick and go to the network analysis page location where you want the data to live in a report template. I usually go to Dashboards because it's the easiest way to create a template with a good amount of data. On most pages you'll find the Report Designer (Now just called Reporting in the 7.0 code) on the upper right side as shown here on the Dashboards summary page:

→ Report Designer

Summary Dashboard (switch dashboard)
Provides a summary of activity on the appliance

Network   Threats   Intrusion Events   Status ✕   Geolocation Show the Last 1 week ▼ ‖

Once you get the data you want on the page you choose, make sure and set the time window on the page you want for the report. This example was set to 1 week. After you set the time, click on Reporting or Report Designer. The data on the page will then show up as templates that you can edit and even Preview for the time period you set previously.

From here you can Generate the report, add Advanced settings, and Save the template,:

The bottom icons allow you to configure your reports, and displayed from left to right, a bar chart, line chart, pie chapter, add a table view, detail view, add a text section, add a page break, and to finally import sections from Dashboards, Summaries and Workflow.

Advanced Settings

can page, design page,

even

General Settings

Cover Page	☐ Include Cover Page
Cover Page Design	$<Logo>$<Report Title> ✎
Table of Contents	☐ Include Table of Contents
Logo	cisco ✎

PDF Settings

Header	left<Empty> ▼	center<Empty> ▼	right<Empty> ▼
Footer	<Empty> ▼	<Empty> ▼	<Empty> ▼
Page Number Start	1	☐ Number First Page?	

From the Advanced Settings tab you include a cover change the of the cover add a table of contents and add your Logo:

Input Parameters   + Add Input Parameter

Name	Type

Right down there on the bottom right, you can see where you can add an Input Parameter, however you don't want to configure the input parameters if you want to schedule this report to run as it will stop and ask you to input your parameter.

NOTE Exam objective information here-> When creating a report template, you are able to limit the results to only show the activity of a specific subnet.

Summary

We went over a lot of information and examples that were all about Firepower's various dashboards and what they do. You learned how to customize them and even how to make your own.

You now understand the differences in dashboards within a multi-domain environment and found out everything you need to know about reports, the built-in variety and how to make your own if you need additional information included in them.

Chapter 22: FTD QoS

The CCNP Security SNCF exam objectives covered in this chapter are:

2.0 Configuration

> ### 2.5 Configure devices using Firepower Management Center

> > #### 2.5.d QoS

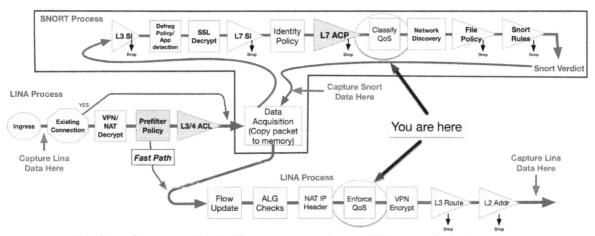

Quality of service (QoS) allows us to assign a different priority to one or more types of traffic over others for different applications, data flows or users so solid performance is maintained on our networks. QoS is also used to manage contention for network resources to ensure a nice, efficient end-user experience. It basically prevents anything in particular from hogging all the network's available bandwidth.

Sounds good right? Not so fast…The catch is that FTD doesn't offer the typical menu of QoS features like application bandwidth assignments, policing, shaping, queuing or dropping. Cisco FTD bestows us with interface policing and that's all we get! We'll explore the differences between IOS and FTD QoS soon.

Take a good look at the figure above the text in this intro. The FTD Packet flow above the QoS policy is configured in the FTD configuration, but the packets don't get a snort verdict. Instead, the QoS is actually enforced in the LINA Egress configuration.

Quality of Service

Modern networks typically see a mix of data, voice and video traffic traversing them and each of these traffic types has different attributes.

This figure pictures the differences in traffic characteristics for data, voice and video:

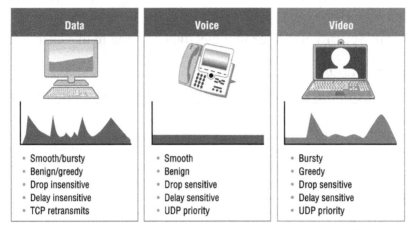

Data traffic is not real-time traffic and it's bursty and unpredictable in nature. Packet arrival time varies quite a bit. Data traffic rarely, if ever requires any special handling these days, especially when TCP is being used.

Today's usual suspect for serious bandwidth consumption is real-time voice traffic, which requires a consistent amount of bandwidth and known packet arrival times.

The voice requirements for one-way traffic include:

- Latency of less than or equal to 150 milliseconds
- Jitter of less than or equal to 30 milliseconds
- Loss of less than or equal to 1%
- Bandwidth of only 30-12k Kbps

Furthermore, there are quite a variety of video traffic types swirling around the Internet these days. Netflix, Hulu and other apps like gaming and remote collaboration require streaming video, real-time interactive video and video conferencing.

Which leads us to the video requirements for one-way traffic:

- Latency of less than or equal to 200-400 milliseconds
- Jitter of less than or equal to 30-50 milliseconds
- Loss of less than or equal to 0.1-1%
- Bandwidth 384 Kbps to 20 Mbps or greater

QoS can ensure that applications with a required bit rate get the bandwidth they need to work properly. Clearly, this doesn't factor in much on networks with plenty of bandwidth, but the more limited your bandwidth is, the more important QoS becomes!

Interface Policing with FTD QoS

We're going to talk about the difference between FTD and the IOS QoS now because you need to know about that before we get into configuring QoS with Firepower/FTD. That's where we'll put some action on packets with things like bandwidth assignments, policing, shaping, queuing or dropping. For example, if some of your traffic exceeds bandwidth, it might be delayed, dropped or even remarked to avoid congestion.

Policers and shapers are two tools used to identify and respond to traffic problems. Both are rate-limiters and this figure shows how they differ:

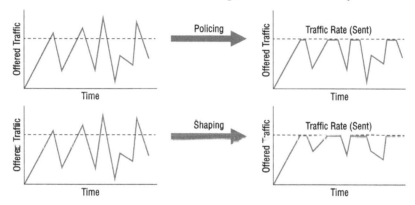

Policers and shapers identify traffic violations in a similar way but they differ in their responses:

Policers
Since the policers make instant decisions you want to deploy them on the ingress if possible. This is because you want to drop traffic as soon as you receive it if it's going to be dropped anyway, right? Still, you can place policers on an egress to control the amount of traffic per class. When traffic is exceeded, policers don't delay it by introducing jitter or delay, they just check the traffic and drop or remark it. So it's important to know that due to the higher drop probability, you can end up with a whole bunch of TCP resends!

Shapers
Shapers are usually deployed between an enterprise network and the ISPs on the egress side to make sure you stay within the contract rate. If the rate is exceeded, it gets policed by the provider and dropped, which ensures the traffic meets the Service Level Agreement (SLA). Shaping introduces jitter and delay and results in fewer TCP resends than policers.

"tip"

Basically, just remember that policers drop traffic and shapers delay it. Shapers introduce delay and jitter and policers do not. Policers can cause significant TCP resends but shapers do not.

Configuring QoS for FTD

To perform policy-based rate limiting, configure and deploy QoS policies to managed devices. Each QoS policy can target multiple devices and each device can only have one QoS policy deployed at a time:

1. Choose `Devices>QoS`

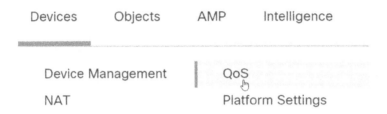

2. Click New Policy to create a new QoS policy and assign target devices. They can also be assigned after policy creating as well. I'm going to name the Policy and add Bob's device that we created back in the Domain chapter now:

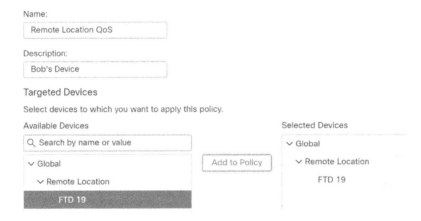

3.Configure QoS rules.

The Rules in the QoS policy editor lists each rule in evaluation order and displays a summary of the rule conditions and rate limiting configurations. Understand that these rules aren't an ACL so all rules will be evaluated on a packet.

Okay so first name the rule and then provide the other parameters, which I'll go through with you here:

Name:*	Bobs Device	☑ Enabled
Apply QoS On:	Interfaces in Source Interface Ob ▾

Traffic Limit Per Interface

Download Limit:	Unlimited	Mbits/sec (Range: 0.008–100000 Mbits/sec)
Upload Limit:	Unlimited	Mbits/sec (Range: 0.008–100000 Mbits/sec)

Enabled
Specify whether the rule is Enabled.

Apply QoS On
Choose the interfaces you want to rate limit—either Interfaces in Destination Interface Objects or Interfaces in Source Interface Objects. Your choice has to correspond with a populated interface constraint (not any).

Traffic Limit Per Interface
Enter a Download Limit and an Upload Limit in Mbits/sec. The default is the value of Unlimited to prevent matching traffic from being rate limited in that direction.

Traffic Limit Per Interface
A QoS rule enforces rate limiting independently on each of the interfaces you specify with the Apply QoS On option. You can't specify an aggregate rate limit for a set of interfaces—you rate limit traffic by Mbits per second. The default value of Unlimited prevents matching traffic of a rule from being rate limited.

Download and upload traffic is rate limited independently. The system determines download and upload directions based upon the connection initiator. If you specify a limit greater than the maximum throughput of an interface, the system won't rate limit matching traffic. Maximum throughput may be affected by an interface's hardware configuration, which you specify in each device's properties, (Devices > Device Management).

You can't save a QoS rule that rate limits all traffic. For each QoS rule, you must apply QoS on either of these two options:

Interfaces in Source Interface Objects
This choice rate limits traffic through the rule's source interfaces. If you go with this option, you have to add at least one source interface constraint that can't be "any".

Interfaces in Destination Interface Objects
Going with this will rate limit traffic through the rule's destination interfaces. If you choose this option, you've got to add at least one destination interface constraint—again, it can't be "any".

Rule Conditions

Conditions specify the kind of traffic the rule handles. You can configure each rule with multiple conditions and traffic must match all conditions in order to match the rule. Each condition type has its own tab in the rule editor. You can rate limit traffic using:

Conditions

Click the corresponding condition you want to add. You must configure a source or destination interface condition, corresponding to your choice for Apply QoS On.

Interface Objects	Networks	Users	Applications	Ports	URLs	SGT/ISE Attributes	Comments

- Interface (FTD routed only; required)

- Network

- User, Realm, and ISE Attribute Conditions (User Control)

- Application Conditions (Application Control)

- Port and ICMP Code

- URL Filtering

- Custom SGT Conditions

- Comments

It's a good idea to think about each rule a bit with an eye on exactly what it is you really want to limit bandwidth-wise. Take a look at the two rules in the example below. In the figure following this first one, you'll see that the first rule, "Marketing SM", is set to only 5 Mbps up/down for social media. Remember way back in the ACP chapter where I created a rule that allowed Marketing to SM using an AD group? I did the same thing here, which completely allows marketing to SM, but limits their bandwidth. So if your boss says they need access, they get it. Sure doesn't mean they get unlimited bandwidth though! This is a great example of a situation where you'd want to limit an allowed connection.

I'm going to give you two screen shots to break up the rule so this figure doesn't end up in nanotype that's way too small to read. Here's the left side of the rules:

#	Name	Source Interface Objects	Dest Interface Objects	Source Networks	Dest Networks	Users	Applicat...
1	⚠ Marketing SM	Inside Outside	Inside Outside	Any	Any	AD/Marketing	Any
2	Limit NetFlix	Inside Outside	Inside Outside	Any	Any	Any	Filter: netflix

Rule #1 shows this error:

This is definitely a bug, but it's not an issue unless you don't have things configured correctly with an identity policy. Anytime you add a group to the conditions, it'll throw this error at you regardless if it's correctly configured or not!

Rule #2 limits an Application using the application condition in the rule. You can easily test this from an inside host using the URL www.fast.com, which just happens to be netflix's bandwidth testing site.

Now it's time to check out the right side of the rule, which shows the ports, urls, download/upload speed and the source interfaces that'll provide the policing:

Source Ports	Dest Ports	URLs	Source SGT	Download	Upload	Applied On	
Any	Any	Social Network	Any	5 Mbits/sec	5 Mbits/sec	Source interfac 0	
Any	Any	Any	Any	7 Mbits/sec	7 Mbits/sec	Source interfac 0	

Depending on the rule type and the devices in your deployment, you can use predefined interface objects called security zones or interface groups to build interface conditions. I rarely if ever configure this type of rule, but you can if you want.

"tip"

One of the best ways to improve system performance is by constraining rules via interfaces. If a rule excludes all of a device's interfaces, that rule won't affect its performance.

Objects used in an interface condition must be of the same type, just as all interfaces in an interface object must be of the same type. Because devices deployed passively don't transmit traffic, you can't constrain rules by destination interface in passive deployments.

Tunnel Zones vs Security Zones

It's possible to use tunnel zones instead of security zones to constrain interface conditions in your configuration. Tunnel zones allow you to use prefiltering to tailor subsequent traffic handling to certain types of encapsulated connections.

Verification and Testing of FTD QoS Interface Policing

There isn't a lot of verification for the QoS policy on your FTD devices. If you look at the FTD flow on the first page of this chapter, you can see that the QoS is configured in the Snort process, but it'senforced in the Lina egress area. The best way to test is to go to an inside host, before !oS config and after deployment, and test the bandwidth. A DSL bandwidth meter should show the limitation nicely.

You can't get too much data on QoS into the FMC analysis section, but here are a couple things you can do:

1. Type show running-config on your FTD and verify the interface policing configuration. This can definitely be a little cumbersome because they use a proprietary number to identity the rule instead of the name you used:

```
>show running-config
[output cut]
policy-map policy_map_Inside
 match flow-rule qos 268437516
  police input 5000000 156250
  police output 5000000 156250
 match flow-rule qos 268437517
  police input 7000000 218750
  police output 7000000 218750
 class class-default

policy-map policy_map_Outside
 match flow-rule qos 268437516
  police input 5000000 156250
  police output 5000000 156250
 match flow-rule qos 268437517
  police input 7000000 218750
  police output 7000000 218750
 class class-default
```

Notice there's an Inside and Outside policy map created for each rule, (assuming you are using both zones):

| Network | Threats | Intrusion Events | Status | Geolocation | QoS × | + |

▶ QoS-Dropped Traffic by Device	— ×	▶ QoS-Dropped Traffic by Interface	—
Device	▼ Total QoS-Dropped Bytes (KB)	Interface	▼ Total QoS-Dropped Bytes (KB)
FTD 19	70,444.85	FTD 19: Inside	70,444.85

2. Go to *Overview>Dashboards>QoS* tab to see the data that was limited. On this view it takes a while to get this data to show up:

It's important for you to remember that this data is provided by the classification in the Snort process, not by what was actually limited on your interface. It should be the same, you just can't really tell if it is actually working other than if you test from an inside host.

Here's the output on www.fast.com (NetFlix) after deployment of my rules. Even though I set the Netflix rule to 7mbps up/down, the example here is pretty close, and most of the time it's spot on:

FAST

Your Internet speed is

6.2 Mbps ⟳

Latency		Upload
Unloaded	Loaded	Speed
10 ms	**12** ms	**5.9** Mbps

Summary

Quality of service (QoS) refers to the way the resources are controlled so that the quality of services is maintained.

In this chapter, you learned that the Cisco Firepower/FTD is essentially QoS policing and about the limitations associated with it. We configured QoS and covered the configuration and output.

Chapter 23: Network Analysis Policy

Even though there aren't any CCNP Security SNCF exam objectives covered in this chapter, I've included NAP, the Network Analysis policy, in this book because there's a lot of key information in it, and this is a Mastering Firepower book after all.

We'll be referring to the figure below throughout the chapter:

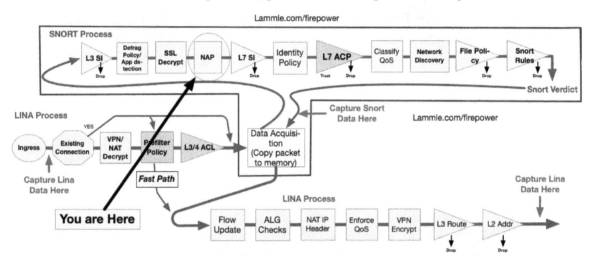

We're at a great point in this book to focus on NAP, which happens to be pretty much buried in the Firepower web user interface. In fact, it's so buried you can't even find it via the menu system! Kind of makes you think that the folks at Cisco don't want most of us messing with it, right? It's true—they don't—because this policy just so happens to contain some of the most complex Snort settings there are! NAP is primarily dedicated to the configuration of Snort's preprocessors. I'm going to get into some of the policy's history and cover key NAP configuration highlights in this chapter.

So let's go back in time and take a look at the underlying architecture of the Firepower system. Prior to its acquisition by Cisco in 2013, the Firepower IPS was a product of Sourcefire. Founded in 2001 by Martin Roesch, Sourcefire provided a commercial intrusion detection system based upon the Snort open-source software. At its inception, the commercial Sourcefire product could've arguably been called "Snort with a nice paint job," but it quickly evolved with enhancements in the user interface and features like Real-time Network Awareness (RNA).

RNA was the original name for the system's ability to passively collect host information and build an internal host database. Couple this with customized high-performance hardware and you have a recipe for a successful IPS.

Snort Configuration

At the core of the system is—and always has been—the open-source Snort intrusion detection system. Snort is essentially a network packet sniffer/analyzer with a rich rules language that's designed to efficiently search through packets for attacks, malware, or anything else the rule writer is interested in. Snort software is configured through text configuration files the same way nearly all Linux software is and typically takes the form of a single file named **snort.conf**. This file contains pretty much all the possible settings that control the operation of Snort's detection. The **snort.conf** file is actually several hundred lines long, containing **include** statements, which refer to additional configuration and rules files.

Snort rules are primarily found in plain-text configuration files and are written in the appropriately named Snort rules language. Snort can also process rules written in object code, but "shared object" rules don't use the Snort rules language. They're often use in advanced detection situations to overcome limitations with Snort keywords. Still, the vast majority of rules use the rules language and are found in plain text on the Snort sensor.

Fast forward to 2016 and you can still find these same text files at Snort's core. Yes, there have been significant improvements in speed and the legion of new rule keywords added to improve detection accuracy. But if you dig deep into the command line of a Firepower or FTD device, you'll eventually find text files containing the familiar Snort rules and configuration parameters.

When deployed, the intrusion and network analysis policies that you create in the Firepower user interface translate to the text Snort configuration files I mentioned earlier. There's actually so much more going into the processing of traffic on a device now because new hardware models and FTD architecture are considerably more complex than just a Linux box running Snort. Firepower and FTD devices implement multiple layers of inspection and include features from the Adaptive Security Appliance (ASA) firewalls as well as malware and file inspection.

Preprocessors

The contents of Snort configuration files can be classified into two categories:

- **Snort rules**: These handle most of the actual detection, and they're configured within the intrusion policy of the Firepower system.
- **Snort configurations**: Even though there's a ton of other options when it comes to how Snort processes traffic, I'm including these in the configuration category. Most of these configurations can be found in the Network Analysis policy, but you'll also see a few turn up as advanced settings in the Access Control policy.

Most of the settings within the NAP have to do with preprocessors, which are designed to modify packet data and remove anomalies so Snort rules can work properly. Keep in mind that packet data isn't modified with the goal of changing it en route to its destination. It's altered to remove conditions like fragmentation and encoding, which can be used to obscure packet data in an attempt to bypass detection. This modified packet data is used for inspection, but as long as the traffic isn't blocked, the original packet data will still exit the device.

There aren't a lot of preprocessors that actually modify network packets, and here's the most important thing to remember about them: If the preprocessor is misconfigured, you can bet the rules that depend on it won't function properly. Think of the preprocessor as being upstream of the rules—if the stream isn't preprocessed correctly, the rules will suffer.

This leads into the second most important thing to remember: Unless you seriously know what you're doing, leave the preprocessor settings alone! They come preset from Talos to function with standard protocols and rules, and they're designed to balance performance and detection demands really well. Talos rules are tested using the default base policy configuration provided, so misconfiguring preprocessors will painfully impact performance, detection, or both!

This definitely used to be a bigger issue than it is today. Early on, it was just way too easy to misconfigure the system. Now, there's a lot more intelligence between the user interface and the actual configurations to prevent people from shooting themselves in the foot. Still, don't push your luck. Before making changes to preprocessor configurations, be absolutely sure you know the ramifications, and if in doubt—even a little—call Cisco TAC to validate any changes you plan to make!

Preprocessor Basics

There are a few key things to know about preprocessors that'll definitely help you understand more about how the system operates.

Preprocessor Rules

Nearly all preprocessors can generate one or more alerts courtesy of preprocessor rules. These rules aren't like the other Snort rules you might be familiar with—here are some major differences:

- They can't use variables. Snort variables like HOME_NET and EXTERNAL_NET aren't available to preprocessors. As a result, they're generally not aware of the direction of a connection or whether it's from client to server or vice versa.

- They don't use ports or IP addresses. Preprocessor rules don't have a traditional rule header—it's basically just the rule action, which is almost universally "alert."

- Their detection is always in compiled/object code. Looking at a preprocessor rule offers little or no insight into what the rule was looking for because the actual detection is performed by compiled code. So if you're good at dissecting source code, you can download the Snort source from www.snorg.org, but beyond that there's not much to see here.

- Most of them are disabled. In the Connectivity and Balanced intrusion policies, there are no preprocessor rules enabled. The Security over Connectivity (SoC) policy does enable a few, but they mostly just generate noise. Remember, the main function of most preprocessors is to normalize traffic for the real Snort rules, *not* to generate events! Enabling or disabling a preprocessor rule has no impact on its normalization capabilities.

The GID

All Snort rules (preprocessor or not) have two numbers assigned: The generator ID (GID) and the Snort ID (SID). The GID indicates which part of Snort will generate the event. The SID is the rule number, which is unique within a given GID. Snort rules have a GID of 1 for a text rule and 3 for a shared object rule. Each preprocessors has one or more GIDs assigned to it, and these GID numbers will be 100 or greater. So, when you see an intrusion event or search through the Intrusion policy for rules, you can find and identify preprocessor rules by their GID.

When you see intrusion events in the FMC interface, each one will have the GID and SID with a colon separating them. Events for rules written in the Snort rules language will start with a 1 and have numbers like 1:1024 or 1:32230. Events generated by preprocessors will have the preprocessor GID such as 119:20 or 123:5.

So each Snort component has one or more assigned GIDs, and you can check out a few of these from the Firepower online help how here:

ID	Component	Description
1	Standard Text Rule	The event was generated when the packet triggered a standard text rule.
2	Tagged Packets	The event was generated by the Tag generator, which generates packets from a tagged session. This occurs when the tag rule option is used.
3	Shared Object Rule	The event was generated when the packet triggered a shared object rule.
102	HTTP Decoder	The decoder engine decoded HTTP data within the packet.
105	Back Orifice Detector	The Back Orifice Detector identified a Back Orifice attack associated with the packet.
106	RPC Decoder	The RPC decoder decoded the packet.
116	Packet Decoder	The event was generated by the packet decoder.
119, 120	HTTP Inspect Preprocessor	The event was generated by the HTTP Inspect preprocessor. GID 120 rules relate to server-specific HTTP traffic.
122	Portscan Detector	The event was generated by the portscan flow detector.
123	IP Defragmentor	The event was generated when a fragmented IP datagram could not be properly reassembled.

Snort's GID assignment makes it easy to identify and enable or disable rules for a specific preprocessor. Remember the filter search bar in the Intrusion policy? You can type in a search term like "GID:119" and it'll return the HTTP preprocessor rules only.

Configuring and enabling preprocessor rules can be baffling—a by-product of the decision to split the advanced settings out of the Intrusion policy. Prior to version 5.4, preprocessors were configured within the Intrusion policy, so you could quickly jump from a preprocessor to look at its rules via a link in the Intrusion policy. Now, you've got to jump back and forth between the Network Analysis and Intrusion policies to configure the settings or rule states for a given preprocessor.

Global and Target Based

When looking through several of the preprocessor configurations, you'll notice a pattern emerging. They contain two types of settings: global and target based.

Global settings govern the overall operation of the preprocessor. You'll find settings like packet depth, fragment size, and maybe some options for different modes. Know that if a preprocessor has a global configuration, it probably also has a target-based section.

Target-based settings are configured based upon factors like operating system or web server type. They allow changing Snort's normalization settings for different host protocol stacks. The need for target-based settings arises from inconsistencies between different operating systems and how they process certain types of traffic. While you can adjust these target-based settings yourself, Firepower also uses a number of techniques to automatically adjust the settings to properly normalize traffic based on the OS or application target.

The Network Analysis Policy (NAP)

Now that you've got a basic understanding of Snort preprocessors, let's go over the settings in the NAP. We're going to do this from a high level and only stop at some of the more commonly modified settings. Remember, you can always use the online help or user guide to get more detailed information about any of these settings.

The first challenge is to *find* the Network Analysis policy! There's no handy menu item to navigate there—all we get is a link to this policy in two places only—the Access Control policy and the Intrusion policy pages. Sure enough, there it is in the upper right of the quick links area:

NOTE Exam Objective information here: The current SNCF exam is based on an older code, so the NAP policy could only be found on the main page of the ACP, not on the IPS page.

The user interface for editing the Network Analysis policy is a lot like the one for the Intrusion policy. If there are existing policies, they'll appear in a list. You can create new policies and delete or edit existing policies.

Clicking the Create Policy button brings up the dialog shown next. Here, you can give your policy a name and a description and select the Inline mode. The Inline mode is the same as the Drop while Inline check box we covered back when creating an IPS policy.

Notice the default is Balanced—this base layer *should match your base IPS policy* or else! I named this Cisco Recommended because it's their default, and as usual, I'm going to tell you not to use the defaults and to use SoC instead. Of course, I'm assuming you're using SoC as an IPS policy base layer, which you should be.

Okay—so Network Analysis policies consist of layers and have a base policy just like the Intrusion policy does. NAP configuration even looks like the Intrusion policy, only there are no rules:

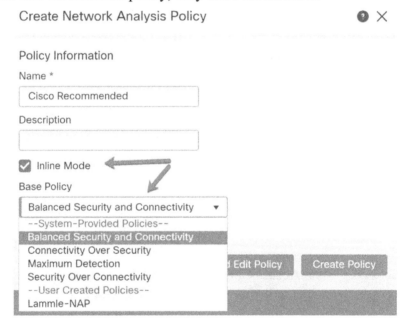

The next figure shows the enabled preprocessors when using the Cisco defaults.

There's a list of settings on the left along with the two default layers—My Changes and the base layer.

As it is when working with the Intrusion policy, it's important to remember that the links on the left that show various settings are only showing us the *enabled* settings in this policy.

Clicking on the Settings link reveals all the policy settings and whether they're enabled or not.

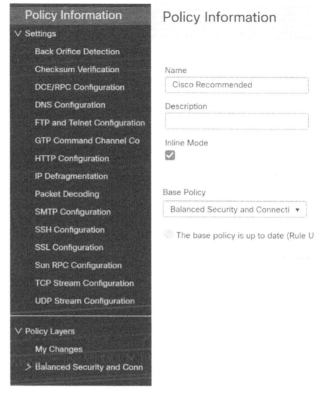

Did you notice that the SIP, IMAP and POP preprocessors don't show up in the list of links on the left? That's because they're currently *disabled*, although the figure only reveals SIP. The rest are further down the page and not shown:

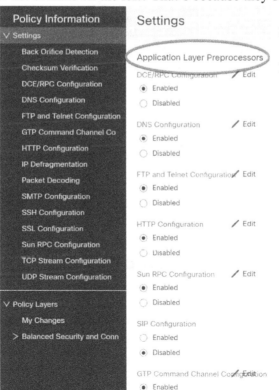

If you were to scroll down on the page that I show above, you'll see that the preprocessors are broken up into four categories as listed here:

1. Application Layer Preprocessors
2. SCADA Preprocessors
3. Transport/Network Layer Preprocessors
4. Specific Threat Detection

Let's discuss these four categories in detail now.

Application Layer Preprocessors

These preprocessors are designed to normalize and inspect traffic for a number of well-known, ubiquitous applications.

DCE/RPC – GID:133

The DCE/RPC preprocessor is dedicated to Distributed Computing Environment and Remote Procedure Call traffic. In short, this means traffic to/from Microsoft Windows systems. This also includes the Server Message Block (SMB) protocol, which, while primarily used on Windows hosts, is

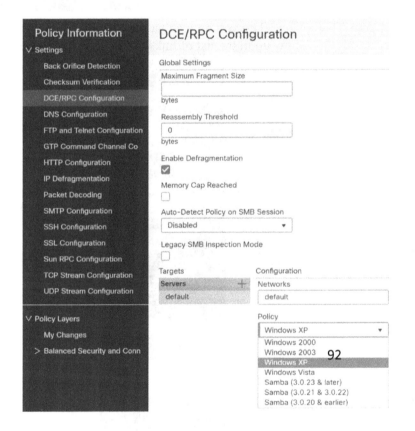

supported on other operating systems too.

The DCE/RPC is a pretty complex preprocessor with a number of options. It's one I don't see modified in the field very often because of that cardinal rule I already mentioned.

Unless you know your environment is using atypical ports or DCE/RPC options, just leave this one alone. But most people reading this can probably figure out I'm using the newer Window Vista file system, included in 7, 8, and 10, and that the old system is the default (XP and below).

So, the default setting here is basically telling me, "You use the old 1995 version of Windows file system for packet fragmentation and reassembly, right? No? Oh wow, too bad." Of course, it'll still work, it'll just be completely inefficient! Isn't that what the Cisco defaults do most of the time anyway? So yep—I changed this one to the "new" file system of 1998, Vista (which includes 7, 8, 10). Maybe I'm just getting to the point where I'm not going with the defaults anymore…just saying!

DNS – GID:131

The DNS preprocessor is one of the few that actually doesn't perform any normalization to traffic. It's an alert-only preprocessor and it'll do so upon several irregularities—if the associated rules are enabled.

FTP and Telnet GID:125,126

Two preprocessors in one, these look for specific commands and anomalous activity in File Transfer Protocol (FTP) and Telnet traffic.

HTTP Configuration GID:119,120

The HTTP inspection preprocessor is one of the most important due to the double-edged sword of the sheer volume of HTTP traffic and the attacks it carries with it. I'm going to slow down a bit here to point out some features.

If you compare some of the settings in the Network Analysis policies provided by Talos, you'll notice some differences. If you're curious, you can create a couple of policies based upon different Talos policies and run a comparison report.

Here's a screen shot of the Cisco defaults. Notice those Compressed/Decompressed Data Depth settings? These are actually mid/late 1990s settings—back when we used modems!

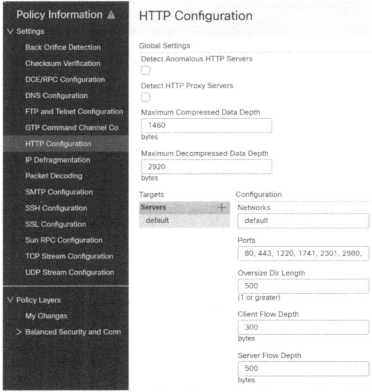

If you scroll down, you'll see the other settings that aren't enabled but need to be, like normalizing HTTP headers, etc.

The differences in the HTTP configuration show up in the next figure. I want to point out that I did this for the Balanced Security and Connectivity and Security over Connectivity policies. The Balanced Security and Connectivity policy is on the left and the Security over Connectivity policy is on the right:

Demo NAP (2016-10-01 15:49:08 by admin)		SoC (2016-10-03 22:06:02 by admin)	
Settings		**Settings**	
HTTP Configuration		HTTP Configuration	
Global Settings		Global Settings	
Maximum Compressed Data Depth	1460	Maximum Compressed Data Depth	20000
Maximum Decompressed Data Depth	2920	Maximum Decompressed Data Depth	20000
Servers		Servers	
default		default	
Ports	80, 1220, 1741, 2301, 2980,	Ports	36, 80, 81, 82, 93, 84, 85, 86
Client Flow Depth	300	Client Flow Depth	0
Server Flow Depth	500	Server Flow Depth	0
Normalize HTTP Headers	No	Normalize HTTP Headers	Yes
Inspect HTTP Cookies	No	Inspect HTTP Cookies	Yes
Inspect HTTP Responses	No	Inspect HTTP Responses	Yes
		Inspect Compressed Data	Yes
		Decompress SWF File (LZMA)	Yes
		Decompress SWF File (Deflate)	Yes
		Decompress PDF File (Deflate)	Yes
Log URI	No	Log URI	Yes
Log Hostname	No	Log Hostname	Yes

94

You can see there are some key settings that are different in the more secure policy on the right! Here's a quick brief on them:

- **Maximum compressed/decompressed data depth**: We go from decompressing a single packet (1460 bytes) on the left to up to 20,000 bytes of data on the right. This is for server responses that use gzip compression.
- **Ports**: The list runs off the page, so just know that there's a bunch of additional ports in the more secure policy.
- **Client and server flow depth**: This determines how deep Snort will inspect an HTTP flow depending on where it's going. The policy on the left looks at 300 bytes into a flow to a client and 500 bytes into a flow to a server. Over on the right, the zero indicates that the depth is unlimited, meaning I've normalized and inspected the entire flow in either direction!
- **Inspect Compressed Data**: I'm only doing an inspection of compressed data when using the Security over Connectivity policy.

Like so many settings within Snort, these represent the tension between performance and security well. The balanced base policy must allow the Firepower device to perform at its rated throughput, but the security base policy is weighted more toward detection at the cost of performance. The settings I just highlighted perfectly illustrate that while it's much more thorough to inspect deeper into the HTTP flows and decompress more data, that activity comes at a cost to device performance.

So, what can we change in the HTTP configuration that won't cost too much in device performance? Aside from the settings I just talked about, here are some common ones you can adjust, which are helpful in some network environments without hurting too much:

- **Ports:** The port list is actually more dynamic than it looks. Snort can identify HTTP by itself and normalize the traffic even if it occurs on a port not listed here. Still, to ensure that you're processing all HTTP, only add ports where HTTP services aren't listed.

  A little note about port 443: If you're performing SSL decryption either externally or via your Firepower device, add port 443 as well as any other decrypted traffic ports to this list.

- **Extract Original Client IP Address:** This comes is very handy when you have an IPS that's external to your proxy server. Snort can extract the client's original IP address if it's populated in the HTTP header by the proxy. Two of the most common fields are listed here: X-Forwarded-For and True-Client-IP. You can change their priority or add your own if your proxy uses a different header field for this information.

- **Log URI and Log Hostname:** These options extract the raw URI and hostname (if present) in the first HTTP header. These values are then displayed in their respective columns in intrusion events.

Sun RPC GID:106

This preprocessor reassembles fragmented Sun RPC traffic.

SIP GID:140

This one allows the use of various SIP rule keywords to inspect Session Initiation Protocol (SIP) telephony traffic.

GTP Command Channel GID:143

The General Service Packet Radio (GPRS) Tunneling Protocol (GTP) preprocessor permits the use of various GTP keywords in Snort.

IMAP GID:141 and POP GID:142

These preprocessors inspect server-to-client Internet Messaging Application Protocol (IMAP) and Post Office Protocol (POP) traffic. If the associated rules are enabled, they can alert on anomalous traffic. They can also extract and decode email attachments.

SMTP GID:124

Like its IMAP and POP brethren, the Simple Mail Transport Protocol (SMTP) preprocessor can alert on anomalous traffic and extract filenames, addresses, and header data for intrusion events triggered by SMTP traffic.

SSH GID:128

The Secure Shell (SSH) preprocessor detects several types of common SSH attacks. By default, it stops inspecting SSH sessions after it sees 20 encrypted packets.

SSL GID:137

The Secure Sockets Layer (SSL) preprocessor analyzes SSL handshake messages and is required for rules that detect exploits like Heartbleed. It stops intrusion and file inspection of packet payloads for encrypted traffic.

SCADA Preprocessors

SCADA stands for Supervisory Control and Data Acquisition. It's the term used for industrial control systems like those used in chemical, power, manufacturing, and a host of other industries.

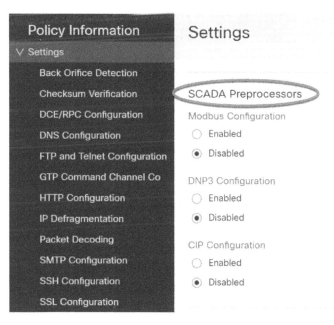

There are two protocols supported by Snort—Modbus and DNP3.

These preprocessors should be enabled if you're protecting SCADA systems along with enabling the PROTOCOL-SCADA Snort rule category.

The Modbus preprocessor uses GID:144 and DNP3 uses GID:145.

Transport/Network Layer Preprocessors

The Transport/Network layer preprocessors operate at the packet layers that carry the same names. The Network layer is where we see the Internet Protocol (IP) and the Transport layer sits right on top. This is also where we see the Transmission Control Protocol (TCP) and the User Datagram Protocol (UDP).

These preprocessors specialize in fragmentation reassembly.

These can also trigger alerts for anomalous traffic if the associated rules are enabled.

Checksum Verification

At a basic level, this verifies if packets have been tampered with.

Inline Normalization

The Inline Normalization preprocessor is one of the few that people typically modify in the Network Analysis policy. The guidance from Cisco is as follows: If your device is inline, this preprocessor should be enabled and includes modes like routed or switched too. Basically, anytime the device processes packets and sends them back out.

There are loads of options you can enable with this preprocessor, so be *really careful* if you decide to "tweak" this one! This preprocessor actually has the ability to *change* packets as they pass through the device, which can be a good thing, but it can also be pretty dangerous.

If you start changing flags or attributes of packets that were working just fine before, it could break a delicate business-critical application, and that could totally ruin your day! So, if you do make changes here, be sure to test thoroughly, however, with all that said - ENABLE THIS.

If you use the Cisco default policy, this preprocessor is disabled! Enable it.

The reason Cisco recommends enabling this preprocessor has to do with fragmentation reassembly. The preprocessor can "clean up" malicious fragmentation, which is sometimes used to evade detection.

I could go on about malicious fragmentation for days and even though it's truly riveting, I'm not going into that here. Just know to turn this on.

IP Defragmentation GID:123

This preprocessor handles packet reassembly at the IP layer. If you haven't noticed yet, fragmentation is a huge deal when it comes to packet inspection. Fragmentation can happen at so many layers, and it's absolutely critical that fragments are properly reassembled before Snort rule inspection!

This wouldn't be so complicated if there weren't seven different ways used to reassemble overlapping IP fragments. And this target-based preprocessor can use all of these methods, depending on the operating system being targeted! So I'm going to refer you to that Judy Novak paper on the Snort website for a detailed discussion of why this is a big deal and how Snort deals with it.

Packet Decoding GID:116

The packet decoder actually decodes the packet data before it gets sent to the other Transport/Network layer preprocessors. It starts decoding at the Data Link layer and moves on up through the Transport layer. There's a whole bunch of rules related to packet decoding; plus, you can alert on a variety of protocol anomalies.

TCP Stream GID:129

If you thought fragmentation was a pain at the IP layer, it just gets worse at the TCP layer. There are 13 different ways Snort can use to defragment TCP data! Some operating systems like Microsoft Windows even change their reassembly method for different versions. The next figure pictures the Policy drop-down menu on the TCP Stream settings page.

Notice the default fragment/reassembly is late 1990s, meaning Win98, WinME, etc. ...really? For crying out loud! Clearly, change this to Vista/7/8, you know, something people actually use:

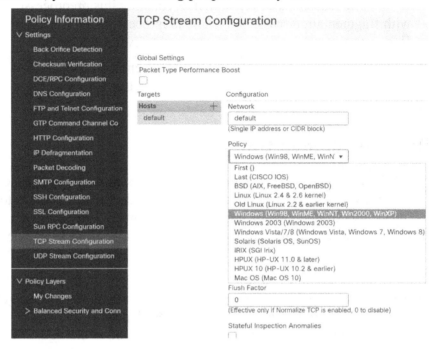

The TCP Stream preprocessor is vital due to the huge amount of TCP traffic traversing modern networks. It's also is required for multiple Snort rule keywords, including the **flow** keyword that's used in nearly every rule.

This preprocessor also maintains a state table that identifies active sessions as well as which specific host is the client and which one is the server in a given conversation.

UDP Stream GID:129

We're going to wrap up this section with the UDP Stream preprocessor, which provides state and session tracking a lot like the TCP preprocessor does, only for the UDP protocol instead. At first, this might seem a little strange because UDP is by definition a "stateless" protocol, but lots of applications use UDP as their transport protocol and maintain state at the Application layer. This preprocessor can detect all this and update the state table with entries even if the session is using UDP.

Specific Threat Detection

The preprocessors in this section don't really fit the classic definition because they don't normalize traffic for rules. Instead, they're designed to detect activity that Snort rules can't.

Detecting the activity in question requires a complex calculation— a time-based component. This just can't be accomplished via the Snort rule language, not even with a pre-compiled rule.

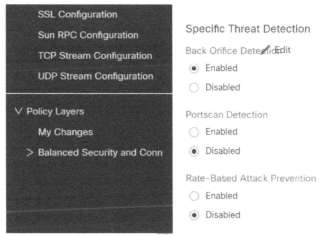

Back Orifice Detection GID:105

The Back Orifice preprocessor is designed to detect traffic from the similarly named remote administration tool. Calling it a remote administration tool is actually a bit generous since it can be installed without user interaction, and it can takes steps to hide it on the target system. This software debuted in 1998, but ancient operating systems still exist, and because it's the only tool for Snort to detect Back Orifice, the preprocessor defaults to enabled.

There aren't any configuration settings. Oddly enough, while the preprocessor is enabled in all Cisco Network Analysis policies, the GID:105 rules are disabled in the Connectivity over Security intrusion policy. Since the only real reason this preprocessor exists is to alert on Back Orifice traffic, either enable the rules or just disable this preprocessor.

Portscan Detection GID:122

Portscan detection is a feature that looks for a large number of reset (RST) or ICMP unreachable packets coming from a host. When its sensitivity is increased, it also looks for a large number of sync (SYN) packets going to a host. Either one of these events could be an indication that the host is being port scanned, which was awesome years ago when a

Snort sensor had a single CPU. Today, with modern devices and multiple instances of Snort, this preprocessor isn't as effective.

The key behind its decreased clout has to do with Firepower's load balancing of flows across CPUs. Because no single CPU gets to "see" all the traffic, portscan activity is divided among various Snort instances. So basically, the more CPUs, the less sensitive the device is to detecting scans. Of course, you can still enable this preprocessor, but your mileage will definitely vary and you could even end up getting a bunch of false positives and negatives!

Rate-Based Attack Prevention GID:135

The last setting I'm going to cover is Rate-Based Attack Prevention, which allows for the creation of rules to detect and potentially stop rate-based attacks. Mitigating evils like denial of service (DOS) attacks and limiting the number of established connections permitted to a host can be achieved via these rules. The former basically prevents network resources from being exhausted, and the latter prevents an attacker from using up most or all of the available connections to a single host.

Enabling this feature effectively enables the appropriate GID:135 rules automatically. Just know that these rules will still show as disabled in the Intrusion policy—manually activating these rules has no effect.

Let's *Not* Use the Cisco Default

So let's have some fun and change the defaults in a Cisco policy plus the NAP! If you've got SoC on your IPS policy(s), you should also have SoC on your NAP, right?

The key here is to understand that it's all about the settings. Let's focus on the SoC: First thing to notice here is that Inline Normalization is enabled by default—what a concept!

So, just using the NAP with a base layer of SoC makes your network more secure and efficient because of the default settings.

Let's check out the HTTP preprocessor now:

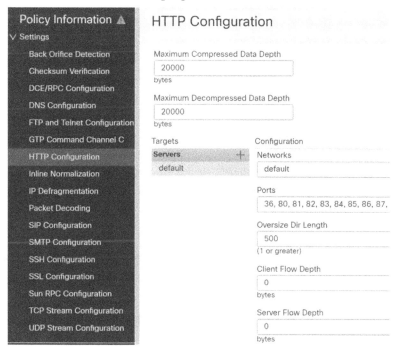

The best advice here is to make sure your IPS policies are using SoC and tune all the IPS policies weekly using your newfound skills as a Firepower Advanced Network Analyst.

Then, set your NAP to be SoC. No changes needed to the policy, just add it to the Advanced tab in your ACP and deploy. You're golden with the NAP SoC defaults.

Last pointer… If you're feeling totally taken for granted at work, just go with Maximum Detection on both your IPS policy and NAP. You'll definitely become the center of attention stat!

Check out the NAP HTTP preprocessor with Max detection as a base policy in the next figure. Notice the amount of depth this processor is using to scrutinize the data flow:

Security over Connectivity (SoC) is clearly the superior NAP base policy over the Cisco defaults!

Summing this part up

Before we move on in this book, I'm going to wrap up NAP with a bow for you, but still not call this a plain ol' Summary, because, well, no one reads summaries, do you? I don't.

We covered a legion of settings and left the majority at their defaults because misconfiguring preprocessors can have a terrifying effect on Snort rules and ruin your life. Firepower's innate design has gone to great lengths to minimize the potentially apocalyptic damage we can do with this policy.

Back when Firepower was FireSIGHT, if you happened to disable a key preprocessor like IP Defragmentation or TCP Stream, you'd get a thoughtful warning that some rules would no longer work properly. In fact, the system would actually prevent you from saving an Intrusion policy with these vital preprocessors disabled. But nowadays, the system won't complain at all —go right ahead and disable every last one of the key preprocessors in the NAP and… Not a peep! You can deploy policies all day long and the system will merrily comply. You might say, "Wait, didn't I just completely handicap the Snort rules?" Nope—you didn't—the system will just enable the appropriate preprocessors so your detection hums along just fine!

You can see this real-time by going to the device and digging into the Snort configuration files. All the preprocessor settings are right there. Even so, as I said, it's best to turn on SoC and just leave it be!

While Cisco has certainly given you configuration options in the NAP, you really have to go out of your way to screw it all up, so you can basically configure away till your heart's content. One caveat—yes, you *can* adjust buffer sizes or misconfigure ports and other options to the extent that Snort detection will be rolled back, but bottom line, it's not something to lose sleep over. Basically, if you only make minor tweaks and *fully understand* their ramifications, your Firepower system will soldier on detecting and ending cyber-evils! You're welcome.

Chapter 24: Correlation Policy

The following CCNP Security SNCF exam objectives are covered in this chapter:

2.3 Configure these features using Cisco Firepower

2.3.c Correlation

Just so you know, this policy is only configured on the FMC, but it's not deployed to the devices, which is why it's missing in the figure depicting the FTD flow.

Maybe because the tools of the Correlation policy are subtler than the Firepower System's more illustrious intrusion and malware detection weapons, it tends to be at least partially overlooked. It shouldn't be, though. The Correlation policy's highly useful features focus on ferreting out the kinds of unusual activity than can alert us to some really evil stuff that's either happening or about to! Correlation rules, white lists, and traffic profiles help us detect network and host behaviors that can be harbingers of malicious activity.

We're going to review the options available for creating rules, lists, and profiles to identify certain types of activity even when there aren't Snort rules at hand to detect a specific threat.

Correlation Overview

Correlation essentially focuses on identifying network behaviors, traffic patterns, and events normally considered exceptional or abnormal—stuff that's definitely worth alerting on. Its rules expose conditions we want to know about from a particular intrusion event to an unusually large HTTP connection. Understand that by itself, a rule does nothing. What we really need is a response, which is generated by the Defense Center and can be any one of the built-in notification types: Syslog, SNMP, or Email.

A response can also take the form of a remediation—a script or program that runs on the Defense Center. The rule and response are linked together with the Correlation policy and this relationship is illustrated in the table below. The left column pictures all the different types of activity that a correlation rule can detect, and the column on the right shows the responses available, linking rule to response:

Rule based on:	Response
Intrusion event	Syslog
Discovery event	SNMP
User activity	Email (SMTP)

Host input event	Built-in remediation
Connection event	Custom remediation
Traffic profile change	
Malware event	
White list*	
Correlation policy links the rule with the response	

* A white list is slightly different because it operates like a rule but technically isn't one.

So yes, correlation certainly provides a powerful, flexible alerting mechanism, but there's more to it than that. With the remediation feature, you can trigger a built-in or custom script in response to a Correlation rule. This means the Defense Center can react with a custom alert or whichever action you can write a script to perform. We'll go deeper into remediations coming up.

Correlation Rules, Responses, and Policies

It's tempting to start off with the Correlation policy when setting out to create a custom response to an event, but remember, the policy only links the correlation rule with the response. So before you can create the actual policy, you've got to have both the rule and the response already finished to be ready for the policy.

Correlation Rules

Let's start with a simple rule example (and I'm going to leave this in the legacy theme because it is easier to view for this policy): You've determined that pretty much all HTTP connections originating from your network are less than 5 MB in total size, so you want to be alerted anytime there's an HTTP connection from your network that's larger than that. Good strategy, because in fact, a connection over 5 MB typically indicates either malicious or unauthorized activity! Rather than trying to create a Snort rule looking for specific data in a packet, you clearly need a way to get a fix on anytime a host sends or receives more than 5 MB in an HTTP connection. Assuming you're already logging connection events, this is a perfect application for a correlation rule!

To get started, go to **Policies>Correlation**, then click the Rule Management tab. If it's your first time here, you'll see an empty rule list like this one:

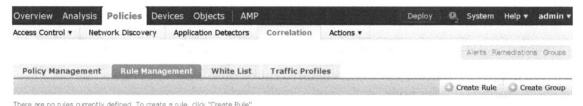

Clicking the Create Rule button on the right takes you to the Rule

The Rule Name and Description fields are pretty straightforward, and while the Name field is required, the Description is optional.

Below this is the Rule Group option. Initially, the only option available is Ungrouped. Rule groups are similar to folders, and they're a great way of keeping rules organized, especially if you write lots of them. By default, all rules will exist in a single flat list. You can add groups on the Rule Management tab by clicking Create Group.

Next up is the meat of the correlation rule—selecting the event. To get that done, I'll create a sentence beginning with *if*. The rest of the sentence defines the kind of activity the rule will target for detection. Clicking the drop-down displays the types of events I can write rules for:

- Intrusion events

- Discovery events

- User activity

- Host input events

- Connection events
- Traffic profile changes
- Malware events

Here's a snapshot of the drop-down list:

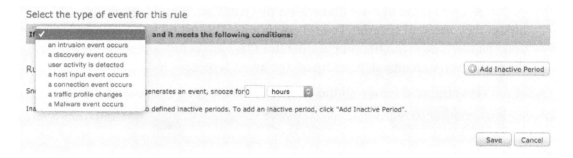

Event types

Since I'm looking for a specific type of HTTP connection, I'm going to go with, "a connection event occurs." After I choose an event type, a second drop-down list usually appears offering some more options depending on the type of event selected. Picking the connection event option opens the drop-down with options for beginning, end, or either:

Event criteria

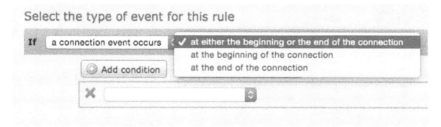

The second drop-down can contain either a few items or a bunch of them. In the case of intrusion events, it won't be displayed at all. Deciding what to choose here is pretty intuitive because I'm just building a sentence describing the type of activity I want detected.

Since I'm hunting for large HTTP connections, I'll go with the default setting for most connection rules using "at either the beginning or the end of the connection". However, I'm still going to be as specific as possible for this one because that'll reduce, even eliminate false positives! Information about large connections is only available at the end of the connection, so I'll opt for "at the end of the connection" for this rule.

Next, I'll add conditions to the rule. The example mentioned these criteria, so I'll include them now:

- Application protocol is HTTP

- Source is our internal network

- Larger than 5 MB

Keep in mind that we don't want this rule matching connections unless they meet all criteria! To add conditions, I'll just pick the options and connect them with the proper operator ("is" or "is not"). Again, the drop-down will change depending on the event type selected.

This figure displays all the criteria available for a connection event:

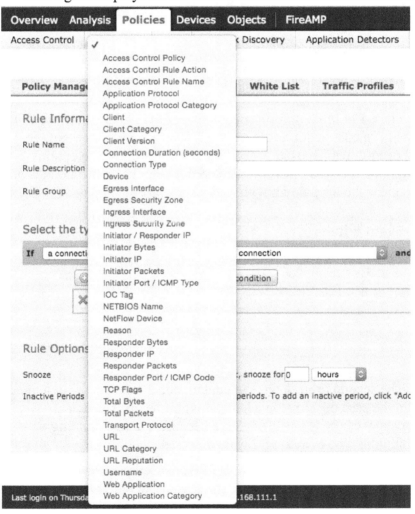

Connection event criteria

Moving on, I'll get started with the application protocol. Once this is selected, the rest of the options in the condition will be populated. After that, I'll pick "is" or "is not" and choose a protocol:

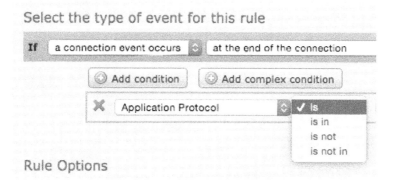

Predictably, the list of application protocols available is super long—there's an arrow to scroll for more choices and as you can see, I've just gotten to the ones that start with *I*!

The next figure shows my progress so far:

Rule Conditions

Let's add some more criteria… If I connect the criteria up with an AND or an OR, I can make the rule broader. The next figure demonstrates that I've added the source network and connection size using the AND operator to make the rule more specific:

Completed rule criteria

Select the type of event for this rule

If	a connection event occurs	at the end of the connection	and it meets the following conditions:

Add condition | Add complex condition

✖ Application Protocol | is | HTTP

AND ✖ Initiator IP | is in | 192.168.0.0/16

✖ Total Bytes | are greater than | 5000000

Just to confuse everyone, the usual terms *source* and *destination* aren't used with connection events. Instead, we get *Initiator* and *Responder*, which also happen to be analogous to *client* and *server*. The reasoning here is that because clients initiate connections, they're "initiators," and servers respond to connection requests, making them "responders."

Rule Options

Okay—so below the rule criteria there are options for Snooze and Inactive Periods, which can come in handy with a few rule types.

Snooze

Snooze cuts down on how many times a rule will trigger. What do you think the rule I just created would do if there were a bunch of big HTTP connections initiated from the same host during a very short period of time? That's right—it would trigger like crazy, and if it was linked to an email response—well, holy Defense Center Spam Storm! *No one* needs that… A single email alert is all the heads-up anyone needs, thank you.

This is where the Snooze option comes in. You can snooze the rule for a user-defined period of seconds, minutes, or hours, which will thankfully cause the Defense Center to trigger the rule the first time it matches during the snooze period *only*.

Here's a look at what a set snooze period looks like:

Rule Options

Snooze	If this rule generates an event, snooze for 10 minutes

Inactive Periods

Similar to Snooze, the Inactive Periods option also works to reduce the number of alerts a rule will hit you with. Let's say this kind of big HTTP connection behavior is normal during business hours so you only want this kind of traffic detected afterward, when it shouldn't be happening. Just add an inactive period to make this rule inactive during the workday!

To get this done, click the Add Inactive Period button on the right and select the period—daily, weekly, or monthly. Continue with the day of the week, start time, and minutes of inactivity. In this example, I'm going to create five different inactive periods for each day of the workweek, as shown here:

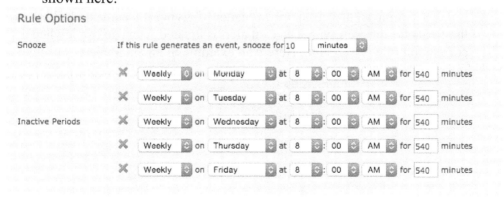

Clicking the Save button will take you back to the rules list.

Responses

Next, I'm going to make sure I've got the proper response in place. Keep in mind that a response is an action performed on the Defense Center when a correlation rule triggers. Responses can range from a simple email message to a highly complex customized remediation script that executes an action on a remote device or system. They fall into two, broad categories—Alerts and Remediations:

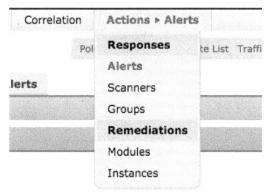

Alerts

Alerts are notifications generated by the Defense Center, and there are three built-in types available:

- Email SMTP sent to the mail relay configured in the System policy.
- SNMP—SNMP versions 1, 2, and 3 are supported
- Syslog—standard SYSLOG sent to port 514/UDP.

Let's head over to **Policies> Actions> Alerts** to configure these alerts. Once here, I'll click the Create Alert button on the right, which will display the drop-down used to create any of the three alert types.

Creating an alert is simply a matter of giving it a name and filling in the fields for the alert type. Once an alert is created, you can use it when a correlation rule is triggered. Here's an example of an email alert:

Remediations

A remediation is just another type of response only a lot more complex. It's essentially a script or program that runs on the Defense Center in response to a correlation rule being triggered. Remediations are powerful tools that equip the Defense Center with the ability to deploy a specific action in response to a correlation event. There are several built-in responses, but you can also create custom responses to upload to the Defense Center.

To get an idea of the kind of responses available, go to **Policies> Actions> Modules**. You'll find modules under the Remediations heading on the menu, which will bring up the screen shown below.

Installed Remediation Modules

Module Name	Version	Description
Cisco IOS Null Route	1.0	Block an IP address in a Cisco IOS router
Nmap Remediation	2.0	Perform an Nmap Scan
pxGrid Adaptive Network Control (ANC) Policy Assignment	1.0	Apply or clear an ANC policy for the endpoint at the involved IP addresses
pxGrid Mitigation	1.0	Perform a pxGrid mitigation against the involved IP addresses
Set Attribute Value	1.0	Set an Attribute value

There are five built-in remediation modules (the amount here depends on your code):

1. **Cisco IOS Null Route** adds a null route entry to a remote Cisco IOS router.

2. **Nmap Remediation** runs an Nmap scan.

3. **PxGrid Adaptive Network Control (ANC) Policy Assignment performs** apply or clear and ANC policy for the endpoint at the involved IP addreses

4. **pxGrid Remediation** performs an Nmap scan from a device or the Defense Center.

5. **Set Attribute Value** sets the value of a host attribute.

Built-in remediations come un-configured, and to use them, you've got to create at least one instance. An instance represents a specific set of configuration values for the remediation. For example, if you have four Cisco IOS routers you want to use with the Cisco IOS Null Route remediation, you will create four instances. After you've created an instance, you can add specific remediations, which can then be used in the Correlation policy.

To show you how this works, I'm going to walk you through setting up one of the built-in remediation modules—the Cisco IOS Null Route.

Setting Up the Cisco IOS Null Route Remediation

First, let's go to the modules page at **Policies> Actions> Modules** as shown in the figure above and click on the magnifying glass icon far to the right of the Cisco IOS Null Route remediation. This will bring up the configuration page for this module, pictured next:

Click the Add button to create a new instance, which brings up the Edit page for this remediation as shown in the next figure. Remember to create an instance for each router you want to control.

This configuration page is actually built from an XML file created by the author of the remediation module itself! The page contains information the module needs to function.

To configure this instance, fill in the applicable values on the form. Keep in mind that this is one of the few places in the Firepower user interface where you can't use spaces in the name field.

Once you've filled out the required fields, click Create and the Configured Remediations section will appear at the bottom of the page:

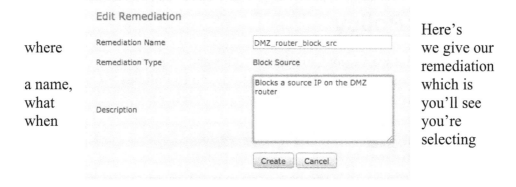

Configured Remediations

Remediation Name	Remediation Type	Description

No configured remediations available

Add a new remediation of type | Block Destination ▼ | Add

Block Destination
Block Destination Network
Block Source
Block Source Network

We have four remediation types for this particular instance:

1. Block Destination
2. Block Destination Network
3. Block Source
4. Block Source Network

These were built into this remediation by the author, and some can carry out more actions than others. We're going to pick the Block Source remediation type and click the Add button, which takes us to the Edit Remediation page:

Edit Remediation

where
Remediation Name   DMZ_router_block_src

Remediation Type   Block Source

a name,
what   Blocks a source IP on the DMZ
              router
when   Description

Here's
we give our
remediation
which is
you'll see
you're
selecting

Create   Cancel

remediations in the Correlation policy.

With that in mind, it's wise to pick one that's nice and descriptive so you'll know what you're selecting. Remember—don't pick a name with spaces in it or you'll get an error! The figure above has a good example of a descriptive name for a remediation in it.

The last step is to click the Create button to save your new remediation.

Creating Custom Remediations

One of the best things about remediations is the ability to create and upload your own! By following the *Firepower System Remediation API Guide*, you can create a custom remediation to do pretty much whatever you want.

Your remediation will run on the Defense Center and you can code it using one of the following:

- Perl
- Shell script
- Precompiled, statically linked C program

A custom remediation is actually a combination of an XML file called `module.template` and the remediation program itself. You can even provide a help file with your remediation. If you use Perl, you can also include any required Perl modules that aren't already found on the Defense Center.

The remediation files are packaged into a gzipped tarball (`.tar.gz` or `.tgz`) and uploaded to the Defense Center from the main module page. For more information on this, refer to the API guide.

Correlation Policy

Now that we've got Correlation Rules and responses, we need to implement them with a policy. To create one, go to **Policies > Correlation**. Policies are shown on the Policy Management tab here:

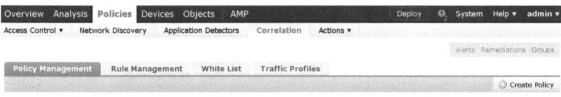

As you can see, there aren't any policies by default, so to create a new policy, click the Create Policy button, which loads the page shown here:

Next, you've got to name it and add and an optional description. Click the Add Rules button to load the list of existing correlation rules:

To add a rule, click the rule check box and then the Add button. I added the example HTTP rule created earlier.

A quick look at the Responses column shows that I haven't selected anything yet. You can create a correlation policy without configuring responses, but most people find that adding notifications and/or remediations is really helpful. If you configure a rule without a response, it'll still generate a correlation event, but that's just not good enough, so I'm going to add some key responses now.

Clicking on the red flag icon to the far right (not shown in figure) loads the responses dialog where I'm going to add responses to the policy.

Choosing an unassigned response and clicking the ^ symbol lets me assign one or more responses to the rule. When I'm done, the Update button updates the policy with the new settings. In the figure below, you can see that I added the email response and the Cisco IOS remediation configured earlier.

Responses for Large HTTP from Internal Net

Assigned Responses

ᵛ ᴧ

Unassigned Responses

DMZ_router_block_src
Email to Security Operations

Update   Cancel

Remember when I told you that giving your rules/alerts/remediations descriptive names is a really good idea? The reason why should be crystal clear now... If I had just named the SMTP alert "Email alert," I'd have absolutely no idea is *who's* being emailed!

I can add multiple rules to the correlation policy and each one can have its own specific responses assigned. Just don't forget to click the Save button after editing the correlation policy. Once you do that, you'll be sent back to the Policy Management tab:

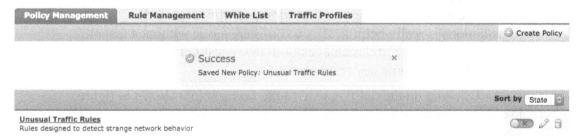

| Policy Management | Rule Management | White List | Traffic Profiles |

⦿ Create Policy

⊘ Success
Saved New Policy: Unusual Traffic Rules   ✕

Sort by State ⬍

Unusual Traffic Rules
Rules designed to detect strange network behavior

One last thing before we're done... When you create a new correlation policy, the default state is disabled. So if you want the policy to actually do something, you've got to enable it by clicking on the switch icon on the right. Once you do that, you'll get a confirmation message and the switch icon will change, indicating the policy has been enabled.

Create Policy

Success   ×
Activated Policy: Unusual Traffic Rules

Sort by   State

Unusual Traffic Rules
Rules designed to detect strange network behavior

Keep in mind that the policy only needs to be enabled once—if you edit the policy and update your rules/responses, your changes will go into effect as soon as the policy is saved.

Okay—from now on, your policy is active, so you should start getting notifications when correlation rules trigger!

White Lists

Another cool Firepower feature in the correlation category is called a white list, which isn't the same thing as a Security Intelligence whitelist. In this context, a white list is a set of criteria used to define which OSs, client/server apps, and protocols are *allowed* to run on your network.

So basically, where correlation rules hunt for undesirable stuff, white lists look for desirable things. Rules trigger when they zero in on an event matching specific criteria, but white lists trigger when they find something *other* than what's allowed.

A really simple white list might only specify a single criterion like an operating system. Let's say you only want to allow Linux operating systems on a given network segment. If you create a white list containing only this type of OS, you can be alerted if Firepower detects any other kind on that segment.

White lists consist of two main parts: targets and host profiles. Targets are the IP addresses or ranges to be evaluated by the white list, whereas a host profile can contain the OSs, client or server applications, protocols, and web applications allowed. You can even add specific applications to your white list so that a host that's caught with an application that's not included will generate a violation.

I'll walk you through creating a sample white list to clarify all this.

Again, we're going to start by navigating to **Policy>Correlation**. From here, click the White List tab, which brings up the currently available

Policy Management   Rule Management   White List   Traffic Profiles

Edit Shared Profiles   New White List

121

Name

Default White List
Recommended White List

white lists. Only the Default White List shows up right now because we haven't added any new ones yet:

The Default White List actually contains lots of operating systems and applications, but I'm going to create a new one to apply to a specific network segment. Clicking the New White List link on the right brings up the Survey Network screen shown here:

Policy Management	Rule Management	White List	Traffic Profiles

Add Shared Host Profile   Target Network

Survey Network

Survey a network and generate host profiles based on discovery data.

IP Address	Netmask
0.0.0.0	0

OK   Skip

Now I'm going to choose an IP address/subnet range that my white list will apply to. I could leave it at 0.0.0.0/0, which would make it applicable to all hosts in the Firepower database, but most of the time it's better to restrict things to a certain network segment.

The process of surveying a network actually scans through the existing Firepower database and populates a host profile based upon what turns up. Entering a survey network on this page limits the scope's activity, giving us a host profile that contains all the operating systems, applications, and protocols discovered for hosts within this range. I want to point out that we're not actually scanning the network range in this step, just querying the existing host database to build the profile.

Okay—I'm going to enter the IP range of 192.168.174.0/24 and limit my result to hosts found in the Firepower database within this range:

Policy Management	Rule Management	White List	Traffic Profiles

Add Shared Host Profile   Target Network

⊟ **My White List**

⊟ **Target Networks**

    192.168.174.0/24

⊟ **Allowed Host Profiles**

    Any Operating System

    Microsoft Windows 2000 SP3, XP

    Microsoft Windows 2000, XP, Serv...

    Microsoft Windows XP

White List Information

Name	My White List
Description	
Allow Jailbroken Mobile Devices	☐

Next, I'm going to change the default, My White List, to something more meaningful and add an optional but helpful description. You can see that Firepower Network Discovery has found three different operating system types in this part of the network.

Clicking one of them on the left reveals the details of the operating system, applications, clients, web applications, and protocols—the criterion that'll be used for the white list.

Now would be a good time to verify that the details discovered for these hosts correspond to your organizational policies. You need to get rid of anything discovered that isn't compliant, but you can also add an item to one of the categories by clicking the little, green plus icon in the category heading. Your net result is a "white listed" set of host criteria you can now apply using a Correlation policy.

Again, don't forget to click Save, which will get you right back to the main White List tab:

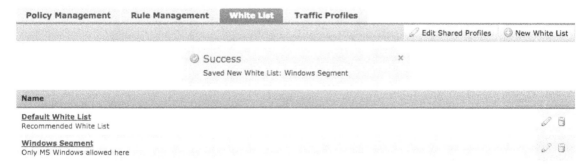

Once the white list has been created, it will be treated the same as a correlation rule—it must be implemented via a Correlation policy.

So now, I'm going to create a new policy for my white list rules back at the Policy Management tab. Here, I've added the new policy and given it a name:

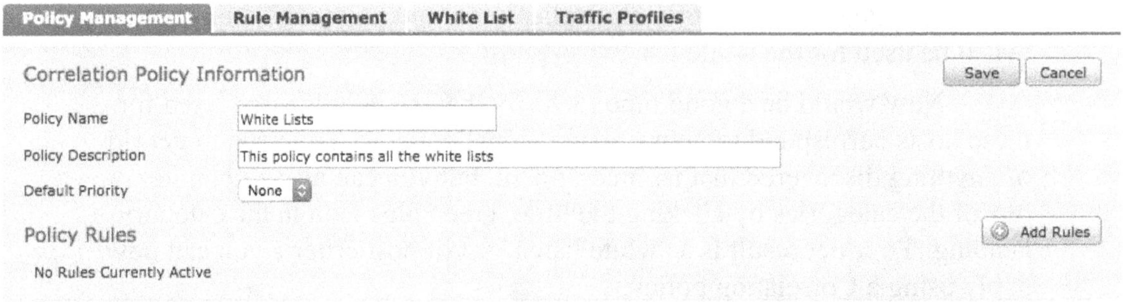

Next up, clicking the Add Rules button will bring up the list of rules and white lists I've created. I'm going to follow the same procedure as before to assign a response and then save and activate the new correlation policy.

When a white list is added to an active Correlation policy, the host(s) in that range will be evaluated as being either compliant or non-compliant. Their status will show up in the host profile via a new host attribute with the same name as the white list. You can view all the non-compliant hosts by heading to **Analysis > Correlation > White List Violations**.

The default workflow reveals the host IP addresses with the white list and a violation count for each. Clicking on the computer icon for a specific host will bring up the host profile.

In the figure below, you can see that this host has an unauthorized SMTP client. Check out the Windows Segment host attribute indicating this host is non-compliant:

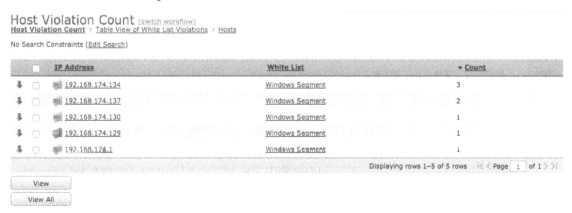

When a discovery event representing a white list violation occurs, it triggers a white list event plus any response(s) that were configured in the policy. These events can be found by navigating to **Analysis>Correlation > White List Events**.

Even though white lists are really cool features that give us visibility to unauthorized software or operating systems, if they're used on a dynamic network segment, things can get pretty crazy. You're going to find a huge amount of non-compliant hosts along with a whole bunch of white list events. People get this under control in two ways:

- Limit white lists to "static" network segments—only apply your white lists to critical hosts that don't typically change. Using a detailed host profile with your white list means you'll be alerted to most software changes on the host(s).
- Limit the number of attributes in your host profile. If your white list covers a legion of dynamic hosts, limit the list to just one or two areas by specifying the operating system(s) allowed but not the applications, protocols, or services. This way, your hosts will only be non-compliant if they're running an unauthorized operating system.

The bottom line is to try to avoid too much noise! Unnecessary alerts are usually ignored anyway, which like crying wolf kills the white list's effectiveness over time!

Traffic Profiles

The last correlation feature up is the traffic profile, which is basically an activity baseline that includes things like the IP address, application protocol, transport protocol, etc. Once activated, the profile collects data points about the traffic over the profile period. After the profile is built, you can add it to correlation rules and specify the deviation that will cause the rule to trigger. As with the other features, add the rule to a Correlation policy and select an appropriate response.

To get this done, go to **Policies>Correlation** and click the Traffic Profiles tab to view existing profiles. By default, this screen is blank.

Policy Management	Rule Management	White List	Traffic Profiles

New Profile

There are no traffic profiles currently defined. To create a traffic profile, click "New Profile".

Choose the New Profile link on the right, which loads the profile configuration screen:

Policy Management	Rule Management	White List	Traffic Profiles

Profile Information   Add Host Profile Qualification

Profile Name
Profile Description

Profile Conditions   Copy Settings

Collect connection information for all traffic that matches the following conditions:

Add condition   Add complex condition

✕

Profile Options   Add Inactive Period

Profiling Time Window   Maintain data for this profile for the last 1   week(s)
Sampling Rate   Sample data every 05 minutes
Inactive Periods   There are no defined inactive periods. To add an inactive period, click "Add Inactive Period".

Save   Save & Activate   Cancel

The Profile Information section contains the profile's name and its optional description.

Next, scroll down to Profile Conditions, where you'll specify the type of traffic you want to profile. If you've already set up some conditions you want to build upon, just click the Copy Settings button to copy from an existing profile. If you need to enter profile conditions, it's a lot like what you've already done in a correlation rule. Basically, you're just defining the conditions for the connection that'll be included in this profile.

Keep in mind that traffic profiles are built from connection events, so you've got to be logging connections for the hosts/applications specified in the traffic profile for this to work. Also, there have to be "end of connection" events.

NOTE: If your traffic profiles are empty, it's probably because your Access Control policy isn't configured to log connections.

Now, add conditions as necessary to limit your profile to the desired traffic. Here, I'm collecting HTTP traffic in the DMZ portion of the network:

Policy Management	Rule Management	White List	**Traffic Profiles**	

Profile Information   ⊙ Add Host Profile Qualification

Profile Name   `DMZ HTTP Traffic`

Profile Description   `HTTP traffic in the DMZ!`

Profile Conditions   🗐 Copy Settings

Collect connection information for all traffic that matches the following conditions:

⊙ Add condition   ⊙ Add complex condition

AND ⬍

✕   Initiator / Responder IP ⬍   is in ⬍   `172.20.5.0/24`

✕   Application Protocol ⬍   is ⬍   `HTTP`

The last section is Profile Options, where you'll determine how long to collect data for the profile plus configure some other parameters.

The duration set to maintain the data is called the Profiling Time Window, or PTW, which can range from hours to days to weeks. The default PTW is 1 week since most traffic patterns generally repeat on a weekly basis.

Once you've selected a PTW, next comes the sample rate. The default is every 5 minutes, but you can change that up to 60 minutes in 5-minute increments.

The combination of PTW and sample rate yields a number of data points in your profile. Keep in mind that this is a statistical sample of data, so a small number of data points won't give you a meaningful sample! You want your traffic profile to have at least 100 data points. The number of data points is calculated via this formula:

Data points = PTW/sample rate

To clarify, if your PTW is 1 day (24 hrs) and your sample rate is one every 60 minutes, the number of data points would be

24/1 = 24 data points

This isn't going to provide a reliable sample, so either increase the time window or decrease the minutes in the sample rate. You can even increase the amount of total samples to make the profile more effective.

Another option when creating the profile is going with inactive periods, which means one or more periods during which the profile doesn't collect any data. This comes in handy by ignoring traffic spikes during known periods like during backups. Profiling backup traffic will likely cause spikes in the profile and trigger a violation when you add it to a correlation rule. So to ignore these known periods of high traffic, just add one or more inactive periods to your profile.

You can also create your profile without any inactive periods and then review the traffic statistics later to add inactive periods as needed.

The completed traffic profile example shown below will do the following:

- Profile all HTTP traffic in the 172.20.5.0/24 network.

- The profile will gather data for 1 week with samples every 5 minutes.

- The profile won't gather data daily at 3:00 a.m. for 50 minutes during the nightly backup. (Yes, it's unlikely that HTTP would actually be used as the backup protocol, but this is just an example, right?)

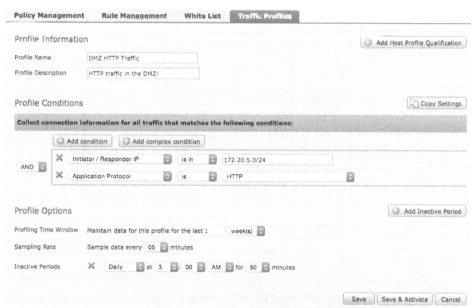

When finished with the profile, click the Save or Save & Activate button. The former saves the profile all set and ready to be activated later, and the latter saves it and starts collecting traffic data immediately.

Clicking the Save button returns to the screen shown below. You can see the switch icon to the right that shows the profile is inactive. Just click the switch to activate the profile when you're ready to begin collecting data.

Success
Saved profile DMZ HTTP Traffic.   ×

Name	Progress	PTW	Sort by State
DMZ HTTP Traffic HTTP traffic in the DMZ!		0 % (1 week)	

The Progress column contains a percentage bar indicating the completeness of the traffic profile. Once activated, this bar will reach 100% at the end of the profile's PTW. You can also view the data collected by a traffic profile by clicking the graph icon to the right of the switch. Initially, this graph will be empty, but over time, as your profile collects traffic information, it'll appear in this graph:

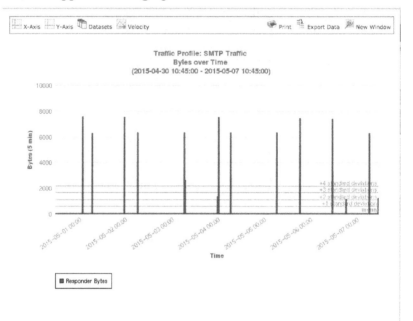

Now that you have one or more traffic profiles, they've got to be added to a Correlation policy to do any good. Because traffic profiles can't be added directly to a policy, I'll need to first create rules to trigger for specific profile conditions.

Okay—going back to the Rule Management tab, I'll again create a correlation rule, only this time, I'll select the option "a traffic profile changes" from the drop-down. Once I've done that, I'll get another drop-down listing all the available profiles. From here I can create the rule the same way I did for previous ones.

Here's the available criteria for a traffic profile rule:

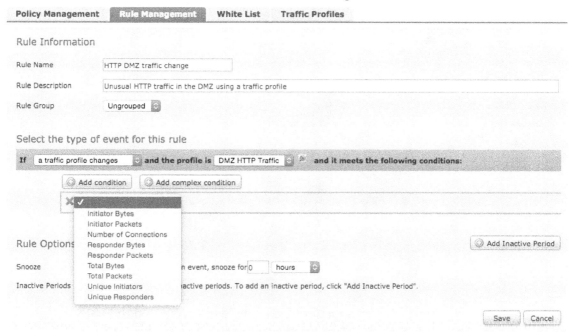

I can select one or more of these counters to cause the rule to trigger:

- Initiator Bytes
- Initiator Packets
- Number of Connections
- Responder Byes
- Responder Packets
- Total Bytes
- Total Packets
- Unique Initiators
- Unique Responders

Using the default 5-minute interval means I'm collecting all this data for each traffic profile every 5 minutes.

Clearly, to create a useful rule, I need to have some idea about what's normal for this profile. This is where the graph above comes in—its information reveals what a "normal" week looks like for HTTP traffic in the DMZ. This key information makes it possible for me to accurately write a rule detecting unusual activity.

The next figure shows that I've finished a rule that's looking for a change in the number of connections or number of unique initiators:

| Policy Management | **Rule Management** | White List | **Traffic Profiles** |

Rule Information

Rule Name	HTTP DMZ traffic change
Rule Description	Unusual HTTP traffic in the DMZ using a traffic profile
Rule Group	Ungrouped

Select the type of event for this rule

If [a traffic profile changes] and the profile is [DMZ HTTP Traffic] and it meets the following conditions:

[Add condition] [Add complex condition]

OR

Number of Connections | are greater than | 2 | standard deviation(s)
use velocity data

Unique Initiators | are greater than | 2 | standard deviation(s)
use velocity data

From here, it's just a matter of creating a Correlation policy or adding the rule to an existing policy and selecting the appropriate response.

Pro tip on traffic profiles… When a traffic profile is created, it doesn't stay static. It's actually a "sliding" window of time that's being constantly updated. This means a seven-day traffic profile will always show the previous seven days, not just the first seven days after it was activated. This is a good thing because it gives flexibility to the profile, allowing it to adjust to the growth of your network.

By using a rule criteria like standard deviation(s), you can detect unusual spikes in traffic while still allowing the profile to adjust to the normal ebb and flow of things.

Summary

The Correlation Policy is an often overlooked but useful feature of the Firepower System. The features available in this area concentrate on detection of unusual activity rather than specific intrusion or malware events and is only configured on the FMC.

By using Correlation Rules, White Lists and Traffic Profiles, we can detect network or host behaviors that are likely indications of malicious activity.

We reviewed the options available for creating rules, lists and profiles to identify activity even when there are no Snort rules available to detect a specific threat.

Chapter 25: SSL

The following CCNP Security SNCF exam objectives are covered in this chapter:

2.0 Configuration

2.2 Configure these policies in Cisco Firepower Management Center

2.2.f SSL

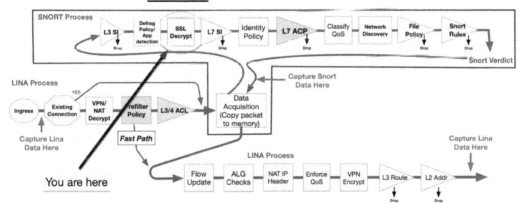

One of the newer punches Firepower FTD packs lies in SSL policies. These give us insight beyond typical packet sniffing detection by helping us bore deeper into potentially compromised hosts and encrypted data.

SSL

We first gained the ability to decrypt Secure Sockets Layer (SSL) communications back in FireSIGHT version 5.4, but it was Firepower v6.0 that actually extended this capability to the ASA with the Firepower FTD platform. Then, v6.1 came along packing some nice improvements to SSL processing that really improved reliability and paved the way for decryption to work well in more situations.

Let's start off with some SSL basics and then get into how we use the SSL policy.

Secure Sockets Basics

SSL use on Internet websites has been steadily growing in popularity. If you check the various browser tabs you have open right now, it's likely that most of them have the familiar "https" and associated lock icon in the site URL. From banking to web mail to your favorite social media site, pretty much everyone is now on board with encrypted communications. This is great—unless you're using an intrusion prevention system (IPS) to try to inspect network traffic—then it's terrible, like staring into a black hole!

After all, secure communications are all about privacy, integrity, and authentication. SSL helps ensure that your network traffic can't be read, that what you send or receive hasn't been modified en route, and that you're actually communicating with the site you think you are.

Of course, SSL isn't really what we're using nowadays. It's actually SSL's successor—TLS, or Transport Layer Security. But everyone still uses the generic term *SSL* when talking about this type of encryption, so we won't split hairs.

While it would be fun to dive into all things SSL, TLS, and symmetric cryptography, I'm going to stay up at a high level to help you nail down what's really important when it comes to Firepower. I'll also take you through creating your own SSL policy and rules.

First, understand that SSL is all about certificates and keys. Certificates are generally used to verify the identity of the server and, optionally, the client. Keys are used to lock (encrypt) data prior to transmission and unlock (decrypt) data after receipt. For Firepower to transparently decrypt SSL communications, it has to be provided with this extremely confidential certificate/key data. Armed with these secrets and positioned properly between the client and server, it can intercept communications and inspect their contents and do it all without triggering any notifications or alarms!

Intercepting and decrypting these communications is successful because the organization doing the decryption owns the keys, basically saying, "It's fine, we're the good guys!" This is commonly referred to as a main-in-the-middle (MITM) attack. Firepower inserts itself between the client and server and pretends to be one or the other, depending on whether you're inspecting inbound or outbound connections. Being positioned in the middle isn't always required, but attempting to perform SSL decryption in passive mode will fail for many connections. This is because newer key exchange mechanisms are designed to prevent passive decryption of SSL traffic even when the secrets are known. The bottom line is if you plan to use SSL decryption, your device should be in routed, switched, or Inline mode.

The SSL Handshake

Having a basic understanding of the SSL handshake is key to understanding how Firepower carries out its MITM function and how some of the latest 6.1 features improve reliability. In a typical SSL connection, there's a client and a server. When a user connects to a secure website, the client is the web browser (Chrome, Firefox, Safari, etc.) and the server is an application like Apache or NGINX running a secure website.

The two goals of SSL are as follows:

1.   Verify for the user staring at the screen that the site that says it's www.yourbank.com is really your bank and not some imposter.

2.   Ensure that communications can't be intercepted and viewed by anyone except www.yourbank.com.

The mission is accomplished with a carefully orchestrated handshake that confirms all the right conditions are present on the client and the server. When the handshake is complete, you can be confident in the authenticity of the site and the security of your data—let the banking begin!

We're going to look at this handshake from a very high level without getting into the weeds to focus on what's vital to configuring Firepower SSL decryption.

Here are the steps the process takes:

1. The client sends the "client hello." This contains the client's SSL version number, randomly generated data, and cryptographic information, including which encryption protocols the client supports. For the client and server to communicate, they must agree on a protocol or language they both understand.

2. The server responds with the "server hello." The server sends its SSL version number, cryptographic information, and its digital certificate.

3. The client uses the server's certificate information to verify the authenticity of the server. This includes whether the certificate matches the site name, whether the certificate is expired, and if the certificate authority is trusted. If this fails, you get a warning that the site shouldn't be trusted.

4. The client and server exchange secret key information. This can occur via several methods and is designed to establish and securely exchange the keys that'll be used in the rest of the conversation.

5. The handshake is completed, and the SSL session has begun. All further communications will be encrypted using the agreed-upon encryption algorithm.

Firepower SSL Decryption

When using Firepower to decrypt SSL traffic, the first decision is whether to decrypt inbound or outbound traffic.

Inbound SSL Decryption

Inbound traffic means SSL sessions to your servers. In this case, because you own the servers, you have both the certificate and private key information they use. This private key information is some of the most carefully protected data on the Internet! A compromise of this information would allow an attacker to impersonate your website without a user's knowledge. These keys are generally kept in offline or air-gapped systems and controlled very carefully.

When you configure inbound SSL decryption, you load this certificate and key data onto the Firepower system. This allows it to perform the MITM "attack," decrypt and inspect traffic, and then re-encrypt before sending it to the actual server. No changes on the web server or the client are required to make the connection because the Firepower system impersonates both sides to the other, so neither the server nor the client realize their traffic is being sniffed. Clearly, this has tremendous security implications and illustrates the reason these private keys are so closely guarded!

Outbound SSL Decryption

The other type of decryption you may want to implement is outbound. In this case, you're decrypting sessions that are initiated by clients within your network as they connect to external SSL servers. Since you don't own them, you don't have the secret key information for those external servers. Firepower can perform the MITM action and decrypt the session by replacing the server's certificate with its own, but the client (web browser) will definitely recognize this and give the user a dire warning as shown in the next two figures. The warning is letting them know that the site they're connecting to doesn't have the correct certificate, meaning someone or something is tampering with their connection.

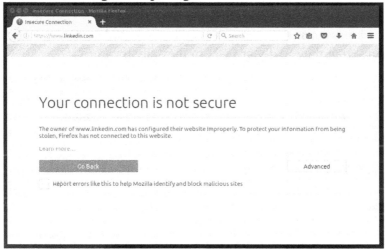

Users can usually bypass these warnings and proceed to the website, but the last thing you want to do is train your users to bypass this type of warning on their system.

It's a legit warning that means there's something wrong with the site's certificate, which could mean someone's intercepting their traffic and data!

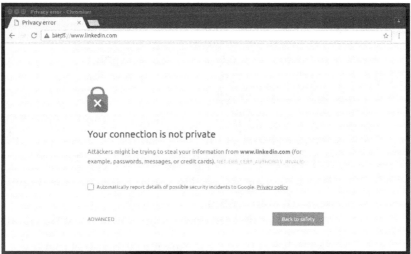

In the examples in the figures above, that's exactly what it means. These screen shots are the result of implementing an outbound SSL policy without using a trusted certificate.

It's all about the certificate chain of trust, which is established by cryptographic signatures. Web browsers and operating systems have built-in root certificate authorities that they trust. These come from organizations you've probably heard of like Verisign, Thawte, Entrust, etc. The concept is basically, "If the root certificate authority (CA) trusts this certificate, then so do I." Because web browsers come with these trusts built in, we can go to a well-known site that's been vetted by a trusted authority with confidence that they really are whom they say they are.

The reason your users can get the warning shown in the last two figures is because the certificate used by Firepower to re-sign the outbound communication wasn't trusted by the web browser. Since you "own" the clients in your organization, you can get around this warning by using your own internal certificate authority to generate and sign the certificate used by Firepower. When your clients see that the certificate Firepower is using is from your trusted certificate authority, they'll treat the SSL connection as legitimate.

Because you have to add this internally generated certificate to all of your web browsers, outbound decryption isn't as simple to implement as inbound. Still, most of the work is done up front updating all of your client browsers with the trusted internal CA certificate. Once over this hurdle, things become much easier. If your organization has already deployed an internal Public Key Infrastructure (PKI), then implementing outbound SSL decryption with Firepower is even more of a breeze.

SSL Objects

Once you decide on the type of SSL decryption you want to use, you need to configure the appropriate objects found in the Objects menu. Three of them relate to SSL decryption:

1. Cipher Suite List: If you want to customize your SSL rules to match a subset of the complete list of supported ciphers, you can create a custom object and add specific cipher suites.

2. Distinguished Name: This object matches the distinguished name field in a server's certificate. You can use this in rules to enable or disable decryption for the specific site name.

3. PKI: This contains the various certificates that have either been generated or imported/signed by external authorities.

They're used to sign or re-sign communications as part of the MITM function.

SSL Policy

Decryption, logging, and blocking of SSL traffic are all implemented in the SSL policy. It's technically associated with an Access Control policy but has its own set of traffic processing rules. Keep in mind that SSL policy rules are implemented before traffic is processed by access control rules.

The SSL policy, along with the rest of the detection policies, is found under **Policies>Access Control>SSL**. There are no SSL policies by default, so to create one, click the New Policy button in the upper right.

Enter the name, an optional description, and the default action for your policy and click Save.

New SSL Policy

Name:

Description:

Default Action:
- Do not decrypt
- Block
- Block with reset

After that, you'll be taken to the main policy editing interface where there are three tabs: Rules, Trusted CA Certificates, and Undecryptable Actions. The Trusted CA Certificates tab (the *CA* stands for *certificate authority*) contains the trusted root certificates I talked about earlier. The list is a like the ones in your own web browser and includes an array of trusted certificate services.

By default, the trusted CA group, Cisco-Trusted-Authorities, is selected; it contains nearly every item from the Available Trusted CAs column on the left. The exception would be any CAs you've added yourself. If you want these to be trusted, you need to add them to the Cisco-Trusted-Authorities group either by means of another group or by adding a specific entry.

The Trusted CA Certificates tab is pictured here:

The Undecryptable Actions tab determines the action that should be taken if the SSL traffic is undecryptable. There's a number of reasons for this listed on this tab, and they vary from things like errors to unknown or unsupported cipher suites. Your choices on how you want to handle this traffic are pretty straightforward:

- **Inherit Default Action**: Do whatever the default action in the policy is set to.

- **Do not decrypt**: Allow the session to pass encrypted. This means you'll have limited visibility into the session.

- **Block**: Block the traffic without resetting the session.

- **Block with reset**: Block the traffic and send a TCP reset to the client and server.

The Rules tab is where you'll spend most of your time configuring this policy. There are three categories: Administrator, Standard, and Root. To be honest, these options aren't really all that useful and actually seem to be more of a throwback to the pre-6.x versions of Firepower. The default is to add rules into the Standard category, which works just fine.

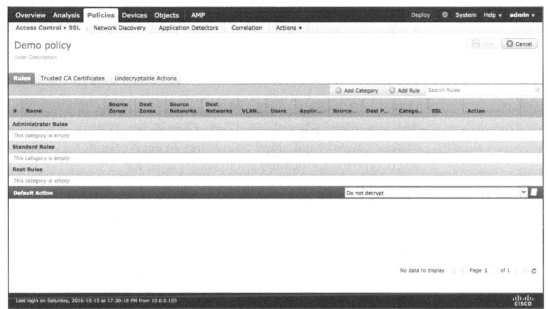

Next up is to configure the default action at the bottom of the rules list and enable logging using the scroll icon to the right. The Rules tab is shown below.

Clicking the Add Rule button brings up the Add Rule dialog. Each rule has a Name field, an Action field, and several tabs that can be used to select the traffic the rule should apply to:

Let's take a quick look at the SSL rule options:

- **Name**: Pretty self-explanatory. The name for your rule, no more than 30 characters.

- **Insert**: Where you want the rule inserted. Can be into a category or above/below an existing rule.

- **Action**:

- o Decrypt – Resign: Decrypt the traffic and re-sign with a previously uploaded CA certificate. This is typically used for outbound decryption. A drop-down list appears for selection of an internal or uploaded CA certificate.

- o Decrypt – Known Key: Match the server certificate data to a previously uploaded server certificate. If it matches, use the uploaded private key to decrypt and re-encrypt the application data. This is used for inbound decryption. A drop-down list appears to select an available certificate.

- o Do not decrypt: Do not decrypt the data in the SSL session.

- o Block: Block the traffic without sending a TCP reset.

- o Block with reset: Block the traffic and send a TCP reset to the client and server.

- o Monitor: Do not decrypt but log a connection event for the traffic.

- **Rule Conditions**: Except for the Logging tab, most tabs are used to limit the traffic a rule applies to. Leaving all these tabs at their defaults will cause the rule to match *all* traffic. Many of these tabs are the same as those found in the Access Control policy so I'm only going to cover the ones that are specific to SSL rules:

- o Certificate: If you've uploaded an external certificate, you can add it here. Only traffic encrypted with this certificate will match the rule.
- o DN: Distinguished name, a site name, or part of a site name with a wildcard, such as, for example, CN=*.mozilla.org. The rule will match traffic that contains the value in the specified attribute. You can add up to 50 conditions in a single rule.
- o Note: The Certificate and DN tabs aren't available for the Decrypt – Known Key action because this information is already in the certificate object.
- o Cert Status: Look for the presence or absence of various certificate attributes. For example, to block sessions using expired certificates, select Yes for the Expired status in a block rule.
- o Cipher Suite: Match sessions using specific cipher suites.

○ Version: Restrict the rule to only match selected SSL/TLS versions.

SSL Rule Examples

I'm going to walk you through some examples of practical SSL rules now.

Outbound Decryption

If you want to decrypt outbound SSL, there are a few things you need to remember. First, since you don't want your users to get the browser warnings you saw previously, you'll need your own internal certificate authority (CA). Then, you'll need to include the CA certificate in the trusted certificates store on all your users' computers.

Next, you'll have to configure Firepower to re-sign SSL communications using a certificate signed by your CA. To do this, go to **Objects>PKI** and select Internal CAs. Then click the Generate CA button to open the following dialog:

the

Generate Internal Certificate Authority	? ×
Name:	
Country Name (two-letter code):	
State or Province:	
Locality or City:	
Organization:	
Organizational Unit (Department):	
Common Name:	
Generate CSR	Generate self-signed CA	Cancel

See

Generate CSR and Generate Self-Signed CA buttons at the bottom? For testing, it's good to generate a self-signed CA, but doing that will cause your browsers to warn you that the site is insecure. So for production, you want to generate a certificate signing request (CSR), which is a file you would then have your CA sign and import back into your FMC. Once that's done, your devices can sign communications under the authority of your internal CA that's now trusted by all of your browsers. Since you have a properly signed internal CA, you can get on with the SSL rules next.

But wait, before you add rules to decrypt outbound sessions, stop and think about the types of traffic you really should *not* decrypt. Do your users do online shopping? What about banking or logging into their healthcare provider's website? These are golden examples of the kind of communications you don't want to be inspecting!

So, what now? You need a do not decrypt rule to identify any sites you want to avoid decrypting via the DN, or if you have the URL Filtering license, do it by the site category.

What's more, there are less obvious sites, which fall into the do not decrypt category—those known to have issues when they're decrypted. For these, Cisco has created a group of Distinguished Name objects you can easily plug into your rules. The object group named Cisco-Undecryptable-Sites contains site CNs for sites where attempting to decrypt the traffic will actually break the underlying application. This is usually because the application uses non-standard SSL parameters or other modifications. Know that as time goes on, you'll probably discover more of these that happen to be specific to your particular organization. You can add the new finds to the rule when you need to.

Okay—next, think about any sites you don't want users going to. For these, add a Block or Block with Reset rule to prevent users from connecting to sites with self-signed or expired certificates—and others should the need arise.

Finally, add your Decrypt – Resign rule and select the signed internal CA you created.

To check out a sample policy with these rules, take a look at the following figure... The default action is set to Do Not Decrypt, which will allow traffic to pass if Firepower can't decrypt it.

I chose to provide more connectivity then security here, but if your organization wants stricter standards, go with one of the block actions as your default:

Inbound Decryption

  Decrypting inbound SSL is a lot easier to configure because you don't need to worry about decrypting users' private information or installing new root certificates on all your web browsers. All you need to do is convince the keepers of your web server's secret keys to share them with you.

  As with outbound SSL, your journey starts in the Objects menu. Go to **Objects>PKI>Internal Certs** where you'll click the Add Internal Cert button and import the certificate and private key from each of the websites you want to decrypt. These can be files (in DER or PEM format), or the cert and key data can be pasted into the appropriate fields.

  The Add Known Internal Certificate dialog is pictured in the this figure:

After this, you can create rules in your SSL policy to decrypt the inbound traffic. Your rule or rules will use the Decrypt – Known Key action shown next.

When using this rule action, you've got to choose one or more internal certificate objects. Clicking the field to the right of the action or the Edit link will bring up the Select Internal Certificate Objects dialog.

You can create several rules or add multiple certificates to a single rule. The rule will only match SSL sessions using the selected certificates.

If you want to restrict the rules further, you get that done with the options on the Networks or Ports tab. Unless you're decrypting all inbound SSL, it's good to leave the default action in this policy to Do Not Decrypt. Here's a simple rule for a single SSL website:

SSL Troubleshooting

Okay, now that you've created and deployed your shiny new policy, it's time to see if it's actually working! To do this, you've got to have logging enabled via the Logging tab in your rules in the SSL or Access Control policy. No worries here—enabling it in both policies won't give you multiple connection events.

Go to **Analysis>Connections>Events** to check out your connection data. The default workflow and table view don't show the SSL information columns—you have to enable some key SSL fields to see that, here is how you do that:

First, click on the Table View of Connection Events link near the upper left of your connection event view, which will take you to a table view of your connections that reveals a bunch of additional columns. The SSL data you are looking for is still hidden though, and one way to expose it is to click on one of the gray X icons to the right of a column heading:

Clicking that X by a column brings up a list of all the columns available in the table view where you can pick the ones you want to add or remove. Scroll down in the list of columns to get to the ones that give you SSL information about the connection way at the bottom:

As you can see, they're all unchecked, so check them and click the Apply button to get all the information there is about an SSL connection. Some of the columns, like the ticket and session ID, really aren't worth much though.

The information in these columns will clue you into if your SSL decryption is working as you thought it would, plus it'll help pinpoint any issues you need to tackle:

SSL Rule	SSL Flow Flags		SSL Flow Messages
Linkedin	VALID, INITIALIZED, SSL_DETECTED, CERTIFICATE_DECODED, FULL_HANDSHAKE, SERVER_SESSION_ID_SEEN, CLIENT_HELLO_SRSSTKT, CH_PROCESSED, SH_PROCESSED, CH_CIPHERS_MODIFIED, CH_CURVES_MODIFIED, CH_EXTENSION_REMOVED, CH_ALPN_HAS_H2		CLIENT_HELLO, SERVER_HELLO, SERVER_CERTIFICATE
Linkedin	VALID, INITIALIZED, SSL_DETECTED, CERTIFICATE_DECODED, FULL_HANDSHAKE, SERVER_SESSION_ID_SEEN, CLIENT_HELLO_SESSTKT, CH_PROCESSED, SH_PROCESSED		CLIENT_HELLO, SERVER_HELLO, SERVER_CERTIFICATE
Linkedin	VALID, INITIALIZED, SSL_DETECTED, CERTIFICATE_DECODED, FULL_HANDSHAKE, SERVER_SESSION_ID_SEEN, CLIENT_HELLO_SESSTKT, CH_PROCESSED, SH_PROCESSED		CLIENT_HELLO, SERVER_HELLO, SERVER_CERTIFICATE
Linkedin	VALID, INITIALIZED, SSL_DETECTED, CERTIFICATE_DECODED, FULL_HANDSHAKE, SERVER_SESSION_ID_SEEN, CLIENT_HELLO_SESSTKT, CH_PROCESSED, SH_PROCESSED		CLIENT_HELLO, SERVER_HELLO, SERVER_CERTIFICATE
Default Rule	VALID, INITIALIZED, UNDECRYPTABLE, PRE_DECISION_ERROR, SSL_DETECTED, CLIENT_HELLO_SESSTKT, CH_PROCESSED, SH_PROCESSED		CLIENT_HELLO, SERVER_HELLO
Default Rule	VALID, INITIALIZED, UNDECRYPTABLE, PRE_DECISION_ERROR, SSL_DETECTED, CLIENT_HELLO_SESSTKT, CH_PROCESSED, SH_PROCESSED		CLIENT_HELLO, SERVER_HELLO
Default Rule	VALID, INITIALIZED, UNDECRYPTABLE, PRE_DECISION_ERROR, SSL_DETECTED, CLIENT_HELLO_SESSTKT, CH_PROCESSED, SH_PROCESSED		CLIENT_HELLO, SERVER_HELLO
Default Rule	VALID, INITIALIZED, UNDECRYPTABLE, PRE_DECISION_ERROR, SSL_DETECTED, CLIENT_HELLO_SESSTKT, CH_PROCESSED, SH_PROCESSED		CLIENT_HELLO, SERVER_HELLO
Default Rule	VALID, INITIALIZED, UNDECRYPTABLE, PRE_DECISION_ERROR, SSL_DETECTED, CLIENT_HELLO_SESSTKT, CH_PROCESSED, SH_PROCESSED		CLIENT_HELLO, SERVER_HELLO

SSL Status	SSL Flow Error	SSL Actual Action	SSL Expected Action	SSL Certificate Status	SSL Version	SSL Cipher Suite	SSL Policy
Decrypt (Resign)	Success	Decrypt (Resign)	Decrypt (Resign)	Valid	TLSv1.2	TLS_ECDHE_RSA_WITH_AES_128_GCM_SHA256	Outbound SSL
Decrypt (Resign)	Success	Decrypt (Resign)	Decrypt (Resign)	Valid	TLSv1.2	TLS_ECDHE_RSA_WITH_AES_128_GCM_SHA256	Outbound SSL
Decrypt (Resign)	Success	Decrypt (Resign)	Decrypt (Resign)	Valid	TLSv1.2	TLS_ECDHE_RSA_WITH_AES_128_GCM_SHA256	Outbound SSL
Decrypt (Resign)	Success	Decrypt (Resign)	Decrypt (Resign)	Valid	TLSv1.2	TLS_ECDHE_RSA_WITH_AES_128_GCM_SHA256	Outbound SSL
Do Not Decrypt (Handshake Error)	MASTER_KEY_INVALID (0xb900035d)	Do Not Decrypt	Unknown	Not Checked	TLSv1.2	TLS_ECDHE_ECDSA_WITH_AES_128_GCM_SHA256	Outbound SSL
Do Not Decrypt (Handshake Error)	MASTER_KEY_INVALID (0xb900035d)	Do Not Decrypt	Unknown	Not Checked	TLSv1.2	TLS_ECDHE_ECDSA_WITH_AES_128_GCM_SHA256	Outbound SSL
Do Not Decrypt (Handshake Error)	MASTER_KEY_INVALID (0xb900035d)	Do Not Decrypt	Unknown	Not Checked	TLSv1.2	TLS_ECDHE_ECDSA_WITH_AES_128_GCM_SHA256	Outbound SSL
Do Not Decrypt (Handshake Error)	MASTER_KEY_INVALID (0xb900035d)	Do Not Decrypt	Unknown	Not Checked	TLSv1.2	TLS_ECDHE_ECDSA_WITH_AES_128_GCM_SHA256	Outbound SSL
Do Not Decrypt (Handshake Error)	MASTER_KEY_INVALID (0xb900035d)	Do Not Decrypt	Unknown	Not Checked	TLSv1.2	TLS_ECDHE_ECDSA_WITH_AES_128_GCM_SHA256	Outbound SSL

SSL decryption is a pretty complex process, so it figures there's a ton of stuff that can go wrong, which I could go on about forever. But you're in luck because I can't do that here!

Remember back a bit when I talked about the SSL handshake? One of the things established during it is the cipher suite that'll be used, which has to be one that the server accepts and the client supports. During the client hello, the client transmits the list of cipher suites it knows to the server, which chooses one of them before the session can proceed.

Sounds simple—what could go wrong? One snag that can crop up here is if the client and server agree on a cipher suite that Firepower doesn't support. In previous versions of Firepower, this would mean the session couldn't be decrypted.

Thankfully, someone finally provided a feature for that in version 6.1, which works by modifying the client hello to remove any cipher suites or other things Firepower doesn't like. So now, we can be confident that the agreed-upon encryption method will be one that we can decrypt as well!

You can see this happening in the messages here:

SSL Flow Flags
VALID, INITIALIZED, SSL_DETECTED, CERTIFICATE_DECODED, FULL_HANDSHAKE, SERVER_SESSION_ID_SEEN, CLIENT_HELLO_SESSTKT, CH_PROCESSED, SH_PROCESSED, CH_CIPHERS_MODIFIED, CH_CURVES_MODIFIED, CH_EXTENSION_REMOVED, CH_ALPN_HAS_H2

Here you can see the various flags Firepower has noted in this session. Of particular interest are any that start with *CH*, meaning they were part of the client hello. Notice the "MODIFIED" flags… These indicate that we modified the client hello on its way back to the server and removed some data that might have caused the session to be undecryptable.

This is pretty cool stuff!

As promised, I'm not going into troubleshooting at length, but now you know about how to determine why SSL decryption might not be working so well and how fix it.

Don't forget the online help either—there's a slew of useful information regarding SSL decryption with Firepower there!

Summary

In this chapter, we looked at a somewhat newer feature in Firepower with SSL policies.

The SSL policy of these provide visibility beyond typical packet sniffing detection by providing additional insight into potentially compromised hosts or encrypted data.

Chapter 26: Cisco Threat Response

The following CCNP Security SNCF exam objectives are covered in this chapter:

4.0 Integration

4.4 Describe using Cisco Threat Response for security investigations

Cisco Threat Response (CTR) is a cloud-based console that integrates information from several of Cisco's security tools. We're going to hit the key features of CTR and cover the steps to integrate it into your Cisco Firepower Management Center.

Of course, this chapter is to help you prepare for the Cisco Threat Response objectives of the CCNP Security exam, but it'll seriously kickstart being able to implement real-world FMC integration with CTR as well.

To actually run CTR, you need an additional subscription license above what you'd normally get with Firepower alone, but you don't need one for this chapter's journey through an awesome integration that can really turbocharge your cybersecurity event investigations!

For exam study material like videos, downloadable supplemental material, and practice questions, head over to www.lammle.com

What Is Cisco Threat Response (CTR)?

Cisco Threat Response (CTR) offers us a great way to tie together information from a whole group of Cisco's major security products while adding context to security events by pulling events and intelligence from multiple sources.

Current integrations include the following products:

- Cisco Advanced Malware Protection (AMP) for Endpoints

- Cisco Threat Grid
- Cisco Umbrella
- Cisco Email Security (ESA)
- VirusTotal
- Cisco Firepower NGFW/NGIPS

Very cool is the fact that if you happen to get yourself one of these fine security products, CTR is included for free! But before we dive into everything CTR can provide, I'm going to fill you in on what all of these great tools can do.

Cisco AMP for Endpoints

AMP stands for Advanced Malware Protection and AMP for Endpoints was the first security innovation to use the AMP cloud.

The AMP cloud is the dominant method most of Cisco's threat-focused creations use to size up a given file to figure out if it's malicious.

AMP for Endpoints predictably runs on hosts or endpoints and supports all the major desktop and server operating systems like Microsoft Windows, Apple MacOS, and Linux—even mobile versions that run on Android and Apple IOS. Of course, since Windows is the most ubiquitous as well as the most vulnerable, you'll find the vast majority of AMP installations on Windows OS.

Once AMP for Endpoints is installed, all management takes place from the Cisco public cloud. There's also a private cloud version available for organizations that want to minimize the amount of company data that's stored off site. Originally, AMP for Endpoints was marketed as an add-on to traditional antivirus solutions, but today, a traditional signature-based antivirus engine can now be deployed as part of the AMP solution. Signature updates are either downloaded from the Cisco cloud or distributed through on-premise AMP update servers for larger deployments.

Here's a snapshot of AMP for Endpoint's main Dashboard:

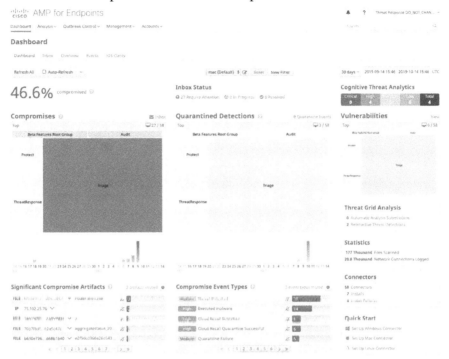

Similar to Firepower's Malware and File policy, the main tool AMP for Endpoints uses to determine a file's disposition is SHA-256. Even so, AMP for Endpoints includes several more engines that perform functions like these:

- Detecting malicious behavior in processes
- Keeping AMP files and processes tamper free
- Blocking connections to known malicious IP addresses

One of the major AMP for Endpoints benefits is its use of the Cisco cloud to aggregate information on files and processes on each endpoint. Because of this, once a file is deemed malicious, AMP knows every endpoint that's been in contact with the file! Via retrospective detection, known malicious files can be quarantined even if several days have passed since the file was last moved, copied, or executed—nice!

Cisco Threat Grid

Cisco Threat Grid is a dynamic file analysis tool used by Cisco solutions like AMP for Endpoints, Cisco Email Security, and Cisco Web Security.

You can log in to Cisco Threat Response at **https://visibility.amp.cisco.com** and then log in with Threat Grid, as shown here:

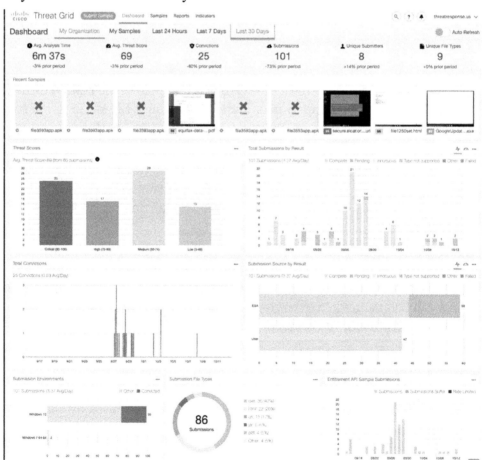

Once you log in, you'll be taken to the Threat Grid dashboard where you can see real-time analysis:

You can get more detailed information for the last month by clicking on the Reports tab:

Dynamic file analysis files are uploaded to Threat Grid and run in a "sandbox" environment. As the file is executed, Threat Grid monitors its activity, including system calls, network traffic, other files created, etc. The file is then given a score from 0 to 100 based upon the number and type of potentially malicious behaviors that were spotted. If the file scores over a given threshold, then Threat Grid "pokes" the AMP cloud and convicts the SHA-256 as malicious.

Keep in mind that Threat Grid doesn't convict files, it just gives them a score. The AMP cloud is still the only source of truth on file dispositions, so it's possible for the Threat Grid disposition to be overridden by automated or manual processes in the AMP cloud. This also means that just because a file gets a Threat Grid score below the conviction threshold, that doesn't mean it's clean. A score below the conviction threshold just means Threat Grid didn't find enough evidence to poke the AMP cloud.

Just like AMP for Endpoints, Threat Grid has cloud-based and on-premise versions, so those who want to maintain control of their files can opt for a hardware-based Threat Grid appliance.

Cisco Umbrella

Cisco Umbrella is a cloud-delivered enterprise security solution that offers different levels of protection available in various packages. At the minimum, Umbrella becomes your DNS server. DNS is the address book of the Internet, and nearly all connections, good and evil, use it to determine where to go. So when security is added to the DNS layer, Umbrella can detect and intercept connections to malicious hosts before they start. Umbrella even includes an endpoint component so they can be protected on their home network or away.

Log in to umbrella from **https://login.umbrella.com,** where you'll see the login splash page for Cisco Umbrella:

At the mid-level, Umbrella adds selective web proxy capability for risky domains, which allows us to block and/or inspect traffic that's likely to be malicious.

We gain use of the Investigate console and an on-demand API for enhancing security incident investigations at this level.

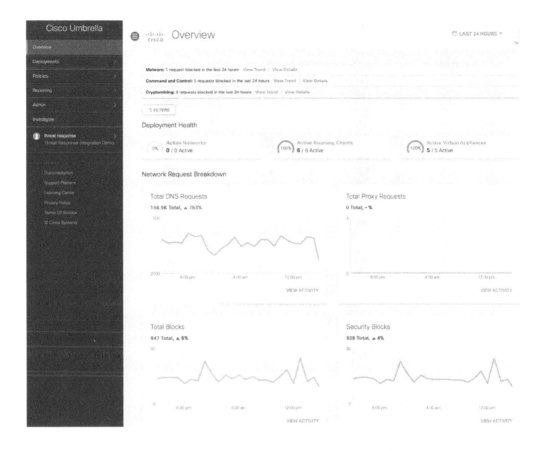

The primo level includes a Secure Internet Gateway (SIG)—a full cloud-based web proxy that arms us further with Cisco Threat Grid file analysis and a cloud access security broker (CASB).

Cisco Email Security

Cisco Email Security (ESA) with NGSMA enables users to communicate securely. It helps organizations combat business email compromise (BEC), ransomware, malware, phishing, spam, and data loss with a multilayered approach to security. All of this is achieved via advanced threat protection agents that detect, block, and remediate threats faster; prevent data loss; and secure key information in transit with end-to-end encryption.

AsyncOS 12.0 for Email Security buffs things up with new capabilities like the ability to consume External Threat Feeds (ETF), support for DNS-based Authentication of Named Entities (DANE), and Sender Domain Reputation (SDR).

At its most basic, the Cisco Email Security is a device that sits between your mail server(s) and the outside world inspecting and blocking malicious emails.

The ESA uses the Cisco AMP cloud to determine if email attachments are malicious in addition to detecting and stopping phishing attacks and other SPAM:

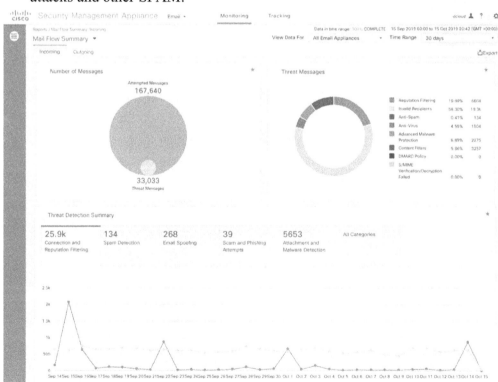

Because people don't usually notice if there's a slight delay getting emails, the ESA has more leeway to upload files to Threat Grid for dynamic analysis if necessary. This means that the appliance can block files that have been discovered as malware even if they've never been seen before!

VirusTotal

VirusTotal is a free service with over 70 antivirus scanner and URL/domain blacklisting services. It's a non-Cisco module that allows people with an API key to query VirusTotal during CTR investigations and use the results to enhance their data. So if you have an optional VirusTotal account, just add your API key to CTR and you're golden.

Oh, and since this is a free service, you can grab it right now and install it. It's actually very cool—even fun! Here's where you go to do this, plus a screen shot too:

https://www.virustotal.com/

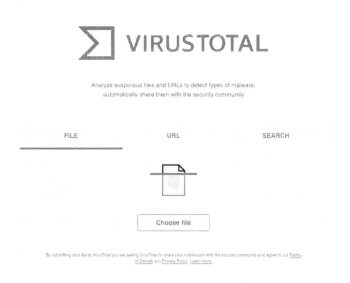

Cisco Firepower

Last but not least, the one and only Firepower is also among the sources that can be leveraged by CTR. When malware inspection is configured, Firepower can carve files out of network flows, then use the AMP cloud to run a variety of checks. It's even possible to upload the file for dynamic analysis in Threat Grid! If the file turns out to be malicious based upon the file hash, it can be blocked before the transfer completes.

Firepower can even upload files to Threat Grid for dynamic analysis, but unlike the ESA, it doesn't actually hold the file while Threat Grid does the analysis. So, if the file is determined to be malware, a retrospective alert is triggered. The file can then be blocked from that point on if the policy is configured to do that.

The FMC is automatically configured to connect to Threat Grid for dynamic analysis, and you're allowed to send up to 100 files a day per device. If you have an enterprise-level agreement (ELA), you're free to send up to 3000 files a day per device.

You can connect or change the connection your FMC has to the Threat Grid by going to **AMP>Dynamic Analysis Connections** and clicking on the green arrow at the right. You'll then be directed to Threat Grid to log in.

Here's a shot of the Cisco Firepower AMP Connection:

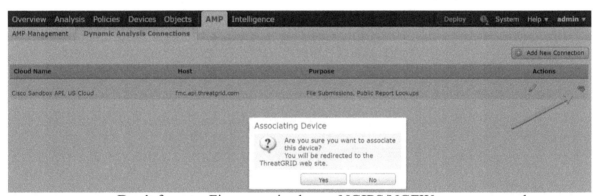

Don't forget—Firepower is also an NGIPS/NGFW, so events and data from intrusion and security intelligence events can really boost your CTR investigations!

Integrating Threat Response and Firepower

The process of integrating Cisco Threat Response with Firepower involves a number of steps. The first thing is to decide if you're going to use the Cisco Security Services Proxy or not. Your choice really comes down to your Firepower version—Firepower 6.4 or higher can send events directly to the cloud, but v6.3 and lower use a proxy for that:

- In Firepower 6.3, you send syslog events to Cisco Security Services Proxy (CSSP). From there, they go to Security Services Exchange (SSE) and then to CTR.
- 6.4 or greater code allows you to send events directly to the SSE from Firepower. From there, they go to CTR.

Since Firepower 6.3 is actually classified as an interim release, it's just better to skip the hassle of setting up a CSSP and go directly to v6.4 + to implement CTR.

The steps on the Firepower Management Center are the easy part…Just go to **System >Integration >Cloud Services** and enable the Cisco Cloud setting:

Once you've done that, the two "Click here" links will take you either to Cisco Cloud configuration or directly to CTR.

Here again, the Firepower online help is your friend. A quick peek at the help reveals an online guide with steps to integrate your Firepower event feed into CTR. Here's a look at the Firepower help topic:

Event and Asset Analysis Tools > Analyze Events Using External Tools > Event Analysis with Cisco Threat Response

Event Analysis with Cisco Threat Response

Rapidly detect, investigate, and respond to threats using Cisco Threat Response, the integration platform in the Cisco Cloud that lets you analyze incidents using data aggregated from multiple products, including Firepower.

For general information about Cisco Threat Response, see https://www.cisco.com/c/en/us/products/security/threat-response.html.

To integrate Firepower with Cisco Threat Response, see the *Firepower and Cisco Threat Response Integration Guide* at https://www.cisco.com/c/en/us/support/security/defense-center/products-installation-and-configuration-guides-list.html.

- View Event Data in Cisco Threat Response

Clicking the link to the *Cisco Threat Response Integration Guide* gets you to the main page for FMC configuration guides, where a brief search for "integration" within the page brings you to the link singled out by the red arrow:

This guide outlines detailed steps for integrating your Firepower system with the CTR cloud for the first time. You can also refer to it for the most current information on how to link your different Smart Accounts.

Cisco Threat Response Investigations

Okay, so as I said, when you go to CTR (https://visibility.amp.cisco.com), you log in with the appropriate Cisco Security or Threat Grid account, depending on how you purchased/licensed CTR.

If you're already using AMP for Endpoints, you'd go with the Log In with Cisco Security button on the initial Threat Response screen:

Once you login you'll find yourself at the main Threat Response page:

To start your investigation, type or paste in entries like IP address, domain, SHA-256, username, etc. as pictured here:

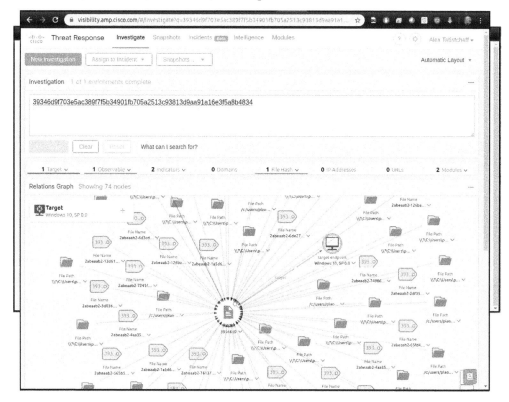

CTR will then show how your information ties into various detections, hosts, URLs, etc. across the entire Cisco cloud! It's also really easy to see if there are any sightings within your own environment:

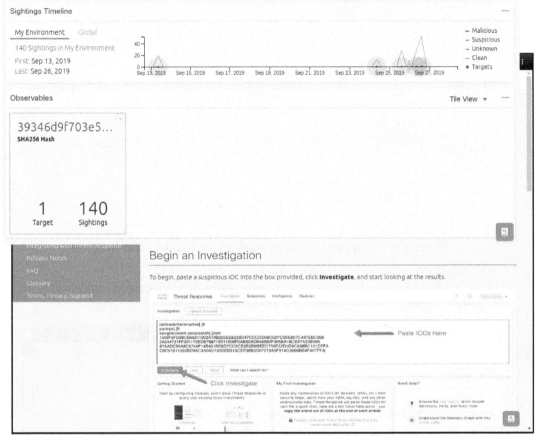

These steps are a nice way to get started with Cisco Threat Response. If you want more detailed information, the CTR portal offers excellent online help and a Quick Start page.

Just click on the help icon at the top ⑦ and you can read about how to use CTR and even watch an introductory video

Cisco Threat Intelligence Model

There's definitely a whole bunch of less than intuitive new terms allied with CTR, so to help you navigate and understand how the incident analysis process works, I'm going to walk you through the Cisco Threat Intelligence Model now.

The Cisco Threat Intelligence Model (CTIM) is an open-source model that is loosely based on STIX (Structured Threat Information Expression). STIX is an XML-based standard language for passing on data about security threats, and one of its main purposes is to allow sharing of information about cyber threats both within and between organizations.

CTIM helps break down the details generated during malware and incident analysis and provides a model where the details can be stored, retrieved, and enriched. Basically, CTIM supplies a language and definitions that make it easier to catalog, store, discuss, and share cyber threat information.

Here are some key CTIM terms and concepts:

- **Target**: A device, identity, or resource a threat has targeted, identified by one or more observables. Targets are always part of a sighting.
- **Sighting**: A record of an Observable showing up at a given date and time.
- **Observable**: An attribute of a possible security incident, which can be IP addresses, file hashes, devices, users, PKI certificate numbers, etc. This is what you start with when beginning an investigation.
- **Disposition**: Observables can be classified with a disposition based on what Cisco knows about it. Dispositions are a key concept within the AMP cloud that indicate whether the observable is considered:

  - Clean = explicitly allowed
  - Malicious = explicitly blocked
  - Suspicious = potentially harmful
  - Unknown = not enough data to make a determination

- **Judgement**: Associating a disposition with an observable. These are valid for an exact span of time.
- **Indicator**: Describes a pattern of behavior or a set of conditions that indicate malicious behavior.
- **Snapshot**: You can save a moment in time for an investigation and keep a record for yourself or share it with others in your organization. These are available to anyone in your organization and are *not* confidential to individuals.
- **Incident**: This feature allows you to triage, investigate, and track high-confidence security incidents in CTR. An incident consists of the sightings and associated threat intelligence that's been sent to CTR.

- **Casebook**: A powerful tool for saving, sharing, and enriching your threat analysis. Think of this as a journal to keep notes and track information as you follow leads in CTR.
- **Module**: CTR can ingest information from a number of Cisco security products. To maximize your visibility, be sure to configure modules for each of your supported Cisco products.

Okay—let's use some of those terms in a paragraph.

Billy logs into CTR and enters observable information into the Investigate field. He then sees one or more sightings where his observable information was actually revealed. These include judgements as well as disposition verdicts. Billy notices there are three modules reporting information on his observable—VirusTotal, Talos Intelligence, and Umbrella—so he creates a snapshot so he can share it with is co-worker Alice, who's on the incident investigation team. Billy then creates a new case and adds the information to a casebook.

That was actually a pretty awesome paragraph.

Summary

This chapter was an overview of CTR and the various Cisco security products that can be integrated. CTR is a great way to combine threat intelligence from a number of sources to enrich cyber threat investigations. CTR saves us from not having to pull information from a myriad of consoles and interfaces when attempting to correlate threat activities.

Chapter 27: Multi-instance

The following CCNP Security SNCF exam objectives covered in this chapter:

1.0 Deployment

1.3 Implement high availability options

1.3.c Multi-instance

Even though Firepower is an awesome NGFW and Firepower/FTD is chock-full of great features that make life wonderful, sometimes a single firewall just isn't flexible enough.

For instance, say you manage the firewall for an entire office building with lots of businesses under its roof. You could manage everyone inside an Access Control policy but that could get pretty messy. Keeping all those rules organized is downright frightful, and worse, you're only one mistake away from causing a huge outage when working on the rule base!

Another case would be when you want to ensure the guest network traffic is completely separated from the production networks because designing a wireless controller to dump the guest WLAN traffic directly to the firewall is a really common setup.

Maybe you want multiple firewalls to give you vault-tight control over how traffic is routed between zones. This can be a terrific way to go if you want to split your network into an internet zone for external traffic and a trusted zone for your data center.

The downside to having multiple firewalls is that it gets pricey quick, especially if you're buying a bunch of devices just to make management easier. Thankfully, Cisco has our backs with the multi-instance feature, which lets us spin up as many separate instances of FTD we need! I'm going to start with talking about the legacy ASA way of providing this with something called contexts. After that, we'll move on to the current and future ways of creating multiple virtual firewalls on a single FTD device known as multi-instance.

ASA Contexts

Before Cisco came out with Firepower, ASAs solved the single firewall problem with a feature called contexts. No, you don't need to know about contexts for the exam, but it's still really good to know why Cisco settled on the multi-instance feature for Firepower.

Traffic Separation

Contexts allow you carve your firewall up into smaller, logical ones. To give you a good picture of this, I'm going to set up two contexts on an ASA to simulate two different tenants with their own Internet connections and switches:

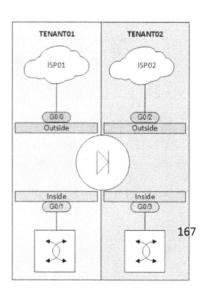

To enable this feature, type in **mode multiple**. Be warned that this is going to cause the ASA to reboot, so don't do this in the middle of the workday if your ASA is in production:

```
ASAx1(config)# mode multiple
WARNING: This command will change the behavior of the device
WARNING: This command will initiate a Reboot
Proceed with change mode? [confirm]
Convert the system configuration? [confirm]
!
The old running configuration file will be written to flash

Converting the configuration - this may take several minutes for a large configuration

The admin context configuration will be written to flash

The new running configuration file was written to flash
Security context mode: multiple
ASAx1(config)#


***
*** --- START GRACEFUL SHUTDOWN ---
***
*** Message to all terminals:
***
***    change mode
Shutting down isakmp
Shutting down webvpn
Shutting down sw-module
Shutting down License Controller
Shutting down File system
```

When the ASA is backup, create your contexts and decide which interfaces they're going to use. This is a lot like virtual routing and forwarding (VRF), where you put the interface into a different routing table. You can have your contexts share an interface if you want them to use a common interface to the Internet, etc.:

```
ASAx1(config)# context TENNANT01
Creating context 'TENNANT01'... Done. (3)
ASAx1(config-ctx)# allocate-interface g0/0
ASAx1(config-ctx)# allocate-interface g0/1
ASAx1(config-ctx)# config-url flash:/tennent1.cfg
INFO: Converting flash:/tennent1.cfg to disk0:/tennent1.cfg

WARNING: Could not fetch the URL disk0:/tennent1.cfg
INFO: Creating context with default config

ASAx1(config-ctx)# context TENNANT02
Creating context 'TENNANT02'... Done. (4)
ASAx1(config-ctx)# allocate-interface g0/2
```

```
ASAx1(config-ctx)# allocate-interface g0/3
ASAx1(config-ctx)# config-url flash:/tennent2.cfg
INFO: Converting flash:/tennent2.cfg to disk0:/tennent2.cfg

WARNING: Could not fetch the URL disk0:/tennent2.cfg
INFO: Creating context with default config


ASAx1(config)# changeto context TENNANT01
ASAx1/TENNANT01(config)# show int ip br
Interface               IP-Address      OK? Method Status              Protocol
GigabitEthernet0/0      unassigned      YES unset  down                down
GigabitEthernet0/1      unassigned      YES unset  down                down
```

I'm not going to go into the tenant configuration here; just know you would configure each context as if it was its own ASA. You can even allow people to SSH directly into their context so they can manage it without gaining access to the other contexts.

Dual Internet

One simple requirement that isn't so simple to set up is having more than one Internet connection on an ASA. Since you can only have one active default route in your routing table, you have to get creative with routing tricks like placing a 128.0.0.0 netmask on your ISP static routes to try to load balance traffic. Using backup links or SLA monitors are another couple of tricks, but they can be a hassle.

Multiple contexts really save the day. Each context can have its own default route, meaning you don't have to jump through a bunch of hoops to make things like NAT work on the secondary connection—so nice!

The setup is a lot like the last one. Create a context for each Internet connection, then advertise each default route to the core switch with OSPF or EIGRP and adjust the metrics as needed for your network. Most of the time I'd also add an SLA monitor on each connection to make sure the Internet is working before advertising the default route to the network.

Here's a snapshot of a typical dual Internet topology using contexts:

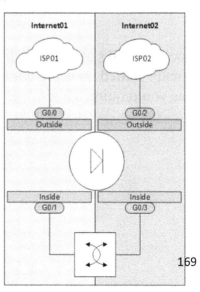

169

The Downside

A couple caveats to contexts: They can be a pain to manage because you really have to jump around between contexts to get your configuration done. Plus, they don't support all of the features you can run in single context mode.

Here's a list of tools that are off limits in a context:

- RIP
- OSPFv3
- Multicast routing
- Threat Detection
- Unified Communications
- QoS
- Remote access VPN

Some of these we can usually do without—if RIP isn't supported, you'd just go with OSPF, EIGRP, and BGP anyway. Also, since you can do ASA with Firepower, you would probably do that instead of FTD.

But others are deal breakers. For instance, what if you need to do remote access VPN or multicast routing? Well, you either can't do contexts or you'll need some serious engineering skills to make some of these services work without buying another firewall to host them!

FTD Multi-instance

It took the folks at Cisco awhile to figure out the best successor to contexts, but they finally settled on using containers to allow you to spin up as many FTD instances as you require. This solves the limitation problems that contexts had because you're actually creating a full-featured FTD instance that just happens to live in a container.

Once it's created, just add the container to your FMC and manage it like any other FTD. The only downside is that currently, multi-instance is only supported on the 4100 and 9300 series appliances, though Cisco is working on bringing it to smaller models.

Let's take a look at how to create some container instances in our lab's Fircpowcr 4100.

Interfaces

The first thing I'm going to do here is log into Firepower Chassis Manager and adjust the interfaces. (I covered FCM in the first book if you

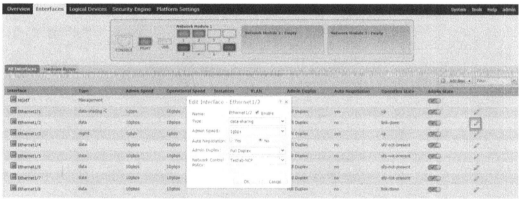

need a refresher.) When creating containers, use the data-sharing interface type in order to allow containers to share the same physical interfaces and go with the data interface type. This would mean each container would need unique interfaces. Check out the interface page here:

For this example, I want Ethernet1/1 and Ethernet1/2 to be the data-sharing type and I'll verify the configuration like this:

Interface	Type	Admin Speed	Operational Speed
MGMT	Management		
Ethernet1/1	data-sharing	1gbps	1gbps
Ethernet1/2	data-sharing	1gbps	1gbps
Ethernet1/3	mgmt	1gbps	1gbps
Ethernet1/4	data	1gbps	10gbps
Ethernet1/5	data	10gbps	10gbps
Ethernet1/6	data	10gbps	10gbps
Ethernet1/7	data	10gbps	10gbps
Ethernet1/8	data	10gbps	10gbps

Logical Devices

So now that the interfaces are ready, I'm going to go to Logical Devices and add a standalone instance. Just so you know, I could also choose to add a cluster in container mode, but I'm not going to complicate things by doing that right now.

The next figure shows adding a standalone instance

Adding an instance is actually done the same way I demonstrated back in the FMC section of the first volume, except the instance type is container instead of native. Here's the config for adding a standalone container:

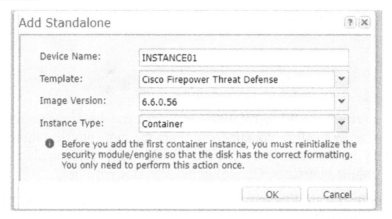

Now I'm going to configure the instance on the provisioning page. First, I'll select the data ports the instance will use—Ethernet1/1 and Ethernet1/2. Notice that the interfaces have the data-sharing icon.

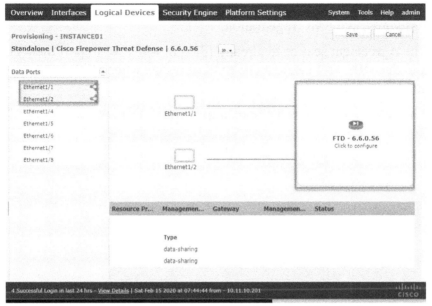

Okay, now I can click on the FTD box to add in the bootstrap configuration for the instance.

Next, I'm going to give the instance an IP address in the bootstrap configuration's general information section. The instance also needs a management instance, and keep in mind that I can use the same one for all my containers.

Last up is to specify the resource profile. Firepower Chassis Manager comes with a **Default-Small** out of the box, which allocates six cores per container instance. I want to point out that in a production environment, you probably want to create a new resource profile that matches your network's needs better.

You can see the General Information Bootstrap settings here:

The settings tab is where I'll configure the rest of the settings like DNS, passwords, and FMC registration.

The Agreement section is already filled in when we import the FTD image into the 4100, so I can just click OK and save when all the information is entered.

The next figure shows the bootstrap Settings section:

To give us more containers to play with, I went ahead and added three more instances. Notice that because each instance is using 6 cores, the

4100 has 46 more cores available—enough for seven more instances if needed:

Command-Line Interface

At this point I can go ahead and add the containers to my FMC, but first I want to show you how to access the FTD CLI if you need to. Once I SSH into the 4140, I'll connect to module 1 because the platform only supports one module:

```
A4140-1# connect module 1
  console  Console
  telnet   Telnet


A4140-1# connect module 1 console
Telnet escape character is '~'.
Trying 127.5.1.1...
Connected to 127.5.1.1.
Escape character is '~'.

CISCO Serial Over LAN:
Close Network Connection to Exit
```

Next, I'm going to connect to the instance I want to access with the `connect ftd <instance name>` command like this:

```
Firepower-module1>connect ftd INSTANCE01

============================== ATTENTION ==============================
You are connecting to ftd from a serial console. Please avoid
```

```
executing any commands which may produce large amount of output.
Otherwise, data cached along the pipe may take up to 12 minutes to be
drained by a serial console at 9600 baud rate after pressing Ctrl-C.

To avoid the serial console, please login to FXOS with ssh and use
'connect module <slot> telnet' to connect to the security module.
====================================================================

Connecting to container ftd(INSTANCE01) console... enter "exit" to return to boo
tCLI

User enable_1 logged in to firepower
Logins over the last 1 days: 1.
Failed logins since the last login: 0.
Type help or '?' for a list of available commands.
firepower> Cryptochecksum: 69a996b2 48e55186 7bbb71a8 cf246364

3060 bytes copied in 0.160 secs
```

Once I'm logged in, the CLI is the same as what I'd get if I SSH'd into a regular FTD box:

```
> show network
===============[ System Information ]===============
Hostname                 : instance01.sfgtc.local
Domains                  : sfgtc.local
DNS Servers              : 127.0.0.11
Management port          : 8305
IPv4 Default route
  Gateway                : 10.11.10.1
  Netmask                : 0.0.0.0


==================[ management0 ]===================
State                    : Enabled
Link                     : Up
Channels                 : Management & Events
Mode                     : Non-Autonegotiation
MDI/MDIX                 : Auto/MDIX
MTU                      : 1500
MAC Address              : A2:B2:90:00:00:46
---------------------[ IPv4 ]---------------------
Configuration            : Manual
Address                  : 10.11.10.221
Netmask                  : 255.255.255.0
Gateway                  : 10.11.10.1
---------------------[ IPv6 ]---------------------
Configuration            : Disabled
```

Multi-instance containers must be managed by FMC! Firepower Device Manager (FDM) isn't supported just yet.

Adding Instances in FMC

I'm going to devote the rest of the chapter to demonstrating how to add the containers to the FMC and prove there really aren't any differences in the configuration compared to what you've seen previously.

Adding Instance

Adding a container is easy—just go to Devices and click the Add button. I went ahead and created four groups, one for each container. I'm also going to create a separate Access Control policy because one of the big advantages to multi-instance is being able to manage each device independently.

Here's a screen shot of the Devices page in FMC:

In the Add instance's IP registration key, ACP, and then can see how the Device page, I'll add the information and assign it a group and an enable licensing. You settings look here:

To save a bit of time, I went ahead and added the other containers. Check out the end result:

Name	Model	Version	Chassis
∨ TENANT01 (1)			
🔘 INSTANCE01 10.11.10.221 - Routed	FTD on Firepower 4140	6.6.0	▦ A4140-1.sfgtc.local:443 Security Module - 1 (Container)
∨ TENANT02 (1)			
🔘 INSTANCE02 10.11.10.222 - Routed	FTD on Firepower 4140	6.6.0	▦ A4140-1.sfgtc.local:443 Security Module - 1 (Container)
∨ TENANT03 (1)			
🔘 INSTANCE03 10.11.10.223 - Routed	FTD on Firepower 4140	6.6.0	▦ A4140-1.sfgtc.local:443 Security Module - 1 (Container)
∨ TENANT04 (1)			
🔘 INSTANCE04 10.11.10.224 - Routed	FTD on Firepower 4140	6.6.0	▦ A4140-1.sfgtc.local:443 Security Module - 1 (Container)

Instance Device Configuration

I'll enable AnyConnect licensing in the instance configuration because it's not allowed in the ASA configurations.

This is actually a pretty big deal since you really want to have at least one of your Firepower devices supporting remote access VPN most of the time. Take a look at the Licensing dialog section of the instance here:

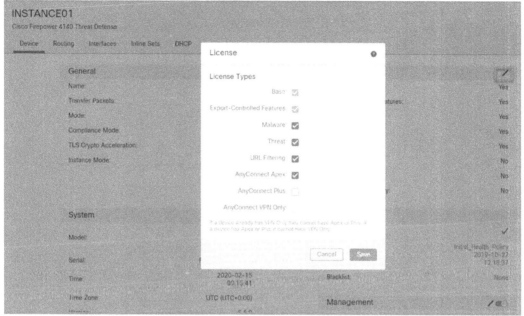

This needs some interface configuration, so I'm going to add Ethernet1/1 to the inside zone and give it an IP. I'll give Ethernet1/2 to the outside zone and give it an IP as well. See that blue icon? It's showing us that FMC is aware I'm using data-sharing interfaces. Here's the interface's configuration result:

To allow the instance to reach everything it needs to, I'll also set up OSPF for all interfaces. I can also opt to set up static, RIP, or BGP from this page, and EIGRP can be configured through FlexConfig since apparently Cisco doesn't want to add an EIGRP section just yet.

The next figure shows the OSPF configuration:

The instance also needs a static route for it to reach the Internet. Here's the default route:

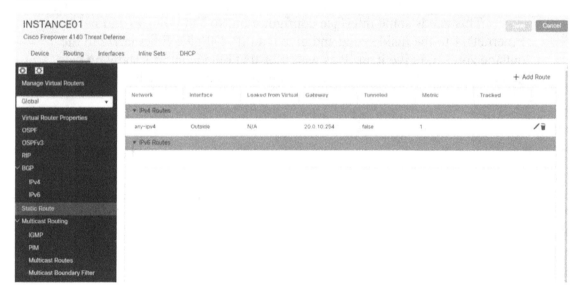

Since there are three more FTD instances to configure, use the Push Device Configuration feature now to save some time. Doing this pushes the full configuration to the other containers, which is wonderful because I only need to change a few values instead of adding everything from scratch—over and over and over!

The next figure showcases this time-saving superhero feature! Checking into INSTANCE02 demonstrates that everything is almost perfectly configured for me. The only tweaks needed are device-specific settings like interface IPs and the default gateway:

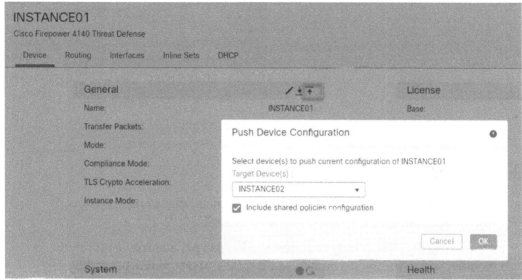

And here's the final interface config:

Access Control Policies

Most of you probably believe me about the instances being treated normally by now, but just in case, let's head over to the Access Control Policy page. See that? Each instance has its own ACP, so each "tenant" gets to have its own policies! I could've just as easily had all the containers share a policy—whichever way lines up to your business requirements best:

Q   Overview   Analysis   Policies   Devices   Objects   AMP   Intelligence   Deploy   🔍 ⚙ ❶ admin ▾

Object Management | Intrusion | Network Analysis Policy | DNS | Import/Export

New Policy

Access Control Policy	Domain	Status	Last Modified	
20	Global	Targeting 1 devices *Out-of-date on 1 targeted devices*	2020-02-03 09:13:44 Modified by "admin"	🖺 📑 ✎ 🗑
Appliance_ACP	Global	Targeting 1 devices *Up-to-date on all targeted devices*	2020-02-05 14:46:01 Modified by "admin"	🖺 📑 ✎ 🗑
TENANT01-ACP	Global	Targeting 1 devices *Up-to-date on all targeted devices*	2020-02-15 00:48:12 Modified by "admin"	🖺 📑 ✎ 🗑
TENANT02-ACP	Global	Targeting 1 devices *Up-to-date on all targeted devices*	2020-02-15 00:55:06 Modified by "admin"	🖺 📑 ✎ 🗑
TENANT03-ACP	Global	Targeting 1 devices *Up-to-date on all targeted devices*	2020-02-15 00:56:47 Modified by "admin"	🖺 📑 ✎ 🗑
TENANT04-ACP	Global	Targeting 1 devices *Up-to-date on all targeted devices*	2020-02-15 00:59:41 Modified by "admin"	🖺 📑 ✎ 🗑
VFMC20-ACP	Global	Targeting 2 devices *Out-of-date on 1 targeted devices*	2020-02-04 11:49:06 Modified by "admin"	🖺 📑 ✎ 🗑

Licensing

By now, you're probably pretty convinced that multi-instance is really cool, but what about the licensing costs?

Happily, Cisco only requires one license per security engine / module, which means if you have a Firepower 4100, you have to buy one license for each type of security engine. If you have a Firepower 9300, you've got to score two since it has two engines.

Remote Access VPNs

The last thing I want to bring up about instances is the fact that you can enable both remote access VPNs and site-to-site VPNs on them.

This is no small thing when you consider that we can create instances as long as we still have resources available on the box because it adds a ton of flexibility to the design. You can choose to add a crew of instances that only handle the remote access VPN and create others to handle the site-to-site traffic!

Here's a shot of the remote access VPN page:

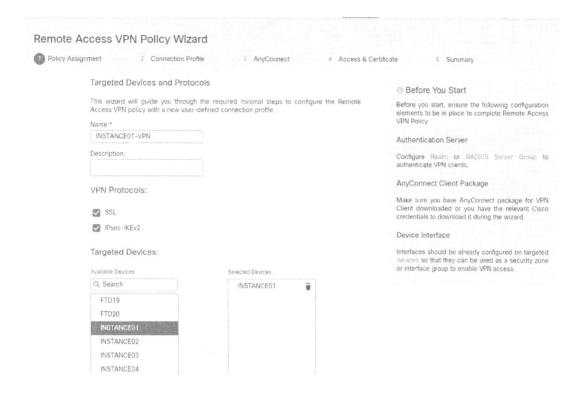

Remote Access VPN Policy Wizard

1 Policy Assignment   2 Connection Profile   3 AnyConnect   4 Access & Certificate   5 Summary

Targeted Devices and Protocols

This wizard will guide you through the required minimal steps to configure the Remote Access VPN policy with a new user-defined connection profile.

Name:*

INSTANCE01-VPN

Description:

VPN Protocols:

☑ SSL

☑ IPsec-IKEv2

Targeted Devices:

Available Devices

🔍 Search

FTD19
FTD20
INSTANCE01
INSTANCE02
INSTANCE03
INSTANCE04

Selected Devices

INSTANCE01   🗑

Before You Start

Before you start, ensure the following configuration elements to be in place to complete Remote Access VPN Policy.

Authentication Server

Configure Realm or RADIUS Server Group to authenticate VPN clients.

AnyConnect Client Package

Make sure you have AnyConnect package for VPN Client downloaded or you have the relevant Cisco credentials to download it during the wizard.

Device Interface

Interfaces should be already configured on targeted devices so that they can be used as a security zone or interface group to enable VPN access.

Summary

Now you know all about the multi-instance feature, including some insight into ASA contexts.

You discovered why single instance firewalls can present a challenge or two and learned how using the multi-instance feature offers serious flexibility for beating design jams.

Next, we created a batch of instances in Firepower Chassis Manager and added them into the FMC. You found out how to push configuration to other instances to save oodles of time and confirmed that there are no configuration limitations about using containers.

We ended with a quick brief on multi-instance's licensing requirements and how you only need one license of each type and for each security engine in use.

Chapter 28: PxGrid

This chapter is a bonus chapter and found at
www.lammle.com/firepower

Chapter 29: Rapid Threat Containment (RTC)

The following CCNP Security SNCF exam objectives are covered in this chapter:

4.0 Integration

4.6 Describe Rapid Threat Containment (RTC) functionality within Firepower Management Center

We're going take pxGrid to the next level by showing off the feature's ability to tie different security solutions together into a comprehensive security fabric. By integrating AMP, Firepower, and ISE, I'll show you how the security fabric quarantines a switchport with a compromised host attached—a great strategy known as Rapid Threat Containment.

Note: Make sure you're really comfortable with Malware & File policy, correlation, and ISE with pxGrid before tackling this chapter!

For some great exam study tools like videos, downloadable supplemental material, and practice questions, head over to www.lammle.com

Rapid Threat Containment

In Chapter 28, we got pxGrid up and running between our Firepower Management Center and ISE deployment. After the integration, we could share information like Security Group Tags between the solutions and use them in Firepower access control rules.

Traditionally, security solutions all worked independently. Your anti-malware would scan your endpoint and decide whether to quarantine a file, but it wouldn't let your firewall or any other solution in on the matter. This means that unless your anti-malware can fully contain the threat, you could be up to watch dawn break.

Except that now we have Rapid Threat Containment (RTC)! It takes advantage of the comprehensive security intelligence gathered by all the security solutions that can be joined to pxGrid. So while sharing all that intel is great, what's even better is that RTC actually uses the information to empower ISE as your network enforcer when a security threat is detected!

Let's check out an example with RTC set up. If your anti-malware detects a threat, that info can be shared through pxGrid, and because Cisco ISE is a robust Network Access Control (NAC) solution, it can place the switchport that connects the compromised endpoint into quarantine by changing the port's 802.1X authorization.

Here's a picture of Rapid Threat Containment in action:

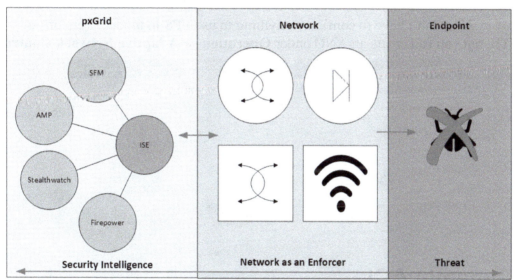

So get ready because I'm going to take you through a whole lot of configuration for the rest of the chapter. Our mission is for Cisco AMP to notify Firepower when it detects a threat and then have ISE place the port in quarantine until a successful scan is completed.

To achieve our goal, we'll be working with these components:

- Cisco ISE
- Firepower Management Center
- Cisco 3750 switch

Identity Service Engine

Components

It's true that the Firepower exam doesn't require you to know much about Identity Services Engine (ISE), but we definitely need to dig deeper into the solution for you to understand how Rapid Threat Containment really works.

Endpoint Protection Service (EPS)

Endpoint Protection Service (EPS) provides a way to quarantine an endpoint through an API, but it's fairly limited so it's actually been succeeded by a new version called Adaptive Network Control (ANC). The problem is, Firepower's pxGrid doesn't yet support ANC at the time of this writing.

Note: EPS is also known as Adaptive Network Control 1.0.

You don't have to configure anything to use EPS in modern versions of ISE, but you can create an ANC under **Operations > Adaptive Network Control**:

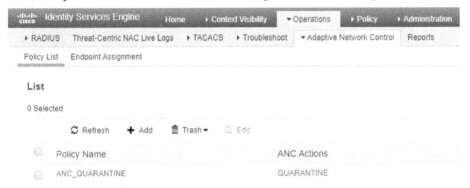

Dynamic ACL

Sadly, there isn't a magic button in ISE that just puts a port in quarantine, but we could have ISE deny all traffic to it and call it a day. Only problem with that is then we couldn't un-quarantine the port since the endpoint won't let us know a scan has finished.

So we need another plan: We're going to use a dynamic ACL—an ACL that's pushed to the switch by ISE—to restrict access to private networks but not the Internet. AMP lives in the cloud so the endpoint has to be able to reach the Internet for this example. In the real world, I'd be more restrictive so the malware can't phone home!

Here's the DACL we'll be using:

```
permit udp any any range
67 68
permit udp any any eq 53
deny ip any 192.168.0.0
0.0.255.255
deny ip any 172.16.0.0
0.0.15.255
deny ip any 10.0.0.0
0.255.255.255
permit ip any any
```

You've probably configured an ACL for guest access before: one that permits DNS and DHCP so the endpoint can get an IP address and ensures private IPs are blocked and everything else is allowed.

Authorization Profile

So now that our DACL has been built, we need an authorization profile to apply it. I created a profile named QUARANTINE that hollers out to the dynamic ACL I also called QUARANTINE.

I could also place the port in a separate VLAN but I'm trying to keep this example really straightforward:

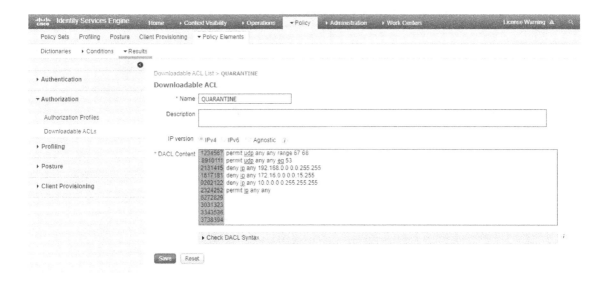

ISE Policy

Policy sets in ISE can get pretty complicated, so the actual 802.1X configuration is definitely beyond the scope of this book. But if you just have to know all about this, ISE does have its own CCNP Security exam.

Anyway, to make RTC work, I'm going to create a global exception rule, which will let some rules be enforced before the rest of the rule set is evaluated. The rule matches an Endpoint Protection Service status that's set to quarantine, then applies the quarantine authorization profile we just talked about.

To future proof the rule, I also matched an ANC policy called ANC_QUARANTINE, but it won't actually do anything for us in this lab. Check it out:

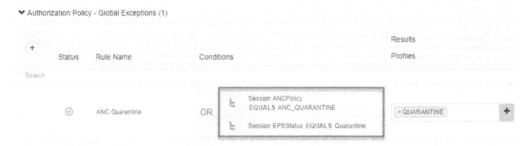

This is all that needs to be done on ISE. We'll get to the rest in Firepower.

Firepower Configuration

Now I'm going to put a correlation rule together inside the Firepower Management Center by creating an instance under **Policies>Actions> Instances**:

Next step is to create a pxGrid Mitigation module by selecting it in the drop-down and clicking Add:

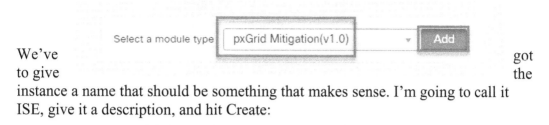

We've got to give the instance a name that should be something that makes sense. I'm going to call it ISE, give it a description, and hit Create:

The module supports mitigating the source or the destination, so I'm going to select Mitigate Source from the dropdown and hit Add:

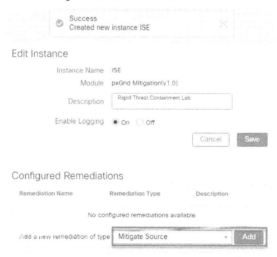

Now I've got to pick a name inside the remediation configuration. I'll go with RTC-QUARANTINE-SOURCE and select a migration action.

Here are three options you can choose and what they mean:

- **Quarantine** = Set the EPS to quarantine the host.

- **Unquarantine** = Set the EPS to remove the quarantine status.
- **Shutdown** = Send a shutdown action to the port, which doesn't require a policy rule in ISE.

Again, I'm going with quarantine as the action:

Edit Remediation

Remediation Name	RTC-QUARANTINE-SOURCE
Remediation Type	Mitigate Source
Description	I
Mitigation Action	quarantine ▾
White List (an *optional* list of networks)	

Cancel   Create

I'm also going create another remediation to carry out the unquarantine action and save the instance when I'm done:

Edit Remediation

Remediation Name	RTC-UNQUARANTINE-SOURCE
Remediation Type	Mitigate Source
Description	
Mitigation Action	unquarantine ▾
White List (an *optional* list of networks)	

Cancel   Create

Edit Instance

Instance Name	ISE
Module	pxGrid Mitigation(v1.0)
Description	Rapid Threat Containment Lab
Enable Logging	● On ○ Off

Cancel   Save

Configured Remediations

Remediation Name	Remediation Type	Description	
RTC-QUARANTINE-SOURCE	Mitigate Source		✏ 🗑
RTC-UNQUARANTINE-SOURCE	Mitigate Source		✏ 🗑

Add a new remediation of type | Mitigate Destination ▾ | Add

Okay—now that I've got the instance created, I'm going to move on to **Policy > Correlation** and choose Rule Management:

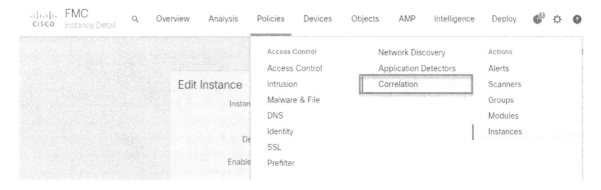

To keep things nice and clean, I'll create a group called PxGrid. This is optional if you want to skip it:

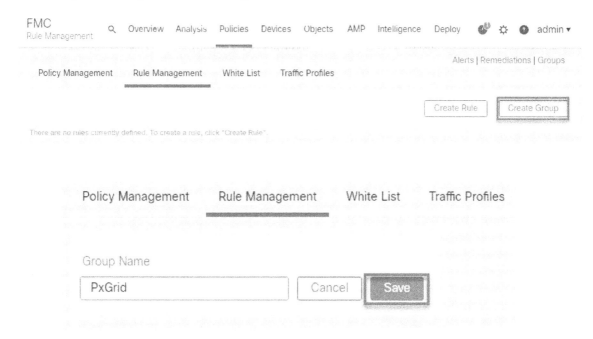

Now we can start working on our actual rules:

So the first rule will run if a malware alert is detected by an endpoint-based malware detection event—what you'd want to happen for AMP running on a computer. You could also choose network based if you want Firepower to detect the threat. There's also a retroactive option, which is when a known file is deemed a threat afterward.

There's a bunch of event types that range from when a threat is detected to when a quarantine fails. In the real world, it makes a lot more sense to opt for Quarantine Failure because that's actually a huge threat that AMP can't put a stop to right away!

But since this is a lab, I'll pick Threat Detected so it's easy to trip the alert:

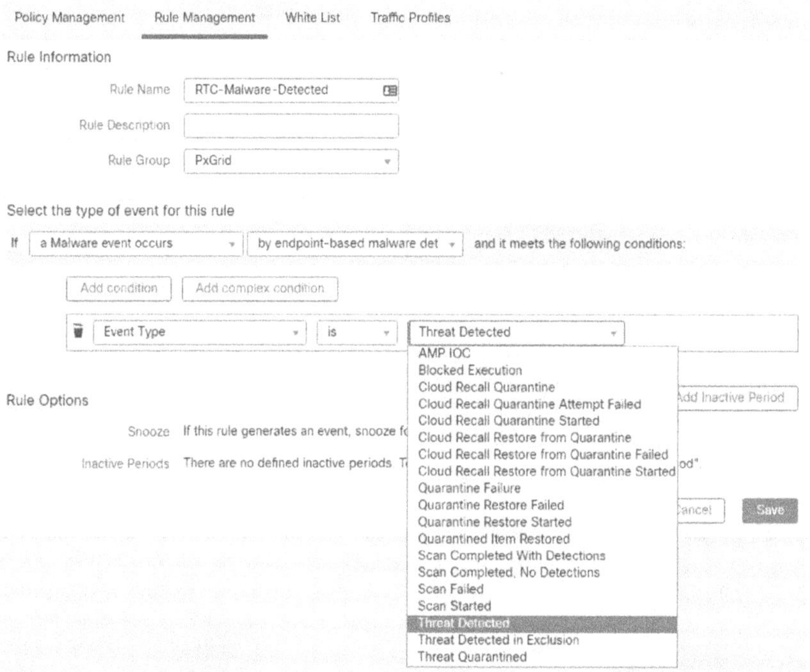

also
to
a rule
run
a

I'm
going
make
that'll
when

malware scan is completed with no threats detected so we can get back on the network when running a scan.

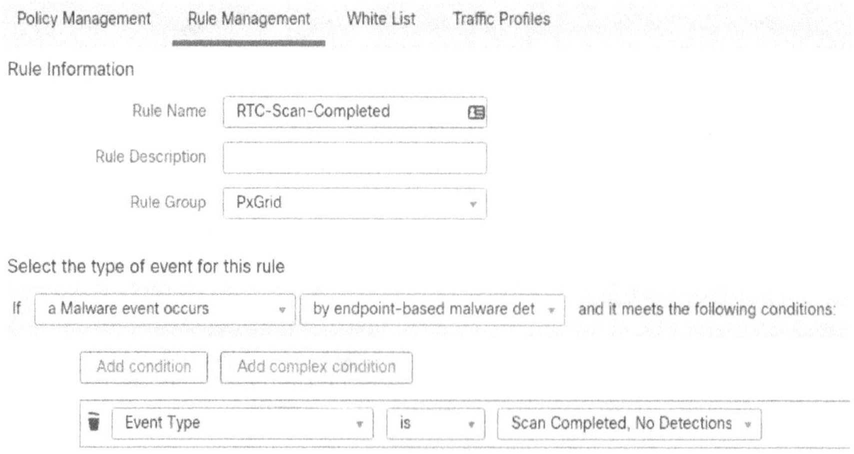

Okay—with our rules formed, the last thing to create is a policy under Policy Management:

I'll give it a name and add the Malware Detected rule:

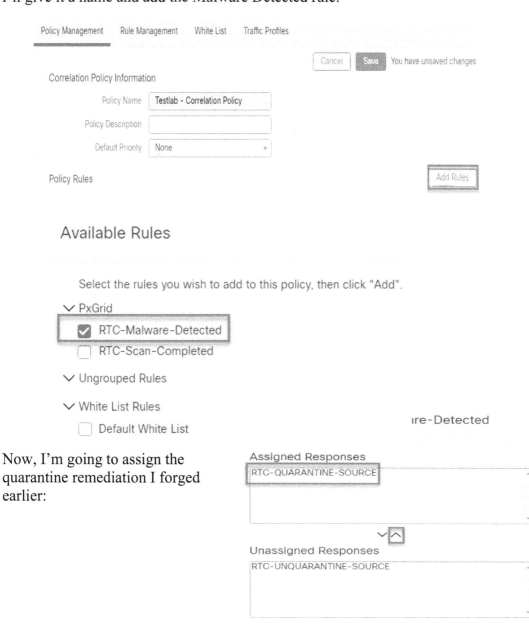

Now, I'm going to assign the quarantine remediation I forged earlier:

And do the same thing with the Scan Completed rule:

Available Rules

Select the rules you wish to add to this policy, then click "Add".

∨ PxGrid
- ☑ RTC-Scan-Completed

∨ Ungrouped Rules

∨ White List Rules
- ☐ Default White List

Next, I'll assign the unquarantine action:

Responses for RTC-Scan-Completed

Assigned Responses

RTC-UNQUARANTINE-SOURCE

∨ ∧

Unassigned Responses

RTC-QUARANTINE-SOURCE

Cancel   Update

Last up, I'll save the policy and activate the policy by clicking on the toggle switch:

Success
Saved New Policy: Testlab - Correlation Policy   ✕

Name   Sort by
                                                  State
Testlab - Correlation Policy

Activated Policy: Testlab - Correlation Policy

Name   Sort by
                                                  State   194
Testlab - Correlation Policy

Testing

It definitely took a bunch of configurations to get here, but now we can try it all out. I've got a Windows 10 desktop that's set up for 802.1X connected to a Cisco switch and I'm using Cisco AnyConnect for the NAC agent. Native Windows would work fine as well, and we've installed AMP too:

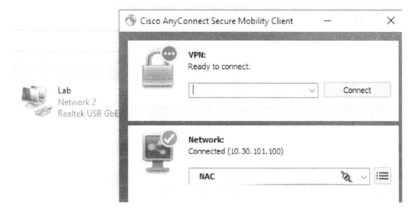

The easiest way to get a virus without going to shady websites on the Internet is by using Eicar's test malware file, although they only carry the https files now, but here you can see I still had access to the old site.

I'll download the zip file now:

As soon
as I
click the

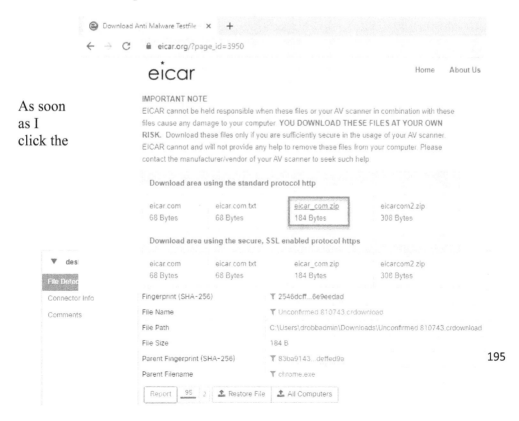

download link, AMP pops up and quarantines the threat. If we check the AMP console, we can check out more information about the malware. Here, you can see it's been recognized as Eicar ransomware:

And about 5 seconds later, ISE pushes the quarantine DACL to the switchport:

Result

Class	CACS:0a140b20Xc_C5lyMPFa4LLn7O53fbEpqfuVeKdC8C3UU7X0lcPw:ise-psn01/379256572/395
cisco-av-pair	ip:inacl#1=permit udp any any range 67 68
cisco-av-pair	ip:inacl#2=permit udp any any eq 53
cisco-av-pair	ip:inacl#3=deny ip any 192.168.0.0 0.0.255.255
cisco-av-pair	ip:inacl#4=deny ip any 172.16.0.0 0.0.15.255
cisco-av-pair	ip:inacl#5=deny ip any 10.0.0.0 0.255.255.255
cisco-av-pair	ip:inacl#6=permit ip any any

Here's the console messages seen on the switch as it pushes the ACL:

```
C3750-SW01# OLICY_REQ: IP 0.0.0.0| MAC 3023.038d.f757| AuditSessionID
0A1E0AF000000049059C816F| AUTHTYPE DOT1X| EVENT APPLY
*Mar  2 02:09:03.667: %EPM-6-AUTH_ACL: POLICY Auth-Default-ACL| EVENT Auth-
Default-ACL Attached Successfully
*Mar  2 02:09:03.667: %EPM-6-AAA: POLICY xACSACLx-IP-QUARANTINE-5ec4d44c| EVENT
DOWNLOAD-REQUEST
*Mar  2 02:09:03.809: %EPM-6-AAA: POLICY xACSACLx-IP-QUARANTINE-5ec4d44c| EVENT
DOWNLOAD-SUCCESS
*Mar  2 02:09:03.809: %EPM-6-POLICY_APP_SUCCESS: IP 10.30.101.100| MAC
3023.038d.f757| Audit
```

Verify this by checking the 802.1X status on the port. I can see that an ACL called xACSACLx-IP-QUARANTINE-5ec4d44c has been applied—a per-user ACL that applies to the port:

```
C3750-SW01#show authentication sessions interface g1/0/1
            Interface:  GigabitEthernet1/0/1
          MAC Address:  3023.038d.f757
           IP Address:  10.30.101.100
            User-Name:  drobbadmin
               Status:  Authz Success
               Domain:  DATA
      Security Policy:  Should Secure
      Security Status:  Unsecure
       Oper host mode:  multi-auth
     Oper control dir:  both
        Authorized By:  Authentication Server
          Vlan Policy:  N/A
              ACS ACL:  xACSACLx-IP-QUARANTINE-5ec4d44c
```

```
   Session timeout:  N/A
      Idle timeout:  N/A
 Common Session ID:  0A1E0AF00000004D05ABDADF
  Acct Session ID:   0x0000006F
            Handle:  0x0C00004E

Runnable methods list:
      Method   State
      dot1x    Authc Success
```

On Firepower, we can view the correlation events under **Analysis > Correlation Events**:

I can verify the ACL is working by trying a ping to one of my local servers:

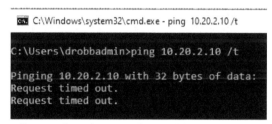

Now all I need to do to undo all this is run a scan that doesn't detect any malware—no problem since AMP quarantined the malware when I first downloaded it:

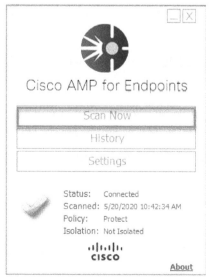

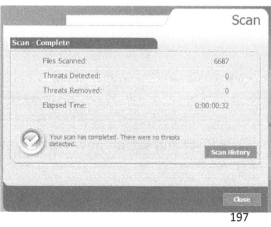

Once the scan is complete, ISE removes the DACL from the port and I've got sweet connectivity again:

```
*Mar  2 02:23:03.601: %EPM-6-POLICY_REQ: IP 10.30.101.100| MAC 3023.038d.f757|
AuditSessionID 0A1E0AF00000004A059C8C58| AUTHTYPE DOT1X| EVENT REMOVE
C3750-SW01#
*Mar  2 02:23:03.819: %AUTHMGR-5-START: Starting 'dot1x' for client
(3023.038d.f757) on Interface Gi1/0/1 AuditSessionID 0A1E0AF00000004B05A9567D
*Mar  2 02:23:04.633: %DOT1X-5-SUCCESS: Authentication successful for client
(3023.038d.f757) on Interface Gi1/0/1 AuditSessionID 0A1E0AF00000004B05A9567D
*Mar  2 02:23:04.633: %AUTHMGR-7-RESULT: Authentication result 'success' from
'dot1x' for client (3023.038d.f757) on Interface Gi1/0/1 AuditSessionID
0A1E0AF00000004B05A9567D
*Mar  2 02:23:04.641: %EPM-6-P
C3750-SW01#OLICY_REQ: IP 0.0.0.0| MAC 3023.038d.f757| AuditSessionID
0A1E0AF00000004B05A9567D| AUTHTYPE DOT1X| EVENT APPLY
*Mar  2 02:23:05.078: %AUTHMGR-5-SUCCESS: Authorization succeeded for client
(3023.038d.f757) on Interface Gi1/0/1 AuditSessionID 0A1E0AF00000004B05A9567D


C3750-SW01#show authentication sessions interface g1/0/1
            Interface:  GigabitEthernet1/0/1
          MAC Address:  3023.038d.f757
           IP Address:  10.30.101.100
            User-Name:  drobbadmin
               Status:  Authz Success
      Security Policy:  Should Secure
      Security Status:  Unsecure
       Oper host mode:  multi-auth
     Oper control dir:  both
         Authorized By:  Authentication Server
          Vlan Policy:  N/A
      Session timeout:  N/A
         Idle timeout:  N/A
    Common Session ID:  0A1E0AF00000004B05A9567D
      Acct Session ID:  0x0000006D
               Handle:  0x4200004C

Runnable methods list:
      Method   State
      dot1x    Authc Success
```

One last thing… checking Firepower, we can see that the malware scan has been detected:

	♦ Time ×	Source IP ×	Source User ×	Description ×
▼ ☐	2020-05-21 02:05:54	10.30.101.100	Testlab\drobbadmin (LDAP)	Malware: Scan Completed, No Detections, US Cloud, 10.30.101.100 -> ::, File: N/A, SHA: N/A, URI: N/A

All set and secure now—awesome!

Summary

If the raw power of this feature isn't crystal clear to you by now, I just don't know what else to say. RTC equips your network to automatically react in a flash to security events—*much* faster than your Security team could ever hope to sitting there, poring logs! Even better, it doesn't require complicated scripting like SIEM remediations do.

I took you through a lot of configuration, which will serve you well for the exam as well as life in network security.

Chapter 30: Threat Intelligence Director (TID)

The following CCNP Security SNCF exam objectives are covered in this chapter:

4.0 Integration

4.3 Implement Threat Intelligence Director for third-party security intelligence feeds

According to Greek mythology, Talos was a giant automaton made of bronze that carried out three security sweeps a day circling island shores to protect Europa in Crete from pirates and invaders. Lofty name to live up to, and Cisco's Talos actually does a decent job inspecting more than 300 billion emails each day! To get that done, it draws upon layering detection technologies like outbreak filters, machine learning-based reputation filters, and Cisco's Advanced Malware Protection (AMP).

Talos isn't the only act in town though. In this chapter, I'm going to guide you through setting up Firepower's Threat Intelligence Director (TID) feature. TID allows your FMC to ingest Cyber Threat Intelligence (CTI) from third-party sources, beefing up Firepower's security effectiveness by acting on Indicators of Compromise from a whole crew of threat feeds!

Threat Intelligence Director

TID has a lot in common with pxGrid in that it accepts information from third-party sources. The difference is that TID consumes security intelligence from assorted external cybersecurity feeds and normalizes it so Firepower can take action when a threat blows in.

A big advantage here is that if a third-party feed becomes aware of a compromised domain or some new malware before Cisco Talos figures it out, you're still protected by TID! Using FMC as your central security dashboard is pretty sweet too, because it can present information from a bunch of different sources.

Another nice benefit is that, because TID actions happen instantly, you don't have to redeploy your policies when you make changes as you do with a regular ACP. So, go right ahead and immediately blacklist a connection, because you don't have to wait for the policy to get pushed to all your firewalls!

TID also hands you tighter control over the things you can filter compared to standard Security Intelligence (SI). SI only lets you whitelist or blacklist an object, but TID equips you to filter more deeply based upon their individual components. Objects are also called indicators, and we'll get to them more in a bit.

Setup

Using TID requires that you're on FMC 6.2.2 firmware at least, and the appliance must have at least 15 GB of RAM. The feature also needs REST API enabled on the FMC, but it's actually enabled by default these days.

If you do need to enable REST API, go to **System>Configuration>REST API Preferences**:

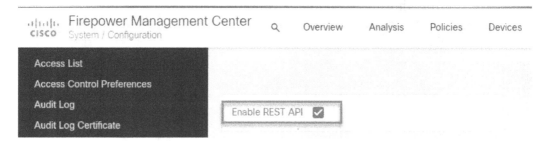

Once REST API is enabled, turn TID on inside your Access Control policy under **Advanced>General Settings>Enable Threat Intelligence Director**. Then push the policy to the firewalls:

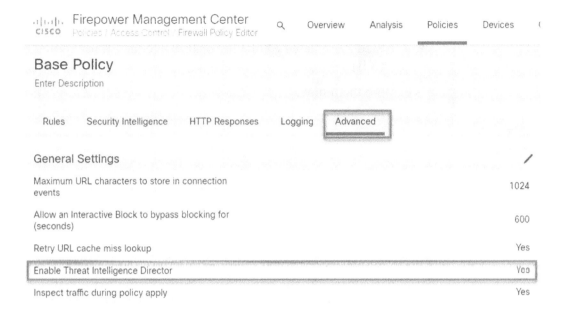

High Availability

Understand that if you're doing high availability with your FMC, the TID configuration and data aren't synchronized to the standby appliance. This means you need to be backing up your TID data nightly in case you need to fail over.

To make that happen, check the Back Up Threat Intelligence Director box in the Create Backup page:

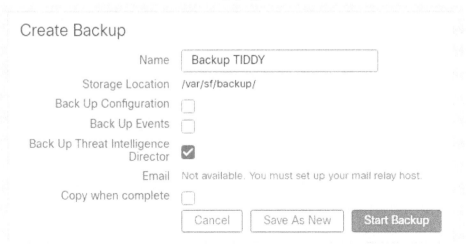

Components

There are two key components here:

- Structured Threat Intelligence eXpression (STIX)
- Trusted Automated eXchange of Intelligence Information (TAXII)

Let's explore them now.

STIX

Structured Threat Intelligence eXpression (STIX) is an open standard for sharing and using threat intelligence information. It's a structured language that allows feeds to describe threat motivations, abilities, capabilities, and responses.

Right now, FMC STIX files must be in STIX versions 1.0, 1.1, 1.1.1, or 1.2.

TID uses a few STIX terms you should know about before we dig into the feature:

- Observables

- Elements

- Indicators

- Incidents

Observables are variables that TID matches from a feed as the Indication of Compromise. Here's the full list of possible values that FMC can currently use:

Observable Name	Description
SHA-256	Matches on SHA-256 hash values.
Domain	Matches on domain names that follow RFC 1035.
URL	Matches on URLs as per RFC 1738. TID adjusts the URL by normalizing any port, protocol, or authentication information before processing. So

	`https://remote.testlab.com:44444/index.html` becomes `remote.testlab.com/index.html`.
IPv4	Matches IPv4 addresses as per RFC 791.
IPv6	Matches IPv6 addresses as per RFC 4291.
Email To	Matches the To field in an email message.
Email From	Matches the From field in an email message.
Email Sender	Matches the Sender field in an email message.
Email Subject	Matches the Subject field in an email message.

Note: You don't actually need to remember the RFCs referenced here, but it definitely doesn't hurt to know what each one considers valid or not.

Observables are then published to the elements—the Firepower devices managed by FMC. Elements monitor traffic and report any found observations to the FMC when the firewalls find any of the observables. They're controlled by the ACP. You can check out the status by going to Intelligence, then Elements. The page will show you the health of the FTD nodes and the ACP that's applied:

FMC Elements	Q	Overview	Analysis	Policies	Devices	Objects	AMP	Intelligence	Deploy			

5 Elements

Name	Element Type	Registered On	Access Control Policy
FTD01	Cisco Firepower Threat Defense for VMWare	May 18, 2020 7:48 PM EDT	Base Policy
FTD02	Cisco Firepower Threat Defense for VMWare	May 18, 2020 7:50 PM EDT	Base Policy
FTD03	Cisco Firepower Threat Defense for VMWare	May 18, 2020 7:52 PM EDT	Base Policy
FTD04	Cisco Firepower Threat Defense for VMWare	May 18, 2020 7:53 PM EDT	Base Policy
FTD31	Cisco Firepower Threat Defense for VMWare	May 31, 2020 6:47 PM EDT	Base Policy

Indicators are a list of observables to be matched. A simple one would only match on one observable, such as, for example, matching on a domain name from a   security feed:

Observable A

You can employ more complex indicators by using Boolean operators like AND, which creates an indicator that matches a domain plus an IPv4 address.

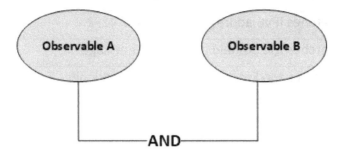

You can even mix and match operators to get more advanced results.

Basically, just remember that incidents are when FMC detects traffic that should by monitored or blocked based on the TID information.

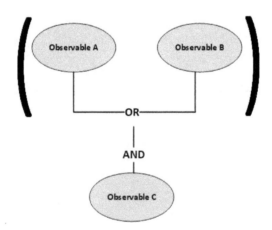

TAXII

Trusted Automated eXchange of Intelligence Information (TAXII) is specifically designed to help transport STIX traffic. You don't really need to understand how TAXII works for the exam since Firepower consumes the provided service.

But in case you're curious, there are three common sharing models you can use. The first is Source/Subscriber, employed when there's a single source of information that's being shared to subscribers.

and Spoke just the

Hub is like

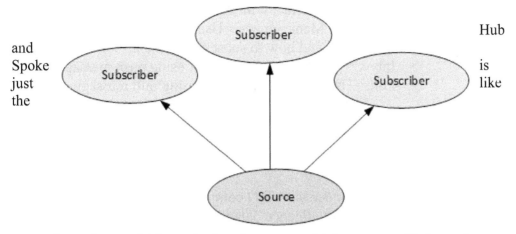

network topology and it's used when there are multiple sources of information that's shared with the hub. Spokes can consume information, send information, or both.

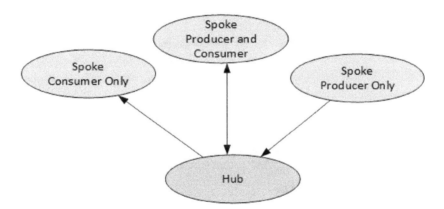

The last model is Peer-to-Peer, which is used when multiple groups share information:

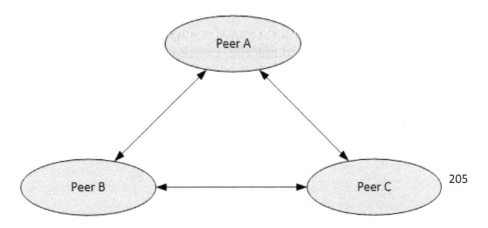

TAXII has four services that can be shared using the models I just talked about:

- Discovery = Used to learn which services an entity supports and how to interact with them.
- Collection Management = Used to learn about data collections and how to subscribe to them.
- Inbox = Used to receive content using push messaging.
- Poll = Used to request content using pull messaging.

Sources

Now that you understand TID components a bit, let's work on getting some Security Intelligence data into the solution. Threat Intelligence Director supports three sources for its Security Intelligence feeds: Manual, STIX, and TAXII.

To add a source, click on the Intelligence tab and select Sources:

Manual – Flat File

The easiest way to get information into TID is by manually uploading flat files. The downside to this is that it can lead to information being out of date since it has no way of getting newer results.

To try this out, I just created a simple text file that has the URL I want to block. To upload this file, I click the plus icon and select Upload for the for .txt file. From here, I get a few options:

- **Type**: In this example, this will be flat file, which could also be STIX.

- **Content**: The observables we talked about—in this case, it'll be domain.

- **File:** Where I'll select the `block.txt` file I created.

- **Name**: This is the name of the source. It can be anything I want, but it should be descriptive.

- **Description:** You can optionally add a description to explain what the source is.

- **Action:** What FMC will do when an incident is created. I can block or monitor, and in this case I'll block connections to the URL.

- **TTL (Days):** How long the source will be considered active without an update.

- **Publish**: Controls if the source is active or not.

After all that, I'll hit Save. An easy way to make sure my file worked is to go to the Indicators tab. If everything imported correctly, I should see my custom rule here:

Now if I try to get to the URL, the page says it can't be reached because of DNS failure:

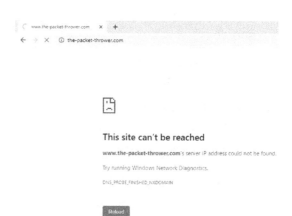

We can check out the incidents
by going to **Intelligence>Incidents**. This page creates a new incident every time
the observable element is seen on the network, so my single attempt actually
created several incidents. This is because of DNS trying to resolve the URL in the

text file on each of its DNS servers:

Clicking on an incident gives you more detailed information so your team
can understand the incident better. Here's where I can name the incident, give it a
description and a category, and change other fields if necessary. Just so you know,
the incident can also be deleted if it's a false alarm:

We can also check out the incident by looking at Security Intelligence Events Analysis. In this case, there's a TID Domain Name Block:

URL – Flat File

It's really a lot more practical to use a URL feed so FMC can periodically download updates and things don't get stale. I'm going to pull some IPs from `https://www.badips.com/get/list/any/2` for the next example.

I'll use curl to see what the content of the feed is. Turns out, it's a bunch of IP addresses:

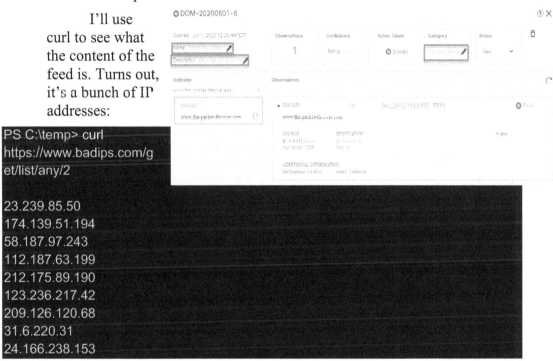

```
PS C:\temp> curl
https://www.badips.com/g
et/list/any/2

23.239.85.50
174.139.51.194
58.187.97.243
112.187.63.199
212.175.89.190
123.236.217.42
209.126.120.68
31.6.220.31
24.166.238.153
```

So I'm going to select URL when adding the source this time. Because it's just an IP list, the type will be a flat file again. The context will be IPv4, and if the URL requires a login, I'd enter a username and password. Not this time though.

The action will be set to block again, and I'll choose how often FMC will update the list. It's 1440 minutes by default, but it can go as low as 30:

Now I'm going to make sure the source is working by checking indicators again. We'll see a lot more entries this time because it's a real list. In fact this list actually has about five hundred thousand entries, so it'll take about 10 minutes to fully parse! Even though the TID is still protecting traffic during this period, it might miss some indicators:

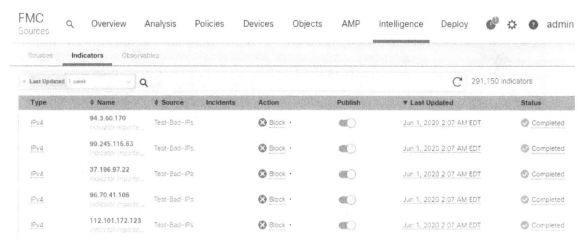

I can search for specific indicators since I'm at this page again. I can search by name, source, observable value, the action being taken, if it's published to the elements, and when it was last updated:

Note: Because the flat file is just a list of values, it can only use simple indicators because there's no room for logic.

Okay—to test it out, I'll ping from my lab to generate some traffic on the FTD element:

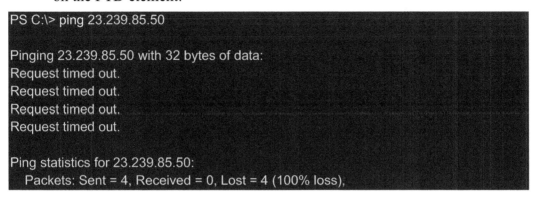

```
PS C:\> ping 23.239.85.50

Pinging 23.239.85.50 with 32 bytes of data:
Request timed out.
Request timed out.
Request timed out.
Request timed out.

Ping statistics for 23.239.85.50:
    Packets: Sent = 4, Received = 0, Lost = 4 (100% loss),
```

Check it out—an incident has been created because of visiting the bad IP (I cleaned up the previous incidents so the page doesn't get too messy):

URL – STIX

So far, flat files have been working just fine. But STIX was developed to be a heck of a lot more secure and scalable! It also lets us use complex indicators. Only trouble here is that I'll have to use the monitoring action instead of having FMC automatically block the traffic.

You can also use STIX with manual uploads, but most people pull the feed from somewhere.

Select URL again, but this time the type will be STIX. I grabbed a sample URL from
https://stix.mitre.org/language/version1.0.1/samples.html:

Because the sample is only one entry, it's parsed pretty much instantly. Over at the indicator page we can see our sample is a complex type:

Clicking the indicator name gets me more details:

Inside is info we've seen before like the name, the description, and the source. I can unpublish the rule, but I can't change the action because only monitoring is supported.

The most interesting info is the indicator pattern, which shows what the complex rule is matching.

You can also choose to download the STIX XML file, which comes in handy for more in-depth troubleshooting. It can even be used to help create your own STIX files.

You're probably thinking this is all great stuff, but how do I block bad traffic? From **Analysis>Security Intelligence**, scroll to the right until you see the observables you want to block, right-click them, and choose to blacklist:

Here, it's a DNS request, but the same goes if you select an IP.

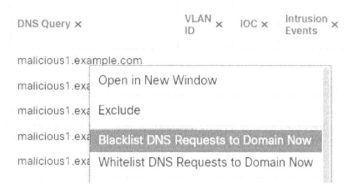

TAXII

Next up, I'll show you how to hail a TAXII by using http://hailataxii.com/, a free open-source TAXII feed that's really helpful for meeting security needs.

So again, I'm going to add a source only this time, I'll go with the TAXII tab. The service does have a login, but just use guest/guest for the username and password.

I want to point out a difference here… Because TAXII is more of a distribution method for STIX, I can pick the feeds I'm interested in. I'll go ahead and add all of them just for fun:

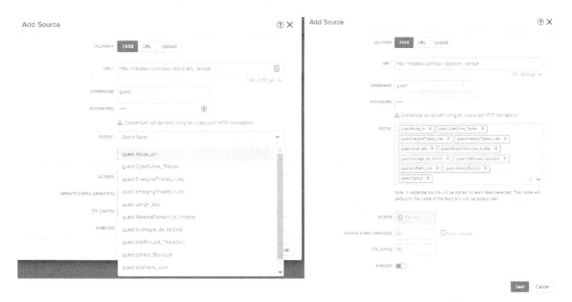

When you enable multiple feeds, they'll show up as individual sources, making it easy to remove feeds you don't want anymore. Just know this can get pretty annoying if you want to completely delete all of them! Check it out:

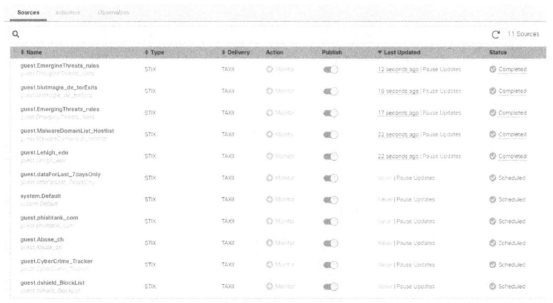

TAXII makes you import the rules with a monitoring action, but you can change them in the indicators page by selecting the action and changing it to block.

Summary

We confirmed Threat Intelligence Director up and running by default and then I talked about how it is components, STIX and TAXII work.

After that, we kicked the tires by playing with manual flat files and moved on to URL feeds before having a look at proper STIX and TAXII examples.

You learned that all in all, TID is a great feature that adds a lot more flexibility to the security of your network and it doesn't require a ton of configuration!

Chapter 31: Remote Access VPN Site to Site

The CCNP Security SNCF exam objectives covered in this chapter are:

2.0 Configuration

> ***2.5 Configure devices using Firepower Management Center***

> > ***2.5.c VPN***

It's time for us to dig into both varieties of secure access VPNs: site to site and remote access. These two technologies could definitely use a set of protocols and a decent way to provide security for the traffic passing between parties, but at least they can use the same framework.

We'll get started with a brief introduction and then jump straight into configuring site-to-site VPN options. Just so you know, we'll be diving deep into remote access VPN in the next chapter.

Site-to-Site VPN

Site-to-site VPN is not exactly new—it's been around for a few decades now and give us a secure way to connect two or more sites virtually over insecure public connectivity like the Internet. I say "virtually" because those two or more sites aren't directly or physically connected to each other, meaning we really leverage other direct connections to virtually connect our sites.

Site-to-site VPN uses the very complex IPsec as the framework to encapsulate and encrypt the traffic passing between the sites. IPsec has a whole bunch of protocols that work together to create a secure tunnel for transferring our data securely.

IPsec's key crew of protocols include Authentication Header (AH), Encapsulating Security Payload (ESP), and Internet Key Exchange (IKE).

The AH protocol ensures the data hasn't been tampered with in transit by calculating a hash of the traffic received and comparing it with the hash sent from the initiator. If the value is different, the packet is discarded.

ESP encrypts the traffic at layer 3 of OSI model, which can be done with any supported algorithm we define in our site-to-site VPN configuration. Some of the old algorithms either have been removed from newer security devices like DES or 3DES or they will be soon because they're so weak they can be cracked by a 10-year-old.

On the other side of things is IKE, a vital management protocol, which manages the key material that'll be negotiated between the site-to-site VPN's parties. IKE also creates the IPsec security associations (SAs) where all the security parameters that've been agreed upon will reside.

Here's how that works: When a device encrypts or decrypts a packet, it looks at the matched SA first before getting busy with encryption or decryption because it bases its operation on the settings included within it. You can think about the SA as a logical container where all the parameters used when we configure the site-to-site VPN live together.

IKE has two flavors: IKEv1 and IKEv2. The main difference between them is using IKEv2 results in fewer messages being exchanged between the site-to-site VPN parties because it simplifies the negotiation process. There are only four messages instead of the six exchanged by IKEv1 in Main mode. IKEv2 also supports EAP authentication, a very cool, secure authentication method, and also checks to see if the remote peer is still alive with a slew of consecutive probes before declaring a remote peer "dead."

Remote Access VPN

Clearly, remote access VPN is mainly used to support remote workers. The technology serves up a flexible way for remote workers to connect to the corporate networks remotely and securely. With remote access VPN, there's no issue concerning the remote clients' public IP addresses because they can source from any public IP and still securely connect to our corporate networks.

Of course, there's always bad news too. Protocols can be used on the client side to connect to our VPN. The old Cisco IPsec VPN client uses IPsec as the underlying framework to establish the VPN tunnel, but thankfully, that doesn't work out all that great for remote workers nowadays. In modern public spaces like airports, coffee shops, etc., IPsec just wouldn't make it through the firewalls, effectively blocking remote workers from being able to establish a remote tunnel to the corporate network.

To clear this little snag, Cisco came up with the new AnyConnect client that allows using the traditional HTTPS port 443/tcp for establishing the VPN tunnel. In today's networks, port 443/tcp would likely be opened on any firewall in the outbound direction. AnyConnect only goes with port 443/tcp for backup if it isn't allowed to use its first choice, port 443/udp. This optimizes performance serving low-latency traffic like audio and video.

The AnyConnect client can also be configured to use IPsec, which definitely gives us some flexibility. If our remote workers tend to use public connections, then it's fine to have them use the AnyConnect client SSL VPN. If they usually work from home, or from another office where IPsec can be put on the firewall outbound, we can make them use IPsec.

When it comes to both site-to-site and remote access VPN connections, there are different ways to decide on the traffic to protect if we want to send it across the tunnel. We also have three main tunnel types to choose from: split tunnel, tunnel all, and exclude tunnel. Split tunnel allows us to selectively decide which traffic to send across the tunnel, leaving anything else to be locally broken out to the Internet. Tunnel all means we send all the traffic between the two parties over the tunnel. Exclude tunnel is a great option for when we want to tunnel all traffic except for a few specific subnets—for example, when we want to allow remote clients to use their local LAN accesses like printers yet still tunnel all the traffic over the VPN.

Authentication between VPN parties can happen via pre-shared keys or certificates. Certificate authentication offers more security, and we can also use it to make sure incoming connections are only initiated from corporate devices. A good example here would be a home laptop that doesn't have the corporate certificate installed. If our AnyConnect remote access VPN policy is configured to allow authentication via certificates issued by our internal CA only, no one can authenticate to the VPN unless they do that from a corporate laptop.

A key factor with VPN connections is NAT exemption, which people sometimes call Identity NAT. Basically, what Identity NAT does is translate the source and destination to themselves—their IP addresses don't change. Identity NAT's main purpose is to allow the private IP addressing in each end to reach each other. If Identity NAT isn't applied, the traffic sent by a remote host is translated to the public IP address of its gateway or to another public IP address that's configured on that gateway.

This means the VPN traffic between the two ends wouldn't match the encryption domains, which are the subnets defined in the crypto access lists. It also means the traffic will be routed out of the VPN tunnel and wouldn't succeed between the two end hosts! So yes, Identity NAT absolutely has to be configured to prevent things like this.

I'm sure it's becoming really clear that there's a world of components involved with the VPN. Going through all their details would take a whole book, so we're going to focus on covering the 300-710 SNCF exam topics here instead.

We're still going to have some fun configuring the site-to-site and remote access VPNs. No worries—I'll cover all the options that FMC offers and tell you about everything you need to master this topic!

I'm going to get started by talking about each option we have in the site-to-site and remote access VPN sections and then we'll dive straight into configuring VPN site to site.

Site-to-Site VPN Configuration

On the Devices tab, click Site-to-Site:

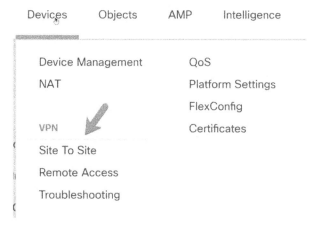

The Create New VPN Topology screen appears, which is where we'll configure the site-to-site VPN. Let's go through all those fields now and get this tunnel up:

Here's a description of our configuration options, starting from the very top:

Topology Name
The topology name is just the name you provide for the site-to-site VPN tunnel.

Network Topology
Network Topology gives us three options, and how we would use each one depends on our VPN design:

- Point to Point is used when a site-to-site VPN between two peers is configured. This is the most common topology for site-to-site VPNs.
- Hub and Spoke is used when we have multiple remote sites that'll connect to the same peer. The remote sites are called spokes, and the main site where all those VPN connections will be terminated is called the hub.
- Full Mesh is similar to Hub and Spoke. The main difference is that with Full Mesh, all the VPN peers establish a direct VPN tunnel to each other in addition to the Hub.

IKE Version

As the name implies, the IKE Version option lets us pick the IKE version to use for our VPN tunnel. We can select IKEv1, IKEv2, or both at the same time. A great case for using both presents itself when one of the peers is transitioning from IKEv1 to IKEv2.

Endpoints Tab

The Endpoints tab lets us configure the local peer, which is actually our firewall, plus the remote peer, which is the firewall at the remote site: The exception here is the full mesh VPN, where all the peers involved in the tunnel are configured in the same section.

For the Point-to-Point topology, node A is the local peer and node B is the remote peer. In each of these two sections, we've got to give a name to each peer, the interface on which VPN traffic will be terminated, as well as the protected networks. The name can be anything you come up with. The VPN interface will be the firewall outside interface, and finally, the protected networks are the subnets we want to encrypt over the tunnel. This means any traffic sent to those subnets will be encrypted.

A super important thing to keep in mind is that with Firepower, there's no security level concept like the ASA. This means we have to define some rules on the Access Control policy so the VPN traffic will be successful!

Device Name

The Device name menu will list all the Firepower devices that've been registered to the FMC. There's one more option in there, Extranet. It's used to define the remote peer, which isn't managed by this FMC. That would be Node B. For Node A, I'll just select the Firepower appliance we want to configure for this VPN tunnel.

Okay—so to start the tunnel configuration, click the plus sign (+) on the right side of the Node A line. Then configure Node B by clicking the plus sign (+).

When you click the plus sign to add a node in the Point-to-Point Endpoints tab, you'll get a window a lot like this one:

Add Endpoint   ? ×

| Empty | ❗ |

Interface:* | Empty |

IP Address:* | Empty |

                   ☐ This IP is Private

Connection Type: | Bidirectional |

Certificate Map: | + |

Protected Networks:*

◉ Subnet / IP Address (Network)   ○ Access List (Extended)

+

Let's define the options on this page:

Interface
As I said earlier, the interface is basically the segment where the VPN tunnel will be terminated. So, if we have two interfaces configured on our

Firepower appliance called INTERNAL and EXTERNAL, the interface to select in this case would be EXTERNAL because that interface will be the one facing the remote peer. The interfaces that'll be listed in the Interface menu are specific to the selected Firepower appliance.

IP Address

The IP Address option is used to define our local VPN peer. But that option gets populated automatically when we select the Firepower appliance interface. The only exception is when we select Extranet to define the remote peer, but that's in the Node B section. The check box This IP is Private, right there below the IP Address field, must be ticked when the Firepower appliance's selected interface is behind a NAT device. In that case, the interface IP address will probably be in the RFC 1918 range.

Connection Type

There are three connection types: Originate Only, Answer Only, and Bidirectional. Most of the time people go with Bidirectional, which allows the local peer to initiate the VPN tunnel with the remote peer, or permits it to respond to the VPN tunnel negotiation initiated by the remote peer. (This has nothing to do with allowing the VPN traffic through the Access Control policy!) The second most popular option is Originate Only, which will ensure that the VPN tunnel is always initiated by the local peer. Word to the wise is that this feature doesn't dictate any extra security bits; it just ensures the VPN tunnel isn't initiated by the remote peer.

Certificate Map

A certificate map is used to map a certificate to a specific VPN tunnel. This works by defining a certificate map with some specific attributes that must be matched exactly for the certificate to be used for authentication.

Protected Networks

We can use either option to define the encryption domains that'll dictate the type of traffic to be sent over the VPN tunnel. The main difference between using a subnet or an IP address and using an extended access list for the VPN traffic comes down to just how granular we want to get when defining it. If we use the Subnet / IP Address (Network) option, it'll point to our network objects and result in having an extended access list created with the local and remote peer objects. If we use the Access List (Extended) option instead, it'll point to our access list's container and give us more granularity. Here's what I mean…Let's say we want to define an access list for the VPN traffic that would actually protect the traffic going to one of our servers *on a specific port*. There's just no way to get this level of granularity with the Subnet / IP Address (Network) option, since doing that will just create an extended access list without specifying any ports! We absolutely have to go with the extended option for that.

IKE Tab

We typically use the IKE tab to define the IKE policy and authentication type. The options you'll get from this tab depend on the IKE version you use:

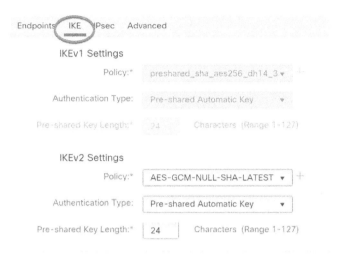

Let's check out all the options both IKE versions offer:

Policy:* drop-down menu

The IKEv1 policy is a container where you can define all IKE attributes related to phase 1—you can define the priority, encryption, hash, DH, lifetime, and authentication method.

IKEv2, serves up more options, like Pseudo-Random Function (PRF), the algorithm IKEv2 uses to derive the keying material and the hash value. This version supports much more secure encryption and hash algorithms compared to IKEv1!

You can either shop the policy menu to pick one of the pre-defined policies, or you can create a new policy by clicking the plus sign (+) there, on the right side of the Policy:* menu.

Here's a look at the two pages you get when you choose IKEv1 and IKEv2:

New IKEv1 Policy

Name:*

Description:

Priority: (1-65535)

Encryption:*
aes-128

Hash:*
SHA

Diffie-Hellman Group:*
14

Lifetime:* seconds (120-2147483647)
86400

Authentication Method:*
Preshared Key

Cancel   Save

New IKEv2 Policy

Name:*

Description:

Priority: (1-65535)

Lifetime: seconds (120-2147483647)
86400

Available Algorithms		Selected Algorithms
Integrity Algorithms	MD5	Add
Encryption Algorithms	SHA	
PRF Algorithms	SHA512	
Diffie-Hellman Group	SHA256	
	SHA384	
	NULL	

Cancel   Save

Name (IKEv1/2)

The name field lets you name the new policy. Be sure there aren't any spaces in it!

Description (IKEv1/2)

The description is just there to reference what you're using the policy for.

Priority (IKEv1/2)

The priority is basically the order of operation the policy will be checking for. For instance, if there are a whole bunch of policies on the FTD with priority 10, 20, 30 etc. but you want your new policy to get checked before them, just set your new policy's priority to a number between 1 and 9 and it'll get checked before all the others.

The strategy behind doing this is because when we have multiple policies, we usually set a higher priority for the most secure one. Say we've got three IKEv1 policies: one with AES-256, another with AES-192, and the third one with AES-128. In this case we'd set the AES-256 policy to get the highest priority and be checked first, followed by the AES-192 policy next and the AES-128 as the last one up.

Think about priority as preference—the higher the priority, the more preferred the policy is. Why do we have multiple IKEv1 policies instead of having only one? Because we might have multiple site-to-site VPN tunnels with multiple peers, but not all the peers are using the same encryption, hash, and DH parameters. So, in this case, we'd set up all our policies and give the most secure one the highest priority, making it preferred over the others. This way, when the IKEv1 phase 1 tunnel is negotiated, the most secure policy will get selected due to its preference that we defined as priority.

Encryption (IKEv1) / Encryption Algorithms (IKEv2)
The encryption algorithm is used to encrypt the phase 1 traffic, which could be the phase 2 encryption algorithm as well unless you use PFS in phase 2. More about this soon. For now, know that you can select one of the supported encryption algorithms, with the highest encryption algorithm as the most secure one for encryption over the tunnel.

Hash (IKEv1) / Integrity Algorithms (IKEv2)
The hash is used for integrity, which means each peer being able to verify if the received traffic was truly received by the remote peer and wasn't manipulated in transit. When the peer receives the traffic from the other peer, it calculates the traffic's hash value and will pass integrity if the calculated hash value matches the one sent by the remote peer.

Diffie-Hellman Group (IKEv1/2)
Diffie-Hellman is used to exchange values between the two peers and calculate a unique keying material between them. The power of DH is that it allows two peers to exchange those values over public media without any risk of compromising the keying material the peers agreed upon. This is because that keying material will never be sent across the wire! Each peer can calculate the unique keying material locally based on the values that were exchanged between them to derive the encryption and hash keys.

Lifetime (IKEv1/2)
The lifetime value defines the duration of the phase 1 encryption key used between peers. A new encryption key will be generated that'll replace the old one before it expires.

Authentication Method (IKEv1)
The authentication method can be either a pre-shared key or certificates. Your choice of one of these depends on your implementation, but I recommend going with certificates wherever possible since they're more secure.

PRF Algorithms (IKEv2)
Pseudo-random function (PRF) is the algorithm used by IKEv2 to derive the keying material and the hash value.

Authentication Type (IKEv1/2)
This allows you to choose if you want to use pre-shared key or certificates for the VPN topology. But here, you get options for the type of pre-shared key type: manual or automatic. Manual is the traditional key and the automatic pre-shared key automatically generates the pre-shared key between the two peers. You can only opt for automatic if the two FTD

appliances are managed by the same FMC.

Pre-shared Key Length (IKEv1/2)
This lets you define the length of the pre-shared key with a value between 1 and 127. The longer the key, the more secure the encryption key will be. You can only use this value if you've chosen the automatic key option.

Now, why do we have Authentication Type options when we could've defined it already in the policy? Well first, the authentication method you chose in the policy has to match the Authentication Type on the IKE tab. You'll just get an error if you try to do something different. Second, when we define the Authentication method in the policy, we don't specify any settings for it. So, if you select pre-shared key in the policy, that just allows you to define the method you want to use, it doesn't require you to define the pre-shared key itself.

Same kind of thing goes for certificates… If you select certificate as the authentication method, that just defines the method. It won't ask you to define the trust point to be used.

IPsec Tab

The IPsec tab is all about IKE phase 2 parameters. You can define all the phase 2 settings here, and the number of options depends on if you've selected IKEv1 or IKEv2:

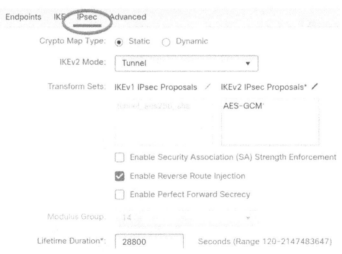

Crypto Map Type (IKEv1/2)
Here's where you can opt to go with a static or dynamic crypto map. You'd want a dynamic crypto map if you're setting up a VPN tunnel with a remote peer that doesn't have a static IP address.

IKEv2 Mode (IKEv2)

IKEv2 Mode is where you choose to use Tunnel or Transport mode. The main difference between the two is that in Transport mode, the client IP header won't be encrypted. From the IKEv2 menu, you specify if the Transport mode should be required or preferred, and if you select preferred, the encapsulation mode will fall back to tunnel mode if the peer doesn't support transport mode.

Transform Sets (IKEv1/2)

The transform sets are the containers where we define the Encapsulating Security Payload (ESP), encryption, and hash algorithms. IKEv2 offers a lot more options with much more secure algorithms. You can opt for one of the pre-defined sets, but you can also create a new set by clicking the pencil sign and then the plus sign on the Available Transform Sets page.

Enable Security Association (SA) Strength Enforcement (IKEv2)

This option is used to guarantee the encryption algorithm used by the child. Just remember that IPsec SA is not stronger than the parent, IKEv2 SA.

Enable Reverse Route Injection (IKEv1/2)

Choose this option if you want to allow the FTD to inject the VPN protected networks routes into a downstream L3 device. For instance, the FTD can be running OSPF with a downstream router, and if so, the FTD will inject the remote VPN protected networks into the OSPF route. As a result, the downstream L3 device will have a route to the remote VPN encryption domains via the FTD.

Enable Perfect Forward Secrecy (IKEv1/2)

If you enable this option, it'll allow the FTD to generate new keying material for phase 2 that's not derived from the DH keying material that was used for phase 1. This is a nice option because it gives us more security since the phase 1 and 2 keying materials will be independent of one another. When you enable this option, you've got to select the DH group from the drop-down menu.

Lifetime Duration (IKEv1/2)

Here's where you define the lifetime length before the encryption key is replaced with a new one. Again, a new key will be generated before the current encryption key expires.

Scroll down on the screen to check out your options:

| Lifetime Duration*: | 28800 | Seconds (Range 120-2147483647) |
| Lifetime Size: | 4608000 | Kbytes (Range 10-2147483647) |

▼ ESPv3 Settings

☐ Validate incoming ICMP error messages
☐ Enable "Do Not Fragment" Policy
    Policy: [▼]
☐ Enable Traffic Flow Confidentiality (TFC) Packets

    Burst: ☑ Auto   bytes (1-16)
    Payload Size: ☑ Auto   bytes (64-1024)
    Timeout: ☑ Auto   seconds (10-60)

Lifetime Size (IKEv1/2)

Similar to the Lifetime Duration, this option determines the lifetime based on how many kilobytes have been transferred over the tunnel before regenerating the encryption keys.

ESPv3 Settings

This section is all about the ESP version 3.

Validate incoming ICMP error messages

This allows the FTD to validate ICMP error messages passing over the VPN tunnel.

Enable "Do Not Fragment" Policy

We use this to define how the FTD will deal with the packets that have the Do-Not-Fragment (DF) flag set in the IP header. You pick out one of the options from the Policy drop-down menu to decide how to deal with the DF traffic. If you want to ignore the DF, just choose Clear.

Enable Traffic Flow Confidentiality (TFC) Packets

This option makes the FTD able to hide the actual length of the packets transferred over the VPN tunnel. It works by adding extra padding to the packets and sending dummy packets with different lengths at random intervals. You can manually define the Burst, Payload Size, and Timeout parameters to generate random length packets at random intervals, or use the auto option to allow the FTD to automatically set those values. Why would anyone want to do this? It really helps to mitigate any traffic analysis attacks monitoring how much traffic is passing across our networks. In a word, stealth!

Advanced Tab

Under the Advanced tab, there are three submenu items on the left that we're going to run through now:

IKE (IKEv1/2)

There are two sections in the submenu with IKE: ISAKAMP Settings and IKEv2 SA Settings. Let's start at the top:

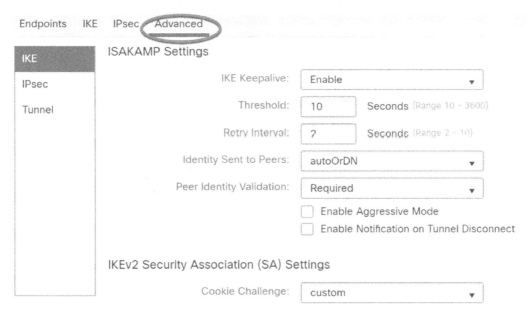

ISAKAMP Settings

IKE Keepalive
IKE Keepalives are messages exchanged between the peers to check if they're still alive. You can disable or enable them and even enable infinite, which means the device never starts keepalive for monitoring itself.

Threshold
Keepalive thresholds are the values you set for a device telling it how long to wait before starting keepalives monitoring.

Retry Interval
The retry interval value is to specify how many seconds the device waits before retrying to send keepalives.

Identity Sent to Peers

During the IKE negotiation, the peers try to identify themselves. Choose an option from the drop-down menu to select the identification method:

autoOrDN, the default, allows the peer to send its IP address for identification when a pre-shared key is used. When a certificate is used, it allows the peer to send its certificate DN value, but this option isn't supported anymore.

ipAddress allows the peer to send its IP address for identification.

Hostname allows the peer to send its FQDN for identification.

Peer Identity Validation

Peer identity validation can be enabled or disabled on a per-tunnel-group basis. It's used with certificate authentication, and when it's enabled, the peers will validate each other using the Subject Alternative Name (SAN) from the presented certificate.

Enable Aggressive Mode

We can use this option in Hub-and-Spoke VPN topology. It's a good choice if the remote peer IP address is unknown and the DNS resolution isn't defined on the peers.

Enable Notification on Tunnel Disconnect

Use this option if you want the peer to receive an IKE notification message for inbound packets received on an SA that don't match the traffic selectors for that SA.

IKEv2 Security Association (SA) Settings (IKEv2)

There are four settings under SA settings for IKEv2:

Cookie Challenge

This option allows sending cookie challenges to the peers in response to SA initiate packets. By default, cookie challenges are used when 50% of the available SAs are in negotiation, and using them can really help defeat denial of service (DoS) attacks!

Threshold to Challenge Incoming Cookies

This option lets you define the percentage of the total amount of SAs allowed in negotiation. Any future SA negotiation will trigger cookie challenges.

Number of SAs Allowed in Negotiation

Here's how we limit the maximum number of SAs that can be in negotiation at any given time. If you use this option with cookie challenges, know that you've got to configure the cookie challenges threshold to be lower than this value!

Maximum number of SAs Allowed

This option is to limit the number of allowed IKEv2 connections. The default is to use the maximum supported on the FTD platform in use.

IPsec

The IPsec Settings options in the IPsec submenu are shown here:

Enable Fragmentation Before Encryption

This option is enabled by default and it's all about allowing for the fragmentation of packets before encryption. How it works is when the remote peer receives this traffic, it's able to start decrypting and building the fragmented packet without having to wait for the whole packet in order to decrypt it.

Path Maximum Transmission Unit Aging

Use this option to enable Path Maximum Transmission Unit (PMTU) aging.

Tunnel

There are three settings in the Tunnel submenu:

IKE	NAT Settings
IPsec	☑ Keepalive Messages Traversal
Tunnel	Interval: 20 Seconds (Range 10 - 3600)

Access Control for VPN Traffic

☐ Bypass Access Control policy for decrypted traffic (sysopt permit-vpn)

Decrypted traffic is subjected to Access Control Policy by default. This option bypasses the inspection, but VPN Filter ACL and authorization ACL downloaded from AAA server are still applied to VPN traffic.

Certificate Map Settings

☐ Use the certificate map configured in the Endpoints to determine the tunnel
☑ Use the certificate OU field to determine the tunnel
☑ Use the IKE identity to determine the tunnel
☑ Use the peer IP address to determine the tunnel

NAT Settings

Keepalive Messages Traversal

Use this option if the peer is setting behind a NAT device. Enabling it will trigger NAT keepalive messages to be sent to the remote peer. The default value is 20 seconds.

Access Control for VPN Traffic

Bypass Access Control policy for decrypted traffic

Some people think this command was born in FTD with 6.3 code, but it really isn't new—it's actually the old ASA command `sysop permit-vpn`! Anyway, if you enable this option, VPN traffic will bypass the security inspection on the local peer, meaning the incoming traffic over the VPN won't be subject to the Access Control policy. Even so, you can still apply a VPN filtering access list or use a downloadable access list pushed by the AAA server.

Certificate Map Settings

Use the certificate map configured in the Endpoints to determine the tunnel

This option lets you to point to the certificate map that was defined or referenced when you added the endpoint in the Endpoints tab.

Use the certificate OU field to determine the tunnel

This one allows the peer to use the OU value from the certificate to determine the VPN tunnel.

Use the IKE identity to determine the tunnel

If the "Use the certificate OU" option is enabled and the peer wasn't determined by the OU value, then the certificate-based IKE sessions are mapped to a tunnel based on the content of the phase1 IKE ID.

Use the peer IP address to determine the tunnel

If neither the "Use the certificate OU" nor the "Use the IKE identity" option is matched, this option allows the use of the established peer IP address to determine the tunnel.

Site-to-Site VPN with Pre-shared Automatic Key Configuration

Coming up, I'm going to show you how to actually configure a site-to-site VPN between two FTDs using FMC Pre-shared Automatic Key! This feature lets us offload the creation of the pre-shared key to the FMC and even tells it how long the pre-shared key will be. For Pre-shared Automatic Key to work, both FTD appliances must be managed by the same FMC because the FMC can't just push the auto generated key to a remote device that it doesn't manage. Makes sense, right?

We'll be using IKEv1 in this lab, and the FTD appliances will be called FTDv-01 and FTDv-03. FTDv-01 is running unified code 6.5.0.4 and FTDv-03 is running unified code 6.6.0. The FMC we'll be using is running 6.6.0 code.

First, to get our site-to-site VPN tunnel up and running, we'll create a new VPN topology and define all the phase 1 and 2 settings. Once that's done, we'll configure a rule in our access control policies to allow the outbound traffic from our internal encryption domain to get to the remote encryption domain. Just so you're clear, "encryption domain" is just another way of referring to protected networks—the very networks we want to protect over the VPN tunnel. Oh, and we'll be going with split tunnel for our VPN topology.

Another component we'll configure is Identity NAT, so we'll be creating an Identity NAT rule on each FTD appliance. Identity NAT is actually just another name for NAT exemption, which is a really common requirement for VPN connections. What's cool is that NAT exemption can even be used in other environments where there isn't a VPN. It all depends on your specific situation and business requirements. The Identity NAT concept is basically translating the source and destination to themselves, which results in having the same source and the same destination for any traffic passing between the VPN subnets. Basically, it just means that there won't be any changes to the source or destination for that traffic flow.

Okay—so why do we need that? Because…privacy! We want to keep the same private IP addresses for the VPN traffic, and if we don't apply Identity NAT rules, traffic passing between the two VPN subnets will get translated by another NAT/PAT rule, effectively breaking the traffic flow between the two subnets!

Moving on, our two encryption domains are referred to as FLAT, which is the subnet 172.16.1.0/24, and VLAN_33, which is the subnet 192.168.33.0/24.

Okay, now let's build a tunnel!

Configuring Site-To-Site with Automatic Key

Configuring site-to-site VPN involves five steps: activate the FTD, create the New VPN topology, configure the ACP with Identity NAT, create the Identity NAT rules, and verification.

Step 1: Activate FTD

Traverse to **Devices>VPN>Site To Site** and click on Firepower Threat Defense from either location:

Step 2: Create the New VPN Topology

Next, create the new VPN topology:

1. Give the new VPN topology a name.
2. Select IKEv1 and deselect IKEv2.
3. Click the plus sign to add Node A. It doesn't matter which FTD device you start with here:

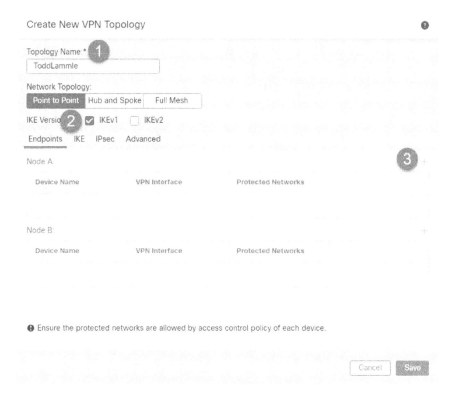

When you click on the plus sign (+), the Add Endpoint menu appears.

1. Select one of the FTD appliances that'll be forming the VPN tunnel.

2. Choose the interface that'll be facing the remote peer. This will probably be the external interface.

3. Click the plus sign to add the encryption domain.

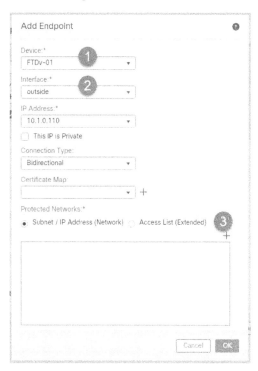

I'm going to pause here a second and go through the other options with you. The first one, **This IP is Private**, is what you'd go with when the FTD appliance is sitting behind a NAT device.

Next up is **Connection Type**, which by default, is bidirectional. You can set it either to Originate Only, if you don't want the remote peer to be able to initiate the VPN tunnel, or to Answer Only, if you don't want this FTD to initiate the connection.

Keep in mind that this isn't a security feature! No matter which of these two options you choose, when the VPN tunnel is established, the traffic will still pass through unrestricted unless you applied some rules on the ACP, and that's *only* if you aren't using `sysopt connection permit-vpn` or going through a VPN filter!

Now, choose the networks you want to include in the Protected Networks field:

1. Select the network object you've created to define the local encryption domain, which sits behind the FTD Node A.
2. Click the Add button to add it to Selected Networks
3. Click OK.

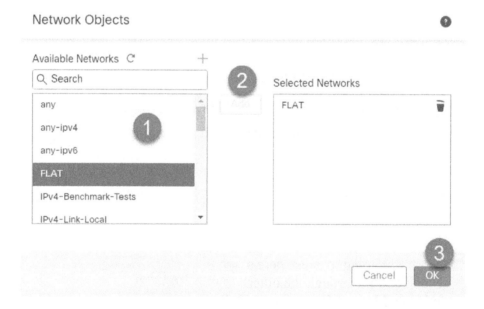

When you select the *Subnet / IP Address (Network)* option, the FMC creates an extended access list with the local encryption domain as the source. The destination of this access list will be defined within the Node B configuration coming up next.

If you select the Access List (Extended) option, you can use any extended access list you've have created or create a new one from the configuration screen. The key difference between these two options is that using the first one will create the extended access list with no reference to any port. Going with the second option lets you build up a customized access list to map to your specific requirements..

The Node B configuration is a lot like Node A's with the main differences being the device, interface, and the encryption domain:

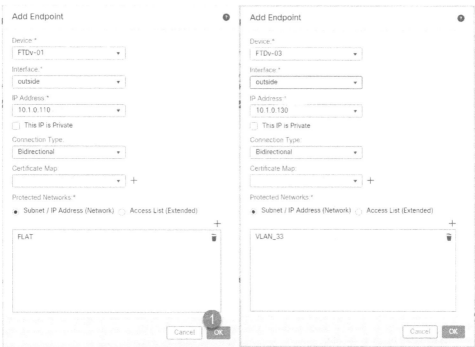

Okay—both node configurations are done, so next, we'll head over to the IKE tab and configure phase 1 settings:

1. Click on the IKE tab.
2. Click the plus sign to configure a new IKEv1 phase 1 policy.

On the New IKEv1 Policy screen, name the policy.

1. Set the priority value. Remember, the lower the number, the higher the priority, meaning the higher the preference will be if both peers agree on the policy set values.

2. Select the encryption algorithm. I recommend choosing the higher supported algorithm, but

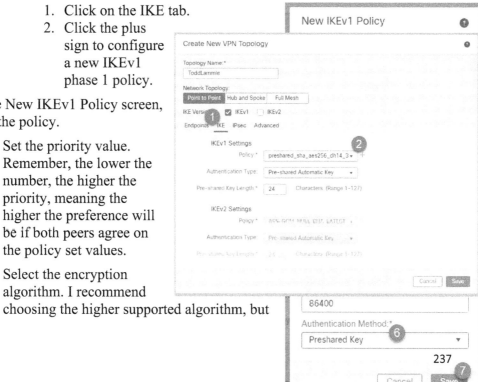

237

keep in mind that the higher the algorithm, the more CPU resources it requires.

3. Select the hash algorithm for integrity check. Whatever you do, steer clear of MD5 because it's a notoriously weak algorithm!

4. Select the Diffie-Hellman group—should be DH group 14 at a minimum.

5. Select Preshared Key as the authentication method and then…

6. Click Save.

1. Back on the IKEv1 settings page, select the new IKEv1 policy we created from the drop-down menu.

2. Set the Pre-shared Key Length value, which can be any value between 1 and 127. The longer the key, the more secure the encryption will be.

3. Click on the IPsec tab to configure IKEv1 phase 2 settings.

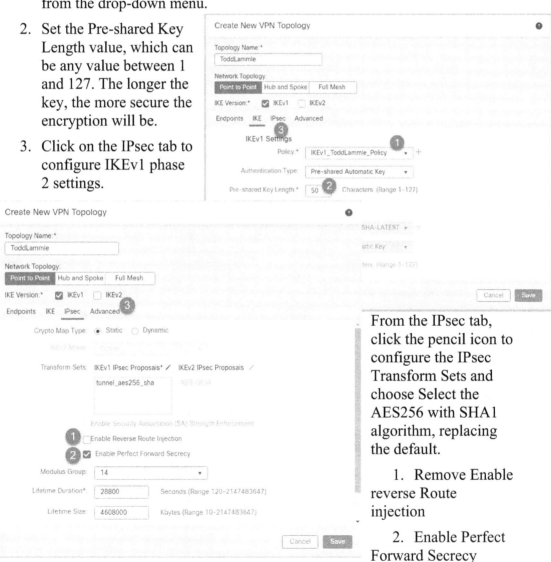

From the IPsec tab, click the pencil icon to configure the IPsec Transform Sets and choose Select the AES256 with SHA1 algorithm, replacing the default.

1. Remove Enable reverse Route injection

2. Enable Perfect Forward Secrecy

3. Click on the Advanced tab

1. Change IKEv1 to 128_sha

2. Deselect Enable Reverse Route Injection because we don't have a downstream router to advertise the remote VPN subnet

3. Choose Perfect Forward Secrecy, which allows the IKEv1 phase 2 to generate new keying material to encrypt the traffic over the VPN tunnel. The new keying material will be independent of the one created for Phase One.

4. Move on to the Advanced tab.

From the Advanced tab:

1. Select **ipAddress** from the Identity Sent to Peers option to allow the VPN peers to identify themselves by their IP addresses. This identification is used to match the tunnel group that'll be configured on each FTD appliance.

2. Leave all the other options at their defaults and move on to the Tunnel section.

At the Tunnel side menu:

1. Deselect the NAT Traversal Keepalive Messages—we don't need those since our FTD appliances are directly connected to the public shared segment and aren't behind NAT devices.

2. Click Save.

Sweet—we're done creating the new VPN Topology! Next, we'll create the access control policy rules plus the Identity NAT rules.

Step 3: Configure the ACP with Identity NAT

Go to **Policies>Access Control**.

We're going to edit two Access Control policies: the ACP_FTDv-01 and the ACP_FTDv-03. Each policy is associated with the respective FTD appliance.

We're going to configure the new rules so we can have one single rule to match the VPN traffic sourcing from our local encryption domain (FLAT) that's destined to the remote encryption domain VLAN_33 and vice versa:

Click the pencil icon to edit Access Control policy ACP_FTDv-01 and click Add Rule:

1. Name the rule VPN Traffic.

2. Go to the Zones tab.

3. Select both the FLAT and LAB_OUTSIDE security zones and add them to the Source Zones area.

4. Select both the FLAT and LAB_OUTSIDE security zones and add them to the Destination Zones area.

5. Move on to the Networks tab:

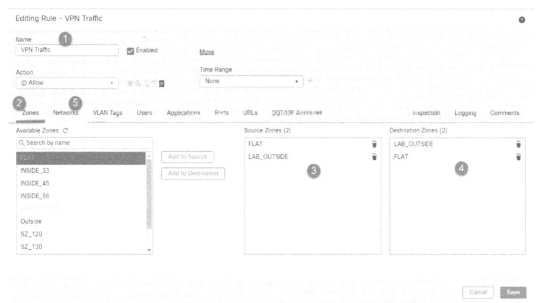

1. Select both the FLAT local encryption domain and the VLAN_33 remote encryption domain and add them to the Source Networks area.

2. Select both the FLAT local encryption domain and the VLAN_33 remote encryption domain and add them to the Destination Networks area.

3. Move on to the Logging tab:

1. Enable Log at Beginning of Connection.

2. Click Add to add your new rule.

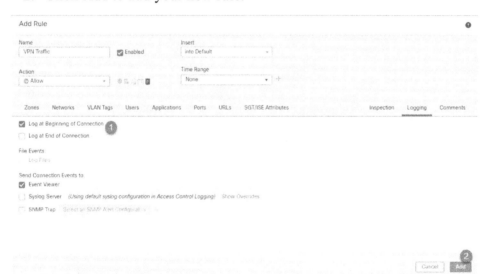

3. Don't forget to save the newly added rule!

Next up, we'll do pretty much the same thing for the FTDv-03 Access Control policy.

So, you can see that the changes we applied to the ACP_FTDv-03 access policy rule are a lot like the ones for ACP_FTDv-01, with the main differences being the source and destination security zones.

Now it's finally time to go to the NAT section to create our Identity NAT rules before deploying our changes!

Step 4: Creating Identity NAT Rules

Go to **Devices > NAT**.

There's a bunch of NAT policies here, but we'll focus on tweaking the FTDv-01 and FTDv-03 policies only. Each one is applied to the respective FTD appliance:

Click the pencil icon to edit the FTDv-01 NAT policy, then Add Rule:

Next, we'll hop through the steps for the NAT rule:

1. Go to Interface Objects tab.

2. Select the source security zone and add it to the Source Interface Objects list.

3. Select the destination security zone and add it to the Destination Interface Objects list

4. Head to the Translation tab

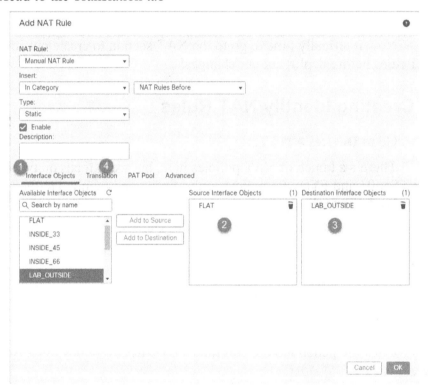

From the Translation tab:

1. Choose the local encryption domain from the Original Source drop-down menu.

2. Choose the remote encryption domain from the Original Destination drop-down menu.

3. Choose the local encryption domain from the Translated Source drop-down menu.

4. Choose the remote encryption domain from the Translated Destination drop-down menu.

5. Move on to the Advanced tab

1. Enable "Do not proxy ARP on Destination Interface" option.
2. Enable "Perform Route Lookup for Destination Interface."

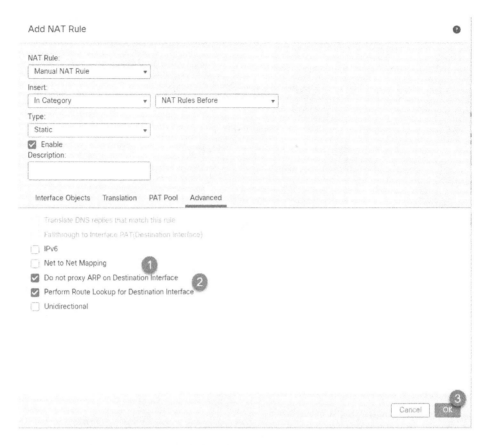

Did you notice we didn't have to add the source and destination in the same way as we did in the Access Control policy? That's because the NAT rules are bidirectional by default with this configuration!

If you want to set a manual NAT rule as unidirectional, from the Advanced tab, select Unidirectional

3. Press OK and don't forget to…

4. Save the NAT policy changes:

We'll do pretty much the same thing on the FTDv-03 NAT policy:

Finally, it's time to actually deploy the changes to our devices!

Step 5: Verification

Once the deployment is finished, we need to verify the tunnels of course. Doing this isn't exactly a walk on the beach with Firepower, but I'll be using both a GUI and a CLI to get it done.

I'm going to use two Windows clients to verify our tunnel. One of the hosts resides behind FTDv-01 in the FLAT subnet 172.16.1.0/24, and the other host is behind FTDv-03 located in VLAN33.

The host's IP address behind FTDv-01 is 172.16.1.40, and the one behind FTDv-03 has IP address 192.168.33.40.

Let's shoot over some traffic from a client connected to each encryption domain to bring up the tunnels, then verify the VPN tunnel from the FTD appliances.

Okay—so right after I get a successful ping, I'll head over to the FTD appliances and verify how the VPN tunnels look, including both phase 1 and 2.

Verifying the Hosts with ifconfig

The output below shows how each client looks with the IP addressing configuration and the ICMP traffic result.

This output is from the client on the FLAT subnet: 172.16.1.40. Focus on the second window that demonstrates I can ping the remote host 192.168.33.40:

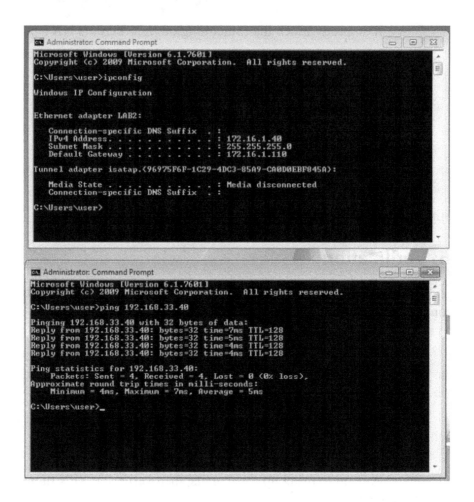

This output is from the host on VLAN_33 with the IP address 192.168.33.40. Clearly, it can ping the remote host, 172.16.1.40:

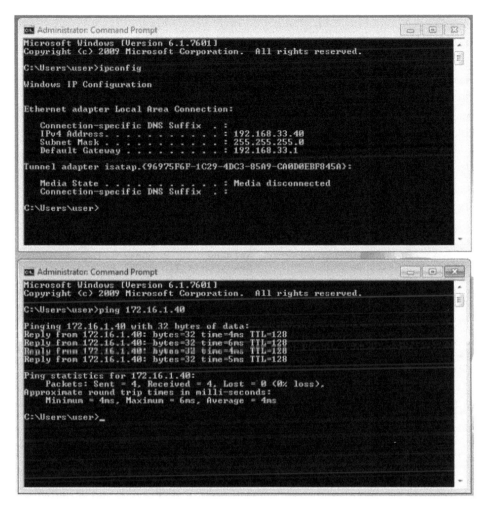

We can see ICMP traffic is successful between the two clients, meaning the VPN tunnel came up just fine between the two FTD appliances.

Next, we'll verify the VPN tunnels have been successfully established with the right security associations on both the FTD appliances!

Verifying the FTD Devices

From the FTD appliance's CLI, type the commands **show vpn-sessiondb detail l2l** and **show crypto ipsec sa** to see everything we need to verify phase 1 and 2, as well as the SAs used to encrypt and decrypt the VPN traffic. Check out the commands at work here:

```
########## FTDv-01 ##########

show vpn-sessiondb detail l2l
```

```
Session Type: LAN-to-LAN Detailed

Connection    : 10.1.0.130
Index         : 76                    IP Addr      : 10.1.0.130
Protocol      : IKEv1 IPsec
Encryption    : IKEv1: (1)AES256  IPsec: (1)AES256
Hashing       : IKEv1: (1)SHA1  IPsec: (1)SHA1
Bytes Tx      : 660                   Bytes Rx     : 660
Login Time    : 23:23:38 UTC Mon May 18 2020
Duration      : 0h:21m:43s
Tunnel Zone   : 0

IKEv1 Tunnels: 1
IPsec Tunnels: 1

IKEv1:
  Tunnel ID    : 76.1
  UDP Src Port : 500                   UDP Dst Port : 500
  IKE Neg Mode : Main                  Auth Mode    : preSharedKeys
  Encryption   : AES256                Hashing      : SHA1
  Rekey Int (T): 86400 Seconds         Rekey Left(T): 85097 Seconds
  D/H Group    : 14
  Filter Name  :

IPsec:
  Tunnel ID    : 76.2
  Local Addr   : 172.16.1.0/255.255.255.0/0/0
  Remote Addr  : 192.168.33.0/255.255.255.0/0/0
  Encryption   : AES256                Hashing      : SHA1
  Encapsulation: Tunnel                PFS Group    : 14
  Rekey Int (T): 28800 Seconds         Rekey Left(T): 27497 Seconds
  Rekey Int (D): 4608000 K-Bytes       Rekey Left(D): 4608000 K-Bytes
  Idle Time Out: 30 Minutes            Idle TO Left : 17 Minutes
  Bytes Tx     : 660                   Bytes Rx     : 660
  Pkts Tx      : 11                    Pkts Rx      : 11
```

Okay—there are three main sections in the show vpn-sessiondb detail 121 command output. The top one gives us some details about the remote peer IP address, protocol, encryption, and hash that were used to establish the tunnel. This section also shows how many bytes have been sent and received over the tunnel, the tunnel duration, and the establishing time.

The IKEv1 section reveals a bunch of details that are only related to phase 1, like the tunnel ID, which is automatically generated by the FTD, the port used to negotiate and establish the tunnel (port 500/udp), the authentication method (pre-shared key), the encryption algorithm, hashing, DH group, and the rekey life time (one day, by default).

The last IPsec section is more about phase 2 details. We can see the encryption domains that have been configured for this tunnel, the encryption algorithm, the PFS DH group, hashing, the traffic passed over the tunnel in bytes and packets, the idle timeout, and the rekey values in seconds and bytes. If one of these values is passed, the keying material will be negotiated again.

The `show crypto ipsec sa` command lets us check out the details related to phase 2. This command also reveals the SAs that have been used to negotiate and establish the phase 2 tunnel. The most relevant things we can verify from the output below are the encryption domains—in this case, the two subnets, 172.16.1.0/24 and 192.168.33.0/24, which are the local and the current peers. The `local addr` gives us the local IP address of the device where the output came from, and the `current_peer` reveals the IP address of the remote peer, FTDv-03. We'll see the same shown in the local and remote crypto endpt.

```
show crypto ipsec sa

interface: outside
    Crypto map tag: CSM_outside_map, seq num: 1, local addr: 10.1.0.110

        access-list CSM_IPSEC_ACL_1 extended permit ip 172.16.1.0 255.255.255.0
192.168.33.0 255.255.255.0
        local ident (addr/mask/prot/port): (172.16.1.0/255.255.255.0/0/0)
        remote ident (addr/mask/prot/port): (192.168.33.0/255.255.255.0/0/0)
        current_peer: 10.1.0.130


        #pkts encaps: 11, #pkts encrypt: 11, #pkts digest: 11
        #pkts decaps: 11, #pkts decrypt: 11, #pkts verify: 11
        #pkts compressed: 0, #pkts decompressed: 0
        #pkts not compressed: 11, #pkts comp failed: 0, #pkts decomp failed: 0
        #pre-frag successes: 0, #pre-frag failures: 0, #fragments created: 0
        #PMTUs sent: 0, #PMTUs rcvd: 0, #decapsulated frgs needing reassembly: 0
        #TFC rcvd: 0, #TFC sent: 0
        #Valid ICMP Errors rcvd: 0, #Invalid ICMP Errors rcvd: 0
        #send errors: 0, #recv errors: 0

        local crypto endpt.: 10.1.0.110/0, remote crypto endpt.: 10.1.0.130/0
        path mtu 1500, ipsec overhead 74(44), media mtu 1500
        PMTU time remaining (sec): 0, DF policy: copy-df
        ICMP error validation: disabled, TFC packets: disabled
        current outbound spi: 1170136F
        current inbound spi : 022937BC

      inbound esp sas:
        spi: 0x022937BC (36255676)
            SA State: active
            transform: esp-aes-256 esp-sha-hmac no compression
            in use settings ={L2L, Tunnel, PFS Group 14, IKEv1, }
            slot: 0, conn_id: 76, crypto-map: CSM_outside_map
            sa timing: remaining key lifetime (kB/sec): (3914999/27458)
            IV size: 16 bytes
            replay detection support: Y
            Anti replay bitmap:
             0x00000000 0x00000FFF
      outbound esp sas:
        spi: 0x1170136F (292557679)
            SA State: active
            transform: esp-aes-256 esp-sha-hmac no compression
            in use settings ={L2L, Tunnel, PFS Group 14, IKEv1, }
            slot: 0, conn_id: 76, crypto-map: CSM_outside_map
            sa timing: remaining key lifetime (kB/sec): (3914999/27458)
            IV size: 16 bytes
```

```
  replay detection support: Y
  Anti replay bitmap:
   0x00000000 0x00000001
```

This output also reveals the pkts encaps and pkts decaps—counters for the packets passing over the phase 2 tunnel. The encaps are the packets leaving the local FTD going over the tunnel, and the decaps are the packets that have been received by the remote peer. These packets should be almost equal!

We can check out the SA' status in the inbound and outbound **esp sas** sections. One SA will be used for the outbound VPN traffic leaving the FTD and the other for the inbound VPN traffic coming to the FTD. The SAs' IDs will be the same on both peers, the only difference is that they're actually mirrored. For instance, the inbound SA on FTDv-01 is the outbound SA on FTDv-03 and the outbound SA on FTDv-01 is the inbound SA on FTDv-03.

Verifying the Config on FTDv-03

To wrap up our verification adventure, let's check the configuration on the second FTD devices:

```
########## FTDv-03 ##########

show vpn-sessiondb detail l2l

Session Type: LAN-to-LAN Detailed

Connection  : 10.1.0.110
Index       : 2                  IP Addr      : 10.1.0.110
Protocol    : IKEv1 IPsec
Encryption  : IKEv1: (1)AES256  IPsec: (1)AES256
Hashing     : IKEv1: (1)SHA1  IPsec: (1)SHA1
Bytes Tx    : 660                Bytes Rx     : 660
Login Time  : 23:23:38 UTC Mon May 18 2020
Duration    : 0h:24m:17s
Tunnel Zone : 0

IKEv1 Tunnels: 1
IPsec Tunnels: 1

IKEv1:
  Tunnel ID    : 2.1
  UDP Src Port : 500             UDP Dst Port : 500
  IKE Neg Mode : Main            Auth Mode    : preSharedKeys
  Encryption   : AES256          Hashing      : SHA1
  Rekey Int (T): 86400 Seconds   Rekey Left(T): 84943 Seconds
  D/H Group    : 14
  Filter Name  :

IPsec:
  Tunnel ID    : 2.2
  Local Addr   : 192.168.33.0/255.255.255.0/0/0
  Remote Addr  : 172.16.1.0/255.255.255.0/0/0
  Encryption   : AES256          Hashing      : SHA1
  Encapsulation: Tunnel          PFS Group    : 14
```

```
Rekey Int (T): 28800 Seconds        Rekey Left(T): 27343 Seconds
Rekey Int (D): 4608000 K-Bytes      Rekey Left(D): 4608000 K-Bytes
Idle Time Out: 30 Minutes           Idle TO Left : 14 Minutes
Bytes Tx     : 660                  Bytes Rx      : 660
Pkts Tx      : 11                   Pkts Rx       : 11
```

///

show crypto ipsec sa

```
interface: outside
    Crypto map tag: CSM_outside_map, seq num: 2, local addr: 10.1.0.130

      access-list CSM_IPSEC_ACL_1 extended permit ip 192.168.33.0 255.255.255.0
172.16.1.0 255.255.255.0
        local ident (addr/mask/prot/port): (192.168.33.0/255.255.255.0/0/0)
        remote ident (addr/mask/prot/port): (172.16.1.0/255.255.255.0/0/0)
        current_peer: 10.1.0.110


        #pkts encaps: 11, #pkts encrypt: 11, #pkts digest: 11
        #pkts decaps: 11, #pkts decrypt: 11, #pkts verify: 11
        #pkts compressed: 0, #pkts decompressed: 0
        #pkts not compressed: 11, #pkts comp failed: 0, #pkts decomp failed: 0
        #pre-frag successes: 0, #pre-frag failures: 0, #fragments created: 0
        #PMTUs sent: 0, #PMTUs rcvd: 0, #decapsulated frgs needing reassembly: 0
        #TFC rcvd: 0, #TFC sent: 0
        #Valid ICMP Errors rcvd: 0, #Invalid ICMP Errors rcvd: 0
        #send errors: 0, #recv errors: 0

        local crypto endpt.: 10.1.0.130/0, remote crypto endpt.: 10.1.0.110/0
        path mtu 1500, ipsec overhead 74(44), media mtu 1500
        PMTU time remaining (sec): 0, DF policy: copy-df
        ICMP error validation: disabled, TFC packets: disabled
        current outbound spi: 022937BC
        current inbound spi : 1170136F

      inbound esp sas:
        spi: 0x1170136F (292557679)
           SA State: active
           transform: esp-aes-256 esp-sha-hmac no compression
           in use settings ={L2L, Tunnel, PFS Group 14, IKEv1, }
           slot: 0, conn_id: 2, crypto-map: CSM_outside_map
           sa timing: remaining key lifetime (kB/sec): (4373999/27299)
           IV size: 16 bytes
           replay detection support: Y
           Anti replay bitmap:
            0x00000000 0x00000FFF
      outbound esp sas:
        spi: 0x022937BC (36255676)
           SA State: active
           transform: esp-aes-256 esp-sha-hmac no compression
           in use settings ={L2L, Tunnel, PFS Group 14, IKEv1, }
           slot: 0, conn_id: 2, crypto-map: CSM_outside_map
           sa timing: remaining key lifetime (kB/sec): (4373999/27299)
           IV size: 16 bytes
           replay detection support: Y
           Anti replay bitmap:
            0x00000000 0x00000001


===============
```

Summary

In this chapter, we into both varieties of secure access VPNs: site to site and remote. These two technologies could definitely use a set of protocols and a decent way to provide security for the traffic passing between parties, but at least they can use the same framework.

We started with a brief introduction and then jumped straight into configuring site-to-site VPN options. Just so you know, we'll be diving deep into remote access VPN in the next chapter.

Chapter 32: Remote Access VPN AnyConnect

The following CCNP Security SNCF exam objectives are covered in this chapter:

2.0 Configuration

2.5 Configure devices using Firepower Management Center

2.5.c VPN

In the preceding chapter, we discussed VPN site-to-site configuration, In this chapter, we'll check out the two types of VPN remote access technologies.

Both technologies use a set of protocols plus a way to provide security for traffic passing between interested parties, and they also just happen to use the same framework. This means we can pick up right where we left off in the preceding chapter. And just so you know, you're going to get very familiar with the vitally critical AnyConnect client as well!

Remote Access VPN Configuration

Configuring remote access VPN is actually a bit easier compared to configuring site-to-site VPN, mostly due to the remote access VPN policy wizard. Clicking on "add new remote access VPN configuration" gets us this screen.

The handy Before You Start list lays out all the things we've got to get done before the new SSL VPN will work, but we're not going to deal with that just yet. I'll cover all of these items later in this chapter, where I'll also set up a sweet lab to move you through the list step-by-step, in detail!

For now, we've got give the remote access VPN policy a name, which is actually optional, but I recommend doing that.

VPN Protocols

SSL and IPsec-IKEv2 are the two protocols pictured in the previous figure; let's talk about them now.

SSL

Most people opt for SSL VPN mostly because it offers security and low-latency applications performance. Lots of businesses have moved to SSL VPN for advantages gained from its ease of operation in public hotspots.

SSL VPN uses port 443/tcp and 443/udp, with port 443/tcp tasked with initiating the first connection and in charge of controlling traffic. Also, if the connection over port 443/udp fails, the SSL VPN will fall back to port 443/tcp. But that's it—443/udp is favored because udp is a connectionless protocol with no three-way handshake and no acknowledgments for sent traffic. Applications like audio/video typically don't tolerate latency well, so 443/tcp could really mess with their performance, whereas 443/udp doesn't.

SSL VPN uses port 443/tcp, so if you're on any hotspot Wi-Fi or network, you can send outbound traffic on port 443/tcp across the hotspot firewall. You might be able to via 443/udp, but not always. Firewalls just don't block 443/tcp traffic for the users. What's more, using IPsec could cause some grief by doing things like denying the port 500/udp or port 4500/udp on the public hotspot firewalls—throw in the ESP protocol too!

Happy to say the latest versions of the AnyConnect client do have an embedded browser that's a lot more compatible with SSL VPN.

IPsec-IKEv2

IPsec-IKEv2 is supported with remote access VPN on FTD. It uses a different set of ports and employs the IPsec framework to encrypt VPN traffic. Depending on an organization's policies, some will definitely opt for IPsec over SSLVPN. That's because IPsec is more secure than SSL VPN—it relies on its own secure protocol set and doesn't hand off the security parts to another security protocol. IPsec has also been around for a few decades and it's more robust when it comes to security over SSL protocols. But as I said, remote users would still face challenges connecting to the corporate network using IPsec since the public hotspot's firewalls will usually deny outbound IPsec traffic.

Here's how that looks: The plane you were going to board has a mechanical problem and is delayed, making you an airport inmate for who knows how long. Might as well get some work done right? So you connect via the airport's Wi-Fi to VPN into your corporate network. If you try that with IPsec, the connection will probably fail because the first packet would be sent to port 500/udp. But if you go with SSL VPN instead, you'll probably breeze right through because it utilizes 443/tcp for outbound traffic.

So basically, the IPsec option is a good fit for remote users who have full management of their own firewalls because they can apply security policies that'll allow outbound IPsec traffic.

Targeted Devices

Security policies are definitely all good, but we've still got to assign devices to them! To do that, I'll choose the headend device from the Available Devices list, which will terminate the remote access VPN connection. By the way, you'll only see the FTD devices managed by the FMC on this list. Okay, once I've added the device, I'll click Next to get me to the next screen.

Connection Profiles

As you can see, there are four main sections here:

- Connection Profile
- AAA
- Client Address Assignment
- Group Policy

Connection Profile

The connection profile is the tunnel group name that'll be assigned to the new remote access VPN connection. This name will show up in the drop-down menu when you try to connect from the AnyConnect client, and it doesn't have to be the same as the policy name I gave it in the previous screen. People typically dub it descriptively by matching the name to a specific group, department, or entity, like Employees, Developers, IT Staff, and so on.

Authentication, Authorization & Accounting (AAA)

Next we'll take a look at the AAA options and the server:

AAA Only
This method allows remote VPN users to authenticate against an AAA server with their username and passwords. The AAA server can be a realm like an AD or LDAP or really any RADIUS server like ISE or Windows Network Policy Server (NPS). You can add either one from the same page by clicking on the plus sign.

Client Certificate Only
This option works great if your remote VPN users are going to authenticate with certificates instead of usernames and passwords. Going with this option will get you even more options to define how you want the username to be extracted from the client certificate.

You can choose the complete distinguished name as the username or opt to map different certificate attributes like the CN or the UPN. You can also pick the primary and secondary attribute to be used if required.

Client Certificate & AAA
This is actually a combination of the previous two options together and it's the most secure.

Using the client certificate as well as the username and password serves up two-factor authentication. So if you suddenly dashed to board that plane and forgot your corporate laptop, thieves won't be able to connect to the VPN since the username and password are required plus the client certificate!

Authentication Server

The authentication server is responsible for validating if the presented username exists on it in a realm (AD or LDAP) or a RADIUS server. Authentication happens via AAA only or through certificates.

Authorization Server

The authorization server authorizes user access. The authentication and authorization servers will usually be running on the same entity.

If you leave this field blank and you use RADIUS as the authentication server, the FMC will automatically use the same server for both authentication and authorization.

Accounting Server

The accounting server is predictably where the accounting messages will be sent. These messages come in really handy for tracking down the user's activities, telling you all about what they actually did during their remote VPN session.

Client Address Assignment

This section is responsible for IP address assignments to VPN clients, and again, you get presented with some nice options here:

Use AAA Server (RADIUS Only)

This option allows the RADIUS server to assign an IP address for each remote VPN client. Think of the Cisco ISE where you can set an authorization profile and assign the connected VPN client to a specific VPN group policy with an IP address pool associated to that group. Clearly, you've got to have a RADIUS authorization server configured first to go this route!

Use DHCP Servers

You can configure the FTD to relay clients' DHCP requests to an internal DHCP server where you have a specific pool configured for VPN users to draw from. You can still use the same corporate internal scope to assign IP addresses to VPN clients, just know that this is required if you've got user restrictions at the application levels. If that's the case, all users, whether coming from a VPN connection or locally authenticated, will get an address from within the same range. Any security restrictions will be applied when they try to authenticate against the internal applications.

When you select this option, you've got to set the DHCP server IP address.

Use IP Address Pools

This is a popular option that's basically used to define a local IPv4 or IPv6 address pool that'll be stored on the FTD. If you haven't done so already, you'll need to create a local pool by clicking on the pencil icon, and then on the plus sign from the Network Objects screen. If you've got a pool in place and ready, just click the pencil icon and choose it.

Group Policy

Next, you need to select the group policy you want to associate to the remote access VPN tunnel group. If you haven't created the group policy yet, do that by clicking on the plus sign. We'll dive deeper into the group policy with a cool lab later on in the chapter.

AnyConnect

When you get to the AnyConnect menu of the policy wizard, you'll get the following screen:

From here, select the AnyConnect client package you downloaded from the Cisco website and uploaded to the FMC.

If you haven't uploaded it yet, either click the plus sign or choose **Objects > Object Management > VPN > AnyConnect File > Add AnyConnect File**.

If you've uploaded a bunch of AnyConnect packages for different operating systems, just put them in descending order with the most common one at the top of the list.

Keep in mind that a VPN client will automatically detect the respective AnyConnect package and be prompted to download and install it when it connects to the FTD through the SSL VPN web page.

This screen allows you to select which security zone on the FTD will be used to terminate the remote access VPN. I highly recommend that the interface connected to the Internet be part of that security zone!

Let's look at our options now:

Enable DTLS on member interfaces
Enabled by default, this option is used to enable the 443/udp port, which as I said, will be used for data traffic. If the remote firewall from where the remote access VPN client is coming from doesn't allow outbound traffic on port 443/udp, the AnyConnect client will fall back to port 443/tcp.

Device Certificates
This option is used to define which trust point will be used on the FTD to present the FTD certificate to the VPN clients.

You configure the trust point by clicking the plus sign, or from **Objects>Object Management>PKI >Cert Enrollment**. We thoroughly covered certificates in detail in Chapter 33, so refer back to that chapter if you need to.

Enroll the selected certificate object on the target devices
This option is used to initiate the certificate enrollment on the FTD appliance selected for this remote access VPN policy.

Access Control for VPN Traffic

If you want the remote access VPN to bypass all the security policies on the FTD by bypassing Snort, this is your daisy. Also, if you can see the ASA command was `sysopt permit-vpn`, with this check box you no longer have to use Flexconfig to add this starting in V 6.3. If you opt in on this choice, VPN traffic won't go through any Snort inspection. It will go straight to egress, just like a FastPath.

I have to tell you that if you decide to enable this option, definitely set up some VPN filtering policies like using a VPN filter access list to allow only specific traffic to pass through!

The next page is just a summary page showing all the settings we just went through.

As implied here by the Additional Configuration Requirements section, there could be some more settings to configure, like Identity NAT and Access Control policy. No worries—we'll cover them all in the configuration section next.

Configuring AnyConnect SSL VPN with an ISE Authentication Server

Okay—time to jump into configuring ISE as our authentication server.

AnyConnect users will connect to the FTD device and try to authenticate with their Active Directory username and passwords. The FTD will then relay the authentication requests to ISE in RADIUS format. ISE will look up the usernames and validate their provided passwords, and if solid, ISE will instruct the FTD to authorize the user's access.

ISE will also push a downloadable access list to the user's sessions to limit accesses to only one, single IP address in the network.

Configuring the ISE Authentication Server

ISE configuration involves working through these steps:

1. Join ISE to our Active Directory.
2. Download the AD group that'll be used in the authentication policy where AnyConnect users will reside.
3. Add the FTD appliance as a network device.
4. Create the downloadable access list to be applied to AnyConnect users' sessions.
5. Create an authorization profile that'll be bound to the AnyConnect authorization policy.
6. Create the Allowed Protocols list.
7. Create the policy set for AnyConnect.

Let's get started going through them now!.

Step 1: Join ISE to our Active Directory

1. From the ISE server GUI, traverse to the Administration pull-down menu.
2. Click External Identity Sources.

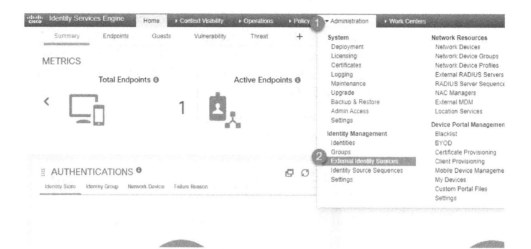

3. Click Active Directory.
4. Click Add.

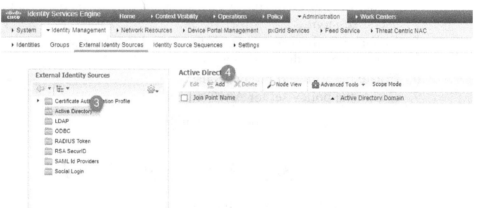

5. Type any reference name to your Active Directory.
6. Type in the Active Directory Domain name.
7. Click Submit.

You don't have to store the credentials on ISE unless you want to use some attributes for profiling, like Active Directory attributes:

8. Type the user account to join the Active Directory. This user account doesn't have to be an administrator but it must have these permissions on the Active Directory.

- Search the Active Directory to check if ISE machine account already exists.
- If there's not an account there already, create Cisco ISE machine account to the domain.

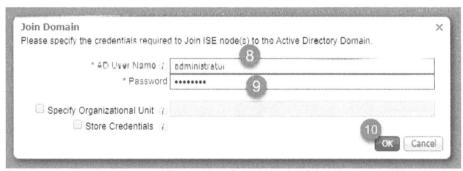

- Set attributes on the new machine account like the machine account password, SPN, and dnsHostname.

9. Type the user account password.
10. Click OK.

You should get a screen like this next one soon. Click Close. The Active Directory join point should now be operational.

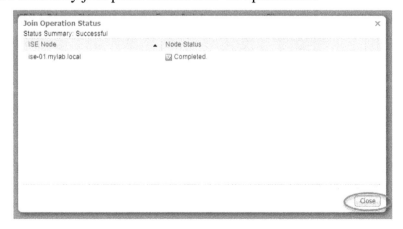

A really common problem arises when there's a time skew between ISE and the Active Directory. So this doesn't happen to you, just use the same NTP server on ISE and the Active Directory. You can also use the

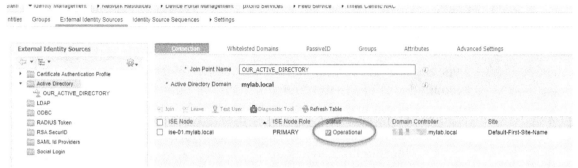

Active Directory itself as the NTP server on ISE.

If you want to make sure all the required services are healthy, use the diagnostic tool as shown as step 12.

11. Select the ISE node.
12. Click Diagnostic Tool.

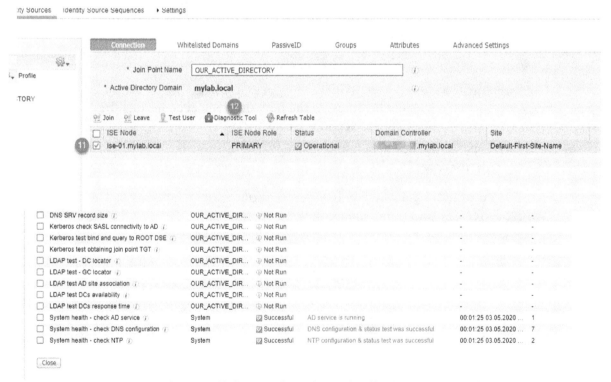

13. Next, choose all the services from the list by enabling the Test Name tick box.

14. Click Run Tests and then click Run All Tests. You should see all the tests marked "Successful."

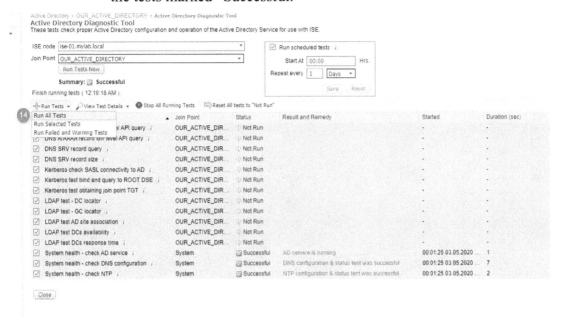

Step 2: Add the Active Directory Group the AnyConnect users will belong to

15. Click Groups.
16. Click Select Groups From Directory.

17. Enter the Active Directory Group name or at least part of it, then click Retrieve Groups.

The asterisk presents a wildcard to search the Active Directory group. I typed Any before the * because our group is called AnyConnect_Users.

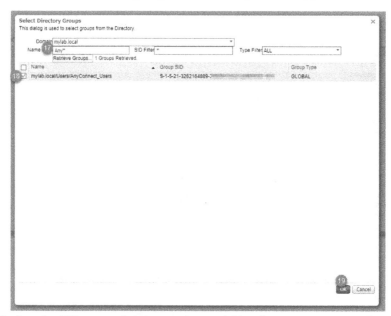

We could also do *Users and the search would be for any group ending with the Users keyword. This search isn't case sensitive.

18. Select the group(s).
19. Click OK.
20. Click Save.

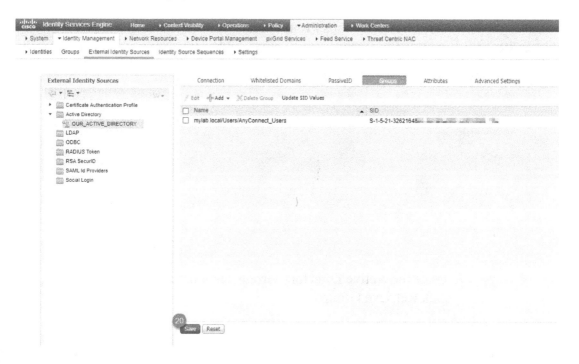

Step 3: Add the FTD appliance as a network device

21. Click Administration.
22. Click Network Devices.

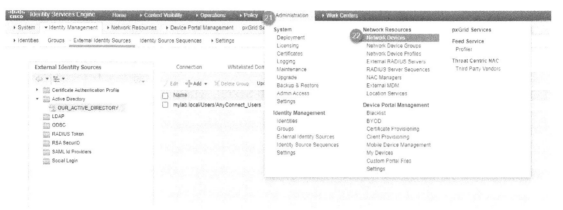

23. Click Add.
24. Give the FTD a name. It doesn't have to be the same as the FTD hostname.
25. Now, type the IP address of the interface you want used to reach

ISE on the FTD appliance.

26. Then, enable the RADIUS Authentication Settings section.

27. Type in the RADIUS Shared Secret, which will be configured on the FTD appliance too.
28. Click Submit.

You should now see a screen like this one.

Step 4: Create the downloadable access list

29. Go to Policy.
30. Click Results.

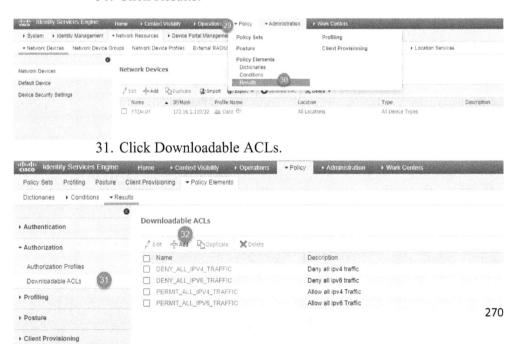

31. Click Downloadable ACLs.

32. Click Add.
33. Next, give the downloadable ACL a name.

34. Now type the downloadable ACL content. Keep in mind that the source must always be an IP! You won't see the source IP if you issue the command `show access-list <the downloadable acl name>` from the FTD because the FTD will replace the any keyword with the connected AnyConnect client IP address. I'll show you a way to verify this coming up soon: Keep in mind that the downloadable ACL has `deny ip any any` at the end just like any Cisco ACL.
35. Click Check DACL Syntax, which should show DACL is valid.
36. Then click Submit.

Step 5: Create the authorization profile

37. Go to Authorization Profiles.
38. Click Add.

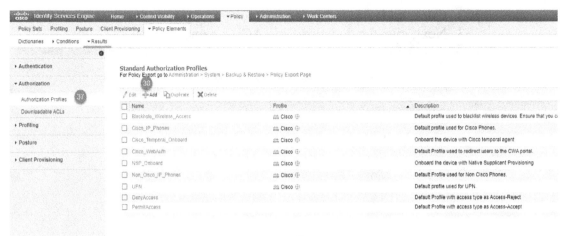

39. Give the authorization profile a name.
40. Enable the DACL Name tick box. The downloadable ACL

created has been automatically selected because there's only one downloadable ACL there right now. So if you've got multiple downloadable ACLs, you have to manually select the one you want associated to the authorization profile.
41. Click Submit.

Step 6: Create the Allowed Protocols list

42. Go to Allowed Protocols.
43. Click Add.

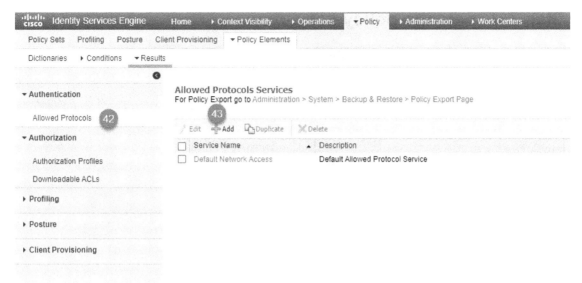

44. Give the Allowed Protocol list a name.
45. Next, deselect all the protocols except Allow PAP/ASCII.

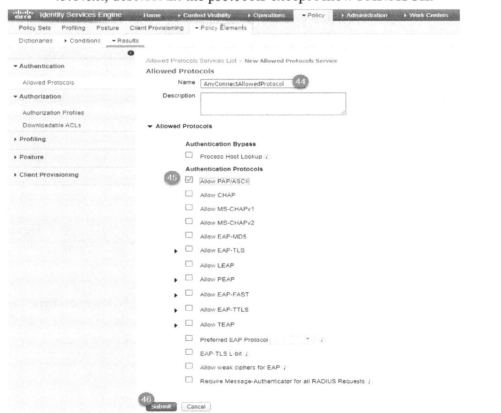

46. Then click Submit.

Step 7: Create the policy set

47. Go to **Policy > Policy Sets**.
48. Click Add.

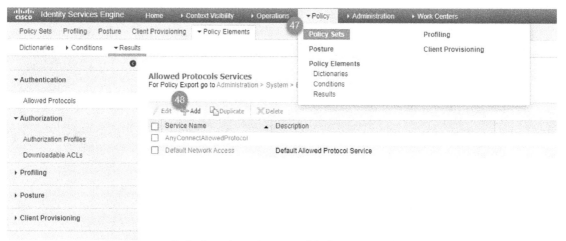

49. Next, click the plus sign to add the new policy set.
50. And give the new policy set a name.
51. Click the Conditions plus sign to add the policy set top conditions.

52. Click the drop-down menu and select Network Access: Device IP Address and type the FTD appliance IP address of the interface that'll be used to reach ISE.
53. Click New.
54. Click the drop-down menu, select Radius NAS-Port-Type, and choose Virtual to match the VPN traffic only as the VPN traffic is classified as Virtual from RADIUS NAS Port Type perspective.

55. Now click Use. You can save this condition by clicking Save.
56. Select the Allowed Protocols list we created.
57. Click Save.

58. Click the right arrow to go into the policy set properties.
59. Expand the Authentication Policy section.

60. Next, select the Active Directory join point we created earlier.

61. And expand the Authorization Policy section.
62. Click the plus sign to add a new authorization rule.
63. Give the authorization rule a name.

64. Click the authorization Conditions plus sign to add the authorization condition.
65. Select the Active Directory join point we created, then select the Active Directory group we mapped from the drop-down menu.

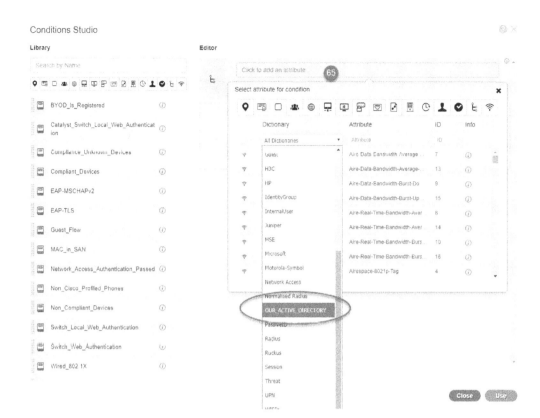

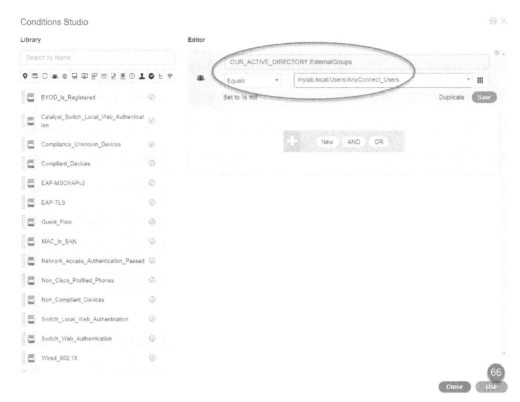

66. Click Use.
67. Now select the authorization profile from the drop-down menu that we created previously

68. Click Save and we're done with ISE configuration!

Creating the Remote Access VPN Policy on

FMC

Now we're going to move over to the FMC to continue configuration.

1. Go to Devices.
2. Click Remote Access.

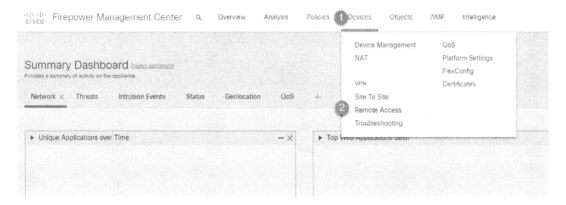

Click Add or click Add a new configuration:

1. Give the Remote Access policy a name.
2. Deselect IPsec-IKEv2.
3. Select the FTD appliance and add it to the Selected Devices list.
4. Click Next.

1. Change the name of the connection profile, which will be the one that'll appear on the AnyConnect drop-down menu.
2. Click the plus sign next to Authentication Server.
3. Select RADIUS Server Group.

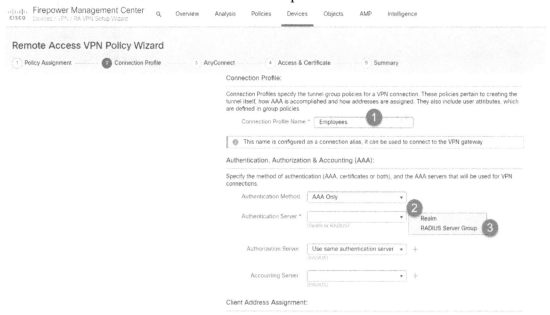

1. Give the RADIUS server group a name.
2. Enable the interim account updates.
3. Even though enabling the dynamic authorization (CoA) on the FTD isn't required for our lab, I highly recommended enabling it in case you add any features that would rely on it!

4. Click the plus sign next to RADIUS Servers.

1. Type the ISE server IP address or hostname. If you use the hostname or FQDN, the FTD must be able to resolve that hostname or FQDN.
2. Type the RADIUS secret we configured earlier on ISE when we added the FTD as a network device.
3. Confirm the RADIUS secret.
4. Select Specific Interface. When you enable the CoA, you've got to choose this option and specify the interface out that you want the FTD to use to talk to ISE.
5. Next, select the interface that FTD will use to reach ISE server.

6. Click Save.

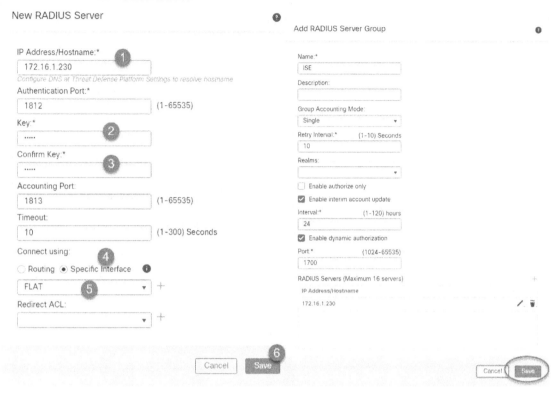

1. Select the ISE RADIUS server group in the Accounting Server drop-down.
2. Click the pencil icon to create the IPv4 local IP address pool.

1. Click the plus sign to create the new IPv4 IP local pool.

2. Give the pool a name.
3. Specify the IP address range you want to assign to AnyConnect clients.
4. Specify the subnet mask.
5. Click Save.
6. Select the new pool and click Add to add it to the Selected IPv4 Pools list.
7. Click OK.

1. **Next, click the plus sign to create a new group policy for AnyConnect**

Authorization Server: | Use same authentication server ▼ | +
(RADIUS)

Accounting Server: | ISE ▼ | +
(RADIUS)

Client Address Assignment:

Client IP address can be assigned from AAA server, DHCP server and IP address pools. When multiple options are selected, IP address assignment is tried in the order of AAA server, DHCP server and IP address pool.

☐ Use AAA Server (RADIUS only) ℹ

☐ Use DHCP Servers

☑ Use IP Address Pools

IPv4 Address Pools: | AnyConnectPool | ✎

IPv6 Address Pools: | | ✎

Group Policy:

A group policy is a collection of user-oriented session attributes which are assigned to client when a VPN connection is established. Select or create a Group Policy object.

Group Policy:* | DfltGrpPolicy ▼ | + **1**

Edit Group Policy

Add Group Policy ⓘ

Name:*
| AnyConnectGroupPolicy | **1**

Description:
| |

General   AnyConnect   Advanced

VPN Protocols	VPN Tunnel Protocol:
IP Address Pools	Specify the VPN tunnel types that user can use. At least one tunneling mode must be configured for users to connect over a VPN tunnel.
Banner	☑ SSL
DNS/WINS	☐ IPsec-IKEv2 **2**
Split Tunneling **3**	

1. Give the new group policy a name.
2. Deselect IPsec-IKEv2.
3. Then head over to Split Tunneling.

Cancel   Save

284

1. Select Tunnel Networks Specified Below.
2. Click the plus sign to create the split tunnel access list.

1. Give the split tunnel standard access list a name.
2. Click Add.

1. Select the local encryption domain that you want AnyConnect to reach.
2. Click Add.

Then Click Save.

Click Save here too.

1. Select the AnyConnect package that you uploaded previously to the FTD. If you haven't done that already, you can click on the plus sign icon and do it from there.
2. Click Next.

1. Select the security zone that the FTD external interface is placed

within.

2. Choose the trust point that you want to associate to the FTD external interface. (I'm using the trust point created in site-to-site VPN with certificate authentication.)

3. Enable Access Control for VPN traffic. Don't worry that this option bypasses all the FTD security checks! The AnyConnect traffic will be restricted based on the downloadable access list we configured on the authorization profile on ISE that we bound to the AnyConnect policy set. That downloadable access list will be pushed by ISE to the FTD and the FTD will apply it to the AnyConnect connected users' sessions—nice!

4. Click Next.

Click Finish and remember to deploy the changes.

Keep in mind that we still need an Identity NAT rule similar to what we did in the previous lab. Here's the NAT rule we applied on FTDv-01 for AnyConnect traffic:

Remote Access Verification

Okay—we've done a boatload of configuration, so now's the time to verify it all! I'm going to walk you through verifying these two vital things:

- Verification with the AnyConnect Client
- Verification from the FTD Device CLI

Verification with AnyConnect Client

By the way, I'm going to use a Windows client to connect to the FTDv-01 via AnyConnect client for this lab.

1. This remote access SSL VPN will authenticate through username and password.
2. The test user we'll use is test1.
3. The FTD will relay the test1 authentication requests to the ISE server.
4. ISE will then check in with the AD to validate the username and password.

5. If they check out, ISE will instruct the FTD to allow the VPN connection. It'll also dynamically push the downloadable access list we configured to the test1 session.
6. This access list will only allow the traffic to the destination IP address 172.16.1.40. All the other traffic is denied.

On the AnyConnect client, type the FTDv-01 FQDN and hit Connect.

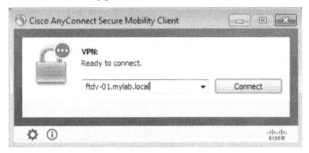

Select the Employees connection profile from the drop-down menu, then type the test1 AD credentials and hit OK.

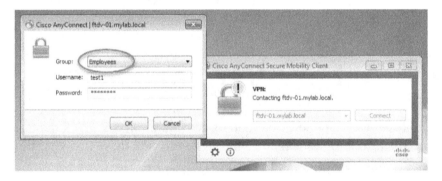

Remember—"Employees" is the connection profile name set up previously in the Remote Access VPN policy.

Yes! The remote access SSL VPN connection has been successfully established.

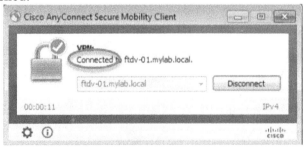

Next, let's have a look at some details from within the AnyConnect statistics and route details pages.

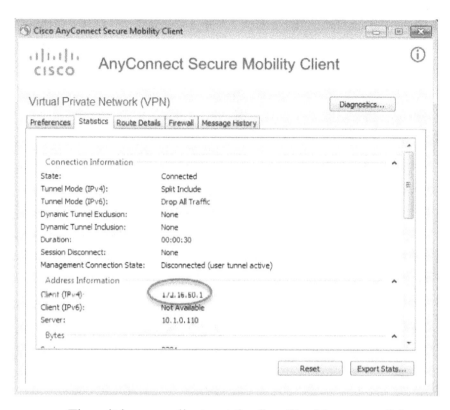

There it is—our client got the first IP address out of the remote access SSL VPN,172.16.50.1.

According to our split tunnel configuration, we only have the subnet 172.16.1.0/24 defined as the protected network. Even so, the test1 user session will be associated with a downloadable access list pushed by ISE and will allow the traffic to the host 172.16.1.40 only. You'll see this in the output coming up, which details a bunch of useful information about our AnyConnect session! There's the connected username, the pool-assigned IP address, and the public IP address of the connected client.

There are also details related to the protocol used for the VPN tunnel, encryption algorithm, hashing, bytes, and packets of the exchanged traffic. That's not all! We can also spot the group policy associated to this VPN tunnel, the connection profile name, the authentication method, and the downloadable access list in it.

Notice also how the AnyConnect tunnel is using both port 443/tcp and 443/udp. Remember, if port 443/udp isn't allowed by a firewall from where the AnyConnect client is connected, the FTD appliance will fall back to use port 443/tcp only.

Verification from FTD Device CLI

Let's use the show vpn-sessiondb detail anyconnect command on the FTD device to see our tunnel information. Check it out:

```
>show vpn-sessiondb detail anyconnect

Session Type: AnyConnect Detailed

Username      : test1             Index       : 79
Assigned IP   : 172.16.50.1       Public IP   : 10.1.0.40
Protocol      : AnyConnect-Parent SSL-Tunnel DTLS-Tunnel
License       : AnyConnect Premium
Encryption    : AnyConnect-Parent: (1)none  SSL-Tunnel: (1)AES-GCM-256  DTLS-
Tunnel: (1)AES256
Hashing       : AnyConnect-Parent: (1)none  SSL-Tunnel: (1)SHA384  DTLS-Tunnel:
(1)SHA1
Bytes Tx      : 16000             Bytes Rx      : 760
Pkts Tx       : 14                Pkts Rx       : 10
Pkts Tx Drop  : 0                 Pkts Rx Drop  : 0
Group Policy  : AnyConnectGroupPolicy  Tunnel Group : Employees
Login Time    : 01:04:19 UTC Tue May 19 2020
Duration      : 0h:04m:55s
Inactivity    : 0h:00m:00s
VLAN Mapping  : N/A               VLAN          : none
Audt Sess ID  : 000000000004f0005ec33093
Security Grp  : none              Tunnel Zone   : 0
```

```
AnyConnect-Parent Tunnels: 1
SSL-Tunnel Tunnels: 1
DTLS-Tunnel Tunnels: 1

AnyConnect-Parent:
  Tunnel ID     : 79.1
  Public IP     : 10.1.0.40
  Encryption    : none              Hashing        : none
  TCP Src Port  : 49377             TCP Dst Port   : 443
  Auth Mode     : userPassword
  Idle Time Out : 30 Minutes        Idle TO Left   : 25 Minutes
  Client OS     : win
  Client OS Ver : 6.1.7601 Service Pack 1
  Client Type   : AnyConnect
  Client Ver    : Cisco AnyConnect VPN Agent for Windows 4.8.03043
  Bytes Tx      : 7940              Bytes Rx       : 0
  Pkts Tx       : 6                 Pkts Rx        : 0
  Pkts Tx Drop  : 0                 Pkts Rx Drop   : 0

SSL-Tunnel:
  Tunnel ID     : 79.2
  Assigned IP   : 172.16.50.1       Public IP      : 10.1.0.40
  Encryption    : AES-GCM-256       Hashing        : SHA384
  Ciphersuite   : ECDHE-RSA-AES256-GCM-SHA384
  Encapsulation : TLSv1.2           TCP Src Port   : 49381
  TCP Dst Port  : 443               Auth Mode      : userPassword
  Idle Time Out : 30 Minutes        Idle TO Left   : 25 Minutes
  Client OS     : Windows
  Client Type   : SSL VPN Client
  Client Ver    : Cisco AnyConnect VPN Agent for Windows 4.8.03043
  Bytes Tx      : 7940              Bytes Rx       : 328
  Pkts Tx       : 6                 Pkts Rx        : 2
  Pkts Tx Drop  : 0                 Pkts Rx Drop   : 0
  Filter Name   : #ACSACL#-IP-AllowanyConnect-5ec32ae6

DTLS-Tunnel:
  Tunnel ID     : 79.3
  Assigned IP   : 172.16.50.1       Public IP      : 10.1.0.40
  Encryption    : AES256            Hashing        : SHA1
  Ciphersuite   : DHE-RSA-AES256-SHA
  Encapsulation : DTLSv1.0          UDP Src Port   : 50806
  UDP Dst Port  : 443               Auth Mode      : userPassword
  Idle Time Out : 30 Minutes        Idle TO Left   : 29 Minutes
  Client OS     : Windows
  Client Type   : DTLS VPN Client
  Client Ver    : Cisco AnyConnect VPN Agent for Windows 4.8.03043
  Bytes Tx      : 120               Bytes Rx       : 432
  Pkts Tx       : 2                 Pkts Rx        : 8
  Pkts Tx Drop  : 0                 Pkts Rx Drop   : 0
  Filter Name   : #ACSACL#-IP-AllowanyConnect-5ec32ae6
```

Notice the downloadable access list we configured on ISE. It's been associated to the AnyConnect client 172.16.1.50 session.

Here's the downloadable access list content:

```
>show access-list #ACSACL#-IP-AllowanyConnect-5ec32ae6

access-list #ACSACL#-IP-AllowanyConnect-5ec32ae6; 1 elements; name hash:
0x8ef3b893 (dynamic)
access-list #ACSACL#-IP-AllowanyConnect-5ec32ae6 line 1 extended permit icmp
any4 host 172.16.1.40 (hitcnt=0) 0x9699ca6d
```

Now let's test the ICMP traffic from the AnyConnect client to our internal server with IP address 172.16.1.40. As per our ISE policy set and the downloadable access list, this traffic should be allowed:

```
Administrator: Command Prompt                                    _ □ ×
Microsoft Windows [Version 6.1.7601]
Copyright (c) 2009 Microsoft Corporation.  All rights reserved.

C:\Users\user>ping 172.16.1.40

Pinging 172.16.1.40 with 32 bytes of data:
Reply from 172.16.1.40: bytes=32 time=6ms TTL=128
Reply from 172.16.1.40: bytes=32 time=3ms TTL=128
Reply from 172.16.1.40: bytes=32 time=3ms TTL=128
Reply from 172.16.1.40: bytes=32 time=3ms TTL=128

Ping statistics for 172.16.1.40:
    Packets: Sent = 4, Received = 4, Lost = 0 (0% loss),
Approximate round trip times in milli-seconds:
    Minimum = 3ms, Maximum = 6ms, Average = 3ms

C:\Users\user>
C:\Users\user>
C:\Users\user>
C:\Users\user>
```

Nice—ICMP traffic is coming through. Now let's try to ping the ISE node with IP address 172.16.1.230. It should not be allowed since our downloadable access list only permits ICMP traffic to the host 172.16.1.40. Any other traffic would be matching the implicit deny ip any any at the end:

Yep—the ICMP traffic destined to ISE node has failed.

```
Reply from 172.16.1.40: bytes=32 time=5ms TTL=128
Reply from 172.16.1.40: bytes=32 time=4ms TTL=128
Reply from 172.16.1.40: bytes=32 time=3ms TTL=128
Reply from 172.16.1.40: bytes=32 time=3ms TTL=128

Ping statistics for 172.16.1.40:
    Packets: Sent = 4, Received = 4, Lost = 0 (0% loss),
Approximate round trip times in milli-seconds:
    Minimum = 3ms, Maximum = 5ms, Average = 3ms

C:\Users\user>
C:\Users\user>
C:\Users\user>
C:\Users\user>ping 172.16.1.230

Pinging 172.16.1.230 with 32 bytes of data:
Request timed out.
Request timed out.
Request timed out.
Request timed out.

Ping statistics for 172.16.1.230:
    Packets: Sent = 4, Received = 0, Lost = 4 (100% loss),

C:\Users\user>
```

Okay, next I'm going to set up a packet capture called DROP on the FTD CLI so it only matches the dropped traffic. Then I'll do show capture DROP to verify the output:

```
>capture DROP type asp-drop acl-drop match icmp host 172.16.50.1 any

>show capture DROP
Target:     OTHER
Hardware:   NGFWv
Cisco Adaptive Security Appliance Software Version 9.13(1)5
ASLR enabled, text region 55c6e0909000-55c6e5d20c81

4 packets captured
   1: 01:20:44.548815       172.16.50.1 > 172.16.1.230 icmp: echo request Drop-
reason: (acl-drop) Flow is denied by configured rule, Drop-location: frame
0x000055c6e2f6cd37 flow (acl-drop)/snp_sp_action_cb:1788

   2: 01:20:49.131356       172.16.50.1 > 172.16.1.230 icmp: echo request Drop-
reason: (acl-drop) Flow is denied by configured rule, Drop-location: frame
0x000055c6e2f6cd37 flow (acl-drop)/snp_sp_action_cb:1788

   3: 01:20:54.123559       172.16.50.1 > 172.16.1.230 icmp: echo request Drop-
reason: (acl-drop) Flow is denied by configured rule, Drop-location: frame
0x000055c6e2f6cd37 flow (acl-drop)/snp_sp_action_cb:1788

   4: 01:20:59.130638       172.16.50.1 > 172.16.1.230 icmp: echo request Drop-
reason: (acl-drop) Flow is denied by configured rule, Drop-location: frame
0x000055c6e2f6cd37 flow (acl-drop)/snp_sp_action_cb:1788
4 packets shown
```

Sure enough, the ICMP traffic sent from our AnyConnect client 172.16.50.1 destined to our ISE node with IP address 172.16.1.230 was showing on the asp-drop acl-drop packet capture. Sweet success—our downloadable access list pushed by ISE to the AnyConnect session is not allowing that traffic!

To wrap up this chapter, here are the RADIUS logs from ISE that are related to our AnyConnect connection:

Summary

In the preceding chapter 31, we discussed VPN site-to-site configuration, In this chapter, we checked out the two types of VPN remote access technologies.

Both technologies use a set of protocols plus a way to provide security for traffic passing between interested parties, and they also just happen to use the same framework.

Chapter 33: Certificates

The following CCNP Security SNCF exam objectives are covered in this chapter:

2.0 Configuration

2.5 Configure devices using Firepower Management Center

2.5.f Certificates

Before we dig into FMC certificate configuration, I'm going to take you through a quick refresher about what they are and why it's important to use them.

These certificates, also known as signatures, are typically used to establish secure channels, as VPN does. We also put them to work securing email communications, application access, and the like, or for securely exchanging documents.

FMC certificates are a digital form of identification that binds the identity of the owner to a pair of asymmetric keys—one private and one public. The private key is often used to sign a message or to decrypt the data that's been encrypted with the public key, a process handled by the owner of both keys.

If anyone happens to nick someone's private key, they've essentially stolen their identity. The thief can then freely impersonate the compromised identity to sign messages and read confidential data that would've been encrypted by the original owner of the public key. So clearly, private keys must be stored securely at all times and never ever shared with anyone! On the other hand, the public key should be readily shared and made available to anyone who needs it for encrypting data to send to the public key's owner.

Here's how it works: The sender first calculates the message digest—a hash value of the original message—before encrypting it with the private key and sending it off with certificate in tow. The sender certificate includes the sender's public key, which is used by the receiver to decrypt the message digest and verify that it matches the hash the receiver will locally calculate. If so, the receiver will assume the sender is whom they claim to be and the message wasn't tampered with in transit.

The sender's public key can also be made available for downloading from somewhere like a web page by the receiver.

Here's how this process looks on both ends:

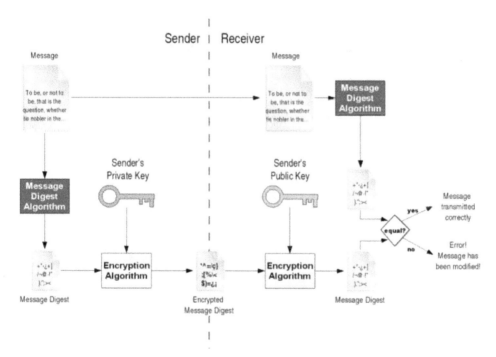

Now we all know there's a problem with that word *assume*, right? We must be able to do better than that—we've got to know *for sure* who that sender is!

That's where PKI comes in. PKI stands for Public Key Infrastructure, which defines a set of standards to be followed by all involved parties. Basically, if a sender wants to communicate with a receiver, both should be enrolled with the same PKI so they can securely identify each other.

PKI can be public like those of GoDaddy, VeriSign, Comodo, and so on, or it can be internal. Nowadays, lots of companies use internal PKI to manage digital certificates, but whether public or private, the PKI concept is still the same.

There's a bunch of different components within the PKI, and each of them is responsible for specific tasks. the root CA, intermediate CA, registration authority, and CRL distribution point are all potential PKI elements, but having all of them involved isn't required. You can have a PKI with root CA only.

The root CA is the entity where everyone involved should be enrolled. It not only validates their identities, but it also ensures the entity or endpoint that's asking to be enrolled matches all required standards. Once it validates the requester's identity, it issues an identity certificate that's signed by the CA and returned. The identity certificate also includes the public key the requester provided to the CA during the enrollment process.

So with PKI in the mix, the sender must send its certificate along with the message and encrypted message digest to the receiver. The receiver trusts the sender's certificate issuer and their certificate includes their public key, which the receiver uses to verify and validate the sender's identity. This is how the process looks on both ends:

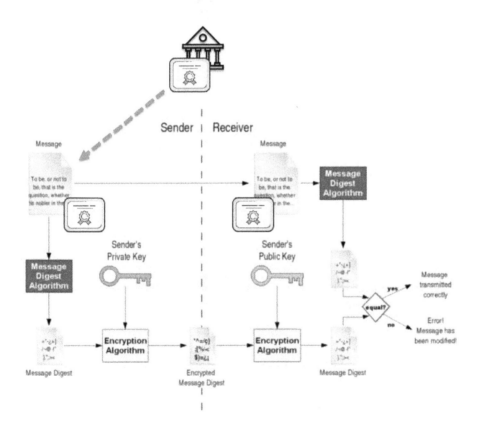

Let's say we've got a PKI with only root CA and two endpoints that want to talk to each other securely. Here's how the enrollment process would work, step-by-step:

1. The endpoints have to trust the PKI root CA, so we'll install the root CA public certificate in the endpoints' trusted root CA container.

2. Each of the endpoints must provide a CSR to the root CA asking it to issue them an identity certificate, which entails generating a key pair with a private and public key. The CSR will also include details like the device's serial number, IP address, FQDN, company department, etc.

3. If the root CA is satisfied with the info the endpoints have provided, it'll issue an identity certificate for each endpoint, including each endpoint's public key.

4. Endpoints A and B can now form a site-to-site VPN using certificates to verify their identities to each other. A certificate asymmetric key pair can be used for encryption and signing. SSL uses a key for encryption but not signing and IKE uses a key pair for signing but not encryption.

5. Both endpoints will calculate a hash value from the messages they want to exchange with each other to negotiate the VPN tunnel.

6. The hash value will then be encrypted by each peer's private key to generate a digital signature.

7. Each endpoint then sends messages along with their certificates. The receiving endpoint will use the root CA public key to decrypt the root CA digital signature included in the sending endpoint's certificate for verification.

8. If the digital signature is verified authentic, the receiving endpoint will assume that the remote peer's certificate is valid and that it's talking to the correct peer.

9. The receiving endpoint decrypts the sender's digital signature using the sender's public key, which is included in the received certificate.

10. Now that the receiving endpoint can see the digital signature in clear text, it begins a hash calculation locally.

11. If the calculated hash matches the one that the sender endpoint sent, the receiving endpoint will trust the sender.

12. This process is the same for the other endpoint and when both have completed it, they'll establish the VPN tunnel.

The FMC has different types of certificates it can use, and we'll explore them next.

HTTPS Server Certificate

These certificates are used by the FMC to present an SSL certificate to web browsers. By default, the FMC uses a server self-signed certificate, but you can replace that by generating a CSR for the PKI team to issue the identity certificate instead. An HTTPS server certificate can also be replaced by importing the identity certificate along with the private key and certificate chain.

Cert Enrollment

This is just another name for an FTD appliance's trust points. From **Objects>Object Management**, add a cert enrollment, associate it with an FTD appliance, and push in trust point format.

This enrollment can be done via a self-signed certificate, SCEP, PKCS12 file, or manually, with each method requiring a different process. The most common one is SCEP since it allows an auto-secure enrollment with the root CA.

External Certs

External certs can be added by importing an external CA certificate, which can't be verified with a trusted CA certificate.

These certs are used in the SSL policy rules to match the traffic encrypted by the external certificates, which can be imported in Distinguished Encoding Rules (DER) and Privacy-Enhanced Electronic Mail (PEM) format.

External Cert Groups

The external certs groups are just groups where you can group some external certs together.

Internal CAs

Internal CAs are created by generating a CSR or a self-signed internal CA or by importing them. They have a private and public key that are stored on the FMC. Your company or organization controls them, and they're used in the SSL policy rules to decrypt outgoing encrypted traffic by re-signing the server certificate with the internal CA.

Endpoints that don't trust internal CAs will get a certificate security warning on their browsers. Also, certain applications might not work so well if they don't have a way to trust internal CAs or if they don't support MITM certificate inspection.

Internal CA Groups

These are groups where you keep a set of your internal CA certificates.

Internal Certs

These server certs are added by importing them along with their private keys and are managed by your organization. They can be used to decrypt traffic arriving at the corporate servers using the known private key in the SSL policy rules. Internal certs are used for integration with an ISE identity source or for authentication in a captive portal and can be imported in DER and PEM format.

Internal Cert Groups

Groups where you can corral your internal certs.

Trusted CAs

Trusted CAs are added to the FMC by importing them. They're used to control encrypted traffic with a certificate signed by the trusted CA or any CA within the chain of trust. They can also be used to establish LDAPs or AN AD connection in the FMC realm as well as for ISE integration with the FMC. Trusted CAs can also be imported in both DER and PEM format.

We're going to run through two labs to get you up to speed on how certificates work in the real world. We'll dig into certificate authentication for a site-to-site VPN tunnel first and move on to certificate authentication for AnyConnect SSL VPN remote access.

LAB 1: Site-to-Site VPN with Certificate Authentication

Okay—to set the stage, I've got two FTD devices named FTDv-01 and FTDv-02. FTDv-01 is managed by an FMC named FMCv-02 and FTDv-02 is managed by an FMC called FMCv-03.

- The encryption domains are 172.16.1.0/24, with the internal subnet of FTDv-01, and 192.168.22.0/24, with internal subnet of FTDv-02.

- Windows 2012 R2 will be my internal CA; it'll issue two identity certificates, one for each FTD. I'll be using SCEP to enroll the two FTD appliances with the internal CA.

- Since FTDv-02 already has a CA, I'm just going to deal with the enrollment process for the FTDv 01 in this lab.

- Creating a crypto CA trust point is a key factor for the site-to-site VPN tunnel with certificate authentication. The Cert Enrollment is just a name the FMC uses to define a crypto ca trust point. You can create the Cert Enrollment from different places in the FMC: Within the site-to-site VPN topology window, via **Objects>Object Management**, or from **Devices>Certificates**.

Remember—If you create the trust point from within the VPN topology or Object Management, you still need to enroll it on the FTD appliance from the **Devices>Certificates** page.

Also, just because the crypto ca trust point will be used for authentication between the two peers in the site-to-site VPN configuration, that doesn't mean it has to be assigned to the FTD external interface. That's because you can have multiple trust points configured on the FTD without assigning them to the FTD outside interface and still authenticate the site-to-site VPN peers. You'll get a clear picture of how this works because the trust point I'm going to create won't be assigned to the FTD's outside interfaces.

Just so you know, this isn't the case with AnyConnect SSL VPN! The trust point used in AnyConnect SSL VPN policy must be associated to the FTD external interface.

 Okay—Let's get started by creating the new VPN topology now…

Deselect IKEv2, choose IKEv1, and click the plus sign to add the local FTD details:

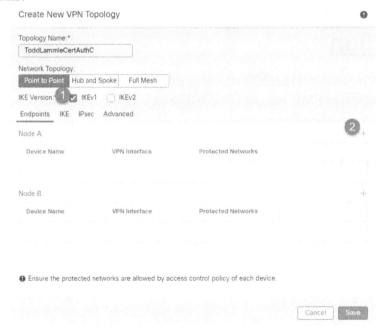

(1) Select FTDv-01, (2) then outside interface, and (3) then the outside interface's IP address. After that, (4) click the plus sign to add the FTDv-01 encryption domain:

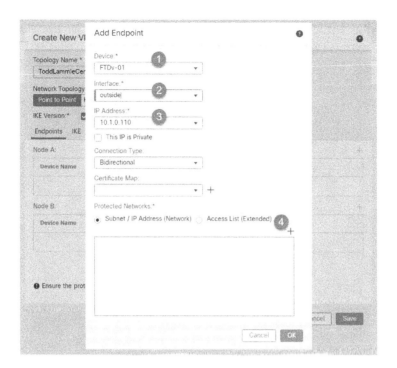

(1) pick the local encryption domain object, (2) click Add, (3) then OK:

I'm going to repeat what I just did, except I'll go with Extranet for the device type in the drop-down because FTDv-02 isn't being managed by FMCv-02. That makes it an extranet device:

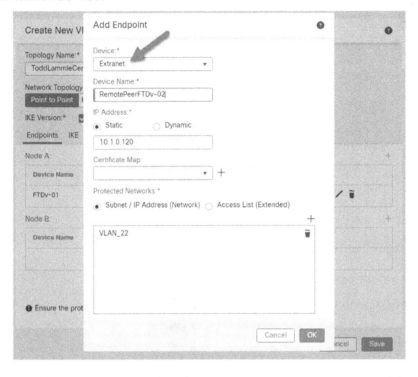

I was careful to come up with a device and a topology name without any spaces in them— always do this when naming anything!

Next, (1) I selected the certificate policy from the Policy drop-down and changed the authentication policy from pre-shared key to certificate.

Then (2) I chose Certificate from the Authentication Type drop-down menu and (3) clicked the plus sign to create the crypto ca trust point:

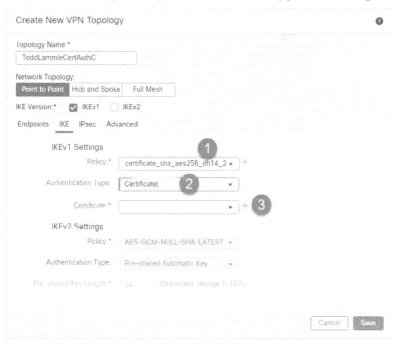

Here's a list describing the next steps:

1. Give the trust point a name.

2. Select SCEP as the enrollment type.

3. Type the SCEP URL. I'm using the default SCEP URL on Windows server in this lab: `https://<SERVER-IP>/certsrv/mscep/mscep.dll`.

4. Insert the fingerprint from the Windows internal CA for SCEP enrollment.

5. Move to the Certificate Parameters tab.

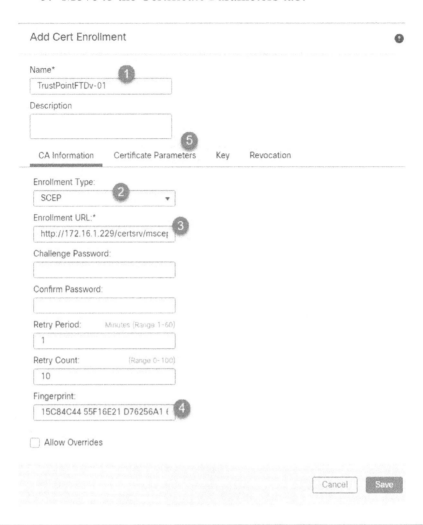

You can configure the certificate revocation check from the Revocation tab if required.

Next (1) I entered FTDv-01 FQDN in the custom FQDN field, (2) typed FTDv-01 FQDN in the CN field, and (3) clicked Save: [FTDv-01 mylab.local in the figure.]

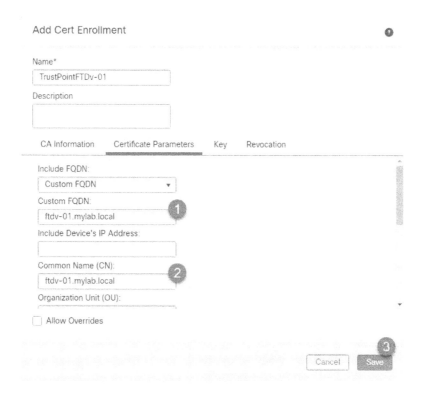

Here's a screen shot of how the Certificate menu should look. Click Save.

Now it's time to enroll the certificate on FTDv-01.

Go to **Devices>Certificates>Add**.

It doesn't matter if you click Add Certificates or the Add button because they do the same thing.

(1) Select the FTD appliance FTDv-01 and (2) then the trust point created from within the VPN topology. (3) Click Add:

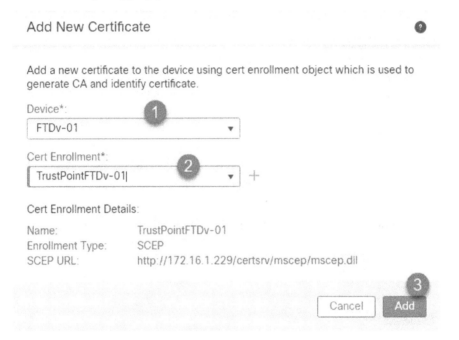

Don't forget that the FTD appliance should have a route to the internal CA server and vice versa!

You should see a similar screen to this one... In progress means that the certificate enrollment is occurring on the FTD appliance:

After a successful enrollment, you should see a screen just like this one. If you click the CA and ID buttons, you'll see the root CA certificate and the FTD identity certificate parameters:

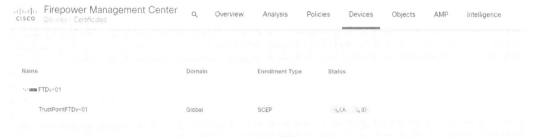

You can also check the trust point and certificates from the FTD CLISH mode or the FMC Threat Defense CLI:

show crypto ca trustpoints TrustPointFTDv-01

```
Trustpoint TrustPointFTDv-01:
    Subject Name:
    cn=WIN-2K12-01-CA
    dc=mylab
    dc=local
        Serial Number: 54f665b209b771xxxxxxxxxxxxxxx
    Certificate configured.
    CEP URL: http://172.16.1.229:80/certsrv/mscep/mscep.dll
```

show crypto ca certificates TrustPointFTDv-01

```
Certificate
  Status: Available
  Certificate Serial Number: 5c0000006807bbea7dfe7xxxxxxxxxxxx
  Certificate Usage: General Purpose
  Public Key Type: RSA (2048 bits)
  Signature Algorithm: SHA256 with RSA Encryption
```

```
Issuer Name:
  cn=WIN-2K12-01-CA
  dc=mylab
  dc=local
Subject Name:
  cn=ftdv-01.mylab.local
  hostname=ftdv-01.mylab.local
CRL Distribution Points:
  [1]   ldap:///CN=WIN-2K12-01-CA,CN=WIN-2K12-
01,CN=CDP,CN=Public%20Key%20Services,CN=Services,CN=Configuration,DC=mylab,DC=l
ocal?certificateRevocationList?base?objectClass=cRLDistributionPoint
  [2]   http://crl.mylab.local/crld/WIN-2K12-01-CA.crl
Validity Date:
  start date: 02:19:44 UTC May 3 2020
  end   date: 02:19:44 UTC May 3 2022
Storage: config
Associated Trustpoints: TrustPointFTDv-01

CA Certificate
Status: Available
Certificate Serial Number: 54f665b209718xxxxxxxxxxxxxxxxxxx
Certificate Usage: Signature
Public Key Type: RSA (2048 bits)
Signature Algorithm: SHA256 with RSA Encryption
Issuer Name:
  cn=WIN-2K12-01-CA
  dc=mylab
  dc=local
Subject Name:
  cn=WIN-2K12-01-CA
  dc=mylab
  dc=local
Validity Date:
  start date: 17:04:13 UTC Sep 6 2018
  end   date: 02:22:37 UTC Apr 17 2030
Storage: config
Associated Trustpoints: TrustPointFTDv-01
```

Now let's move on to the Access Control policy and Identity NAT settings. I'm
not going over all the configuration steps for these here because we covered them
thoroughly back in Chapter 32!

Here's a summary of how I configured the Access Control policy and Identity
NAT rules on FTDv-01:

Of course, you'll need to adjust these settings based on your specific environment.

Let's deploy the changes and test the VPN tunnel now!

Verification

Okay, so we've got two clients for testing —one behind FTDv-01 and the other behind FTDv-02. The client behind FTDv-01 is in FLAT subnet 172.16.1.0/24, and the client behind FTDv-02 is in VLAN-22 subnet 192.168.22.0/24.

Traffic coming from either client destined for the other one would be enough to trigger the VPN tunnel, so I'm going to initiate some ICMP traffic from the client behind FTDv-01 to the client behind FTDv-02 now:

Client on the FLAT subnet

Client on the VLAN_22 subnet

```
Administrator: Command Prompt

Microsoft Windows [Version 6.1.7601]
Copyright (c) 2009 Microsoft Corporation.  All rights reserved.

C:\Users\user>ipconfig

Windows IP Configuration


Ethernet adapter Local Area Connection:

   Connection-specific DNS Suffix  . :
   IPv4 Address. . . . . . . . . . . : 192.168.22.40
   Subnet Mask . . . . . . . . . . . : 255.255.255.0
   Default Gateway . . . . . . . . . : 192.168.22.1

Tunnel adapter isatap.{96975F6F-1C29-4DC3-85A9-CA0D0EBF845A}:

   Media State . . . . . . . . . . . : Media disconnected
   Connection-specific DNS Suffix  . :

C:\Users\user>
```

```
Administrator: Command Prompt

C:\Users\user>
C:\Users\user>
C:\Users\user>
C:\Users\user>
C:\Users\user>
C:\Users\user>
C:\Users\user>
C:\Users\user>
C:\Users\user>
C:\Users\user>
C:\Users\user>
C:\Users\user>ping 172.16.1.40

Pinging 172.16.1.40 with 32 bytes of data:
Reply from 172.16.1.40: bytes=32 time=7ms TTL=128
Reply from 172.16.1.40: bytes=32 time=6ms TTL=128
Reply from 172.16.1.40: bytes=32 time=5ms TTL=128
Reply from 172.16.1.40: bytes=32 time=6ms TTL=128

Ping statistics for 172.16.1.40:
    Packets: Sent = 4, Received = 4, Lost = 0 (0% loss),
Approximate round trip times in milli-seconds:
    Minimum = 5ms, Maximum = 7ms, Average = 6ms

C:\Users\user>
```

Great—ICMP traffic flows just fine between the two clients! Next, I'm going to see if the VPN tunnels have been successfully established with the right security associations on both FTD appliances. I also want to find out if the tunnel is using certificate authentication:

show vpn-sessiondb detail l2l on FTDv-01:

```
Session Type: LAN-to-LAN Detailed

Connection  : 10.1.0.120
Index       : 1                        IP Addr      : 10.1.0.120
Protocol    : IKEv1 IPsec
Encryption  : IKEv1: (1)AES256  IPsec: (1)AES256
```

```
Hashing       : IKEv1: (1)SHA1  IPsec: (1)SHA1
Bytes Tx      : 420                    Bytes Rx      : 420
Login Time    : 22:51:02 UTC Thu Jul 2 2020
Duration      : 0h:00m:25s
Tunnel Zone   : 0

IKEv1 Tunnels: 1
IPsec Tunnels: 1

IKEv1:
  Tunnel ID    : 1.1
  UDP Src Port : 500               UDP Dst Port : 500
  IKE Neg Mode : Main              Auth Mode    : rsaCertificate
  Encryption   : AES256            Hashing      : SHA1
  Rekey Int (T): 86400 Seconds     Rekey Left(T): 86375 Seconds
  D/H Group    : 14
  Filter Name  :

IPsec:
  Tunnel ID    : 1.2
  Local Addr   : 172.16.1.0/255.255.255.0/0/0
  Remote Addr  : 192.168.22.0/255.255.255.0/0/0
  Encryption   : AES256            Hashing      : SHA1
  Encapsulation: Tunnel
  Rekey Int (T): 28800 Seconds     Rekey Left(T): 28775 Seconds
  Rekey Int (D): 4608000 K-Bytes   Rekey Left(D): 4608000 K-Bytes
  Idle Time Out: 30 Minutes        Idle TO Left : 29 Minutes
  Bytes Tx     : 420               Bytes Rx     : 420
  Pkts Tx      : 7                 Pkts Rx      : 7
```

show vpn-sessiondb detail l2l on FTDv-02:

```
Session Type: LAN-to-LAN Detailed

Connection    : 10.1.0.110
Index         : 1                   IP Addr       : 10.1.0.110
Protocol      : IKEv1 IPsec
Encryption    : IKEv1: (1)AES256  IPsec: (1)AES256
Hashing       : IKEv1: (1)SHA1  IPsec: (1)SHA1
Bytes Tx      : 420                    Bytes Rx      : 420
Login Time    : 22:51:02 UTC Thu Jul 2 2020
Duration      : 0h:02m:46s
Tunnel Zone   : 0

IKEv1 Tunnels: 1
IPsec Tunnels: 1

IKEv1:
  Tunnel ID    : 1.1
  UDP Src Port : 500               UDP Dst Port : 500
  IKE Neg Mode : Main              Auth Mode    : rsaCertificate
  Encryption   : AES256            Hashing      : SHA1
  Rekey Int (T): 86400 Seconds     Rekey Left(T): 86234 Seconds
  D/H Group    : 14
  Filter Name  :

IPsec:
  Tunnel ID    : 1.2
  Local Addr   : 192.168.22.0/255.255.255.0/0/0
  Remote Addr  : 172.16.1.0/255.255.255.0/0/0
  Encryption   : AES256            Hashing      : SHA1
```

```
Encapsulation: Tunnel
Rekey Int (T): 28800 Seconds        Rekey Left(T): 28634 Seconds
Rekey Int (D): 4608000 K-Bytes      Rekey Left(D): 4608000 K-Bytes
Idle Time Out: 30 Minutes           Idle TO Left : 27 Minutes
Bytes Tx    : 420                   Bytes Rx    : 420
Pkts Tx     : 7                     Pkts Rx     : 7
```

Nice—the two FTD appliances have formed the site-to-site VPN tunnel using certificate authentication! I'm going to verify the security associations being used for this VPN tunnel now:

show crypto ipsec sa on FTDv-01:

```
interface: outside
    Crypto map tag: CSM_outside_map, seq num: 2, local addr: 10.1.0.110

    access-list CSM_IPSEC_ACL_2 extended permit ip 172.16.1.0 255.255.255.0
192.168.22.0 255.255.255.0
        local ident (addr/mask/prot/port): (172.16.1.0/255.255.255.0/0/0)
        remote ident (addr/mask/prot/port): (192.168.22.0/255.255.255.0/0/0)
        current_peer: 10.1.0.120


        #pkts encaps: 7, #pkts encrypt: 7, #pkts digest: 7
        #pkts decaps: 7, #pkts decrypt: 7, #pkts verify: 7
        #pkts compressed: 0, #pkts decompressed: 0
        #pkts not compressed: 7, #pkts comp failed: 0, #pkts decomp failed: 0
        #pre-frag successes: 0, #pre-frag failures: 0, #fragments created: 0
        #PMTUs sent: 0, #PMTUs rcvd: 0, #decapsulated frgs needing reassembly: 0
        #TFC rcvd: 0, #TFC sent: 0
        #Valid ICMP Errors rcvd: 0, #Invalid ICMP Errors rcvd: 0
        #send errors: 0, #recv errors: 0

        local crypto endpt.: 10.1.0.110/0, remote crypto endpt.: 10.1.0.120/0
        path mtu 1500, ipsec overhead 74(44), media mtu 1500
        PMTU time remaining (sec): 0, DF policy: copy-df
        ICMP error validation: disabled, TFC packets: disabled
        current outbound spi: 2A96EE98
        current inbound spi : 5986B839

    inbound esp sas:
      spi: 0x5986B839 (1502001209)
         SA State: active
         transform: esp-aes-256 esp-sha-hmac no compression
         in use settings ={L2L, Tunnel, IKEv1, }
         slot: 0, conn_id: 1, crypto-map: CSM_outside_map
         sa timing: remaining key lifetime (kB/sec): (3914999/28566)
         IV size: 16 bytes
         replay detection support: Y
         Anti replay bitmap:
          0x00000000 0x000000FF
    outbound esp sas:
      spi: 0x2A96EE98 (714534552)
         SA State: active
         transform: esp-aes-256 esp-sha-hmac no compression
         in use settings ={L2L, Tunnel, IKEv1, }
         slot: 0, conn_id: 1, crypto-map: CSM_outside_map
         sa timing: remaining key lifetime (kB/sec): (3914999/28566)
```

```
        IV size: 16 bytes
        replay detection support: Y
        Anti replay bitmap:
         0x00000000 0x00000001
```

show crypto ipsec sa on FTDv-02:

```
interface: outside
    Crypto map tag: CSM_outside_map, seq num: 1, local addr: 10.1.0.120

        access-list CSM_IPSEC_ACL_1 extended permit ip 192.168.22.0 255.255.255.0
172.16.1.0 255.255.255.0
        local ident (addr/mask/prot/port): (192.168.22.0/255.255.255.0/0/0)
        remote ident (addr/mask/prot/port): (172.16.1.0/255.255.255.0/0/0)
        current_peer: 10.1.0.110


        #pkts encaps: 7, #pkts encrypt: 7, #pkts digest: 7
        #pkts decaps: 7, #pkts decrypt: 7, #pkts verify: 7
        #pkts compressed: 0, #pkts decompressed: 0
        #pkts not compressed: 7, #pkts comp failed: 0, #pkts decomp failed: 0
        #pre-frag successes: 0, #pre-frag failures: 0, #fragments created: 0
        #PMTUs sent: 0, #PMTUs rcvd: 0, #decapsulated frgs needing reassembly: 0
        #TFC rcvd: 0, #TFC sent: 0
        #Valid ICMP Errors rcvd: 0, #Invalid ICMP Errors rcvd: 0
        #send errors: 0, #recv errors: 0

        local crypto endpt.: 10.1.0.120/0, remote crypto endpt.: 10.1.0.110/0
        path mtu 1500, ipsec overhead 74(44), media mtu 1500
        PMTU time remaining (sec): 0, DF policy: copy-df
        ICMP error validation: disabled, TFC packets: disabled
        current outbound spi: 5986B839
        current inbound spi : 2A96EE98

    inbound esp sas:
      spi: 0x2A96EE98 (714534552)
         SA State: active
         transform: esp-aes-256 esp-sha-hmac no compression
         in use settings ={L2L, Tunnel, IKEv1, }
         slot: 0, conn_id: 1, crypto-map: CSM_outside_map
         sa timing: remaining key lifetime (kB/sec): (4373999/28520)
         IV size: 16 bytes
         replay detection support: Y
         Anti replay bitmap:
          0x00000000 0x000000FF
    outbound esp sas:
      spi: 0x5986B839 (1502001209)
         SA State: active
         transform: esp-aes-256 esp-sha-hmac no compression
         in use settings ={L2L, Tunnel, IKEv1, }
         slot: 0, conn_id: 1, crypto-map: CSM_outside_map
         sa timing: remaining key lifetime (kB/sec): (4373999/28520)
         IV size: 16 bytes
         replay detection support: Y
         Anti replay bitmap:
          0x00000000 0x00000001
```

LAB 2: AnyConnect SSL VPN with Certificate Authentication

Time for the next lab! I'm going to show you how to deploy AnyConnect SSL VPN with certificate-based authentication. It's a good bet that the AnyConnect client I'm going to use already has a corporate certificate deployed by the internal CA.

I'm going with FTDv-01 again for my headend device and focus on the certificate authentication steps this time. Again, I won't be taking you through all the settings because we already went over them in Chapter 33.

In this lab, it'll be up to FTDv-01 to authenticate the AnyConnect clients. ISE will only be responsible to authorize the connections, because with certificate-based authentication, certificates won't be passed to ISE in RADIUS packets. This means certificate authentication will always terminate at the FTDv-01.

Another point to keep in mind is that FTDv-01 won't be relying on things like CN or UPN from the client certificates to map the username for the authentication. Its focus will be on checking if the certificate it gets from the client is valid and if it's been issued by the same trusted CA configured in the trust point that's configured to authenticate AnyConnect clients.

Once authentication has happened, the FTD will only pass the username extracted from the certificate for authorization to ISE. By default, the FTD will go with the CN to map the username first. The OU is pretty much backup.

ISE will validate these attributes against a specific Active Directory group configured in the authorization rule within the ISE policy set that'll be used to match AnyConnect connections. If the validation check passes, ISE will instruct the FTD to authorize the client session, and if it doesn't pass, the FTD will be told to deny it.

Time to get started: To create the new Remote Access VPN policy, go to **Devices>Remote Access**:

Click on Add or Add a New Configuration to conjure the new Remote Access VPN Policy Wizard:

1. Give the new Remote Access VPN policy a name.

2. Deselect IPsec-IKEv2.

3. Select the FTD appliance and add it to the Selected Devices list.

4. Click Next.

Remote Access VPN Policy Wizard

5. Give the Connection Profile a name—it will show up in the AnyConnect Group drop-down.

6. Choose Client Certificate Only as the authentication method.

7. Select the UPN attribute for the Primary Field value. Depending on your deployment, you might need to select the attribute you're using on the client certificates.

8. Enter None as the secondary field.

9. Choose ISE as the authorization server. (This is the server created in the AnyConnect lab in Chapter 32, the VPN chapter.)

10. Select ISE as the accounting server. (This server was also created back in the VPN chapter.)

11. Opt for AnyConnectPool as the IP address pool for the IPv4 Address Pools field. (Also created back in the VPN chapter.)

12. Select the AnyConnectGroupPolicy as the group policy. (This group policy was also created in the VPN chapter.)

13. Click Next.

14. Choose the AnyConnect package you've already uploaded to the FTD. If you haven't done that yet, click the plus sign button.

15. Click Next.

16. Pick the security zone that the FTD external interface is part of.

17. Choose the trust point you want to use for the AnyConnect authentication. I went with the trust point created back in the AnyConnect lab in Chapter 33. Because I'm configuring AnyConnect SSL VPN, this trust point will be associated to the FTD external interface—the outside interface of the FTD in this lab. Just remember when you configured the site-to-site VPN labs, the trust point we used wasn't associated to the FTD external interface!

18. Enable Access Control for VPN traffic.

19. Click Next.

20. Click Finish.

But wait! Before I go and deploy these changes, I've got to tweak a couple of options to make the ISE server an authorization server *only*. I also need to enable the option that will deny accesses to users who don't pass ISE validation against the Active Directory group specified in my ISE authorization rule.

Do get this done, I'm going to **Objects>Object Management>RADIUS Server Group**:

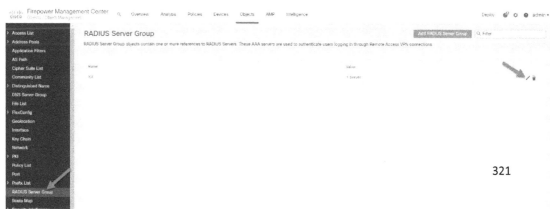

I'm going with Enable authorize only and then I'll hit Save.

Next, I'm heading over to **Devices>Remote Access** to click the pencil icon and edit the Remote Access VPN policy:

Now, I'll click the pencil icon to edit the Employees Connection Profile created previously:

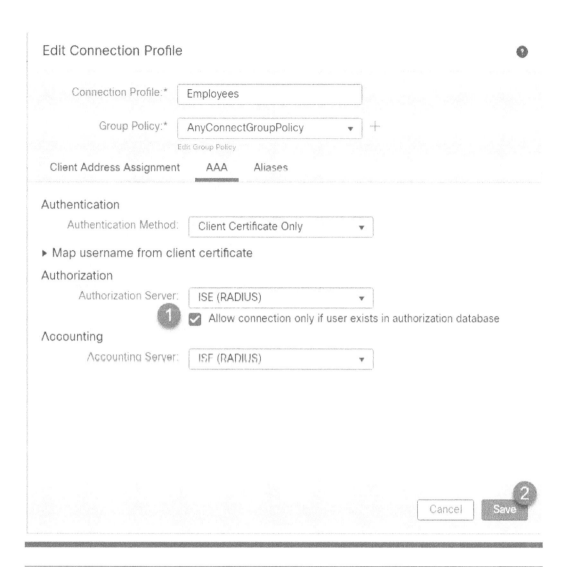

*) From the client certificate section, you can expand the Map Username settings and pick the attribute you want to handle user mapping from the client certificate.

1) In the AAA tab, enable Allow Connection Only If User Exists in Authorization Database.

2) Hit Save and deploy the changes!

Verification

We're going to test this all out now with two users creatively named Test1 and Test7. Both of them have valid certificates issued by the internal CA, but only Test1 is part of the Active Directory group specified in the ISE authorization rule. If all's good, Test7 should fail the authorization and be denied access to the network, but Test1 should sail right through!

Test1 user:

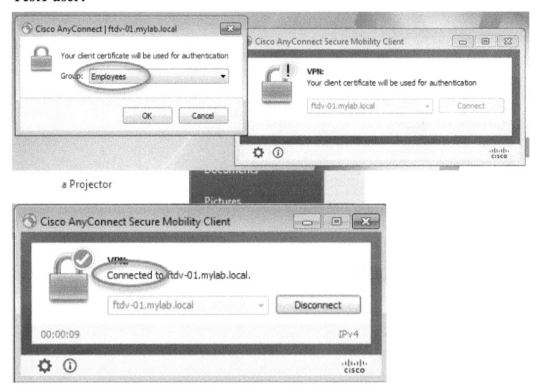

Okay—the remote access VPN has definitely been successfully established and we can check out the connection details with the command `show vpn-sessiondb detail anyconnect` from the FTD CLISH or FMC Threat Defense CLI tool:

```
Session Type: AnyConnect Detailed

Username     : test1@mylab.local      Index       : 8
Assigned IP  : 172.16.50.1            Public IP   : 10.1.0.40
Protocol     : AnyConnect-Parent SSL-Tunnel DTLS-Tunnel
License      : AnyConnect Premium
Encryption   : AnyConnect-Parent: (1)none  SSL-Tunnel: (1)AES-GCM-256  DTLS-
Tunnel: (1)AES256
Hashing      : AnyConnect-Parent: (1)none  SSL-Tunnel: (1)SHA384  DTLS-Tunnel:
(1)SHA1
Bytes Tx     : 16030                  Bytes Rx    : 112
Pkts Tx      : 12                     Pkts Rx     : 2
Pkts Tx Drop : 0                      Pkts Rx Drop : 0
Group Policy : AnyConnectGroupPolicy  Tunnel Group : Employees
Login Time   : 01:09:43 UTC Fri Jul 3 2020
Duration     : 0h:00m:07s
Inactivity   : 0h:00m:00s
VLAN Mapping : N/A                    VLAN        : none
Audt Sess ID : 0a01006e000080005efe8557
Security Grp : none                   Tunnel Zone : 0

AnyConnect-Parent Tunnels: 1
SSL-Tunnel Tunnels: 1
DTLS-Tunnel Tunnels: 1
```

```
AnyConnect-Parent:
  Tunnel ID    : 8.1
  Public IP    : 10.1.0.40
  Encryption   : none                  Hashing      : none
  TCP Src Port : 62069                 TCP Dst Port : 443
  Auth Mode    : Certificate
  Idle Time Out: 30 Minutes            Idle TO Left : 29 Minutes
  Client OS    : win
  Client OS Ver: 6.1.7601 Service Pack 1
  Client Type  : AnyConnect
  Client Ver   : Cisco AnyConnect VPN Agent for Windows 4.8.03043
  Bytes Tx     : 8015                  Bytes Rx     : 0
  Pkts Tx      : 6                     Pkts Rx      : 0
  Pkts Tx Drop : 0                     Pkts Rx Drop : 0

SSL-Tunnel:
  Tunnel ID    : 8.2
  Assigned IP  : 172.16.50.1           Public IP    : 10.1.0.40
  Encryption   : AES-GCM-256           Hashing      : SHA384
  Ciphersuite  : ECDHE-RSA-AES256-GCM-SHA384
  Encapsulation: TLSv1.2               TCP Src Port : 62073
  TCP Dst Port : 443                   Auth Mode    : Certificate
  Idle Time Out: 30 Minutes            Idle TO Left : 29 Minutes
  Client OS    : Windows
  Client Type  : SSL VPN Client
  Client Ver   : Cisco AnyConnect VPN Agent for Windows 4.8.03043
  Bytes Tx     : 8015                  Bytes Rx     : 112
  Pkts Tx      : 6                     Pkts Rx      : 2
  Pkts Tx Drop : 0                     Pkts Rx Drop : 0
  Filter Name  : #ACSACL#-IP-AllowanyConnect-5ec32ae6

DTLS-Tunnel:
  Tunnel ID    : 8.3
  Assigned IP  : 172.16.50.1           Public IP    : 10.1.0.40
  Encryption   : AES256                Hashing      : SHA1
  Ciphersuite  : DHE-RSA-AES256-SHA
  Encapsulation: DTLSv1.0              UDP Src Port : 62327
  UDP Dst Port : 443                   Auth Mode    : Certificate
  Idle Time Out: 30 Minutes            Idle TO Left : 29 Minutes
  Client OS    : Windows
  Client Type  : DTLS VPN Client
  Client Ver   : Cisco AnyConnect VPN Agent for Windows 4.8.03043
  Bytes Tx     : 0                     Bytes Rx     : 0
  Pkts Tx      : 0                     Pkts Rx      : 0
  Pkts Tx Drop : 0                     Pkts Rx Drop : 0
  Filter Name  : #ACSACL#-IP-AllowanyConnect-5ec32ae6
```

Looking good! Next up is the Test7 user.

Test7 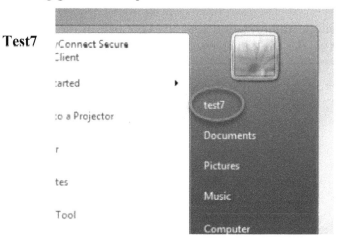 **user:**

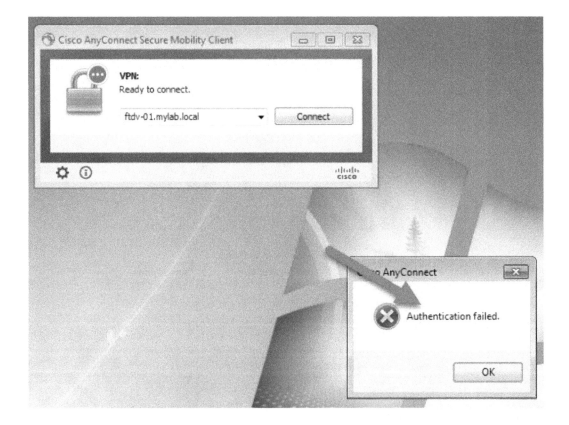

Sure enough, Test7 user failed the authorization since it is not part of the Active Directory group we specified on the ISE authorization rule—success!

ISE logs:

Chapter 34: Troubleshooting

The following CCNP Security SNCF exam objectives are covered in this chapter:

3.0: Management and Troubleshooting

3.1 Troubleshoot with FMC CLI and GUI

3.3 Troubleshoot using packet capture procedures

Things going wrong is a fact of life in IT! No matter how well you configure your firewalls, or how much redundancy and resiliency you add into your firewall design…eventually something that is super important will break at 3:00 a.m. that you need to fix ASAP! Even if your Firepower deployment is perfectly fine, that doesn't mean that some other part of the infrastructure cannot randomly explode in such a way that causes an outage anyway.

If outages do not manage to ruin your night, don't worry! Other departments in your company will often immediately blame the poor firewall if any of their applications are not working perfectly; "Blame the network" is a saying in this field for a reason!

This chapter is going to help you get some peace and quiet by teaching you how to troubleshoot some common issues you might encounter in your Firepower deployment.

Troubleshooting Methodology

A common misconception is that you need to be a senior-level resource to efficiently troubleshoot issues. The truth is, while experience certainly makes things easier since you have a better understanding of how things work, the best way to troubleshoot an issue is to follow a methodology that helps diagnose an issue and then work through it till it's resolved.

Some issues are straightforward to identify; for example, if the Internet at the office dies and you cannot access your firewall, then that is a pretty big clue for you to investigate. Unfortunately, a lot of issues are more along the lines of a user complaining that "the Internet is slow sometimes," which does not give you a lot to go on. Because of this, it is very important to work on properly defining the problem before directly diving into trying to solve the issue. Instead try the formal steps outlined in the following sections.

Gather Information

This step starts when you first learn about the issue you are trying to solve. You can learn about it from a trouble ticket, an alert from a network monitoring solution, a user telling you about it in the hallway, or even by noticing something as you are going about your day-to-day activities.

Since users do not tend to share all the useful information they may inadvertently know when they open a trouble ticket, you may need to talk with people to understand the problem. Once you understand what you are trying to fix, you can check for more information by looking at monitoring solutions for events or looking at whatever logs you have available.

If possible, you should try to replicate the issue on your own so you can get more information and easily test to see if your fix resolved the issue.

Analyze the Information

Once you have gathered a bunch of information, you can start comparing it against your understanding of how the systems should work when the issue is not causing the company grief. For example, if you have a complaint about slow Internet through the firewall, it would be useful if you had a baseline for how fast the Internet was before the issue as well as how fast the Internet was during the issue.

The number of complaints can help you narrow the issue down as well. If a lot of tickets come from the same department or floor, then that can point you to specific network devices or firewall policies that apply to that user base. But if it is a single user, the issue could just be with their computer rather than something the firewall guy needs to care about.

It is also a good idea to check change control records to see if anything was recently done on the network that could be related to the problem.

Eliminate Possibilities

At this point you should be able to eliminate a few possibilities in much the same way you would when trying to answer a certification exam question. For example, if you are trying to troubleshoot all users not being able to get online at an office, it makes sense to assume the firewall is offline.

But if the issue is that only some users can't get on to the Internet, you can eliminate the firewall being offline as a consideration because the device would have to be at least somewhat working since it is allowing some traffic.

The benefit of eliminating options is the same as it is when answering a question in a certification exam; it leaves you with a better chance of picking the right answer.

This does require good information and analysis from the previous steps though. If you eliminate the wrong possibility, then you might accidentally increase your troubleshooting efforts since you will have to eventually circle back to start the process over. To add to our previous example, what if the users that are online are really going through a backup firewall because the primary is down?

Make a Hypothesis

After eliminating a few potential possibilities, you should hopefully be left with a solid idea of what is causing the problem. Now you should be able to put together a proposed solution that should solve the issue. If your company requires change control approval before you can implement your fix, then this would be step where you make your paperwork.

It is best to keep your solution as specific as possible. You don't want to change 10 settings at once because it will be difficult to identify what actually resolved the issue if you use the shotgun approach.

Test the Hypothesis

Finally, it is time to implement your proposed solution. Once the change has been completed, you should test to see if the issue is resolved. If the issue is still occurring, then you should undo what you changed and start this troubleshooting process over at an earlier step.

OSI Layers

Since this is well above CCNA material, I am going to assume you are familiar with the OSI and TCP/IP models, but if you need a refresher for this section, then check out the following reference.

Since we are talking about the OSI/TCP/IP models, let's take a minute to map some troubleshooting tools over to layers.

Application	• File, print, message, database, and application services
Presentation	• Data encryption, compression, and translation services
Session	• Dialog control
Transport	• End-to-end connection
Network	• Routing
Data Link	• Framing
Physical	• Physical topology

Layer 1

The first layer deals with the physical components. This will be items like cabling and basic interface configuration for things like speed, and in the case of the bigger appliances, that would include interface allocations in the chassis manager.

Components	Layer Examples
Firepower appliance	Interface cabling
FTDv	Basic interface configuration
5500-X	Interface allocation

In a Firepower 4100 or 9300 appliance, we use the Firepower Chassis Manager (FCM) to configure the interfaces and allocate them to the FTD instance.

Hardware Bypass is also a layer 1 feature that can be configured to allow FTD to fail open if the physical appliance goes down.

Interface	Type	Admin S...	Operational ...	Instan...	VLAN	Admin Duplex
MGMT	Management					
▸ Port-channel1	data	1gbps	1gbps	FTD		Full Duplex
Ethernet1/1						
Ethernet1/2	data	10gbps	10gbps	FTD		Full Duplex
Ethernet1/3	mgmt	1gbps	1gbps	FTD		Full Duplex
Ethernet1/4	data	1gbps	10gbps			Full Duplex
Ethernet1/5	data	10gbps	10gbps			Full Duplex
Ethernet1/6	data	10gbps	10gbps			Full Duplex
Ethernet1/7	data	10gbps	10gbps			Full Duplex
Ethernet1/8	data	10gbps	10gbps			Full Duplex

We can verify layer 1 is working alright on an FTD by checking the interfaces pages under the devices. If the interface is enabled and has negotiated the correct speed, you should see a green circle next to the interface. If there is an issue with the cable or the speed, then the circle will be red.

If an interface is "missing" from the interfaces page, it was probably not allocated to the FTD instance in FCM. On a virtual appliance, you have accidentally selected an unsupported network interface card (NIC) type.

FTD31

Cisco Firepower Threat Defense for VMWare

Device   Routing   Interfaces   Inline Sets   DHCP

Interface	Logical Name	Type	Security Zones
Diagnostic0/0	diagnostic	Physical	
GigabitEthernet0/0	Outside	Physical	Outside
GigabitEthernet0/1	Inside	Physical	Inside

We can verify the interface allocation using the FXOS CLI:

```
A4140-1# scope ssa
A4140-1 /ssa # show logical-device

Logical Device:
    Name        Description Slot ID    Mode        Oper State
Template Name
    ---------- ----------- ---------- ---------- ------------------------ -----
--------
    FTD                     1          Standalone Ok                        ftd
A4140-1 /ssa # scope logical-device FTD
A4140-1 /ssa/logical-device # show configuration
 enter logical-device FTD ftd 1 standalone
    enter external-port-link Ethernet12_ftd Ethernet1/2 ftd
        set decorator ""
        set description ""
        set port-name Ethernet1/2
    exit
    enter external-port-link Ethernet13_ftd Ethernet1/3 ftd
        set decorator ""
        set description ""
        set port-name Ethernet1/3
    exit
    enter external-port-link PC1_ftd Port-channel1 ftd
        set decorator ""
        set description ""
        set port-name Port-channel1
    exit
```

Layer 2

The second layer deals with MAC addressing, ARP, port channels, and VLANs in a Firepower deployment. On hardware appliances (2100, 4100, 9300) LACP is run on FXOS. On all other platforms, LACP is run on Lina.

Components	Layer Examples
Lina	MAC addressing
FXOS (2100, 4100, 9300)	ARP
	Port channels

The easiest way to verify MAC address information is by hovering your mouse over the interface name under the device page, or by running `show interfaces`.

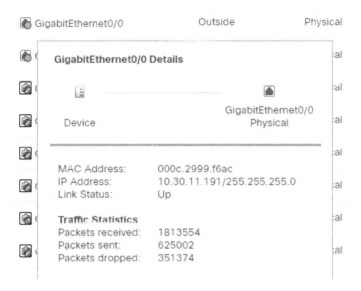

```
> show interface Inside
Interface GigabitEthernet0/1 "Inside", is up, line protocol is up
  Hardware is net_vmxnet3, BW 10000 Mbps, DLY 10 usec
        Auto-Duplex(Full-duplex), Auto-Speed(10000 Mbps)
        Input flow control is unsupported, output flow control is unsupported
        MAC address 000c.2999.f6b6, MTU 1500
        IP address 10.100.10.1, subnet mask 255.255.255.0
        1112520 packets input, 167727655 bytes, 0 no buffer
        Received 0 broadcasts, 0 runts, 0 giants
        0 input errors, 0 CRC, 0 frame, 0 overrun, 0 ignored, 0 abort
        0 pause input, 0 resume input
        0 L2 decode drops
        707255 packets output, 318920425 bytes, 0 underruns
        0 pause output, 0 resume output
        0 output errors, 0 collisions, 0 interface resets
        0 late collisions, 0 deferred
        0 input reset drops, 0 output reset drops
        input queue (blocks free curr/low): hardware (0/0)
        output queue (blocks free curr/low): hardware (0/0)
  Traffic Statistics for "Inside":
        1113253 packets input, 145337250 bytes
        707255 packets output, 309018855 bytes
        792218 packets dropped
      1 minute input rate 1 pkts/sec,   398 bytes/sec
      1 minute output rate 0 pkts/sec,   59 bytes/sec
      1 minute drop rate, 1 pkts/sec
      5 minute input rate 1 pkts/sec,   292 bytes/sec
      5 minute output rate 0 pkts/sec,   49 bytes/sec
      5 minute drop rate, 1 pkts/sec
```

Layer 3

The third layer deals with everything IP related, including IP addressing, routing, and NAT. Everything in this layer is handled in Lina.

Components	Layer Examples
Lina	IP addressing
	Routing
	NAT

You can set or verify the IP address on an interface page yet again.

Edit Physical Interface

General   IPv4   IPv6   Advanced   Hardware Configuration   FMC Access

IP Type:

Use Static IP   ▼

IP Address:

10.100.10.1/24

eg. 192.0.2.1/255.255.255.128 or 192.0.2.1/25

The `show ip address` command is great for seeing IP information on the CLI.

```
> show ip address
System IP Addresses:
Interface              Name          IP address      Subnet mask
Method
GigabitEthernet0/0     Outside       10.30.11.191    255.255.255.0
manual
GigabitEthernet0/1     Inside        10.100.10.1     255.255.255.0
CONFIG
Management0/0          diagnostic    10.30.10.181    255.255.255.0
CONFIG
Current IP Addresses:
Interface              Name          IP address      Subnet mask
Method
GigabitEthernet0/0     Outside       10.30.11.191    255.255.255.0
manual
```

```
GigabitEthernet0/1          Inside              10.100.10.1    255.255.255.0
CONFIG
Management0/0               diagnostic          10.30.10.181   255.255.255.0
CONFIG
```

NAT can be verified with the either the `show nat` or `show running-config nat` command.

```
> show running-config nat
!
object network Testlab-LAN
 nat (Inside,Outside) dynamic interface
```

The routing table can be viewed with the `show route` command.

```
> show route

Codes: L - local, C - connected, S - static, R - RIP, M - mobile, B - BGP
       D - EIGRP, EX - EIGRP external, O - OSPF, IA - OSPF inter area
       N1 - OSPF NSSA external type 1, N2 - OSPF NSSA external type 2
       E1 - OSPF external type 1, E2 - OSPF external type 2, V - VPN
       i - IS-IS, su - IS-IS summary, L1 - IS IS level-1, L2 - IS-IS level-2
       ia - IS-IS inter area, * - candidate default, U - per-user static route
       o - ODR, P - periodic downloaded static route, I - replicated route
       SI - Static InterVRF
Gateway of last resort is 10.30.11.1 to network 0.0.0.0

S*      0.0.0.0 0.0.0.0 [1/0] via 10.30.11.1, Outside
C       10.30.11.0 255.255.255.0 is directly connected, Outside
L       10.30.11.191 255.255.255.255 is directly connected, Outside
C       10.100.10.0 255.255.255.0 is directly connected, Inside
L       10.100.10.1 255.255.255.255 is directly connected, Inside
```

Layer 4

The fourth layer deals with TCP state checking and L4 ACLs. Everything is still handled by Lina.

Components	Layer Examples
Lina	TCP state checking
	Layer 4 ACLs

The best way to see existing connections going through the FTD is the `show conn` command. We will talk about the FTD packet flow later in this chapter and next, but one of the first things FTD does is check to see if the connection is already established.

```
> show conn protocol tcp
5 in use, 51368 most used
```

```
Inspect Snort:
        preserve-connection: 0 enabled, 0 in effect, 32250 most enabled, 0 most
in effect

TCP Inside  10.30.11.191(10.100.10.100):59687 Outside  69.192.196.125:443, idle
0:00:03, bytes 0, flags Ux N
TCP Inside  10.30.11.191(10.100.10.100):49678 Outside  23.49.134.110:80, idle
0:00:18, bytes 221, flags UxO N
TCP Inside  10.30.11.191(10.100.10.100):60765 Outside  52.179.224.121:443, idle
0:00:45, bytes 17150, flags UxIO N
TCP Inside  10.30.11.191(10.100.10.100):49677 Outside  80.254.145.118:80, idle
0:00:18, bytes 214, flags UxO N
TCP nlp_int_tap  10.30.11.191(169.254.1.2):22 Outside  10.30.10.16:14010, idle
0:00:00, bytes 36361626, flags UIO
```

We will be looking at the Access Control policy a lot when we get to the troubleshooting steps. You can use `show access-list` to see the configured ACLs on the FTD. It is, though, a lot cleaner to use the FMC to have a look at the rules.

```
> show access-list
access-list cached ACL log flows: total 0, denied 0 (deny-flow-max 4096)
            alert-interval 300
access-list CSM_FW_ACL ; 13 elements; name hash: 0x4a69e3f3
access-list CSM_FW_ACL_ line 1 remark rule-id 268435458: PREFILTER POLICY:
Testlab - Prefilter - Policy
access-list CSM_FW_ACL_ line 2 remark rule-id 268435458: RULE: DEFAULT TUNNEL
ACTION RULE
access-list CSM_FW_ACL_ line 3 advanced permit ipinip any any rule-id 268435458
(hitcnt=0) 0xf5b597d6
access-list CSM_FW_ACL_ line 4 advanced permit udp any eq 3544 any range 1025
65535 rule-id 268435458 (hitcnt=0) 0x46d7839e
access-list CSM_FW_ACL_ line 5 advanced permit udp any range 1025 65535 any eq
3544 rule-id 268435458 (hitcnt=0) 0xaf1d5aa5
access-list CSM_FW_ACL_ line 6 advanced permit 41 any any rule-id 268435458
(hitcnt=0) 0x06095aba
access-list CSM_FW_ACL_ line 7 advanced permit gre any any rule-id 268435458
(hitcnt=0) 0x52c7a066
access-list CSM_FW_ACL_ line 8 remark rule-id 268435459: ACCESS POLICY: Testlab
- Base - Mandatory
access-list CSM_FW_ACL_ line 9 remark rule-id 268435459: L7 RULE: Block Site
access-list CSM_FW_ACL_ line 10 advanced permit tcp ifc Inside any ifc Outside
any object-group HTTPS rule-id 268435459 (hitcnt=34735) 0x39c06649
```

Layers 5–7

The rest of the layers are mostly handled by the Snort engine except for Lina's Modular Policy Framework (MPF)

Components	Layer Examples
Snort	Application detection & AppID
Lina (MPF)	URL filtering
	IPS

	SSL decryption
	User awareness
	File and malware
	NAP

Common Approaches

Now that you've seen the basic troubleshooting methodology you should follow when trying to work on an issue, and also how the OSI model maps to FTD, we can turn our attention to some of the commonly used approaches.

Bottom Up

This approach has you follow either the OSI or TCP/IP model from the bottom and work your way up to the top. This means you will make sure the physical stuff like the network cable is working properly before you work your way up to checking the Access Control policy (ACP) rules in Firepower.

While a lot of the firewall-specific issues will often be related to things like the rule base, you can still encounter a lot of "lower-layer" issues such as Firepower interfaces not working, routing issues, and general connectivity.

In fact, when we were at a customer recently, we fixed a Firepower deployment where the VLAN used for failover was accidentally deleted from the switch that the firewalls were connected to, which that caused both firewalls to become active!

Top Down

This one is simply the exact opposite of the bottom-up approach. Here you start with the Application layer and work your way down. This tends to make more sense in a firewall setting where a typical ticket would be about a user not being able to access a website or needing an application to work through the firewall.

Divide and Conquer

This approach can be summed up as a the "follow your gut" method. You would pick where you think the problem might be based on your experience and knowledge of the environment to try to save time. For example, if the device has frequent OSPF issues, you might immediately check for Network layer issues to see if that is the problem.

This approach works well if you guess correctly, but if you have not found the issue after a couple guesses, then it will likely be more efficient to fall back to a more structured approach.

Follow the Path

With the follow-the-path approach you would, as the name suggests, "follow the path" a packet would take while moving through your firewall. While using this approach is normally pretty complex since you have to know exactly what your firewall is doing for this to work, Cisco makes this really easy with the `packet-tracer` command, which we'll discuss later in the chapter.

Spot the Difference

Just as with picture games for kids, we simply compare the current configuration to a reference and try to find any differences that should not be there. The reference you use can be anything from a backup configuration to a similar device's configuration that is currently working.

Move the Problem

Moving the problem can be a simple but effective way of isolating an issue. If you have a laptop that cannot get online, you might swap out the network cable to see if that was the problem. You might also try another laptop to see if the issue is just the user's laptop. Or you might try a different switchport if you want to fully rule out the first layer.

This approach does have limitations though; after all, it may not be practical to swap out a network device unless you are trying to solve a pretty big problem.

The Life of a Packet

In the previous section, you learned about some handy troubleshooting approaches you can use to troubleshoot various issues on the network, but for a Firepower (or any NGFW) deployment, the most useful one to use is the follow-the-path approach. The reason is simply that when packets flow through your FTD, they go on quite the epic journey!

Firepower Architecture

Let's take a minute to explore Firepower's architecture so you can understand the path a packet takes while moving through your device. The following picture shows how a virtual FTD is structured.

Here we chose to focus on the FTDv because things are a bit more streamlined when compared to the hardware models, which have PCI buses and potentially fabric interconnects to consider. But the general idea is the same throughout all the models.

The packet enters the firewall through one of the device's interfaces where the traditional ASA side of the firewall, called Lina, applies any firewall features that apply to the packet, such as NAT or QoS. If you have prefilter rules, they can be used to quickly decide the packet's fate. But if the packet does not match the prefilter, it is off the Data Acquisition (DAQ) layer.

The DAQ layer is used to translate packets into a format that Firepower's Snort engine can work with. From there the IPS will identify what the conversation is doing and reach a verdict. If the traffic is permitted, it flows back and out through the firewall the egress port.

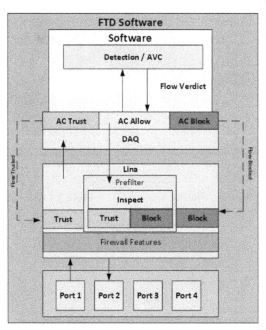

While knowing how the Firepower architecture works is handy for troubleshooting, let's have a look at the actual path a packet takes through an FTD:

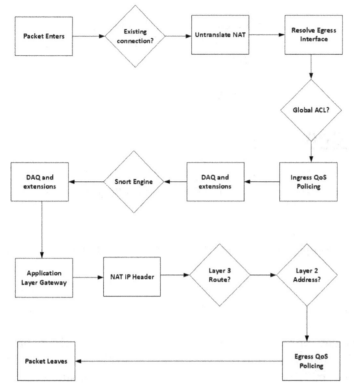

When the packet enters the firewall, FTD first checks if the packet is part of an existing connection. If it is a new connection, NAT will untranslate the packet if necessary, then have a look at the routing table to figure out the egress interface.

Next the packet goes through the Access Control policy to see if the packet should be dropped or not. Assuming the packet is not dropped, ingress QoS policing is applied to the packet if needed by the configuration. Then it is off to the Data Acquisition layer so the traffic can be understood by the Snort engine and the IPS can make its decision. If the traffic is not blocked, the DAQ layer will change the traffic back to its normal format and then apply any applicable ALGs. The rest of the steps deal with getting the packet to the egress interface so it can leave the firewall.

Snort Engine

If that was not complicated enough, here is what a packet goes through when it enters the Snort end of the firewall.

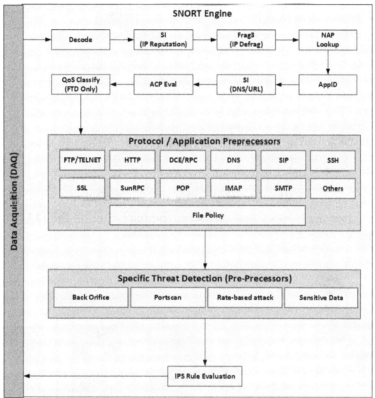

We will talk about this is more detail elsewhere in the book, but for now the packet will first be decoded, and the Snort will do various checks, such as checking the IP reputation or seeing if the packet is defragmented. The application in use will be identified, the ACP will be evaluated, then the packet will go through application preprocessors, checked for specific threat detections, and finally evaluated by the IPS rule base.

Here is the full end to end packet flow. The blue icons are the Lina ASA engine, and the Snort engine is the red icons in the second picture. After the "Ingress QoS Policing" step the packet moves into the DAQ and enters the snort side of things.

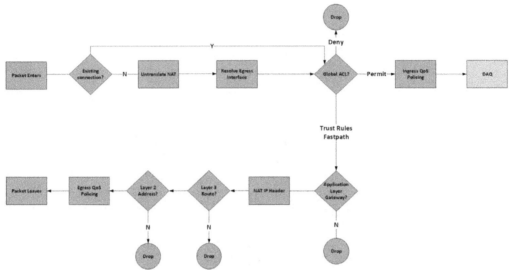

After the "QoS Classify" step, the packet exits the DAQ and continues at the ALG.

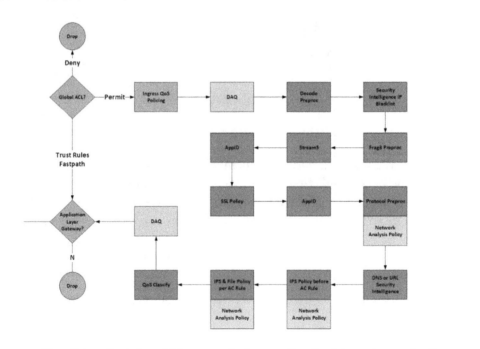

One thing that should jump out at you after looking at a packet's path through the firewall is that there are several points in the above flowcharts that can lead to the packet being dropped. On the other hand, steps like QoS probably are not going to cause a packet to drop in normal operations. To make your troubleshooting more focused, Cisco recommends looking at firewall components in the following order:

- Packet ingress and egress
- DAQ
- Security intelligence
- Access Control policy
- SSL policy
- Active authentication
- IPS
- NAP

Summary

In this chapter, we dove into some of the common troubleshooting steps that you will want use when solving problems in your lab or in the real world. We talked about the OSI model layers as well as common approaches you can use to track down that pesky problem. In the next chapter we will really get into the weeds.

Chapter 35: Troubleshooting Part II

The CCNP Security SNCF exam objectives covered in this chapter include:

3.0: Management and Troubleshooting

3.1 Troubleshoot with FMC CLI and GUI

3.3 Troubleshoot using packet capture procedures

In the last chapter, you learned some effective troubleshooting strategies for your career. This chapter will be a deep dive into Cisco's recommended troubleshooting steps for Firepower issues. Make sure you have a coffee before continuing past this point, this is going to be a long one!

Packet Ingress and Egress

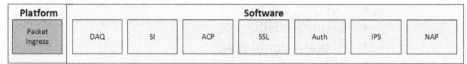

Platform	Software						
Packet Ingress	DAQ	SI	ACP	SSL	Auth	IPS	NAP

The obvious first step in troubleshooting an FTD traffic issue is to make sure the packet is reaching the firewall in the first place. This might not be a problem in a smaller environment, but if your core has a busy routing table with redundant paths, traffic might end up through a device you are not expecting.

Once you know that traffic is flowing through your firewall, you can be certain that if the packet does not make it out the other end, something went wrong! Now at this point this can be anything from the packet being denied along the way or simply ARP failed when trying to get the packet on the egress interface.

Routing

Typically, you get traffic to your firewall by either making a static default route on your core switch or by learning about the route through a dynamic routing protocol.

We will use this simple topology for this section, the network has a router with an IP address of 10.100.252.253/24 that has a MPLS connection and an FTD with the IP address 10.100.252.254/24 with an Internet connection.

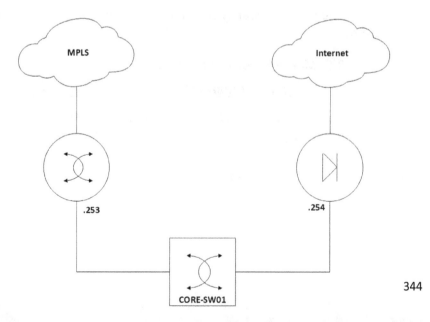

There is not too much that can go wrong with a static route. Either the route is pointing to the correct destination or it is not. It is also possible, though, that a required static route is simply missing. In this example, we are not able to get online from our core switch:

```
Core-SW01#ping 11.11.11.11
Type escape sequence to abort.
Sending 5, 100-byte ICMP Echos to 11.11.11.11, timeout is 2 seconds:
U.U.U
Success rate is 0 percent (0/5)
```

The first thing to note is that we are getting a "U" code back in the ICMP response. This tells us a couple of things; we know up to layer 3 is working because we got a response from the upstream device. Speaking of that response, the "U" means the device has no upstream path, which means the response is probably from the router in the network since an MPLS network does not always have a default route.

One way we can tell we're receiving the ICMP code from the router is that firewalls try to be very secretive so they will not send out information like ICMP since that can be used against you, though it does make troubleshooting a bit harder. Now that we have a pretty good idea that the default route is pointing to the router, we can confirm it by looking at the core switch's routing table.

```
Core-SW01#show ip route | b Gate
Gateway of last resort is 10.100.252.253 to network 0.0.0.0

S*      0.0.0.0/0 [1/0] via 10.100.252.253
        10.0.0.0/8 is variably subnetted, 2 subnets, 2 masks
C          10.100.252.0/24 is directly connected, GigabitEthernet2
L          10.100.252.1/32 is directly connected, GigabitEthernet2
```

This is easy enough to fix; we just need to remove the current static route and add a new one that points to the FTD's IP.

```
Core-SW01#conf t
Enter configuration commands, one per line.  End with CNTL/Z.
Core-SW01(config)#no ip route 0.0.0.0 0.0.0.0 10.100.252.253
Core-SW01(config)#ip route 0.0.0.0 0.0.0.0 10.100.252.254
```

But when I try to ping again, we can see it's still not working.

```
Core-SW01(config)#do ping 11.11.11.11
Type escape sequence to abort.
Sending 5, 100-byte ICMP Echos to 11.11.11.11, timeout is 2 seconds:
.....
Success rate is 0 percent (0/5)
```

A great tool we can see to understand what is happening to packets is the packet-tracer command. This shows us the actual packet flow discussed above and lets us know why the packet is being dropped. We will be using this tool a lot in the real world and likely in this chapter. You can run packet-tracer either from the FTD's CLI or through the FMC.

This time I used the CLI, and we can see the packet was dropped because the routing table didn't know how to reach the destination.

```
> packet-tracer input Inside icmp 10.100.252.100 0 0 11.11.11.11

Result:
input-interface: Inside(vrfid:0)
input-status: up
input-line-status: up
Action: drop
Drop-reason: (no-route) No route to host, Drop-location: frame
0x000055dccfb2ab79 flow (NA)/NA
```

When we check the FTD's routing table, we can see that a default route is not configured!

```
> show route | begin Gate
Gateway of last resort is not set

C       10.100.252.0 255.255.255.0 is directly connected, Inside
L       10.100.252.254 255.255.255.255 is directly connected, Inside
C       20.0.1.0 255.255.255.0 is directly connected, Outside
L       20.0.1.101 255.255.255.255 is directly connected, Outside
```

To fix it, all I need to do is add a default gateway on the FTD and push the changes.

Add Static Route Configuration

Type: ⦿ IPv4   ◯ IPv6

Interface*

Outside   ▾

(Interface starting with this icon 🔁 signifies it is available for route leak)

Available Network C   +   Selected Network

🔍 Search   any-ipv4   🗑

any-ipv4
IPv4-Benchmark-Tests
IPv4-Link-Local
IPv4-Multicast
IPv4-Private-10.0.0.0-8
IPv4-Private-172.16.0.0-12   ▾

Gateway*

20.0.1.254   ▾   +

Metric:

1

(1 - 254)

Tunneled: ☐ (Used only for default Route)

Route Tracking:

▾   +

Cancel   OK

346

Now if I try to ping again from the core switch, everything works fine!

```
Core-SW01(config)#do ping 11.11.11.11
Type escape sequence to abort.
Sending 5, 100-byte ICMP Echos to 11.11.11.11, timeout is 2 seconds:
!!!!!
Success rate is 100 percent (5/5), round-trip min/avg/max = 1/203/1008 ms
```

While the actual exam probably will not ask too many routing-related troubleshooting questions, it is good to keep in mind that even though you may be focused on security, you may still need to solve the odd networking problem.

Connection Events

Once we are sure the firewall is receiving traffic, the best place to start troubleshooting packet egress is through Connection Events under the Analysis tab. This page gives you detailed information about all the connections that are logged by the FTD. It should go without saying, but you need to make sure your all your ACP rules are configured to log all the connections you care about.

The Action tab on the Connection Events page gives a quick Allow or Block answer for each connection.

				FMC	Overview	Analysis	Policies	Devices	Objects	AMP
				CISCO Events						

Bookmark This Page | Reporting | Dashboard | \

Connection Events (switch workflow)

No Search Constraints (Edit Search)

Connections with Application Details   Table View of Connection Events

Jump to...

		↓ First Packet	Last Packet	Action	Reason	Initiator IP	Initiator Country	Responder IP	Responder Country
▼	☐	2020-08-18 00:37:12		Block		192.168.255.2		11.11.11.11	🇺🇸 USA
▼	☐	2020-08-18 00:23:09		Allow		💻 192.168.255.1		11.11.11.11	🇺🇸 USA
▼	☐	2020-08-18 00:07:07		Allow		💻 10.100.252.1		11.11.11.11	🇺🇸 USA
▼	☐	2020-08-17 23:32:52		Allow		💻 10.100.252.1		11.11.11.11	🇺🇸 USA

By default, the page will show more application details. If you want to drill down into more connection-specific info, you can either click the left-most triangle next the connection event or select the Table View of Connection Events tab. This view adds more useful detail, such as what access control rule is being matched. In the case of 192.168.255.2, it is matching a rule called Block Loopback, which is probably why that traffic is being blocked.

Access Control × Policy	Access Control Rule ×	Network Analysis Policy ×	Prefilter Policy ×
Base	Block Loopback	No Rules Active	Testlab - Prefilter Policy
Base	Permit All Traffic	Balanced Security and Connectivity	Testlab - Prefilter Policy
Base	Permit All Traffic	Balanced Security and Connectivity	Testlab - Prefilter Policy
Base	Permit All Traffic	Balanced Security and Connectivity	Testlab - Prefilter Policy

FMC also has a pretty powerful search feature that will let us filter the Connection Events page (and others!) based on everything from the standard IP information you would expect all the way to QoS details.

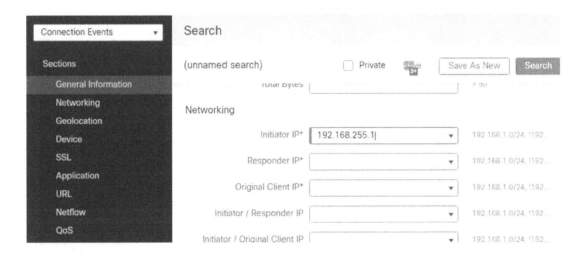

Packet Capture

If the traffic is not creating a connection event, or if FMC says the connection is allowed but the traffic is still not making it through the firewall, then it may be time to try looking at a packet capture tool.

Fortunately, Firepower has one built in that we can use! If you are using the latest version of FMC, you can access the packet capture directly from the Devices page by clicking the three vertical dots on the right side of the firewall and selecting Capture w/Trace.

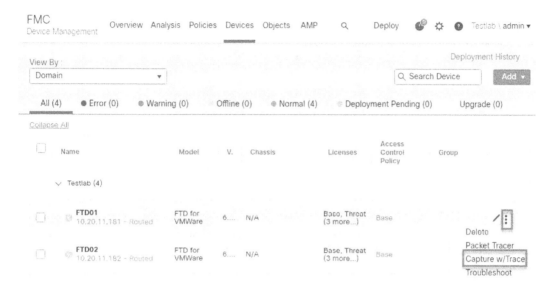

Otherwise, you can access the capture tool through Advanced Troubleshooting on the Health Monitoring page.

To add a capture, click the Add Capture button and enter in the traffic details you want to capture. It is a good idea to check the Trace option at the bottom. This will run a packet tracer on the matched traffic so you can see what is happening through the firewall. You can also choose to adjust the buffer and packet size if needed.

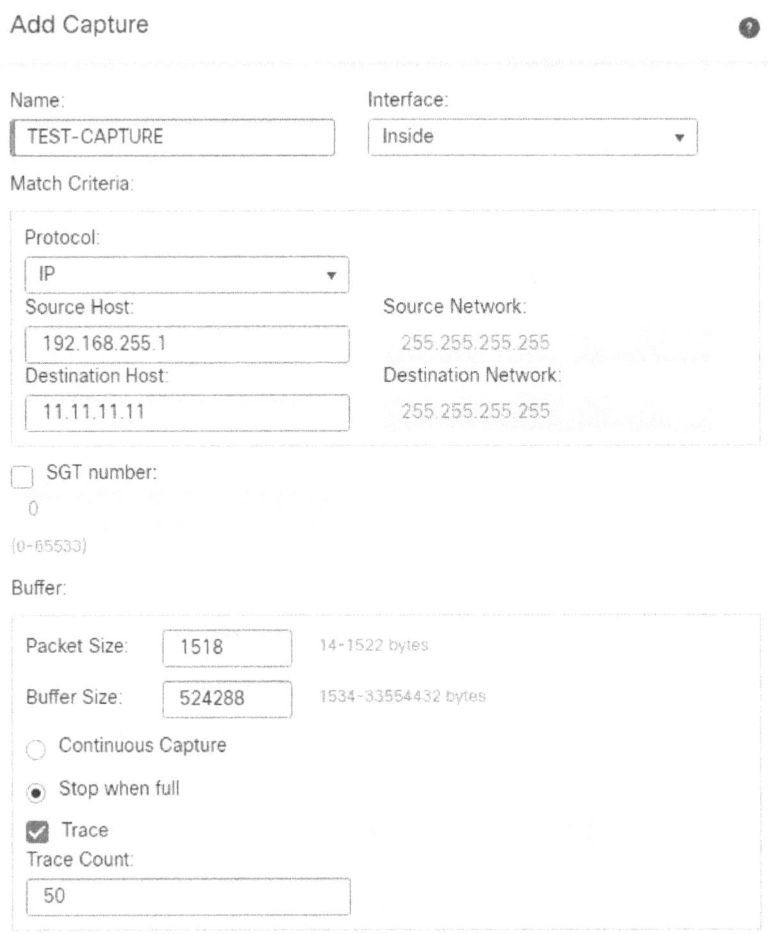

Add Capture

Name:

TEST-CAPTURE

Interface:

Inside ▼

Match Criteria:

Protocol:

IP ▼

Source Host:

192.168.255.1

Source Network:

255.255.255.255

Destination Host:

11.11.11.11

Destination Network:

255.255.255.255

☐ SGT number:

0

(0-65533)

Buffer:

Packet Size: 1518   14-1522 bytes

Buffer Size: 524288   1534-33554432 bytes

○ Continuous Capture

◉ Stop when full

☑ Trace

Trace Count:

50

Once the capture is started, try generating some traffic to re-create the situation. After you are done, either refresh the page or enable auto-refresh to see the captured output. If you left Trace enabled, FMC will show you a trace for every captured session (up to 50 by default); this makes it easy to track down what is happening to your traffic on a larger scale.

If you want a more structured look at the output, you can use the tree format to show each phase as a folder that you can expand or collapse as you please.

You can also choose to save the capture as a PCAP file with the disk icon on the capture page. This lets you open the capture up in Wireshark for more convenient analysis.

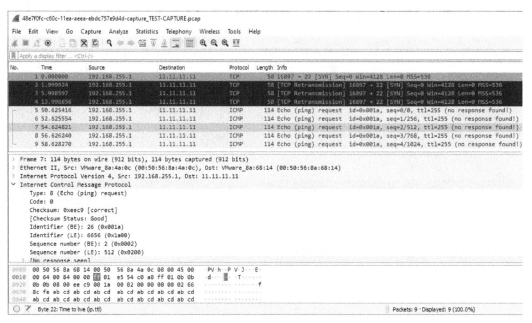

If you need more control over your capture, then you should be using the FTD's CLI to get the job done. To make a capture, you use the `capture` command just as you would with the ASA platform. The CLI gives you a ton of options that you can use to be very selective about what you want in your packet capture.

```
> capture SSH
  buffer               Configure size of capture buffer, default is 512 KB
  circular-buffer      Overwrite buffer from beginning when full, default is non-
circular
  ethernet-type        Capture Ethernet packets of a particular type, default is
IP
  file-size            Configure size of capture file in MB (32 - 10000)
  headers-only         Capture only L2, L3 and L4 headers of packet without data
in them
  include-decrypted    Include IPsec/SSL VPN decrypted packets in the capture
  interface            Capture packets on a specific interface
  match                Capture packets based on match criteria
  packet-length        Configure maximum length to save from each packet, default
is 1518 bytes option with a slow console connection may result in an excessive
amount of non-displayed packets due to performance limitations.
  stop                 Stop packet capture
  trace                Trace the captured packets
  type                 Capture packets based on a particular type
  <cr>
```

The main choice is what interface you want to do the packet capture on. FTD lets you capture from any of your data interfaces but also lets you do it on more specialized ones like the management interface or the control plane. I also opted to turn on the `trace` option for the capture.

```
> capture SSH trace interface
  cplane               Capture packets on controlplane interface
  data-plane           Capture packets on dataplane interface
  management-plane     Capture packets on managementplane interface
```

```
nlp_int_tap          Capture packets on nlp_int_tap interface
Inside               Name of interface GigabitEthernet0/1
Outside              Name of interface GigabitEthernet0/0
Test01               Name of interface Tunnel10
diagnostic           Name of interface Management0/0
```

Once the interface is selected, we need to pick what protocol we are interested in. If you want all traffic, pick IP. I will go ahead and pick TCP since I want to capture SSH traffic in this example.

```
> capture SSH trace interface Inside match
  0-255    Enter protocol number (0 - 255) (0..255)
  ah
  eigrp
  esp
  gre
  icmp
  icmp6
  igmp
  igrp
  ip
  ipinip
  ipsec
  isis     Intermediate System to Intermediate System Protocol
  mac      Mac-address filter
  nos
  ospf
  pcp
  pim
  pptp
  sctp
  snp
  tcp
  udp
```

Next we need to specify the source addresses that will be captured. You enter an IPv4 or IPv6 address or network, or use any for all sources.

```
> capture SSH trace interface Inside match tcp
  A.B.C.D            Source IPv4 address
  X:X:X:X::X/<0-128> Source IPv6 address/prefix
  any                Abbreviation for source address and mask of 0.0.0.0
0.0.0.0
  any4               Abbreviation for source address and mask of 0.0.0.0
0.0.0.0
  any6               Abbreviation for source prefix ::/0
  host               Use this keyword to configure source host
```

The destination choices are the same except we can also specify ranges.

```
> capture SSH trace interface Inside match tcp any
  A.B.C.D            Destination IPv4 address
  X:X:X:X::X/<0-128> Destination IPv6 address/prefix
  any                Abbreviation for destination address and mask of 0.0.0.0
0.0.0.0
  any4               Abbreviation for destination address and mask of 0.0.0.0
0.0.0.0
  any6               Abbreviation for destination prefix ::/0
  eq                 Port equal to operator
```

```
      gt                 Port greater than operator
      host               Use this keyword to configure destination host
      lt                 Port less than operator
      neq                Port not equal to operator
      range              Port range operator
```

Finally, we need to select the destination port.

```
> capture SSH trace interface Inside match tcp any any eq
  1-65535              Enter port number (1 - 65535) (1..65535)
  aol
  bgp
  chargen
  cifs
  citrix-ica
  cmd
  ctiqbe
  daytime
  discard
--- trimmed for brevity ---
```

With all that out of the way, we now have a command that will capture all SSH traffic.

```
> capture SSH trace interface Inside match tcp any any eq 22
> show capture SSH

3 packets captured

   1: 08:02:06.290527        192.168.255.1.17921 > 11.11.11.11.22: S
855355995:855355995(0) win 4128 <mss 536>
   2: 08:02:08.290420        192.168.255.1.17921 > 11.11.11.11.22: S
855355995:855355995(0) win 4128 <mss 536>
   3: 08:02:12.289856        192.168.255.1.17921 > 11.11.11.11.22: S
855355995:855355995(0) win 4128 <mss 536>
3 packets shown
```

If you need more control you can specify the type of packet you are interested in; this lets you easily match more specialized traffic.

```
> capture LAB-SSH type
  asp-drop    Capture packets dropped with a particular reason
  inline-tag  Capture packets with L2 inline SGT
  isakmp      Capture encrypted and decrypted ISAKMP payloads
  lacp        Capture inbound and outbound layer two LACP data on one or more
interfaces
  raw-data    Capture inbound and outbound packets on one or more interfaces
  tls-proxy   Capture decrypted inbound and outbound data from TLS Proxy on one
or more interfaces
  webvpn      Capture WebVPN transactions for a specified user
```

For example, if you want to capture a drop reason, you can use the asp-drop type. While the output only shows a handful of options, there are in fact 468 options that you can pick from!

```
> capture LAB-SSH type asp-drop
  a-module                              Packet is unknown or traced
```

```
  access-list                            Capture asp-drop packets that
match access-list
  acl-drop                               Flow is denied by configured
rule
  all                                    All packet drop reasons
  app-recv-queue-not-ready               Application Recv Queue not
ready
  appid                                  Blocked or blacklisted by the
AppID preprocessor
  async-lock-queue-limit                 Async lock queue limit
exceeded
  back-orifice                           Blocked or blacklisted by the
back orifice preprocessor
  backplane-channel-null                 Backplane channel was NULL
  bad-crypto                             Bad crypto return in packet
--- trimmed for brevity ---
```

I will pick the `acl-drop` ASP just for fun. This will capture any packet that is blocked by an access rule. When I check the output, I can see a couple of VRRP packets and that an OSPF packet was denied.

```
> capture DROP type asp-drop acl-drop match ip any any
> show capture DROP
Target:    OTHER
Hardware:  NGFWv
Cisco Adaptive Security Appliance Software Version 9.15(0)8
ASLR enabled, text region 55dccd55c000-55dcd1968aad

42 packets captured

   1: 00:14:53.414056       20.0.1.252 > 224.0.0.18  ip-proto-112, length 20
Drop-reason: (acl-drop) Flow is denied by configured rule, Drop-location: frame
0x000055dccfb21f24 flow (NA)/NA

   2: 00:14:54.411950       20.0.1.252 > 224.0.0.18  ip-proto-112, length 20
Drop-reason: (acl-drop) Flow is denied by configured rule, Drop-location: frame
0x000055dccfb21f24 flow (NA)/NA


   3: 00:14:57.416726       20.0.1.252 > 224.0.0.5  ip-proto-89, length 44
Drop-reason: (acl-drop) Flow is denied by configured rule, Drop-location: frame
0x000055dccfb21f24 flow (NA)/NA
```

Hopefully, you can see how powerful this is when trying to capture just the traffic you are interested in when you are on a busy production firewall.

Regardless of how you do your packet capture, remember that you will often have to take several captures to get the whole story. For example, you might capture the inside interface to ensure FTD gets the packet and look at the trace for clues. Then capture the outside interface to ensure the packet leaves the interface and to see if the neighbor has any replies.

Packet Tracer

Packet Tracer is simply awesome; it lets you see exactly how the firewall will treat the traffic you are interested in. Once you start to use Packet Tracer, you will start to get annoyed when other vendor firewalls do not have a similar feature!

To access Packet Tracer from the FMC, head back to Advanced Troubleshooting and select Packet Tracer. You can also access it from the device page by clicking the same menu we used in the preceding section.

Advanced Troubleshooting
FTD01
File Download   Threat Defense CLI   Packet Tracer   Capture w/Trace

Select the packet type and supply the packet parameters. Click start to trace the packet.

Packet type:	TCP			Interface*:	Inside
Source*:	IP address (IPv4)	192.168.255.2		Source Port*:	44444
Destination*:	IP address (IPv4)	11.11.11.11		Destination Port*:	22
SGT number:	SGT number... (0-65533)	VLAN ID:	VLAN ID... (1-4090)	Destination Mac Address:	XXXX.XXXX.XXXX
Output Format:	summary				

Clear   Start

On the Packet Tracer page, we need to fill out all the connection details we want to test with. This includes the protocol, the source and destination addresses, and the ports. One thing you might not be used to entering is the source port since we usually concern ourselves with the destination port. Since the source port is typically chosen at random, you can pick any value for this field. The exception would be if you are trying to test returning traffic through the firewall.

To test this out, I am using a loopback on the core switch from the topology above and I am trying to reach the "internet" address 11.11.11.11. I'll explain the various phases we see in the output. Speaking of output, you can also set the format to have more detail, or in an XML format if you are using the feature with automation.

The first phase we see is capture; this is because I did not stop the packet capture from the previous section and the session is matching one of the filters.

```
Phase: 1
Type: CAPTURE
Subtype:
Result: ALLOW
Config:
Additional Information:
MAC Access list
```

Phase 2 is seeing if any mac access-lists apply to the connection, but we can safely ignore this step when the FTD is in routed mode.

```
Phase: 2
Type: ACCESS-LIST
Subtype:
Result: ALLOW
Config:
Implicit Rule
Additional Information:
MAC Access list
```

Phase 3 is the FTD making sure it can determine the egress interface. If the FTD can't figure out where to send the packet, this is usually a routing issue such as your device doesn't have a default route.

```
Phase: 3
Type: INPUT-ROUTE-LOOKUP
Subtype: Resolve Egress Interface
Result: ALLOW
Config:
Additional Information:
Found next-hop 20.0.1.254 using egress ifc  Outside(vrfid:0)
```

Phase 4 is where my firewall is checking the Access Control policy; in this case the traffic is blocked by a rule called Block Loopback. The output also shows the raw ACL entry being matched; the basic syntax is still similar to what you would find on an ASA, so it is easy to understand why the rule is matching in most cases.

```
Phase: 4
Type: ACCESS-LIST
Subtype: log
Result: DROP
Config:
access-group CSM_FW_ACL_ global
access-list CSM_FW_ACL_ advanced deny ip ifc Inside host 192.168.255.2 ifc
Outside host 11.11.11.11 rule-id 268437504 event-log flow-start
access-list CSM_FW_ACL_ remark rule-id 268437504: ACCESS POLICY: Base -
Mandatory
access-list CSM_FW_ACL_ remark rule-id 268437504: L4 RULE: Block Loopback
Additional Information:
```

The last section shows the result and a summary of the decision process including the final action and the drop reason. The tool doesn't always give you a clear-cut solution to your problem, but it does, usually at least, put you on the right path.

```
Result:
input-interface: Inside(vrfid:0)
input-status: up
```

```
input-line-status: up
output-interface: Outside(vrfid:0)
output-status: up
output-line-status: up
Action: drop
Drop-reason: (acl-drop) Flow is denied by configured rule, Drop-location: frame
0x000055dccfb21f24 flow (NA)/NA
```

We can also do this through the FTD CLI, and it does give us a bit more options than FMC does. To run Packet Tracer, type **packet-tracer input** and then select the interface that will input the traffic. I will be using the inside interface.

```
> packet-tracer input
  Inside      Name of interface GigabitEthernet0/1
  Outside     Name of interface GigabitEthernet0/0
  diagnostic  Name of interface Management0/0
```

Then we select the packet type / protocol of the traffic we are testing. I will stick with my SSH example, so I will pick TCP.

```
> packet-tracer input Inside
  esp      Enter this keyword if the trace packet is ESP
  gre      Enter this keyword if the carrier trace packet is GRE
  icmp     Enter this keyword if the trace packet is ICMP
  ipip     Enter this keyword if the carrier trace packet is IP in IP
  rawip    Enter this keyword if the trace packet is RAW IP
  sctp     Enter this keyword if the trace packet is SCTP
  tcp      Enter this keyword if the trace packet is TCP
  udp      Enter this keyword if the trace packet is UDP
  vlan-id  Specify VLAN id for the flow
```

Next, we enter a source address. This can be an IPv4 address, an IPv6 address, or a FQDN. For more advanced examples, you can also enter a username, a VLAN ID if the traffic is tagged, or a security group. Since I know the last address is blocked by my policy, I will select another loopback address to keep things interesting.

```
> packet-tracer input Inside tcp
  A.B.C.D         Enter the Source address if ipv4
  X:X:X:X::X      Enter the Source address if ipv6
  fqdn            Enter this keyword if an FQDN is specified as source address
  inline-tag      Enter this keyword if trace packet is embedded with L2 CMD
Header
  security-group  Enter this keyword if a security group is specified as source
address
  user            Enter this keyword if a user is specified as source address
```

The source port typically does not matter all that much, so just pick a random value. I prefer using 44444 since it's easy to type.

```
> packet-tracer input Inside tcp 192.168.255.1
  0-65535          Enter port number (0 - 65535) (0..65535)
  aol
  bgp
  chargen
  cifs
  citrix-ica
```

```
--- trimmed for brevity ---
```

The destination address is largely the same except you cannot pick the more advanced options since a user is not something you can resolve into a destination. Also, if you enter an IPv6 source address, your only option will be a IPv6 destination.

```
> packet-tracer input Inside tcp 192.168.255.1 44444
  A.B.C.D          Enter the destination ipv4 address
  fqdn             Enter this keyword if an FQDN is specified as destination
address
  security-group   Enter this keyword if a security group is specified as
destination address
```

We will stick with SSH as the destination port. You can enter the port number or the well-known name.

```
> packet-tracer input Inside tcp 192.168.255.1 44444 11.11.11.11
  0-65535          Enter port number (0 - 65535) (0..65535)
  aol
  bgp
  chargen
  cifs
  citrix-ica
--- trimmed for brevity ---
```

The final section lets us do some cool things like actually transmit a generated, packet which can be useful if you want to create a log or see if an upstream device receives it. You also have options for dealing with VPN traffic, and you can adjust the format.

```
> packet-tracer input Inside tcp 192.168.255.1 44444 11.11.11.11 22
  bypass-checks   Bypass all security checks for simulated packet
  decrypted       Treat simulated packet as IPsec/SSL VPN decrypted
  detailed        Dump more detailed information
  persist         Enable long term tracing and follow tracing in cluster
  transmit        Allow simulated packet to transmit from device
  vxlan-inner     Specify inner packet using VLXN encapsulation
  xml             Output in xml format
  |               Output modifiers
  <cr>
```

Now we will have a look at the output of our `packet-tracer` command.

```
> packet-tracer input Inside tcp 192.168.255.1 44444 11.11.11.11 22
```

Phase 1 shows I still have not disabled the packet captures; it is worth noting that the phases only appear when they apply to the connection. If I had remembered to disable the capture, then phase 1 would be the mac access-list match.

```
Phase: 1
Type: CAPTURE
Subtype:
Result: ALLOW
Config:
Additional Information:
MAC Access list
```

Phase 2 will practically always be allow since routed mode does not support MAC ACLs at this time.

```
Phase: 2
Type: ACCESS-LIST
Subtype:
Result: ALLOW
Config:
Implicit Rule
Additional Information:
MAC Access list
```

Phase 3 is the egress routing lookup because this is the same topology; it is still going out the outside interface.

```
Phase: 3
Type: INPUT-ROUTE-LOOKUP
Subtype: Resolve Egress Interface
Result: ALLOW
Config:
Additional Information:
Found next-hop 20.0.1.254 using egress ifc  Outside(vrfid:0)
```

Phase 4 is the ACL lookup, this time we are hitting a rule called Permit All Traffic, which as the name implies is allowing the traffic. But the "Additional information" message notes that traffic will be sent to Snort for further processing.

```
Phase: 4
Type: ACCESS-LIST
Subtype: log
Result: ALLOW
Config:
access-group CSM_FW_ACL_ global
access-list CSM_FW_ACL_ advanced permit ip any any rule-id 268435457
access-list CSM_FW_ACL_ remark rule-id 268435457: ACCESS POLICY: Base -
Mandatory
access-list CSM_FW_ACL_ remark rule-id 268435457: L7 RULE: Permit All Traffic
Additional Information:
 This packet will be sent to snort for additional processing where a verdict
will be reached
```

Phase 5 is any global policy settings that apply to the connection. By default, this will apply a TCP map to normalize connections to prevent certain attacks. There are some cases where you will need to adjust the connection settings for traffic to work properly.

```
Phase: 5
Type: CONN-SETTINGS
Subtype:
Result: ALLOW
Config:
class-map class-default
 match any
policy-map global_policy
 class class-default
  set connection advanced-options UM_STATIC_TCP_MAP
service-policy global_policy global
Additional Information:
```

Phases 6 through 9 are the packet going through NAT and IP options.

```
Phase: 6
Type: NAT
Subtype: per-session
Result: ALLOW
Config:
Additional Information:

Phase: 7
Type: TP-OPTIONS
Subtype:
Result: ALLOW
Config:
Additional Information:

Phase: 8
Type: NAT
Subtype: per-session
Result: ALLOW
Config:
Additional Information:

Phase: 9
Type: IP-OPTIONS
Subtype:
Result: ALLOW
Config:
Additional Information:
```

Phase 10 is where the actual flow would be created in the firewall.

```
Phase: 10
Type: FLOW-CREATION
Subtype:
Result: ALLOW
Config:
Additional Information:
New flow created with id 3815, packet dispatched to next module
```

Phases 11 and 12 are the packet going through the Snort process; ultimately the packet is allowed.

```
Phase: 11
Type: EXTERNAL-INSPECT
Subtype:
Result: ALLOW
Config:
Additional Information:
Application: 'SNORT Inspect'

Phase: 12
Type: SNORT
Subtype:
Result: ALLOW
Config:
Additional Information:
Snort Trace:
Packet: TCP, SYN, seq 316484663
Session: new snort session
AppID: service unknown (0), application unknown (0)
Firewall: allow rule, id 268435457, allow
```

```
Snort id 1, NAP id 1, IPS id 0, Verdict PASS
Snort Verdict: (pass-packet) allow this packet
```

The last two phases have to do with routing the packet out of the firewall.

```
Phase: 13
Type: INPUT-ROUTE-LOOKUP-FROM-OUTPUT-ROUTE-LOOKUP
Subtype: Resolve Preferred Egress interface
Result: ALLOW
Config:
Additional Information:
Found next-hop 20.0.1.254 using egress ifc  Outside(vrfid:0)

Phase: 14
Type: ADJACENCY-LOOKUP
Subtype: Resolve Nexthop IP address to MAC
Result: ALLOW
Config:
Additional Information:
Found adjacency entry for Next-hop 20.0.1.254 on interface  Outside
Adjacency :Active
MAC address 0000.5e00.0154 hits 0 reference 1
```

The result sums up all the steps we just discussed, we can see the action as well as the input and output interfaces.

```
Result:
input-interface: Inside(vrfid:0)
input-status: up
input-line-status: up
output-interface: Outside(vrfid:0)
output-status: up
output-line-status: up
Action: allow
```

Interface Errors

Another area that can cause an incident is interface errors. Usually errors will not fully kill traffic unless they are severe. Rather, you would typically see speed slow down a lot since several packets are dropped for various layer 1 / layer 2 reasons, such as a duplex mismatch.

The easiest way to check for errors is simply do a `show interface` on the FTD. There is not a lot of traffic going through my lab firewalls, but we can see in the bolded sections that my FTD does not have any errors and has low traffic but does have 99316 dropped packets. While a lab firewall having almost 100K dropped packets sounds bad…remember that a firewall's main job is to drop packets.

```
> show interface Inside
Interface GigabitEthernet0/1 "Inside", is up, line protocol is up
  Hardware is net_vmxnet3, BW 10000 Mbps, DLY 10 usec
        Auto-Duplex(Full-duplex), Auto-Speed(10000 Mbps)
        Input flow control is unsupported, output flow control is unsupported
        MAC address 0050.568a.6814, MTU 1500
        IP address 10.100.252.254, subnet mask 255.255.255.0
```

```
    143394 packets input, 11019182 bytes, 0 no buffer
    Received 0 broadcasts, 0 runts, 0 giants
    0 input errors, 0 CRC, 0 frame, 0 overrun, 0 ignored, 0 abort
    0 pause input, 0 resume input
    0 L2 decode drops
    19397 packets output, 1809466 bytes, 0 underruns
    0 pause output, 0 resume output
    0 output errors, 0 collisions, 0 interface resets
    0 late collisions, 0 deferred
    0 input reset drops, 0 output reset drops
    input queue (blocks free curr/low): hardware (0/0)
    output queue (blocks free curr/low): hardware (0/0)
  Traffic Statistics for "Inside":
    143402 packets input, 8285838 bytes
    19397 packets output, 1537908 bytes
    99316 packets dropped
  1 minute input rate 0 pkts/sec,   45 bytes/sec
  1 minute output rate 0 pkts/sec,   8 bytes/sec
  1 minute drop rate, 0 pkts/sec
  5 minute input rate 0 pkts/sec,   40 bytes/sec
  5 minute output rate 0 pkts/sec,   8 bytes/sec
  5 minute drop rate, 0 pkts/sec
```

If you have a Firepower 4100 or higher, it might be useful to check the fabric interconnect for errors as well. This can be done from the default UCS CLI you get when you connect to the Firepower Chassis Manager. Simply go under the `eth-uplink` scope and type the **show stats** command. One nice thing about this output is that the errors and loss stats are separated into different sections.

```
A4140-1# scope eth-uplink
A4140-1 /eth-uplink # show stats

Ether Error Stats:
    Time Collected: 2020-08-19T23:21:14.795
    Monitored Object: fabric/lan/A/pc-1/err-stats
    Suspect: No
    Rcv (errors): 0
    Align (errors): 0
    Fcs (errors): 0
    Xmit (errors): 0
    Under Size (errors): 0
    Out Discard (errors): 0
    Int Mac Tx (errors): 0
    Int Mac Rx (errors): 0
    Deferred Tx (errors): 0
    Thresholded: Xmit Delta Min

Ether Loss Stats:
    Time Collected: 2020-08-19T23:21:14.795
    Monitored Object: fabric/lan/A/pc-1/loss-stats
    Suspect: No
    Single Collision (errors): 0
    Multi Collision (errors): 0
    Late Collision (errors): 0
    Carrier Sense (errors): 0
    Giants (errors): 0
    Symbol (errors): 0
    SQE Test (errors): 0
    Excess Collision (errors): 0
    Thresholded: 0
```

```
Ether Pause Stats:
    Time Collected: 2020-08-19T23:21:14.795
    Monitored Object: fabric/lan/A/pc-1/pause-stats
    Suspect: No
    Recv Pause (pause): 0
    Xmit Pause (pause): 0
    Resets (resets): 0
    Thresholded: 0

Ether Rx Stats:
    Time Collected: 2020-08-19T23:21:14.795
    Monitored Object: fabric/lan/A/pc-1/rx-stats
    Suspect: No
    Total Packets (packets): 34701
    Total Bytes (bytes): 3521163
    Unicast Packets (packets): 1967
    Multicast Packets (packets): 32309
    Broadcast Packets (packets): 425
    Jumbo Packets (packets): 0
    Thresholded: 0

Ether Tx Stats:
    Time Collected: 2020-08-19T23:21:14.795
    Monitored Object: fabric/lan/A/pc-1/tx-stats
    Suspect: No
    Total Packets (packets): 11475
    Total Bytes (bytes): 1579165
    Unicast Packets (packets): 0
    Multicast Packets (packets): 11475
    Broadcast Packets (packets): 0
    Jumbo Packets (packets): 0
    Thresholded: 0
```

If you want to run a `show interface` on a higher-model Firepower appliance, you need to connect to the module and then the FTD instance first.

```
A4140-1# connect module 1 console
Telnet escape character is '~'.
Trying 127.5.1.1...
Connected to 127.5.1.1.
Escape character is '~'.

CISCO Serial Over LAN:
Close Network Connection to Exit

Firepower-module1>connect ftd
Connecting to ftd(FTD) console... enter exit to return to bootCLI

> show interface Port-channel 1
Interface Port-channel1 "Inside", is up, line protocol is up
  Hardware is EtherSVI, BW 1000 Mbps, DLY 10 usec
        MAC address 286f.7f02.b2cd, MTU 1500
        IP address 192.168.10.1, subnet mask 255.255.255.0
  Traffic Statistics for "Inside":
        12 packets input, 1021 bytes
        1 packets output, 28 bytes
        5 packets dropped
      1 minute input rate 0 pkts/sec,  0 bytes/sec
      1 minute output rate 0 pkts/sec,  0 bytes/sec
      1 minute drop rate, 0 pkts/sec
```

```
5 minute input rate 0 pkts/sec,  3 bytes/sec
5 minute output rate 0 pkts/sec,  0 bytes/sec
5 minute drop rate, 0 pkts/sec
```

NAT

Back in the dark days of firewall administration when the Cisco PIX was the fancy new firewall on the market, NAT was used to move all traffic through the firewall. This was called "NAT control," and it caused many sleepless nights!

Nowadays NAT is used more sanely, with the exception of some hairpin topologies and some VPN designs. But now the tricky thing about NAT is that a packet can often route through the firewall even without proper NAT configuration. The upstream device will likely drop the packet, but as far as FTD is concerned, it did its job correctly.

In fact, if you remember our previous Packet Tracer example, I glossed over the NAT section but there was not much there in the output. That is because NAT was not actually matching that traffic. Looking at the NAT configuration, we can see that the rule is matching traffic from the 172.16.0.0/12 private range.

You can also verify the NAT configuration with the `show nat` command on the FTD.

```
> show nat

Auto NAT Policies (Section 2)
1 (Inside) to (Outside) source dynamic IPv4-Private-172.16.0.0-12 interface
    translate_hits = 0, untranslate_hits = 0
```

I fixed the issue by changing the NAT configuration to match the 192.168.0.0/16 private network instead. We can verify the configuration is correct by running the `show nat` command again.

```
> show nat

Auto NAT Policies (Section 2)
1 (Inside) to (Outside) source dynamic IPv4-Private-192.168.0.0-16 interface
    translate_hits = 0, untranslate_hits = 0
```

Now when I run `packet-tracer` again, we see that NAT is translating 192.168.255.1 to the outside interface address 20.0.1.101!

```
Phase: 6
Type: NAT
Subtype:
Result: ALLOW
Config:
object network IPv4-Private-192.168.0.0-16
 nat (Inside,Outside) dynamic interface
Additional Information:
Dynamic translate 192.168.255.1/44444 to 20.0.1.101/44444
```

To see the current translations going on in the firewall, you can use the `show xlate` command. The command has a lot of options to help you filter the output to what you are looking for, such as letting you specify the IP addresses and ports.

```
> show xlate
1 in use, 2 most used
Flags: D - DNS, e - extended, I - identity, i - dynamic, r - portmap,
       s - static, T - twice, N - net-to-net

ICMP PAT from Inside:192.168.255.1/33 to Outside:20.0.1.101/33 flags ri idle
0:00:02 timeout 0:00:30
```

The `packet-tracer` command can also be used to make sure your static NATs are working correctly. Simply enter in the connection information so that it reflects a host on the Internet. In my case I picked 1.2.3.4 as a source, going to a NAT address on my firewall.

```
> packet-tracer input Outside tcp 1.2.3.4 44444 20.0.1.200 443

Phase: 1
Type: ACCESS-LIST
Subtype:
Result: ALLOW
Config:
Implicit Rule
Additional Information:
```

```
Phase: 2
Type: UN-NAT
Subtype: static
Result: ALLOW
Config:
nat (Inside,Outside) source static TEST-SERVER SERVER-GLOBAL
Additional Information:
NAT divert to egress interface Inside(vrfid:0)
Untranslate 20.0.1.200/443 to 10.100.10.100/443

Phase: 3
Type: ACCESS-LIST
Subtype: log
Result: ALLOW
Config:
access-group CSM_FW_ACL_ global
access-list CSM_FW_ACL_ advanced permit ip any any rule-id 268435457
access-list CSM_FW_ACL_ remark rule-id 268435457: ACCESS POLICY: Base -
Mandatory
access-list CSM_FW_ACL_ remark rule-id 268435457: L7 RULE: Permit All Traffic
Additional Information:
 This packet will be sent to snort for additional processing where a verdict
will be reached

Phase: 4
Type: CONN SETTINGS
Subtype:
Result: ALLOW
Config:
class-map class-default
 match any
policy-map global_policy
 class class-default
  set connection advanced-options UM_STATIC_TCP_MAP
service-policy global_policy global
Additional Information:

Phase: 5
Type: NAT
Subtype:
Result: ALLOW
Config:
nat (Inside,Outside) source static TEST-SERVER SERVER-GLOBAL
Additional Information:
Static translate 1.2.3.4/44444 to 1.2.3.4/44444

--- trimmed for brevity ---
```

The last thing to keep in mind about NAT is that it is important to make sure NAT is not accidently affecting your VPN traffic by translating VPN traffic when it shouldn't. After these sections, you should have a pretty good idea at how to troubleshoot packets going through the Firepower device.

Data Acquisition (DAQ) Layer

Platform	Software						
Packet Ingress	DAQ	SI	ACP	SSL	Auth	IPS	NAP

The next component that Cisco recommends we look at is the Data Acquisition (DAQ) layer. We talked about the DAQ earlier in the chapter, but as a refresher, it simply translates the packet format into something that Snort can easily work with and then back again.

In the previous sections, we focused on making sure the firewall is receiving the ingress packets, and we also verified that the firewall can egress packets. So we know that if the packet enters the firewall but does not leave, it should be a software component that is picking on our poor packet.

Because DAQ is the gateway to the Snort engine, our main focus in the following sections is making sure the IPS isn't affecting traffic.

Inline Sets

Using inline sets can be useful when troubleshooting DAQ layer issues because it simplifies the environment but takes components like routing out of the equation. However, they are not always practical to use in a production environment when everything is already set up.

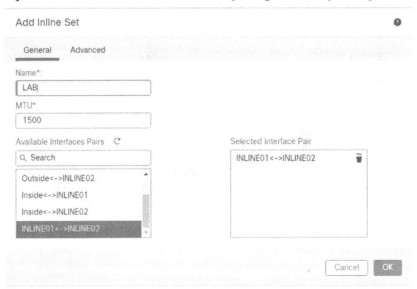

Capture Traffic at the DAQ Layer

We use the `capture-traffic` command to capture traffic at the DAQ layer; this is basically just an alias for `tcpdump` on the Linux system. We will need to tell FTD what domain to capture; global will be for all your data interfaces, and if you have a inline set, then you can capture that traffic as well. Since I just created a inline set, I'll use that. Since the command is using `tcpdump`, it will ask us what `tcpdump` options we want to use for the connection. In this example, I'll just use `-w capture.pcap` in order to name the PCAP file.

```
> capture-traffic

Please choose domain to capture traffic from:
  0 - eth0
  1 - Global
  2 - LAB inline set

Selection? 2

Please specify tcpdump options desired.
(or enter '?' for a list of supported options)
Options: -w capture.pcap
```

Once we have generated the traffic we want to capture, we need to actually get that PCAP file off the firewall. We can use the File Download tab in our handy Advanced Troubleshooting page to download the PCAP file. Simply enter the name and click the Download button.

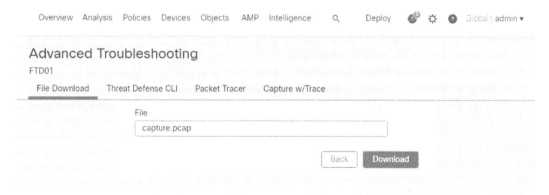

You can also SCP the file off the FTD by using the `file secure-copy` command.

```
> file secure-copy 10.20.2.80 the-packet-thrower /tmp/ capture.pcap
the-packet-thrower@10.20.2.80's password:
copy successful.
```

Because I chose to do a capture on an inline set, we see a lot more traffic than in our last capture since the inline interfaces are connected to my server network.

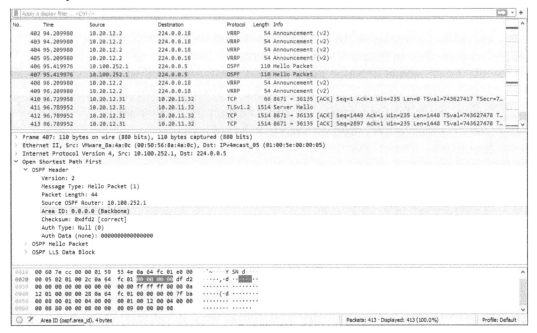

TAP

Once you confirm that traffic is not making it through the firewall, a potential next step is to bypass the FTD inspection phase to see if that helps. The main troubleshooting benefit of using inline sets is that you can easily enable TAP mode. When TAP mode is enabled, Firepower will not be able to enforce any action on a packet. This makes it handy for testing out new policies since you can see what Firepower will do without the risk of an outage.

Pre-filter Policy

Some connections are just not IPS friendly; sometimes the connection keeps getting incorrectly dropped by the policy, and sometimes it is just a waste of resources to inspect, such as the case with backup replication. We can use a fastpath rule in a pre-filter policy to bypass the IPS process for matching traffic. In this example, I created a fastpath rule that will prevent my SSH traffic from being dropped by the custom IPS rule.

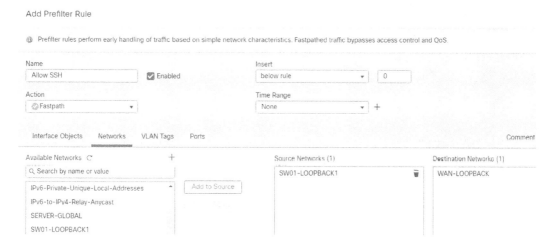

Once the policy is deployed, we can see that the SSH traffic is no longer being dropped!

```
> packet-tracer input Inside tcp 192.168.255.1 44444 11.11.11.11 22

Result:
input-interface: Inside(vrfid:0)
input-status: up
input-line-status: up
output-interface: Outside(vrfid:0)
output-status: up
output-line-status: up
Action: allow
```

Security Intelligence

Since the DAQ just translates the format, the first software component that inspects traffic is Security Intelligence. Fortunately, it is easy to determine if Security Intelligence is affecting your traffic, assuming logging is properly configured. You can ensure logging is enabled from the Security Intelligence tab in your ACP.

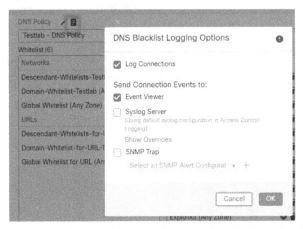

Once logging is working, you simply need to check the Security Intelligence events under the Analysis tab to see any SI events that could be affecting your traffic. Currently, I have four blocks; three of them is from a phishing site that I picked at random, and the other is an Azure site I made for this example.

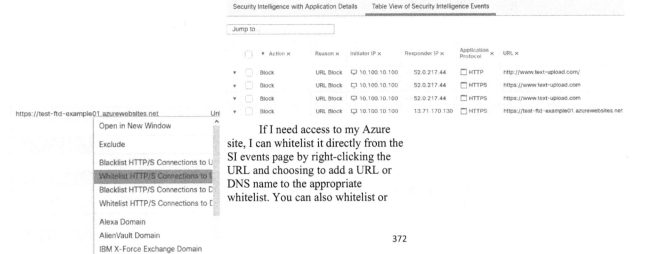

If I need access to my Azure site, I can whitelist it directly from the SI events page by right-clicking the URL and choosing to add a URL or DNS name to the appropriate whitelist. You can also whitelist or

372

blacklist an IP by right-clicking that instead.

FMC does not give you an easy way to view the IPs and URLs learned from SI updates inside the GUI, but you can access them from either the FMC or FTD's expert mode. This is handy for testing out the feature in labs so you know what will trigger a block, though keep in mind that these

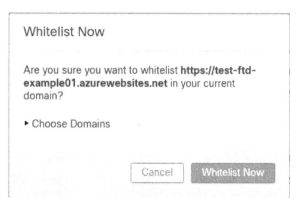

files update frequently, so you may be working with out-of-date information if you copy a file for study.

For the IP ranges you can look in /var/sf/iprep_download:

```
admin@ftd01:~$ grep "31 /var/sf/iprep_download/*
/var/sf/iprep_download/032ba433-c295-11e4-a919-d4ae5275a468.blf:31.210.117.131
/var/sf/iprep_download/032ba433-c295-11e4-a919-d4ae5275a468.blf:31.210.125.99
/var/sf/iprep_download/032ba433-c295-11e4-a919-d4ae5275a468.blf:31.210.125.105
/var/sf/iprep_download/032ba433-c295-11e4-a919-d4ae5275a468.blf:31.184.192.196
/var/sf/iprep_download/032ba433-c295-11e4-a919-d4ae5275a468.blf:31.172.30.4
/var/sf/iprep_download/032ba433-c295-11e4-a919-d4ae5275a468.blf:31.192.228.185
```

For the URL list, you can look in /var/sf/siurl_download:

```
admin@ftd01:~$ grep www /var/sf/siurl_download/*
/var/sf/siurl_download/032ba433-c295-11e4-a919-d4ae5275d599.lf:www.ex.ua
/var/sf/siurl_download/032ba433-c295-11e4-a919-d4ae5275d599.lf:www.x0x1x0.biz
/var/sf/siurl_download/032ba433-c295-11e4-a919-d4ae5275d599.lf:www.riodin.ru
/var/sf/siurl_download/032ba433-c295-11e4-a919-d4ae5275d599.lf:www.dat-media.ru
/var/sf/siurl_download/032ba433-c295-11e4-a919-d4ae5275d599.lf:www.kinoprofi.ru
/var/sf/siurl_download/032ba433-c295-11e4-a919-d4ae5275d599.lf:www.svadbarec.ru
```

For the DNS list, you can look in /var/sf/sidns_download:

```
> expert
admin@fmc01:~$ grep com /var/sf/sidns_download/*
/var/sf/sidns_download/032ba433-c295-11e4-a919-d4ae5275b77b:winsoft1.com
/var/sf/sidns_download/032ba433-c295-11e4-a919-d4ae5275b77b:homebuyline.com
/var/sf/sidns_download/032ba433-c295-11e4-a919-
d4ae5275b77b:www.invis1blearm3333.com
/var/sf/sidns_download/032ba433-c295-11e4-a919-d4ae5275b77b:bttimes.com
/var/sf/sidns_download/032ba433-c295-11e4-a919-
d4ae5275b77b:prcolina.prichaonica.com
```

Access Control Policy

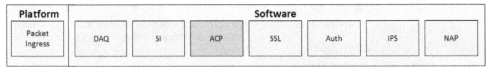

Once we know that SI is not blocking our traffic, the next component to look at is the Access Control policy (ACP). Because the goal of the ACP is to block or permit traffic going through the firewall, you will spend a lot of your troubleshooting efforts figuring out what access rules are causing your issue.

It can be useful to temporarily make a new permit or trust rule to see if it resolves the traffic issue. But if after the following sections you still can't identify the access rule that is matching then you may want to create a new blank policy that permits all traffic to get yourself out of the outage situation.

Capture

A good first move is to run a capture with trace enabled to see what ACL rule is being matched by the traffic. The benefit of a capture is that you can be looser about what you are tracing since every packet that is matched will be traced. In this case we can see that the traffic is hitting the default deny any rule at the bottom of the rule base.

```
> capture SSH trace interface Inside match tcp any any eq ssh
> show capture SSH packet-number 1 trace

5 packets captured

   1: 03:53:27.895476      10.100.10.100.60428 > 11.11.11.11.22: S
3337738250:3337738250(0) win 64240 <mss 1460,nop,wscale 8,nop,nop,sackOK>
Phase: 1
Type: CAPTURE
Subtype:
Result: ALLOW
Config:
Additional Information:
MAC Access list

Phase: 2
Type: ACCESS-LIST
Subtype:
Result: ALLOW
Config:
Implicit Rule
Additional Information:
```

```
MAC Access list

Phase: 3
Type: INPUT-ROUTE-LOOKUP
Subtype: Resolve Egress Interface
Result: ALLOW
Config:
Additional Information:
Found next-hop 20.0.1.254 using egress ifc  Outside(vrfid:0)

Phase: 4
Type: ACCESS-LIST
Subtype: log
Result: DROP
Config:
access-group CSM_FW_ACL_ global
access-list CSM_FW_ACL_ advanced deny ip any any rule-id 268435456 event-log
flow-start
access-list CSM_FW_ACL_ remark rule-id 268435456: ACCESS POLICY: Base - Default
access-list CSM_FW_ACL_ remark rule-id 268435456: L4 RULE: DEFAULT ACTION RULE
Additional Information:

Result:
input-interface: Inside(vrfid:0)
input-status: up
input-line-status: up
output-interface: Outside(vrfid:0)
output-status: up
output-line-status: up
Action: drop
Drop-reason: (acl-drop) Flow is denied by configured rule, Drop-location: frame
0x000055dccfb21f24 flow (NA)/NA
```

Packet Tracer - ACP

Packet Tracer remains a great option for quickly seeing if traffic is matching the wrong rule. I tend to prefer using Packet Tracer since it can be a lot faster than a capture if I know the connection information I am testing.

```
Phase: 3
Type: ACCESS-LIST
Subtype: log
Result: DROP
Config:
access-group CSM_FW_ACL_ global
access-list CSM_FW_ACL_ advanced deny ip any any rule-id 268435456 event-log
flow-start
access-list CSM_FW_ACL_ remark rule-id 268435456: ACCESS POLICY: Base - Default
access-list CSM_FW_ACL_ remark rule-id 268435456: L4 RULE: DEFAULT ACTION RULE
Additional Information:

Result:
input-interface: Inside(vrfid:0)
input-status: up
input-line-status: up
output-interface: Outside(vrfid:0)
output-status: up
output-line-status: up
Action: drop
```

```
Drop-reason: (acl-drop) Flow is denied by configured rule, Drop-location: frame
0x000055dccfb21f24 flow (NA)/NA
```

Firewall Engine Debug

Another good option for figuring out what ACL rule is matching
traffic is the firewall engine debug. This is a conditional debug that matches
the IP information you specify. It is not pretty, but it does tell you exactly
how each packet is processed. You can enable the feature through FTD CLI
with the `system support firewall-engine-debug` command.
After you type it, the system will prompt you for the connection
information you want to match. I will look for traffic going to 11.11.11.11
port 1234.

```
> system support firewall-engine-debug

Please specify an IP protocol: tcp
Please specify a client IP address: 10.100.10.100
Please specify a client port:
Please specify a server IP address: 11.11.11.11
Please specify a server port: 1234
Monitoring firewall engine debug messages

10.100.10.100-60449 > 11.11.11.11-1234 6 AS 1-1 I 0 Got start of flow event
from hardware with flags 00020001
10.100.10.100-60449 > 11.11.11.11-1234 6 AS 1-1 I 0 Logging SOF for event from
hardware with rule_id = 268437512 ruleAction = 4 ruleReason = 0
```

When the packet is denied, the debug returns a simple output that
includes a rule ID. To make it more useful, copy the value and then use
`show access-list` to figure out what rule the ID is referencing.

```
> show access-list | include 268437512
access-list CSM_FW_ACL_ line 16 remark rule-id 268437512: ACCESS POLICY: Base -
Mandatory
access-list CSM_FW_ACL_ line 17 remark rule-id 268437512: L4 RULE: Block Port
access-list CSM_FW_ACL_ line 18 advanced deny tcp ifc Inside any ifc Outside
any eq 1234 rule-id 268437512 event-log flow-start (hitcnt=5) 0x817c1cdd
```

Though if the traffic is permitted, the debug will return a lot more
information, including the proper rule name and details.

```
> system support firewall-engine-debug

Please specify an IP protocol: tcp
Please specify a client IP address: 10.100.10.100
Please specify a client port:
Please specify a server IP address: 11.11.11.11
Please specify a server port:
Monitoring firewall engine debug messages

10.100.10.100-60451 > 11.11.11.11-80 6 AS 1-1 I 1 new firewall session
10.100.10.100-60451 > 11.11.11.11-80 6 AS 1-1 I 1 Starting AC with minimum 2,
'Web Traffic', and SrcZone first with zones 2 -> 1, geo 0 -> 0, vlan 0, source
sgt type: 0, source sgt tag: 0, ISE sgt id: 0, dest sgt type: 0, ISE dest sgt
tag: 0, svc 0, payload 0, client 0, misc 0, user 9999997, icmpType 0, icmpCode
0
```

```
10.100.10.100-60451 > 11.11.11.11-80 6 AS 1-1 I 1 pending rule order 2, 'Web
Traffic', AppID
10.100.10.100-60451 > 11.11.11.11-80 6 AS 1-1 I 1 Starting AC with minimum 2,
'Web Traffic', and SrcZone first with zones 2 -> 1, geo 0 -> 0, vlan 0, source
sgt type: 0, source sgt tag: 0, ISE sgt id: 0, dest sgt type: 0, ISE dest sgt
tag: 0, svc 0, payload 0, client 0, misc 0, user 9999997, icmpType 0, icmpCode
0
10.100.10.100-60451 > 11.11.11.11-80 6 AS 1-1 I 1 pending rule order 2, 'Web
Traffic', AppID
10.100.10.100-60451 > 11.11.11.11-80 6 AS 1-1 I 1 Starting AC with minimum 2,
'Web Traffic', and SrcZone first with zones 2 -> 1, geo 0 -> 0, vlan 0, source
sgt type: 0, source sgt tag: 0, ISE sgt id: 0, dest sgt type: 0, ISE dest sgt
tag: 0, svc 0, payload 0, client 0, misc 0, user 9999997, icmpType 0, icmpCode
0
--- trimmed for brevity ---
```

Connection Events

Assuming logging is properly configured on every rule in the ACP, you can also rely on the Connection Events page on the Analysis page, which is a lot nicer than having to always be connected to your firewall's CLI for everything.

We looked at the search functionality earlier in the chapter, so I will search for packets that have been blocked. A handy feature that I'll mention is that I can save the search for later if I use it a lot, which is handy for operational filters that pop up in production, such as a search that matches your company's servers, for example.

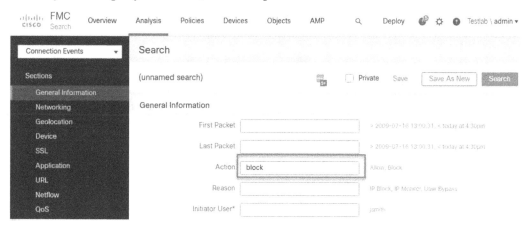

In the connection event's search results, we can see that there are three entries now. The action tab shows us that the packets are blocked, and we can keep scrolling to the right to see more information. I recommend switching to the table view for more details.

	↓ First Packet ✕	Action ✕	Initiator IP ✕	Ingress Security Zone ✕	Egress Security Zone ✕	Destination Port / ICMP Code ✕
▾ ☐	2020-08-20 21:53:27	Block	🖵 10.100.10.100	Inside	Outside	22 (ssh) / tcp
▾ ☐	2020-08-20 21:50:58	Block	🖵 10.100.10.100	Inside	Outside	22 (ssh) / tcp
▾ ☐	2020-08-20 21:46:25	Block	🖵 10.100.10.100	Inside	Outside	22 (ssh) / tcp

Once we scroll to the right enough, eventually we see the Access Control Policy and Access Control Rule tabs, which shows what ACP and rules are matching the traffic.

Access Control Policy ×	Access Control Rule ×	Network Analysis Policy ×	Prefilter Policy ×
Base	Default Action	Testlab – IPS SNORT2 – Policy	Testlab – Prefilter Policy
Base	Block Port	Testlab – IPS SNORT2 – Policy	Testlab – Prefilter Policy
Base	Default Action	Testlab – IPS SNORT2 – Policy	Testlab – Prefilter Policy

Hit Count

A newer feature that Cisco added to Firepower is the ability to see how often a rule is matching from the ACP page. While I think Cisco probably could have done a bit better with this feature (give us real-time hits!), it is still very handy for knowing how busy your rules are.

This is useful for troubleshooting because if you notice a rule is not matching a lot of traffic, you may have a problem with traffic hitting your other rules because of a misconfiguration.

The feature also lets you filter on rules that do not match so you can clean up your rule base a bit. The more you can remove unused rules, the better, since a cleaner ACP will be easier to understand if you do not work with it every day.

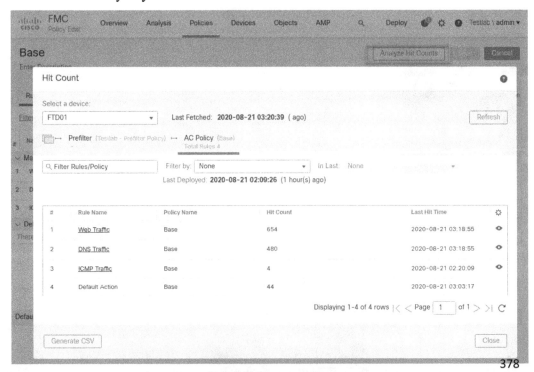

You can also get similar information from the CLI just by looking at `show access-list CSM_FW_ACL_`.

```
> show access-list CSM_FW_ACL_ | exclude hitcnt=0
access-list CSM_FW_ACL_; 11 elements; name hash: 0x4a69e3f3
access-list CSM_FW_ACL_ line 1 remark rule-id 268435458: PREFILTER POLICY:
Testlab - Prefilter Policy
access-list CSM_FW_ACL_ line 2 remark rule-id 268435458: RULE: DEFAULT TUNNEL
ACTION RULE
access-list CSM_FW_ACL_ line 8 remark rule-id 268437511: ACCESS POLICY: Base -
Mandatory
access-list CSM_FW_ACL_ line 9 remark rule-id 268437511: L7 RULE: Web Traffic
access-list CSM_FW_ACL_ line 10 advanced permit tcp ifc Inside any ifc Outside
any object-group HTTP rule-id 268437511 (hitcnt=19) 0x12cf3cb1
  access-list CSM_FW_ACL_ line 10 advanced permit tcp ifc Inside any ifc
Outside any eq www rule-id 268437511 (hitcnt=19) 0x17d1b922
access-list CSM_FW_ACL_ line 11 advanced permit tcp ifc Inside any ifc Outside
any object-group HTTPS rule-id 268437511 (hitcnt=101) 0x39c06649
  access-list CSM_FW_ACL_ line 11 advanced permit tcp ifc Inside any ifc
Outside any eq https rule-id 268437511 (hitcnt=101) 0x2caf1cd4
access-list CSM_FW_ACL_ line 12 remark rule-id 268437507: ACCESS POLICY: Base -
Mandatory
access-list CSM_FW_ACL_ line 13 remark rule-id 268437507: L7 RULE: DNS Traffic
access-list CSM_FW_ACL_ line 15 advanced permit udp ifc Inside any ifc Outside
any object-group DNS_over_UDP rule-id 268437507 (hitcnt=702) 0x757fd84a
  access-list CSM_FW_ACL_ line 15 advanced permit udp ifc Inside any ifc
Outside any eq domain rule-id 268437507 (hitcnt=702) 0x4f03ce25
access-list CSM_FW_ACL_ line 16 remark rule-id 268437512: ACCESS POLICY: Base -
Mandatory
access-list CSM_FW_ACL_ line 17 remark rule-id 268437512: L4 RULE: Block Port
access-list CSM_FW_ACL_ line 18 advanced deny tcp ifc Inside any ifc Outside
any eq 1234 rule-id 268437512 event-log flow-start (hitcnt=5) 0x817c1cdd
access-list CSM_FW_ACL_ line 19 remark rule-id 268435456: ACCESS POLICY: Base -
Default
access-list CSM_FW_ACL_ line 20 remark rule-id 268435456: L4 RULE: DEFAULT
ACTION RULE
access-list CSM_FW_ACL_ line 21 advanced deny ip any any rule-id 268435456
event-log flow-start (hitcnt=21) 0x97aa021a
```

Rule Conflicts

The last ACP specific feature that I will point out to you in this chapter is the Show Rule Conflicts check box. This will generate policy warnings if you have rules that are preempted by a higher-up rule. Aside from inefficiency, you do not want to have rules being preempted because that might accidentally change your intended rule base behavior. For example, if a higher-up rule doesn't have logging turned on or has a different IPS policy, it can cause a headache for you.

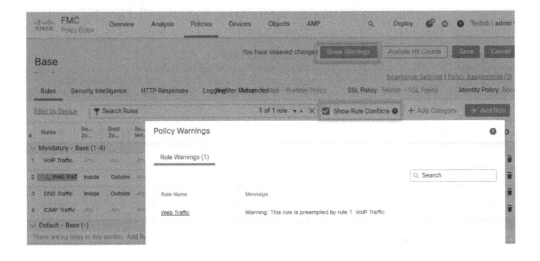

SSL Policy

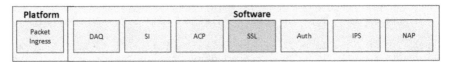

The next component to look at is SSL policies. SSL decryption is becoming more and more vital in today's networks because websites are increasingly moving over to HTTPS for better security. The main issues that can cause your SSL policy to drop traffic are decryption errors and the certificate not meeting current standards.

As per usual, we will want to make sure logging is enabled in the SSL policy so we can see any errors in our Connection Events page.

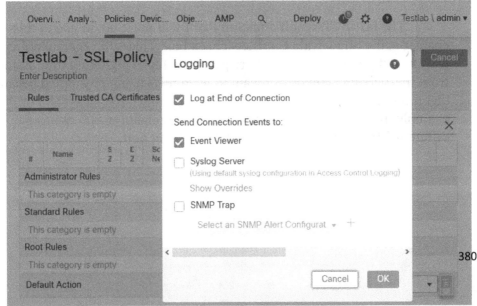

The other thing to keep an eye on is what the default action is set to. By default it will be Do Not Decrypt, but it could be set to block traffic in more secure deployments.

How the policy handles certificates it cannot decrypt can be adjusted in the Undecryptable Actions tab. One thing to note is that a decryption error will always be a blocking action no matter what but the other types will inherit the default action, which will be Do Not Decrypt unless we change to a more explicit action.

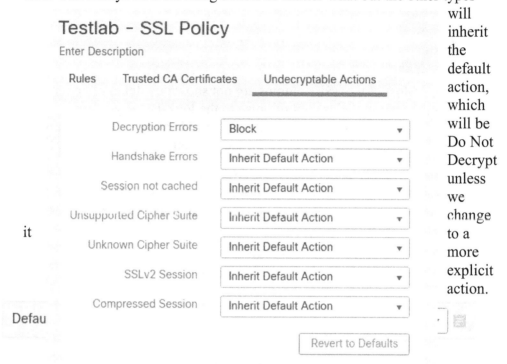

Connection Events - SSL

The easiest way to zero in on SSL policy issues in connection events is to filter on SSL connections in the search page. This will remove any unsecure connections from the results.

Connection Events ▾

Sections

General Information
Networking
Geolocation
Device
SSL
Application
URL
Netflow
QoS

Search

(unnamed search)

SSL

SSL	yes	yes, no
SSL Status		Do Not Decrypt, Block, Decryption Error
SSL Flow Error		SSL_VERSION_NOT_SUPPORTED*, SSL_VERSION_NOT_SUPPORTED (0x6500144f)
SSL Actual Action		Do Not Decrypt, Block
SSL Expected Action		Do Not Decrypt, Block

Most of the SSL columns are not shown by default in connection events because it adds a lot of noise to the logs. But if you are troubleshooting an SSL issue, you can turn them on by clicking the cross on one of the table view columns and then selecting what you want. I use this

Jump to...

		✦ First Packet ×	Last Packet ×	Action ×	Reason ×	Responder IP ×	Ingress Security × Zone	Egress Security × Zone	Destination Port / ICMP Code
▼	☐	2020-08-21 04:25:47	2020-08-21 04:26:19	Block	SSL Block	52	☐ All Columns		
▼	☐	2020-08-21 04:25:43	2020-08-21 04:25:43	Block	SSL Block	52	☑ SSL Actual Action		
▼	☐	2020-08-21 04:25:11	2020-08-21 04:25:43	Block	SSL Block	52	☑ SSL Certificate Status		
▼	☐	2020-08-21 04:25:07	2020-08-21 04:25:39	Block	SSL Block	52	☑ SSL Cipher Suite		
▼	☐	2020-08-21 04:25:06	2020-08-21 04:25:37	Block	SSL Block	65	☑ SSL Expected Action		
▼	☐	2020-08-21 04:25:06	2020-08-21 04:25:06	Block	SSL Block	19	☑ SSL Flow Error		
▼	☐	2020-08-21 04:25:06	2020-08-21 04:25:06	Block	SSL Block	19	☑ SSL Flow Flags		
▼	☐	2020-08-21 04:24:41	2020-08-21 04:26:43	Block	SSL Block	13	☑ SSL Flow Messages		
▼	☐	2020-08-21 04:24:35	2020-08-21 04:25:07	Block	SSL Block	52	☑ SSL Policy		
▼	☐	2020-08-21 04:24:35	2020-08-21 04:24:35	Block	SSL Block	52	☑ SSL Rule		
▼	☐	2020-08-21 04:24:06	2020-08-21 04:24:37	Block	SSL Block	23	☑ SSL Session ID		
▼	☐	2020-08-21 04:24:06	2020-08-21 04:24:06	Block	SSL Block	19	☑ SSL Ticket ID		
▼	☐	2020-08-21 04:24:06	2020-08-21 04:24:06	Block	SSL Block	19	Apply Cancel		

to remove unnecessary columns to make my FMC screen shots a bit more focused.

After we turn on all the SSL columns, we get a ton of information, including whether the SSL policy is blocking traffic or not.

SSL Status ×	SSL Flow Error ×	SSL Actual × Action	SSL Expected × Action	SSL Certificate × Status	SSL × Version	SSL Cipher Suite ×
🔒 Block	Success	Block	Block	Valid	TLSv1.2	TLS_ECDHE_RSA_WITH_AES_256_GCM_SHA384
🔒 Block	Success	Block	Block	Valid	TLSv1.2	TLS_ECDHE_RSA_WITH_AES_256_GCM_SHA384
🔒 Block	Success	Block	Block	Valid	TLSv1.2	TLS_ECDHE_RSA_WITH_AES_256_GCM_SHA384
🔒 Block	Success	Block	Block	Valid	TLSv1.2	TLS_ECDHE_RSA_WITH_AES_256_GCM_SHA384
🔒 Block	Success	Block	Block	Valid	TLSv1.2	TLS_ECDHE_RSA_WITH_AES_256_GCM_SHA384

Connection events will also show you what policy and rule is being matched; in this case we are hitting the default rule. The SSL Flow Flags column is especially valuable since it will show you some insight into why the certificate is having problems; in this case the certificate is deemed "undecryptable."

SSL Policy ×	SSL Rule ×	SSL Flow Flags ×
Testlab - SSL - Policy	Default Rule	VALID, UNDECRYPTABLE, PRE_DECISION_ERROR,
Testlab - SSL - Policy	Default Rule	VALID, UNDECRYPTABLE, PRE_DECISION_ERROR,
Testlab - SSL - Policy	Default Rule	VALID, UNDECRYPTABLE, PRE_DECISION_ERROR,
Testlab - SSL - Policy	Default Rule	VALID, UNDECRYPTABLE, PRE_DECISION_ERROR,

SSL Debug

As usual, we can use the CLI to get much more detailed information than the FMC gives us. The best debug tool to use while troubleshooting SSL issues is the `system support ssl-debug` command.

```
> system support ssl-debug
  Debug parameter for SSL functionality.  Possible options include
debug_policy_verdict, debug_policy_error_callback, debug_policy_matching,
debug_policy_print, debug_nse_version, debug_policy_all,
debug_ssl_preproc_events  tuning parameter
```

You can filter on different parts of SSL functionality, but I will go ahead and turn it all on with the `debug_policy_all` option.

```
> system support ssl-debug debug_policy_all

Parameter debug_policy_all successfully added to configuration file.

Configuration file contents:
  debug_policy_all
```

In older versions, you had to restart Snort with the `pmtool restartbytype DetectionEngine` command, but that is no longer necessary. Generate some traffic with the debug running; then you can check the debug log found in `/ngfw/var/common/ssl_debug_[snort pid]`. My Snort PIDs are 113501 and 113502, so my debug files are `/ngfw/var/common/ssl_debug_113501` and `/ngfw/var/common/ssl_debug_113502`. If you need to find your

Snort PID, just use `ps aux | grep SNORT` to find out the value for your system.

There is a ton of information in the debug file, far more than I could hope to cover in this chapter, so I will simply grep for "error" and we can see that issue is "Unknown session."

```
> expert
admin@ftd31:~$ cat /ngfw/var/common/ssl_debug_113501 | grep error
        2020-08-21 21:16:17.724 (V) [112.0] Verdict callback.
    ssl_policy_decision: SSL flow_info error.
        2020-08-21 21:16:17.724 (V) [112.0]  flow error: NSE:Handshake
    [0xb9000575;code:117;sub:5] Unknown session
        2020-08-21 21:16:30.317 (V) [53.0] Verdict callback.
    ssl_policy_decision: SSL flow_info error.
        2020-08-21 21:16:30.317 (V) [53.0]  flow error: NSE:Handshake
    [0xb9000575;code:117;sub:5] Unknown session
        2020-08-21 21:18:30.288 (V) [98.0] Verdict callback.
    ssl_policy_decision: SSL flow_info error.
2020-08-21 21:18:30.288 (V) [98.0]  flow error: NSE:Handshake
[0xb9000575;code:117;sub:5] Unknown session
```

When we are done looking at the debugs, we can turn it off with the `system support ssl-debug-reset` command.

```
admin@ftd31:~$ exit
logout
> system support ssl-debug-reset

Are you certain that you wish to delete the current SSL debug configuration
file? (y/n) [n]: y

Configuration file successfully deleted.
```

Decrypted Packet Capture

If you are really into the weeds when trying to solve an issue, you can do a unencrypted packet capture for the traffic decrypted by Firepower with the `system debug-DAQ debug_daq_write_pcap` command. You can download the capture file from `/var/common` when you are done.

Do Not Decrypt Rules

The best way to mitigate an SSL decryption issue is to create a new rule in the SSL policy that is set to not decrypt traffic.

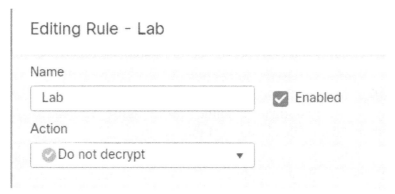

Editing Rule - Lab

Name

> Lab ☑ Enabled

Action

> ✅ Do not decrypt ▼

You might also want to create a new SSL policy with only a Do Not Decrypt action if you just want the feature to not block anything. Or simply turn the feature off in the ACP.

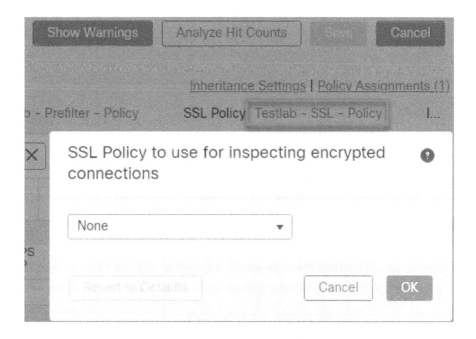

Active Authentication Features

The next component that we should troubleshoot is authentication. If you are using an Identity policy, then the active authentication feature can also drop traffic. Since the feature focuses on web traffic, HTTP and HTTPS traffic can be impacted if the active authentication goes wrong, but other services like DNS or DHCP should not be impacted.

Because passive authentication will not directly lead to dropped traffic, changing the identity rule from active to passive might be a good way to quickly mitigate an authentication issue. You can also take it a step further and completely turn off the feature.

Though if you have rules in your ACP that require user identity, you will have to edit your policy so that it doesn't match on identity in order for traffic to work while you get the feature working again properly.

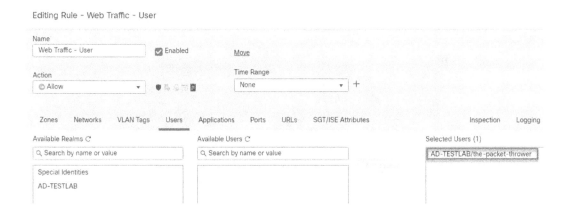

Verify Realm Configuration

The first thing to check when you are troubleshooting an authentication-related issue with all your users is to make sure the Active Directory integration is working correctly. The easiest way to do that is to download users/groups from the realm configuration page by clicking the down-facing arrow icon. After a minute or so you should get a message saying the download was complete.

Host Input Client   Smart Software Sat   Dismiss all notifications

LDAP Download
Download users/groups from AD-TESTLAB

Group DN	Group Attribute	
dc=testlab,dc=com	member	

Now if you go under the realm settings and navigate to User Download, you should see your AD groups. If the groups download properly, you can be sure that the AD configuration is fine; if they do not, you may be dealing with an incorrect service account password etc.

You can configure the user download to download only specific groups, which can be handy if you have a large Active Directory environment. However, if you do choose to filter the downloaded groups, make sure you keep the list up to date because if the sysadmins add a new user group, things will not work until FMC is updated.

AD-TESTLAB
AD Realm

Directory   Realm Configuration   User Download

☑ Download users and groups

Begin automatic download at [8 ▼] [PM ▼] America/New York

[Download Now]

Available Groups ↻

[🔍 Search by name]   [Add to Include]

👥 DHCP Administrators   [Add to Exclude]
👥 Guests
👥 Backup Operators
👥 Help Desk

Verify Redirection

Assuming the AD integration is working properly, the next thing that can go wrong is when FTD tries to redirect traffic to authenticate the user.

FTD will redirect the client to either the ingress interface's IP address or the device's FQDN, depending on what method is selected. If you need a refresher, here is a summary of the authentication methods you can use:

Active Authentication Method	Redirection Type
HTTP Basic	IP address
NTLM	IP address
HTTP Response Page	IP address
Kerberos	FQDN
HTTP Negotiate	FQDN

Regardless of the method you select for the Identity policy rule, FTD will use port TCP 885 for the captive portal redirection. But the catch is that ACP does not magically permit the redirection. So, if you get a "can't reach this page" type of error, check the connection events.

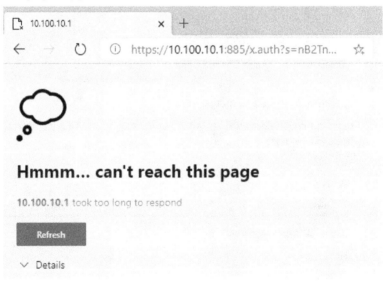

Inside Connection Events we can see that TCP 885 is being blocked from my test PC (10.100.10.100) to the FTD's inside interface (10.100.10.1). It is worth noting that the destination zone is blank since it goes directly to the firewall, though I didn't show that column because I was running out of space for the screen shot.

Connection Events (switch workflow)

▶ Search Constraints (Edit Search Save Search)

Connections with Application Details   Table View of Connection Events

Jump to...

		↑ First Packet ×	Action ×	Initiator IP ×	Responder IP ×	Ingress Security × Zone	Source Port / ICMP Type ×	Destination Port / ICMP × Code
▼	☐	2020-08-23 16:45:24	Block	10.100.10.100	10.100.10.1	Inside	52302 / tcp	885 / tcp
▼	☐	2020-08-23 16:45:02	Block	10.100.10.100	10.100.10.1	Inside	52296 / tcp	885 / tcp
▼	☐	2020-08-23 16:44:43	Block	10.100.10.100	10.100.10.1	Inside	52288 / tcp	885 / tcp
▼	☐	2020-08-23 16:44:40	Block	10.100.10.100	10.100.10.1	Inside	52286 / tcp	885 / tcp
▼	☐	2020-08-23 16:44:19	Block	10.100.10.100	10.100.10.1	Inside	52277 / tcp	885 / tcp

To fix the issue, create an ACP rule that permits traffic to the client-facing firewall interface IP using TCP 885. Ideally you should try to make the rule as specific as possible.

Name	Source Zones	Dest Zones	Source Networks	Dest Networks	Dest Ports	Source SGT	Dest SGT	Action
-5)								
DNS Traffic	Inside	Outside	Any	Any	DNS_over_TCP DNS_over_UDP	Any	Any	● Allow
Web Traffic - User	Inside	Outside	Any	Any	HTTPS HTTP	Any	Any	● Allow
Web Traffic - General	Inside	Outside	Any	Any	HTTPS HTTP	Any	Any	● Allow
ICMP Traffic	Any	Any	Any	Any	ICMP-ANY	Any	Any	● Allow
User Authentication	Inside	Any	Testlab-LAN	FTD31-LAN	TCP (6):885	Any	Any	● Allow

If you are using an authentication method that uses the FQDN, you will need to create a DNS "A" record that points to the client's ingress interface IP on the FTD. There are many ways to create a DNS record, but here is an example of a DNS record on a Windows server using Microsoft's Windows Admin Center tool.

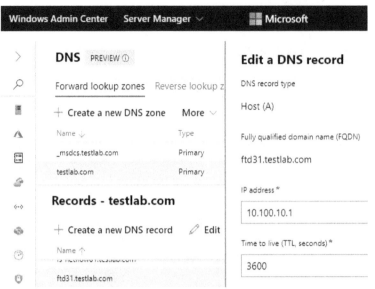

If the redirection is going to the wrong FQDN, there is good chance that the FTD is configured with the incorrect hostname. The best way to troubleshoot it is to connect directly to the FTD CLI.

The best way to verify the configuration is with the `show network` command. This will show the hostname and other useful information like the DNS servers and the management IP settings that are configured.

```
> show network
===============[ System Information ]===============
Hostname                 : ftd30.testlab.com
Domains                  : testlab.com
DNS Servers              : 10.20.2.10
                           10.30.11.10
Management port          : 8305
IPv4 Default route
  Gateway                : 10.30.11.1
  Netmask                : 0.0.0.0

=====================[ eth0 ]=====================
State                    : Enabled
Link                     : Up
Channels                 : Management & Events
Mode                     : Non-Autonegotiation
MDI/MDIX                 : Auto/MDIX
MTU                      : 1500
MAC Address              : 00:0C:29:99:F6:98
---------------------[ IPv4 ]---------------------
Configuration            : Manual
Address                  : 10.30.11.181
Netmask                  : 255.255.255.0
Gateway                  : 10.30.11.1
---------------------[ IPv6 ]---------------------
Configuration            : Disabled

===============[ Proxy Information ]===============
State                    : Disabled
Authentication           : Disabled
```

While we are here, we will also check the IP address on the inside interface since we need to make sure our DNS record is correct.

```
> show ip address Inside
System IP Address:
Interface            Name        IP address      Subnet mask
Method
GigabitEthernet0/1   Inside      10.100.10.1     255.255.255.0
CONFIG
Current IP Address:
Interface            Name        IP address      Subnet mask
Method
GigabitEthernet0/1   Inside      10.100.10.1     255.255.255.0
CONFIG
```

To change the hostname on the FTD, use the `configure network hostname` command.

```
> configure network hostname ftd31.testlab.com
Interface eth0 speed is set to '10000baseT/Full'
```

Verify Certificate

Now that we should have basic connectivity to the captive portal, we need make sure we do not get a certificate error so that the client's user experience is not affected by certificate warnings. If you are getting an error along the lines of ERR_CERT_COMMON_NAME_INVALID, this is due to modern browsers wanting the certificate to have some subject alternate names.

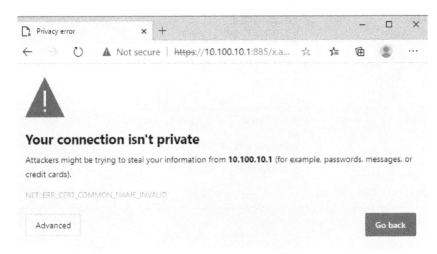

Here is an example of adding the IP address and FQDN as SANs to the certificate.

```
the-packet-thrower@home01:/mnt/c/certs$ cat san.cnf
[req]
default_bits = 4096
distinguished_name = req_distinguished_name
req_extensions = req_ext
x509_extensions = v3_req
prompt = no
[req_distinguished_name]
countryName = CA
stateOrProvinceName = AB
localityName = Calgary
organizationName = Testlab
commonName = ftd31.testlab.com
[req_ext]
subjectAltName = @alt_names
[v3_req]
subjectAltName = @alt_names
[alt_names]
DNS.1 = ftd31.testlab.com
IP.1 = 10.100.10.1
the-packet-thrower@home01:/mnt/c/certs$ openssl genrsa -out ftd31.key 4096
Generating RSA private key, 4096 bit long modulus (2 primes)
.++++
..++++
e is 65537 (0x010001)
the-packet-thrower@home01:/mnt/c/certs$ openssl req -new -key ftd31.key -out
ftd31.csr -config san.cnf
```

Once the certificate is uploaded, head over to the Active Authentication tab in the Identity policy and change the server certificate to the updated certificate. While we are here, you can also change the captive portal port if you want to. Though you would have to also update your ACP rule if you do so.

Testlab - Identity Policy

Enter Description

Rules   Active Authentication

Server Certificate *	FTD31 ▼ +	
Port *	885	(885 or 1025 - 65535)
Maximum login * attempts	3	(0 or greater. Use 0 to indicate unlimited login attempts)

Active Authentication Response Page

This page will be displayed if a user triggers an identity rule with HTTP Response Page as the Authentication Type.

System-provided   ▼   🔍

* Required when using Active Authentication

In a perfect world, FTD should be able to redirect users to the captive portal without any errors provided the proper certificates are installed on the client computer.

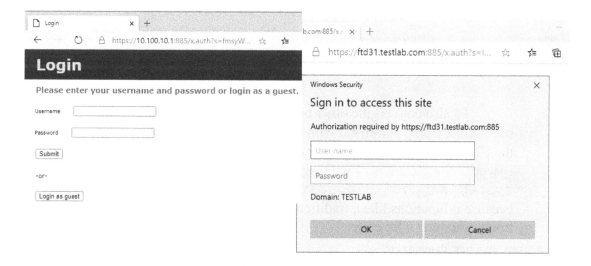

Packet Capture - Redirection

To do a packet capture for the redirection process, we must run two separate captures to get the whole picture. For starters, we simply do a capture for TCP 885.

```
> capture REDIRECT interface Inside match tcp host 10.100.10.100 host
10.100.10.1 eq 885
```

The other capture we need to run is on the tunnel interface that is used to securely redirect the traffic. We can do this by running the tcpdump command in expert mode.

To capture the tunnel interface, add -i tun1 to the command, and while we're at it we'll use -w /ngfw/var/common/redirect-tunnel.pcap to save the capture as a PCAP file in a location where we can use our FMC download tool reach it.

With both our captures up and running, we need to create some traffic to hopefully capture the issue we are troubleshooting, then we can stop both captures.

```
> expert
admin@ftd31:~$ sudo tcpdump -i tun1 -w /ngfw/var/common/redirect-tunnel.pcap

We trust you have received the usual lecture from the local System
Administrator. It usually boils down to these three things:

    #1) Respect the privacy of others.
    #2) Think before you type.
    #3) With great power comes great responsibility.

Password:
HS_PACKET_BUFFER_SIZE is set to 4.
tcpdump: listening on tun1, link-type RAW (Raw IP), capture size 262144 bytes
^C1076 packets captured
1085 packets received by filter
0 packets dropped by kernel
admin@ftd31:~$ exit
logout
> capture REDIRECT stop
```

To also convert the other packet capture we did with capture we can use the copy command with the /pcap switch to convert it. However, the FTD CLI is a bit too rigid for these kinds of commands because of the spacebar completion, so I will use the diagnostic mode CLI with the system support diagnostic-cli command. This CLI is handy because it functions like a traditional ASA device so it can make standard troubleshooting a lot easier.

```
> system support diagnostic-cli
Attaching to Diagnostic CLI ... Press 'Ctrl+a then d' to detach.
Type help or '?' for a list of available commands.

ftd31> en
Password:
```

Once the PCAP file is created, I will move it to our /ngfw/var/common directory so I can download the two captures.

```
ftd31# copy /pcap capture:redirect redirect.pcap

Source capture name [redirect]?

Destination filename [redirect.pcap]?
```

```
!!!!!!!!!!!!!!!!!!!!!!!!!!!!!!!!!!!!!!!!!!!!!!!!!!!!!!!!!!!!!!!!
1856 packets copied in 0.0 secs
ftd31# exit

Logoff

User enable_1 logged in to ftd31
Logins over the last 2 days: 5.  Last login: 21:50:52 UTC Aug 24 2020 from
console
Failed logins since the last login: 0.
Type help or '?' for a list of available commands.
ftd31> exit
Console connection detached.
> expert
admin@ftd31:~$ sudo mv /mnt/disk0/redirect.pcap /ngfw/var/common/redirect.pcap
```

Overv... Anal... Polic... Devi... Obje... AMP Intellig...   🔍   Deploy   👤   ⚙   ❓ admin ▾

Advanced Troubleshooting
FTD31

File Download   Threat Defense CLI   Packet Tracer   Capture w/Trace

File

| redirect-tunnel.pcap |

Back   Download

The IPs will be different between the two captures because the tunnel interface will use the 169.254.0.0/16 loopback range, so it is best to compare the two captures using something like the source port number.

tcp.dstport == 51454 || tcp.srcport == 51454

No.	Time	Source	Destination	Protocol	Length	Info
1534	259.417169	10.100.10.100	10.100.10.1	TCP	66	51454 → 885 [SYN] Se
1535	259.450828	10.100.10.1	10.100.10.100	TCP	66	885 → 51454 [SYN, AC
1536	259.451118	10.100.10.100	10.100.10.1	TCP	54	51454 → 885 [ACK] Se
1537	259.452689	10.100.10.100	10.100.10.1	TLSv1.2	228	Client Hello
1538	259.553407	10.100.10.1	10.100.10.100	TCP	54	885 → 51454 [ACK] Se
1539	259.553423	10.100.10.1	10.100.10.100	TLSv1.2	1434	Server Hello
1540	259.553728	10.100.10.1	10.100.10.100	TLSv1.2	764	Certificate, Server
1541	259.554216	10.100.10.100	10.100.10.1	TCP	54	51454 → 885 [ACK] Se
1542	259.555528	10.100.10.100	10.100.10.1	TLSv1.2	652	Client Key Exchange,
1543	259.555940	10.100.10.1	10.100.10.100	TCP	764	[TCP Spurious Retran
1544	259.556688	10.100.10.100	10.100.10.1	TCP	66	[TCP Dup ACK 1541#1]

In this case, we can see the "server hello" is present in the regular capture but it is not seen in the tunnel capture. This can imply that Snort or another process might have dropped that packet. Additionally, we can see the tunnel capture has some unacknowledged ACKs, which might also indicate some packet loss.

File　Edit　View　Go　Capture　Analyze　Statistics　Telephony　Wireless　Tools　Help

`tcp.dstport == 51454 || tcp.srcport == 51454`

lo.	Time	Source	Destination	Protocol	Length	Info
807	19.831011	169.254.4.11	169.254.0.1	TLSv1.2	621	Application Data
808	19.831281	169.254.0.1	169.254.4.11	TCP	1420	885 → 51454 [ACK] Seq=2373 Acl
809	19.831283	169.254.0.1	169.254.4.11	TLSv1.2	57	Application Data
818	19.873853	169.254.4.11	169.254.0.1	TCP	40	51454 → 885 [ACK] Seq=1354 Acl
1041	29.840340	169.254.0.1	169.254.4.11	TLSv1.2	93	Encrypted Alert
1042	29.840410	169.254.0.1	169.254.4.11	TCP	40	885 → 51454 [FIN, ACK] Seq=38:
1045	29.954596	169.254.0.1	169.254.4.11	TCP	40	[TCP Retransmission] 885 → 51
1046	30.002396	169.254.4.11	169.254.0.1	TCP	40	51454 → 885 [RST, ACK] Seq=13!
1047	30.002435	169.254.0.1	169.254.4.11	TCP	40	[TCP Dup ACK 808#1] 885 → 514
1050	30.224169	169.254.0.1	169.254.4.11	TLSv1.2	93	[TCP Spurious Retransmission]
1052	30.734367	169.254.0.1	169.254.4.11	TLSv1.2	93	[TCP Spurious Retransmission]
1063	31.744207	169.254.0.1	169.254.4.11	TLSv1.2	93	[TCP Spurious Retransmission]

Decrypting SSL Captures

Because we are dealing with encrypted traffic, it will probably be more readable if we decrypt it first! Fortunately, Wireshark makes it easy to make the PCAP file more readable. We can use RSA keys to decrypt the file, but the preferred method is to use the SSLKEYLOGFILE environment variable on the client PC to dump the TLS keys. This method works on Windows, Mac, and Linux operating systems.

The Windows method is simply to create a variable that specifies the location of the log file, with the `setx` command or through Environment Variables in System. You may need to reboot your computer for the log file to be created. Afterward, go ahead and open a modern browser and do a search to trigger redirection.

```
PS C:\> setx SSLKEYLOGFILE C:\Users\the-packet-thrower\Desktop\sslkey.txt

SUCCESS: Specified value was saved.
PS C:\Users\the-packet-thrower\Desktop>
```

Copy over the file to the computer that has the PCAP files. Then in Wireshark, go under Protocols/TLS in Preferences, and set the (Pre)-Master-Secret log to the file with the dumped keys.

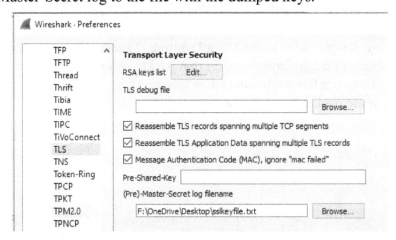

Once we click OK, the capture is magically decrypted! So now we can see the actual HTTP packets, and we can follow the conversation to see the full communication.

There probably will not be too many issues that require this much of a deep dive, but if nothing else this method is handy for understanding how the redirection feature works under the hood.

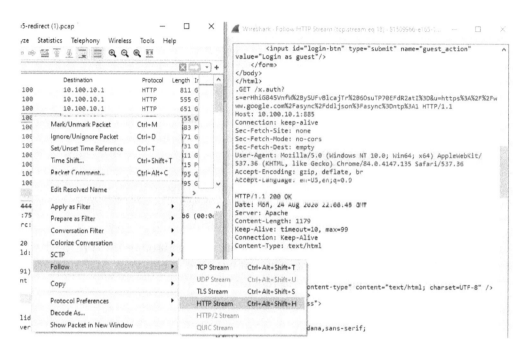

Logging Out

Sometimes you need to be able to restart an active session so you can troubleshoot an intermittent issue, or sometimes you just want to do your lab again and need to clear the session.

To clear an active session, simply go to Active Sessions under Analysis, select the user you want, then click the Logout button. Now when you start a web session on that computer, it will be redirected again.

Jump to...

		↓ Login Time ×	Last Seen ×	User ×	Authentication Type ×
▼	☑	2020-08-24 18:12:08	2020-08-24 18:12:08	👤 packet thrower (AD-TESTLAB\the-packet-thrower, LDAP)	Active Authentication

‹ ‹ Page [1] of 1 › ›   Displaying row 1 of 1 rows

[View]   [Logout]

[View All]

Bypassing Authentication

If you need to mitigate an authentication issue while you troubleshoot it, then the way to do it with the least impact would be to set the authentication rules to be "passive authentication" instead.

That way, if FMC is able to identify users through ISE-PIC or the newly deprecated user agent, you will not have to edit your ACP rules that require a user/group identity to function.

Editing Rule - LAB - Active Authentication

Name

[LAB - Active Authentication]   ☑ Enabled

[Passive Authentication ▼]   **Realm:**

Zones   Networks   VLAN Tags   Ports

Passive authentication should not cause any issues since it lead to dropped traffic, but if you

you can't

Editing Rule - LAB - Active Authentication

Name

[LAB - Active Authentication]   ☑ Enabled

[No Authentication ▼]   Realm:

Zones   Networks   VLAN Tags   Ports

398

want to fully turn off authentication for a rule, you can pick that option. Keep in mind, though, you may need to edit the ACP if you have any user identity rules.

Last, if you want to fully remove the feature, simply change the ACP's Identity policy to None and deploy your changes.

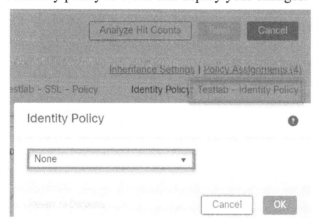

FMC will give you a warning if you forget to edit your rule base before disabling authentication. You can see it by clicking the Warning button in the ACP. FMC will also give you a warning about this every time you deploy a policy to the affected FTDs, so it does try to keep you informed if it thinks you're making a mistake.

Policy Warnings

Rule Warnings (1)

Q Search

Policy Warnings

Rule Warnings (1)

Q Search

Rule Name	Message
Web Traffic - User	Realms, users, and user groups will never match unless an identity policy with active or passive authentication rules is selected.

Intrusion Policy

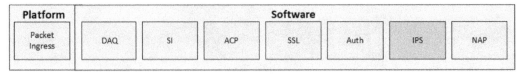

Platform	Software						
Packet Ingress	DAQ	SI	ACP	SSL	Auth	IPS	NAP

If the ACP is the most likely to drop traffic in your network, then the IPS will certainly be a very close second because the Snort rules are constantly updating, and you never know when traffic once considered benign is now a security threat.

In a perfect world, we would be able to tell the business to constantly keep all their applications up to date, but in reality, the company will probably have at least one legacy application that might trigger a false positive or two.

Intrusion Events

The easiest way to see if IPS is blocking your traffic is by going to Intrusion Events under Analysis. This page gives you detailed information about IPS events, including what rule is being matched and the inline result. For example, a down-facing arrow means the traffic is being blocked by the IPS.

You can drill down into the packet view to get a lot more detailed information, including a packet capture of the event. From a troubleshooting perspective, this view will give you a good overview of all the rules that match. It will even show the snort rule information.

Event	Lab Rule - Port 1234 (1:1000000:3)
Timestamp	2020-08-24 20:29:19
Classification	Misc Activity
Priority	low
Ingress Security Zone	Inside
Egress Security Zone	Outside
Device	FTD31
Ingress Interface	Inside
Egress Interface	Outside
Source IP	10.100.10.100
Source Port / ICMP Type	57302 / tcp
Destination IP	1.1.1.1
Destination Port / ICMP Code	1234 / tcp
Destination Country	AUS
Intrusion Policy	Testlab - IPS Policy
Access Control Policy	Testlab - Base
Access Control Rule	Test Port
Rule	alert tcp 10.100.10.100 any -> 1.1.1.1 1234 (sid:1000000; gid:1; msg:"Lab Rule - Port 1234"; classtype:misc-activity; rev:3;)

▸ Actions

Packet Information

FRAME 1 (Expand All)

▸ Frame 1: 66 bytes on wire (66 bytes captured (528 bits)

▸ Ethernet II (Src: 00:0C:29:46:FE:75, Dst: 00:0C:29:99:F6:B6)

▸ Internet Protocol Version 4 (Src: , Dst:)

▸ Transmission Control Protocol (Src Port: 57302 (57302), Dst Port: 1234 (1234), Seq: 0, Len: 0)

▸ Packet Text

▸ Packet Bytes

We can also get some basic information from our trusty Connection Events page. It will not show us what IPS rule is matching, but it will tell us that the traffic is blocking. We can tell the IPS is dropping the traffic because the reason is Intrusion Block.

	First Packet ×	Last Packet ×	✦ Action ×	Reason ×	Responder IP ×	Ingress Security × Zone	Egress Security × Zone	Source Port / ICMP Type ×	Destination Port / ICMP × Code
▼ ☐	2020-08-24 20:29:19	2020-08-24 20:29:19	Block	Intrusion Block	1.1.1.1	Inside	Outside	57302 / tcp	1234 / tcp
▼ ☐	2020-08-24 20:26:49	2020-08-24 20:26:49	Block	Intrusion Block	1.1.1.1	Inside	Outside	44444 / tcp	1234 / tcp
▼ ☐	2020-08-24 20:23:50	2020-08-24 20:23:50	Block	Intrusion Block	1.1.1.1	Inside	Outside	44444 / tcp	1234 / tcp

Packet Tracer - IPS

Packet Tracer is still our MVP tool for testing out connections. I ran it again, but this time our usual SSH session is being blocked by the Snort engine. Unfortunately, Packet Tracer does not give us the name of the blocking rule as it does when an ACL rule denies traffic, but it does give us the SID that we can look up later.

```
> packet-tracer input Inside tcp 192.168.255.1 44444 11.11.11.11 22

Phase: 11
```

```
Type: SNORT
Subtype:
Result: DROP
Config:
Additional Information:
Snort Trace:
Packet: TCP, SYN, seq 1048605527
Session: new snort session
AppID: service unknown (0), application unknown (0)
Firewall: allow rule, id 268435457, allow
IPS Event: gid 1000, sid 1000001, drop
Snort detect_drop: gid 1000, sid 1000001, drop
Snort id 1, NAP id 2, IPS id 1, Verdict BLACKLIST, Blocked by IPS
Snort Verdict: (black-list) black list this flow

Result:
input-interface: Inside(vrfid:0)
input-status: up
input-line-status: up
output-interface: Outside(vrfid:0)
output-status: up
output-line-status: up
Action: drop
Drop-reason: (ips-preproc) Blocked or blacklisted by the IPS preprocessor,
Drop-location: frame 0x000055dcd094e10b flow (NA)/NA
```

Capture - IPS

Along the same lines, we can use the capture tool with the trace option enabled to troubleshoot IPS issues. Just as you saw earlier with the Access Control policy, every packet captured is put through Packet Tracer so you can easily look through all the packet decisions.

```
> capture IPS trace interface Inside match tcp host 10.100.10.100 host 1.1.1.1
eq 1234
> show capture IPS packet-number 1 trace

9 packets captured


--- trimmed for brevity ---
Phase: 13
Type: SNORT
Subtype:
Result: DROP
Config:
Additional Information:
Snort Trace:
Packet: TCP, SYN, seq 232259356
Session: new snort session
AppID: service unknown (0), application unknown (0)
Firewall: allow rule, id 268436484, allow
Snort fpdetect_filter: gid 1, sid 1000000, drop
Snort id 0, NAP id 1, IPS id 0, Verdict BLACKLIST, Blocked by Snort
Snort Verdict: (black-list) black list this flow

Result:
input-interface: Inside(vrfid:0)
input-status: up
```

```
input-line-status: up
output-interface: Outside(vrfid:0)
output-status: up
output-line-status: up
```
Action: drop
Drop-reason: (snort-module) Blocked or blacklisted by snort, Drop-location:
frame 0x0000559f66c02a1b flow (NA)/NA

System Support Trace - IPS

Another way to troubleshoot IPS is to enable a debug with the `system support trace` command. This works just like the firewall engine debug we did in the ACP section; in fact, the first question it asks you is whether or not you also want to enable the firewall engine debug as well.

Once we enter in the connection information we want in the debug, FTD will listen for any matching events and display them.

```
> system support trace

Enable firewall-engine-debug too? [n]: y
Please specify an IP protocol: tcp
Please specify a client IP address: 10.100.10.100
Please specify a client port:
Please specify a server IP address: 1.1.1.1
Please specify a server port: 1234
Monitoring packet tracer and firewall debug messages


10.100.10.100-57302 - 1.1.1.1-1234 6 AS 1-1 CID 0 Packet: TCP, SYN, seq
4174671507
10.100.10.100-57302 - 1.1.1.1-1234 6 AS 1-1 CID 0 Session: new snort session
10.100.10.100-57302 - 1.1.1.1-1234 6 AS 1-1 CID 0 AppID: service unknown (0),
application unknown (0)
10.100.10.100-57302 > 1.1.1.1-1234 6 AS 1-1 I 1 new firewall session
10.100.10.100-57302 > 1.1.1.1-1234 6 AS 1-1 I 1 using HW or preset rule order
6, 'Test Port', action Allow and prefilter rule 0
10.100.10.100-57302 > 1.1.1.1-1234 6 AS 1-1 I 1 HitCount data sent for rule id:
268436484,
10.100.10.100-57302 > 1.1.1.1-1234 6 AS 1-1 I 1 allow action
10.100.10.100-57302 - 1.1.1.1-1234 6 AS 1-1 CID 0 Firewall: allow rule, 'Test
Port', allow
10.100.10.100-57302 - 1.1.1.1-1234 6 AS 1-1 CID 0 IPS Event: gid 1, sid
1000000, drop
10.100.10.100-57302 - 1.1.1.1-1234 6 AS 1-1 CID 0 Snort detect_drop: gid 1, sid
1000000, drop
10.100.10.100-57302 > 1.1.1.1-1234 6 AS 1-1 I 1 deleting firewall session flags
= 0x30001, fwFlags = 0x100
10.100.10.100-57302 > 1.1.1.1-1234 6 AS 1-1 I 1 Logging EOF as part of session
delete with rule_id = 268436484 ruleAction = 4 ruleReason = 64
10.100.10.100-57302 - 1.1.1.1-1234 6 AS 1-1 CID 0 Snort id 1, NAP id 1, IPS id
0, Verdict BLACKLIST
10.100.10.100-57302 - 1.1.1.1-1234 6 AS 1-1 CID 0 ===> Blocked by SSL
Verdict reason is sent to DAQ
```

Suppressions

Checking logs is a great first move for troubleshooting IPS issues. But if rule suppression is configured, it is possible for the FTD to silently drop IPS traffic without informing the FMC. If suppression is incorrectly configured on a Snort rule, then you can delete it under the details section of the rule in the IPS policy.

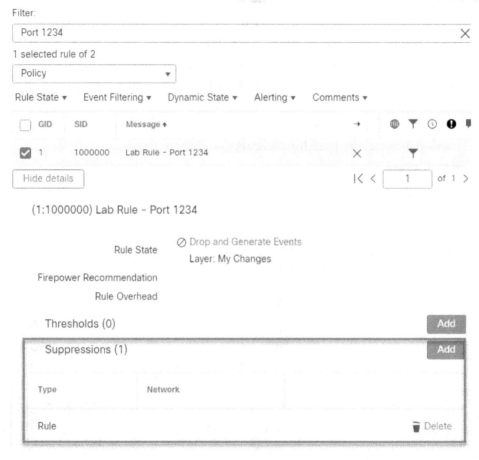

There isn't an easy way in the GUI to see if suppression is enabled for multiple rules, but you can check the `snort_suppression.conf` file under `/var/sf/detection_engine/<uuid>/intrusion/<uuid>/` on the FTD to see a list of suppression rules that you can track down.

You can find out the detection engine UUID with the `de_info.pl` command while in root.

```
root@ftd31:~# de_info.pl
```

—

```
DE Name          : Primary Detection Engine (81509966-e165-11ea-ac14-
d9cfab427eb5)
DE Type          : ids
DE Description   : Primary detection engine for device 81509966-e165-11ea-ac14-
d9cfab427eb5
DE Resources     : 2
DE UUID          : de5b80d0-e165-11ea-b33b-efedab427eb5
```

But you can use the * wildcard to access the file more easily.

```
admin@ftd31:~$ cd /var/sf/detection_engines/*
admin@ftd31:/var/sf/detection_engines/de5b80d0-e165-11ea-b33b-efedab427eb5$
grep -H '^suppress' intrusion/*/snort_suppression.conf
intrusion/dd4f3a30-e384-11ea-80a2-c82c5e4cd26c/snort_suppression.conf:suppress
gen_id 1, sig_id 1000000
```

Adjusting Rule State

Since I created a custom rule to cause the traffic to drop, the easiest way to resolve this issue would be simply to delete the custom rule or simply have it alert instead of drop traffic.

We can do this in the rules section under the IPS policy by changing the rule state. Of course, you probably will not have a ton of custom rules in your IPS policy, but you may need to adjust a rule state if an IPS update causes a problem.

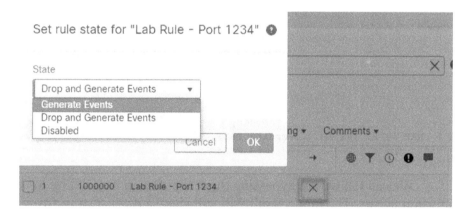

Bypassing IPS

A good way to remove the IPS from the equation is to disable Drop when Inline in the policy. This will prevent IPS from dropping the traffic if it matches. Not only can this get you out of an outage situation, but it is a great way of testing out what an IPS policy will do without affecting your traffic.

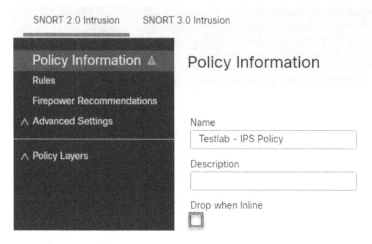

Once Drop when Inline is disabled, Packet Tracer shows that traffic is allowed despite Snort saying the traffic should be blocked.

```
> packet-tracer input Inside tcp 10.100.10.100 44444 1.1.1.1 1234 transmit

--- trimmed for brevity ---

Phase: 13
Type: SNORT
Subtype:
Result: ALLOW
Config:
Additional Information:
Snort Trace:
Packet: TCP, SYN, seq 880741623
Session: new snort session
AppID: service unknown (0), application unknown (0)
Firewall: allow rule, id 268436484, allow
Snort fpdetect_filter: gid 1, sid 1000000, would drop
Snort id 0, NAP id 1, IPS id 0, Verdict PASS, Blocked by Snort
Snort Verdict: (pass-packet) allow this packet
--- trimmed for brevity ---
```

We can tell we are bypassing the IPS policy in the GUI by looking at intrusion events. The inline result will still show a down-facing arrow, but it will be light gray; this means snort "would have dropped" the traffic.

	↓ Time ×	Priority ×	Impact ×	Inline Result ×	Source IP ×	Destination IP ×	Source Port / ICMP Type ×	Destination Port / ICMP Code
▼ ☐	2020-08-24 23:28:36	low	0	↓	10.100.10.100	1.1.1.1	44444 / tcp	1234 / tcp

Another way to solve the issue is to simply change an ACP rule to not use an IPS policy, though this would not be a preferred solution to an IPS issue since you are actively lowering your security level. Because of that, this method is best for quick troubleshooting while you work on a better solution.

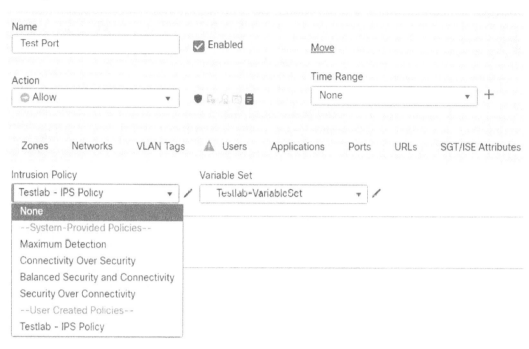

Network Analysis Policy

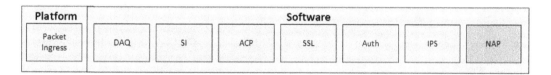

Whew, that took a while to work through, but we are finally at the last phase of Cisco's recommended troubleshooting steps! Last but not least is the Network Analysis policy. This is where all the preprocessors can cause traffic drops. To test this out I made a simple rate-based attack prevention rule that will trigger when I run Nmap on my test PC.

Policy Information	Rate-Based Attack Prevention						< Back
⊟ Settings	⊟ SYN Attack Prevention						⊕ Add
Back Orifice Detection	**Track By**	**Network**	**Rate**			**Drop**	**Timeout**
Checksum Verification	Source ∨	10.100.10.0/24	10	SYNs / 30	seconds ☑	60	seconds 🗑 Delete
DCE/RPC Configuration							
DNS Configuration	⊟ Control Simultaneous Connections						⊕ Add
FTP and Telnet Configuration	**Track By**	**Network**	**Count**			**Drop**	**Timeout**
GTP Command Channel Configurati	Source ∨	10.100.10.0/24	5	connections	☑	30	seconds 🗑 Delete
HTTP Configuration							
IP Defragmentation			Revert to Defaults				
Packet Decoding							
Portscan Detection							
Rate-Based Attack Prevention							

Also, speaking of troubleshooting, I had to switch back to the classic theme for the NAP screen shot because the light theme that we were using throughout this chapter wasn't rendering the fields properly!

System Support Trace - NAP

We can use the trace we used in the last section to troubleshoot NAP preprocessor drops as well. To test it out I will use Nmap to generate a bunch of SYN traffic that should be blocked by the NAP policy above.

```
C:\>nmap -p 1-65535 -T4 -A -v 1.1.1.1
Starting Nmap 7.80 ( https://nmap.org ) at 2020-08-24 22:45 Mountain Daylight
Time
NSE: Loaded 151 scripts for scanning.
NSE: Script Pre-scanning.
Initiating NSE at 22:45
Completed NSE at 22:45, 0.00s elapsed
```

Then I will enable the debug with the `system support trace` command. Notice that the NAP id is 1, which means traffic is hitting the NAP policy. The verdict is "blacklist," and the traffic is "blocked by snort," which means NAP is dropping my NMAP scan.

```
system support trace

Enable firewall-engine-debug too? [n]: y
Please specify an IP protocol: tcp
Please specify a client IP address: 10.100.10.100
Please specify a client port:
Please specify a server IP address: 1.1.1.1
Please specify a server port:
Monitoring packet tracer and firewall debug messages

10.100.10.100-51866 - 1.1.1.1-45254 6 AS 1-1 CID 0 Snort fpdetect_filter: gid
135, sid 1, drop
10.100.10.100-51866 - 1.1.1.1-45254 6 AS 1-1 CID 0 Snort id 0, NAP id 1, IPS id
0, Verdict BLACKLIST
10.100.10.100-51866 - 1.1.1.1-45254 6 AS 1-1 CID 0 ===> Blocked by Snort
Verdict reason is sent to DAQ
```

Intrusion Events

Inside our trusty intrusion events page, we can see that the inline result is a drop along with all the other connection information that we should hopefully be used to by now after this long chapter.

	Impact ×	Inline Result ×	Source IP ×	Destination IP ×	Destination Port / ICMP Code ×	↟ Message ×
▾ ☐	0	↓	10.100.10.100	1.1.1.1	8888 / tcp	INTERNAL_EVENT_SYN_RECEIVED (135:1:2)
▾ ☐	0	↓	10.100.10.100	1.1.1.1	445 (microsoft-ds) / tcp	INTERNAL_EVENT_SYN_RECEIVED (135:1:2)
▾ ☐	0	↓	10.100.10.100	1.1.1.1	38037 / tcp	INTERNAL_EVENT_SYN_RECEIVED (135:1:2)
▾ ☐	0	↓	10.100.10.100	1.1.1.1	58524 / tcp	INTERNAL_EVENT_SYN_RECEIVED (135:1:2)

We can confirm we are matching a preprocessor in the packet view.

Intrusion Policy   Testlab - IPS Policy
Access Control Policy   Testlab - Base
Rule   alert (msg:"INTERNAL_EVENT_SYN_RECEIVED"; sid:1; gid:135; rev:2; metadata:policy max-detect-ips drop, rule-type preproc; classtype:tcp-connection;)

Silent Drops

There is a known quirk with NAP when inline normalization is enabled: it can block traffic without notifying FMC. The reason for this is that the Block Unresolvable TCP Header Anomalies option relies on an IPS rule that is not enabled by default.

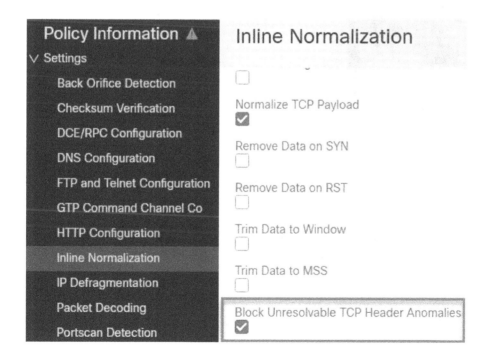

If you encounter this, simply enable "GID: "129" SID:"19" in your IPS policy. After it is turned on, the IPS will generate an alert if traffic is dropped.

Bypass NAP

Just as with the IPS policy, we can turn off inline mode so NAP can no longer block traffic. This is done in the Policy Information section of NAP.

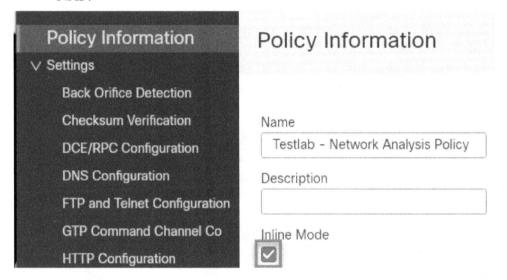

We cannot fully turn off NAP because it is an important part of Firepower's detection engine. But if you need to mitigate an issue with a broken policy, then it is easy to change the active NAP back to a default one by going under the ACP's advanced section.

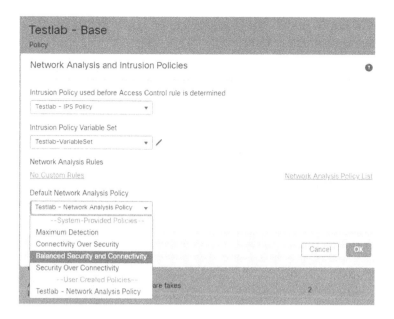

Summary

In chapter 34, you learned some effective troubleshooting strategies for your Firepower network. This chapter dove deep into Cisco's recommended troubleshooting steps for Firepower issues.

Chapter 36: Application detectors

The CCNP Security SNCF exam objectives covered in this chapter include:

2.3 Configure these features using Cisco Firepower Management Center

2.3.b Application detectors (Open AppID)

Firepower discovery and identity includes many parts: host identity sources, realms, controlling users with ISE/ISE-PIC, controlling users with captive portal, controlling users with remote access VPN, controlling users with terminal server agent, controlling users with user agent, identity policies, and finally, network discovery (Firepower) policies. Whew that's a lot of discovery. But wait, there's more!

This chapter will continue on from our other chapters that covered all of the discovery and identities listed above and finally finish this topic with application detectors.

Cisco Firepower Application Detectors

When the Firepower System analyzes your IP traffic, it attempts to identify the most commonly used applications on your network, typically referred to as application awareness. Application awareness is crucial to application control.

There are three types of applications that the system detects:

- Application protocols such as HTTP and SSH, which represent communications between hosts
- Clients such as web browsers and email clients, which represent software running on the host
- Web applications such as MPEG video and Facebook, which represent the content or requested URL for HTTP traffic

The system identifies applications in your network traffic according to the characteristics specified in the specific detectors. For example, the system can identify an application by an ASCII pattern in the packet header, and Secure Sockets Layer (SSL) protocol detectors use information from the secured session to identify the application from the session.

There are two sources of application detectors in the Firepower System:

- System-provided detectors detect web applications, clients, and application protocols.
- Custom application protocol detectors are user created and detect web applications, clients, and application protocols.

The availability of system-provided detectors for applications (and operating systems) depends on the version of the Firepower System and the version of the virtual database (VDB) you have installed.

You can also detect application protocols through what is called implied application protocol detection, which looks for an application protocol based on the detection of a client.

The system identifies only those application protocols running on hosts in your monitored networks, as defined in the network discovery policy. For example, if an internal host accesses an SMB server on a remote site that you are not monitoring, the system does not identify the application protocol as SMB.

The system characterizes each application that it detects. The system uses these characteristics to create groups of applications, called application filters. Application filters are used to perform access control and to constrain search results and data used in reports and dashboard widgets.

Use the Detectors page (**Policies>Application Detectors**) to view the detector list and customize detection capability.

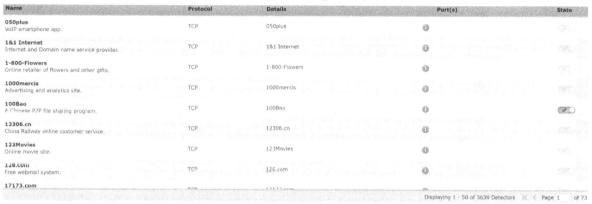

Name	Protocol	Details	Port(s)	State
050plus VoIP smartphone app.	TCP	050plus	ⓘ	
1&1 Internet Internet and Domain name service provider.	TCP	1&1 Internet	ⓘ	
1-800-Flowers Online retailer of flowers and other gifts.	TCP	1-800-Flowers	ⓘ	
1000mercis Advertising and analytics site.	TCP	1000mercis	ⓘ	
100Bao A Chinese P2P file sharing program.	TCP	100Bao	ⓘ	
12306.cn China Railway online customer service.	TCP	12306.cn	ⓘ	
123Movies Online movie site.	TCP	123Movies	ⓘ	
126.com Free webmail system.	TCP	126.com	ⓘ	
17173.com	TCP	17173.com		

Displaying 1 - 50 of 3639 Detectors   K   <   Page 1   of 73

Whether you can modify a detector or change its state (active or inactive) depends on its type. The system uses only active detectors to analyze application traffic.

Cisco-Provided Internal Detectors

Internal detectors are a special category of detectors for client, web application, and application protocol traffic. Internal detectors are delivered with system updates and are always on.

If an application matches against internal detectors designed to detect client-related activity and no specific client detector exists, a generic client may be reported.

Cisco-Provided Client Detectors

Client detectors detect client traffic and are delivered via VDB or system update or are provided for import by Cisco Professional Services. You can activate and deactivate client detectors. You can export a client detector only if you import it.

Cisco-Provided Web Application Detectors

Web application detectors detect web applications in HTTP traffic payloads and are delivered via VDB or

413

system update. Web application detectors are always on.

Cisco-Provided Application Protocol (Port) Detectors

Port-based application protocol detectors use well-known ports to identify network traffic. They are delivered via VDB or system update or are provided for import by Cisco Professional Services. You can activate and deactivate application protocol detectors and view a detector definition to use it as the basis for a custom detector.

Cisco-Provided Application Protocol (Firepower) Detectors

Firepower-based application protocol detectors analyze network traffic using Firepower application fingerprints and are delivered via VDB or system update. You can activate and deactivate application protocol detectors.

Custom Application Detectors

Custom application detectors are pattern based. They detect patterns in packets from client, web application, or application protocol traffic. You have full control over imported and custom detectors.

The following table outlines how the Firepower System identifies detected application protocols:

Firepower System Identification of Application Protocols

Identification	Description
Application protocol name	The Firepower Management Center identifies an application protocol with its name if the application protocol was:
	positively identified by the system
	identified using NetFlow data and there is a port-application protocol correlation in `/etc/sf/services`
	manually identified using the host input feature
	identified by Nmap or another active source
Pending	The Firepower Management Center identifies an application protocol as pending if the system can neither positively nor negatively identify the application.
	Most often, the system needs to collect and analyze more connection data before it can identify a pending application.
	In the Application Details and Servers tables and in the host profile, the pending status appears only for application protocols where specific application protocol traffic was detected (rather than inferred from detected client or web application traffic).
Unknown	The Firepower Management Center identifies an application protocol as unknown if:

the application does not match any of the system's detectors

the application protocol was identified using NetFlow data, but there is no port-application protocol correlation in `/etc/sf/services`

Blank   All available detected data has been examined, but no application protocol was identified. In the Application Details and Servers tables and in the host profile, the application protocol is left blank for non-HTTP generic client traffic with no detected application protocol.

Configuring a Custom Application Detector

In this section we will build a custom application detector to provide a way to identify an application based on the following:

- TLS SNI (Server Name Indication extension) - Mainly used to detect most of HTTPS-based web applications. Basically, the client browser during the TLS handshake process specifies in cleartext which hostname it is attempting to connect to.

- HTTP Host - Mainly used to detect most of HTTP-based web applications. Basically, the client browser specifies in the HTTP request which hostname it is attempting to connect to. (This is valid for HTTP cleartext but not for HTTPS unless it is decrypted.)

Here are the steps:

1. From an inside host of your network, open a browser and go to `coinrail.min.js`.

This coinrail URL is working at the time of this writing. You may need to find another bitcoin miner site for this lab if they take that page down

2. Log in to your FMC and open your Access Control policy.
3. On the right side of the Chrome browser, click on the three dots and choose **More tools>Developer tools** as shown in the following screen shot:

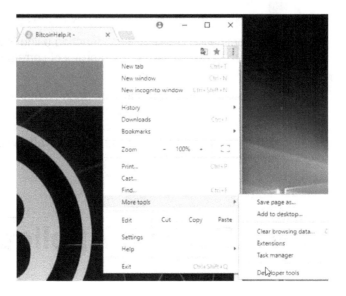

4. From the developer page, click on Network and then JS.

5. Refresh the website and watch the JavaScript load. Notice the output for `coinrail.min.js`. That's the one we want to stop.
6. Back in your FMC, go to **Policies>Application Detectors**.
7. Click on Create Custom Detector.

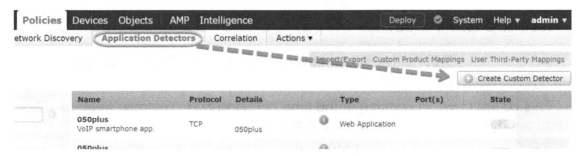

8. From the Create A Custom Application Detector screen, click Add.
9. Name the new detector CoinrailMiner, add the description Bad

Java Site, and click Add.

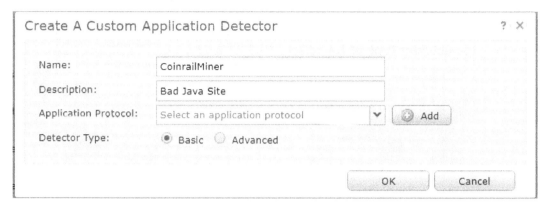

10. In Application Editor, add the name CoinRail-Miner and a description, choose a low business relevance and very high risk, select financial for the category, and click OK.

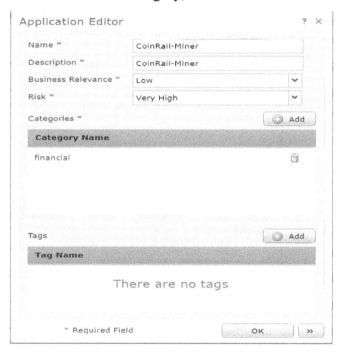

11. You will see a warning stating that Your Snort process will now restart!

12. After you click Yes, you'll be back at the main Application Detector page.
13. Choose CoinrailMiner, add a description, and click OK, leaving the detector type at Basic.

14. On the next page, click Add under Detection Patterns, and enter the following information, and click OK:

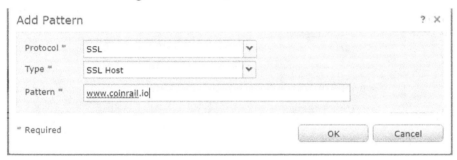

15. Click Add again under Detection Patterns, enter the following, and then click OK:

16. The page should now look like this, and the Application Detector state will come active on the next screen:

17. Click Save in the upper-right corner.
18. Now go to the Name menu on the right side and type in **coinr** to find the detector you just created.
19. Enable the slider bar to activate the application detector:

Name	Protocol	Details	Type	Port(s)	State
CoinrailMiner Bad Java Site	SSL	CoinRail-Miner	Application Protocol		

20. This will start Snort again. You are probably thinking you don't want to do this lab in a production environment unless you can reset Snort a couple times! You should now see this:

Success

Successfully activated 1 detector(s).

OK

21. Click OK.
22. After creating the custom application detector, you need to set up an access control rule in your Access Control policy in order to block that application.
23. Open your ACL and click Add Rule.
24. Set the rule action to Block, and then click on the Applications

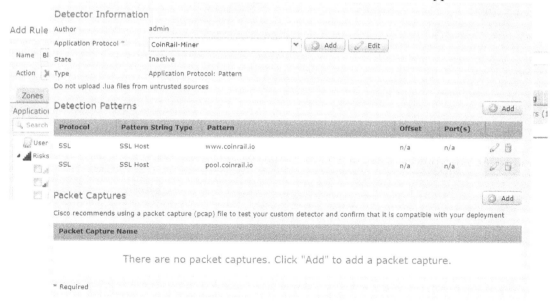

Add Rule

Detector Information

Author   admin

Application Protocol *   CoinRail-Miner   Add   Edit

Name   Bl

State   Inactive

Action

Type   Application Protocol: Pattern

Zones

Do not upload .lua files from untrusted sources

Applicatio

Detection Patterns   Add

Search

Protocol	Pattern String Type	Pattern	Offset	Port(s)	
SSL	SSL Host	www.coinrail.io	n/a	n/a	
SSL	SSL Host	pool.coinrail.io	n/a	n/a	

User

Risks

Packet Captures   Add

Cisco recommends using a packet capture (pcap) file to test your custom detector and confirm that it is compatible with your deployment

Packet Capture Name

There are no packet captures. Click "Add" to add a packet capture.

* Required

tab, find the Coinrail-Miner app, and choose Add to Rule.

25. Click on the Logging tab and click on Log at the beginning of the connection
26. Add the rule anywhere in the ACP, but above your last rule at a minimum.
27. Redeploy your policies to your FTD device.

Verifying Your Custom Application Detector

1. After deployment is complete, go back to your inside host, and with your developer window open, go to **bitcoinhelp.it** again.
2. You should see that `coinrail.min.js` has failed.

3. Go to the FMC and **Analysis>Connection Events** and see the block

Block	10.18.118.20	92.222.84.168	FRA	Inside	Outside
Block	10.18.118.20	92.222.84.168	FRA	Inside	Outside
Block	10.18.118.20	92.222.84.168	FRA	Inside	Outside
Block	10.18.118.20	92.222.84.168	FRA	Inside	Outside

(same output cont)->

Inside	Outside	51166 / tcp	443 (https) / tcp	HTTPS	SSL client	CoinrailMiner	https://pool.coinrail.io
Inside	Outside	51166 / tcp	443 (https) / tcp	HTTPS	SSL client	CoinrailMiner	https://pool.coinrail.io
Inside	Outside	51159 / tcp	443 (https) / tcp	HTTPS	SSL client	CoinrailMiner	https://pool.coinrail.io
Inside	Outside	51159 / tcp	443 (https) / tcp	HTTPS	SSL client	CoinrailMiner	https://pool.coinrail.io

4. Go to Table View of Connection Events to see the web application and more details of the event.

Summary

Firepower discovery and identity includes many parts: host identity sources, realms, controlling users with ISE/ISE-PIC, controlling users with captive portal, controlling users with remote access VPN, controlling users with terminal server agent, controlling users with user agent, identity policies, and finally, network discovery (Firepower) policies. Whew that's a lot of discovery, and in this chapter we added application discovery, which finished our discovery policies.

Chapter 37: Cisco Firepower SafeSearch

Major search engines and content delivery services give us ways to restrict search results and website content. Take CIPA, the Children's Internet Protection Act as a prime example that's used by most schools. The thing is, when restrictions like these are implemented by services and content providers, they can *only* be enforced through tools that work for individual browsers or users.

But the Firepower System smashes through those limitations by handing you control over your entire network!

Firepower enables you to enforce:

Safe Search
Supported in many major search engines, this service filters out explicit and adult-oriented content that most business, government and education environments classify as forbidden. The system doesn't restrict a user's ability to access the home pages for supported search engines.

YouTube EDU
A service that filters YouTube content for educational environments, that enables schools to set access for educational content and limit access to noneducational content. YouTube EDU is different from YouTube Restricted Mode, which enforces restrictions on YouTube searches as part of Google's Safe Search feature. YouTube Restricted Mode is a subfeature

of Safe Search. With YouTube EDU, users access the YouTube EDU home page, rather than the standard YouTube home page.

There are two ways to configure the system to enforce these features:

Method: Access Control Rules
Content restriction features communicate the restricted status of a search or content query via an element in the request URI, an associated cookie or a custom HTTP header element. You can configure access control rules to modify these elements as the system processes traffic.

Method: DNS Sinkhole
For Google searches, you can configure the system to redirect traffic to the Google SafeSearch Virtual IP Address (VIP), which imposes filters for Safe Search including YouTube Restricted Mode. We covered DNS Sinkholes in chapter x in volume I.

Okay, so I'm going to walk you through three specialized, practical labs that'll really help sharpen your Access Control Rules skills:

- Configuring Google SafeSearch
- Configuring Youtube SafeSearch
- Verifying Google SafeSearch

Configuring Google SafeSearch

In this lab, you're going to configure your FTD host to filter out inappropriate content from search results by forcing users to use Browsers with SafeSearch enabled. Let's get started:

1. Go to your ACP, under Policies.

2. Open your last rule and click on the Application tab.

3. Select the SafeSearch link on the right.

4. Next check Enable Safe Search and Select Block as the Action for non-supported engines.

Note: These icons are disabled instead of dimmed if you choose any **Action** other than **Allow** for the rule. You can't enable Safe Search and YouTube EDU restrictions for the same access control rule.

5. Next, select the browsers in the Application Filters table. In the Application Filters type, "safesearch" and you'll see a supported and unsupported tag.

6. Choose "**safesearch supported'** plus, All apps matching the filter and then "Add to Rule". The Categories filter search engine is populated by default:

Note: You must have an active SSL policy for this to work!

7. Now, create a new SSL Policy Rule that's set to "Decrypt – Resign" with your SSL Certificate and make it your first rule.

8. Under Application Filters, select "search engine" as the Category, plus "All apps" matching the filter, then click "Add to Rule".

9. Save, but don't deploy yet! We're going to move on to the next lab first.

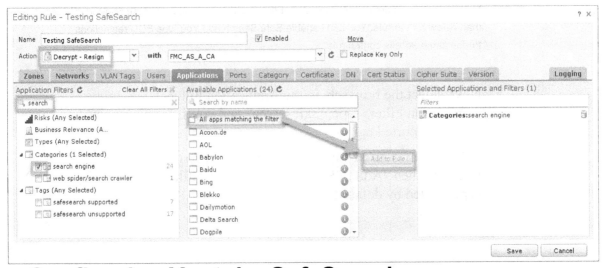

Configuring Youtube SafeSearch

1. Create an ACP Rule and on the Applications tab, click the YouTube EDU link.
2. Enable YouTube EDU.
3. Enter your YouTube EDU ID if you have one. For this lab, just use **1234567890:**

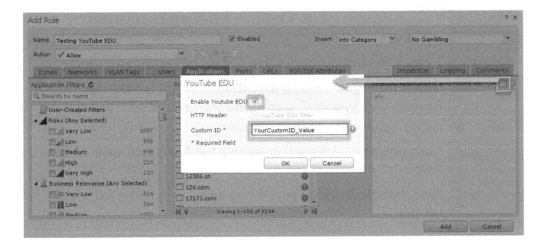

4. Next, add a second rule to your SSL policy for the YouTube safesearch:

5. Save your SSL policy and make sure it's applied in your ACP. After that, it's time to save and deploy your ACP!

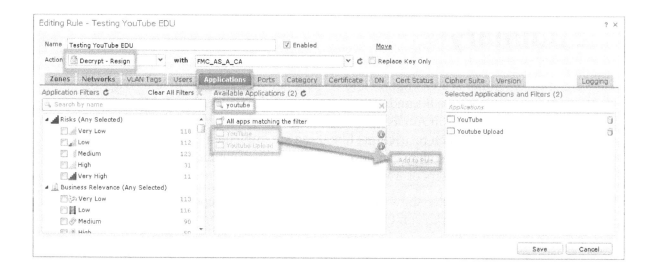

Verifying SafeSearch

Now we're going to verify that we can't disable SafeSearch from an Inside Host by going through the steps here:

1. RDP to an Inside host and open Chrome.

2. Go to Google.com, search for something and verify you see SafeSearch on in the right side of the screen.

3. You shouldn't be able to disable this feature! If you do, the browser should reload with the SafeSearch re-enabled:

Summary

Major search engines and content delivery services give us ways to restrict search results and website content. Take CIPA, the Children's Internet Protection Act as a prime example that's used by most schools. The thing is, when restrictions like these are implemented by services and content providers, they can *only* be enforced through tools that work for individual browsers or users.

This chapter showed you how to use Cisco Firepower to protect your corporate network from Google and Youtube searching.

Chapter 38: Cisco Firepower: Daily Steps for Network Analysis

I'm going to equip you with a great step-by-step guide for ensuring stability and efficiency on the Cisco Firepower/FTD platform. We'll cover all the steps you need to take each day to optimize your Firepower implementation at your organization. Following these steps will also help you to create and modify your security policies.

Six Network Analysis Steps to Start Your Day Off Right:

1. **Fix any health issues**

2. **Go to Context Explorer and set time to 1 day**
   - Resolve all indications of compromise
   - Learn network and apps
3. **Go to Connection Events – verifying time is expanding and 1 day**
   - Perform blacklist IPs and URLs
   - User education
   - Table view
   - Switch workflow
4. **Go to Connections>Security Intelligence Events**

- Table view
- User education
- Switch workflow

5. **Analysis Intrusion Events**
   - Check SID rule number
   - Find out the action
   - Possible user education on DNS sites
   - Documentation
   - Decide on action

6. **Malware Event analysis**
   - Verify files
   - Send to Talos if necessary or run your own sandbox

Step 1: Health Issues

Log in to your Cisco FMC to make sure your health status is green, not red as shown below. If it's green as shown below, awesome—move on to Step 2.

But if it's red, click the red explanation point and resolve each issue.

Looking at the example screenshot below, it's clear that there is a serious issue with an FTD device. If an error such as the one displayed below can't be fixed with some general troubleshooting and possibly rebooting, then you need to open a ticket with TAC asap.

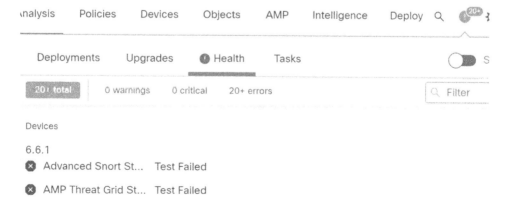

It's important to hold off on Step 2 until you've fixed all health issues.

Step 2: Context Explorer

From your FMC, go to **Analysis>Context Explorer**:

Analysis	Policies	Devices	Objects	AMP	Intelligence

Context Explorer	Hosts	Correlation
Unified Events	Network Map	Correlation Events
	Hosts	Allow List Events
Connections	Indications of Compromise	Allow List Violations
Events	Applications	Status
Security Intelligence Events	Application Details	

2a. Set time

On the right, change the time to 1 day. You want to check out the data from the past 24 hours every morning. If you do this consistently, it gets so much easier to find anything abnormal for your network!

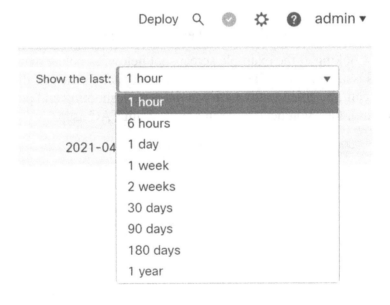

2b. Resolve all indications of compromise

There at the top is a nice graph of traffic. The blue line is your data and the red is attacks. Here, your mission is to optimize your policies so your data line is higher than the red line.

Your Indications of Compromise (IoC) graph is right there under the traffic graph. Drill down into each event and start eliminating the noise by tuning out the false positives.

Left click on each color in the graph and fix each snag until all IOCs are resolved:

Traffic and Intrusion Events over Time

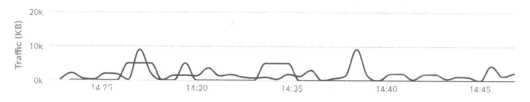

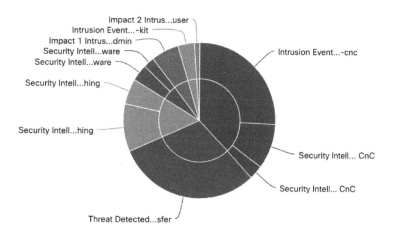

Hosts by Indication

2c. Verify your OS and top talkers

Next, scroll down to find your OS chart and the top talkers. There's nothing wrong here unless you don't know whom those top talkers are. If not, investigate and find out.

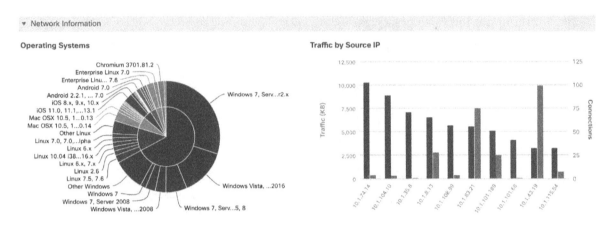

Below this is your connections log hits from your ACP rules and traffic from the destinations.

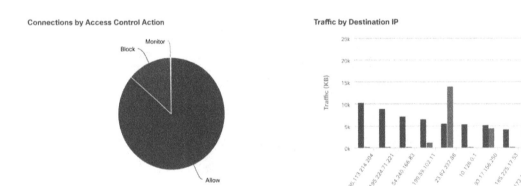

2d. Learn your application risk

Scroll down the page to start learning the application and network information found on the Context Explorer page. By watching the data found here every day, you can benchmark your network and catch anything out of the ordinary a whole lot faster:

2e. Learn about your SI objects

Find the top URLs and IPs by source. Verify top talkers so you'll know that if SI is configured correctly, all of this is dropped data. Some user education may be key here:

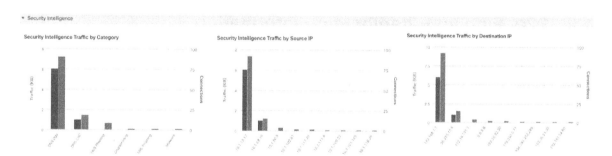

2f. Verify files

Now, scroll down again to verify the different types of files found on your network, the top file names, and the top files sent and received.

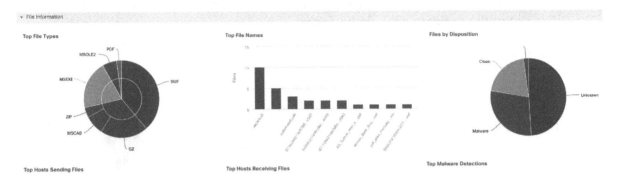

This information isn't really going to tell you if something is wrong. Again, you're looking for anything out of the ordinary. By closely following your application and file flow, you can create and optimize your file policy better.

2g. Find your geolocation information

Another factor you want to be vigilant about is which countries are either initiating connections or attempting to. This information majorly helps you create a solid security policy:

Take a look:

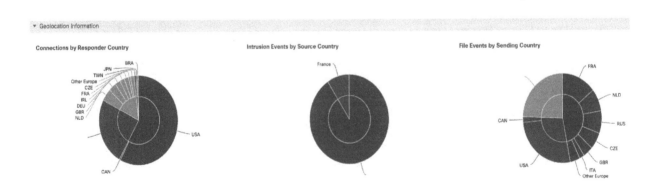

2h. Learn which URL categories are used

Use the information here to help create your URL rules and tweak your security policy if necessary:

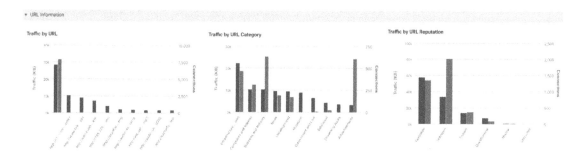

Step 3: Connection Events

From your FMC navigate to **Analysis>Connections>Events**:

Analysis	Policies	Devices	Objects	AMP	Intelligence

Context Explorer	Hosts	Correlation
Unified Events	Network Map	Correlation Events
	Hosts	Allow List Events
Connections	Indications of Compromise	Allow List Violations
Events	Applications	Status
Security Intelligence Events	Application Details	
	Servers	Advanced
Intrusions	Host Attributes	Custom Workflows

3a. Set event time to 1 day

The right side of the Connection Events page tells you that verifying time is expanding and is set to 1 day. The default is 1 hour. Click the URL bar and change the time to 1 day:

Bookmark This Page | Reporting | Dashboard | View Bookmarks | Search

Predefined Searches ▾

‖ 2021-03-06 16:35:00 - 2021-04-06 11:38:30
Expanding

Change the time via this next pop-up screen and click Apply

Events Time Window   Preferences

Expanding Time Window	▼

Start Time

2021-03-06 16:35	16 ↑↓ : 35 ↑↓

|< <   March 2021   > >|

SU	MO	TU	WE	TH	FR	SA
28	1	2	3	4	5	6
7	8	9	10	11	12	13
14	15	16	17	18	19	20
21	22	23	24	25	26	27
28	29	30	31	1	2	3

End Time ☐

2021-04-06 16:37

|< <   April 2021   > >|

SU	MO	TU	WE	TH	FR	SA
28	29	30	31	1	2	3
4	5	6	7	8	9	10
11	12	13	14	15	16	17
18	19	20	21	22	23	24
25	26	27	28	29	30	1

Presets

Last	Current
1 hour	Day
6 hours	Week
1 day	Month
1 week	**Synchronize with**
2 weeks	Audit Log Time Window
1 month	Health Monitoring Time Window

3b. Go through the connection events

Now watch the events that are generated from your ACP unfold in your connection events screen. Pay attention to the action, reason and IPs. Your objective is to really understand your network and verify your traffic:

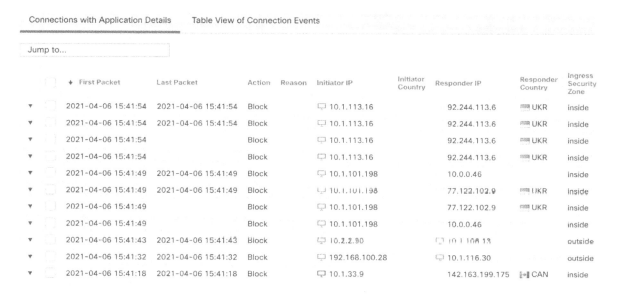

Connections with Application Details   Table View of Connection Events

Jump to...

		♦ First Packet	Last Packet	Action	Reason	Initiator IP	Initiator Country	Responder IP	Responder Country	Ingress Security Zone
▼		2021-04-06 15:41:54	2021-04-06 15:41:54	Block		10.1.113.16		92.244.113.6	UKR	inside
▼		2021-04-06 15:41:54	2021-04-06 15:41:54	Block		10.1.113.16		92.244.113.6	UKR	inside
▼		2021-04-06 15:41:54		Block		10.1.113.16		92.244.113.6	UKR	inside
▼		2021-04-06 15:41:54		Block		10.1.113.16		92.244.113.6	UKR	inside
▼		2021-04-06 15:41:49	2021-04-06 15:41:49	Block		10.1.101.198		10.0.0.46		inside
▼		2021-04-06 15:41:49	2021-04-06 15:41:49	Block		10.1.101.198		77.122.102.9	UKR	inside
▼		2021-04-06 15:41:49		Block		10.1.101.198		77.122.102.9	UKR	inside
▼		2021-04-06 15:41:49		Block		10.1.101.198		10.0.0.46		inside
▼		2021-04-06 15:41:43	2021-04-06 15:41:43	Block		10.2.2.90		10.1.108.13		outside
▼		2021-04-06 15:41:32	2021-04-06 15:41:32	Block		192.168.100.28		10.1.116.30		outside
▼		2021-04-06 15:41:18	2021-04-06 15:41:18	Block		10.1.33.9		142.163.199.175	CAN	inside

3c. Perform blacklist IPs and URLs

Next you want to find blocked traffic and blacklist the IPs. But before you do that, run a WHOIS on the initiator IP to make sure you are not blocking your ISP!

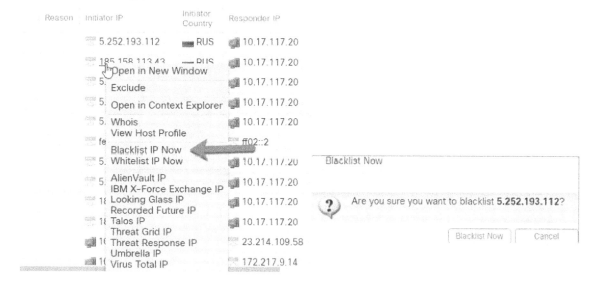

3d. Continue to audit connection events to find any that provide insight into your users.

For instance: "Bob, what the heck is *'chickenkiller'* and why are you going there every day? What's wrong with you?" All good questions....

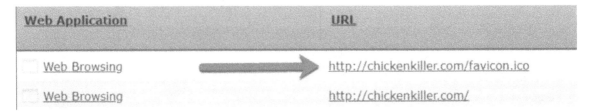

Web Application	URL
Web Browsing	http://chickenkiller.com/favicon.ico
Web Browsing	http://chickenkiller.com/

3e. Click on Table view

If you have packets and you need to find the ACP rule that generated them, go to Table view of Connection Events, scroll to the right, and find the ACP policy and ACP rule, IPS rule and NAP policy responsible. You can now take action on those rules, if necessary.

; ×	Access Control × Policy	Access Control Rule ×	Network Analysis × Policy	Prefilter × Policy	Tunnel/Prefilter × Rule
	ACP 19	ips and file	19	19	
	ACP 19	ips and file	19	19	Default Action
	ACP 19	ips and file, Log	19	19	Default Action
	ACP 19	ips and file, Log	19	19	Default Action
	ACP 19	ips and file	19	19	Default Action
	ACP 19	ips and file, Log	19	19	

3f. Click on Switch Workflow

From Connection Events, there's a bunch of different workflows you can use to find information regarding you network:

Again, there might not be anything ugly here—unless you find something and don't understand the output.

There are 15 different screens that you can use to learn about and find things like hosts associated with huge usage and a high amount of connections to remote servers.

Connection Events

Connection Events
Connections by Application
Connections by Initiator ·
Connections by Port
Connections by Responder
Connections over Time
Traffic by Application
Traffic by Initiator
Traffic by Port
Traffic by Responder
Traffic over Time
Unique Initiators by Responder
Unique Responders by Initiator

Seriously take time to explore and learn this information. You won't catch something wrong here if you don't research and understand the data facing you.

Here's a great example of Connection by Initiator. The only potential problem here is if you don't know who 10.19.119.20 is and why they're showing as top initiator. Spend the time to find out

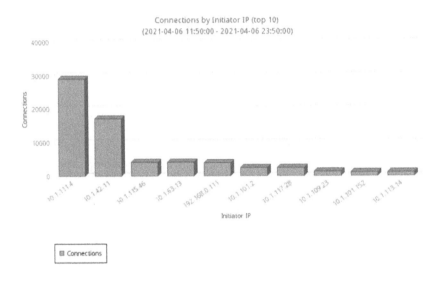

Step 4: Security Intelligence

You probably won't have to take action in this section because everything in here should already be blocked by the Blacklist by IP, ULR or DNS objects. Still important to verify though, so follow along.

4a. Navigate to Connections>Security Intelligence Events:

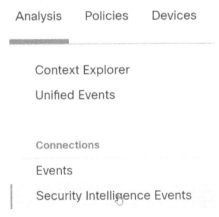

Once you've done that, this screen will appear. Notice the action, reason, and IPs. Right now you're focused on discovering and verifying exactly what your blacklists are blocking:

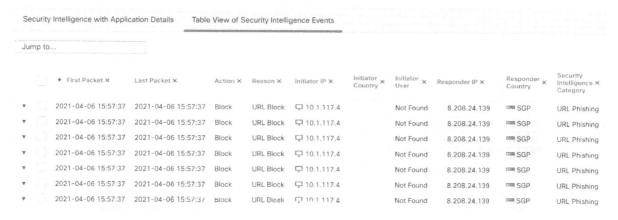

Security Intelligence Events (switch workflow)

No Search Constraints (Edit Search)

Security Intelligence with Application Details | Table View of Security Intelligence Events

Jump to...

		↓ First Packet	Last Packet	Action	Reason	Initiator IP	Initiator Country	Responder IP	Responder Country	Security Intelligence Category
▼		2021-04-06 15:57:00		Block	IP Block	🖥 10.1.103.12		⊗ 89.105.203.184	NLD	CnC
▼		2021-04-06 15:56:58		Block	IP Block	🖥 10.1.103.12		⊗ 89.105.203.184	NLD	CnC
▼		2021-04-06 15:55:40	2021-04-06 15:55:40	Block	URL Block	🖥 10.1.117.27		46.4.115.108	DEU	URL Malware
▼		2021-04-06 15:35:37		Block	IP Block	🖥 10.1.101.93		⊗ 199.59.242.150	USA	Cryptomining
▼		2021-04-06 15:31:37		Block	DNS Block	🖥 10.1.12.10		192.203.230.10	USA	DNS CnC
▼		2021-04-06 15:26:53	2021-04-06 15:31:54	Block	URL Block	🖥 10.1.38.10		185.244.149.74	ROU	URL Malware

4b. Click on Table view

From the URL bar, click on **Table View of Security Intelligence Events**:

Security Intelligence with Application Details | Table View of Security Intelligence Events

Jump to...

		↓ First Packet ×	Last Packet ×	Action ×	Reason ×	Initiator IP ×	Initiator Country ×	Initiator User ×	Responder IP ×	Responder Country ×	Security Intelligence × Category
▼		2021-04-06 15:57:37	2021-04-06 15:57:37	Block	URL Block	🖥 10.1.117.4		Not Found	8.208.24.139	SGP	URL Phishing
▼		2021-04-06 15:57:37	2021-04-06 15:57:37	Block	URL Block	🖥 10.1.117.4		Not Found	8.208.24.139	SGP	URL Phishing
▼		2021-04-06 15:57:37	2021-04-06 15:57:37	Block	URL Block	🖥 10.1.117.4		Not Found	8.208.24.139	SGP	URL Phishing
▼		2021-04-06 15:57:37	2021-04-06 15:57:37	Block	URL Block	🖥 10.1.117.4		Not Found	8.208.24.139	SGP	URL Phishing
▼		2021-04-06 15:57:37	2021-04-06 15:57:37	Block	URL Block	🖥 10.1.117.4		Not Found	8.208.24.139	SGP	URL Phishing
▼		2021-04-06 15:57:37	2021-04-06 15:57:37	Block	URL Block	🖥 10.1.117.4		Not Found	8.208.24.139	SGP	URL Phishing
▼		2021-04-06 15:57:37	2021-04-06 15:57:37	Block	URL Block	🖥 10.1.117.4		Not Found	8.208.24.139	SGP	URL Phishing

You're basically verifying that all of the packets are being blocked. Scroll to the right and you'll uncover more information like the objects that were triggered and the zones that were involved.

Even further to the right, you'll find vital information like the ACP and actual rule that triggered the block.

4c. User education

If you monitor URLs, SI will also tell you about any that are blocked. Most of the time, users will visit known CnC sites only to find they've been blocked, so there's really nothing more to do except contact the user who's persistently trying to visit a nasty malware-ridden site to find out why.

Once users know you're watching them and that unpleasant things can happen to them for going places they shouldn't, you'll definitely see fewer events being triggered.

4d. Switch workflow

Head over to **Analysis>Security Intelligence Events** and click on Switch Workflow to get to the screen after this one:

Browse each option to get accustomed to your traffic.

Your goal here is to have your network's normal patterns down so well you'll know something is off right away.

Step 5: Intrusion events

This is probably one of the most important things you'll do each morning. Pretty detailed too because you've got to sift through every IPS event that's occurred and do something about it.

Start by going to **Analysis>Intrusion>Events** and make sure your time is expanding and set to one day:

Analysis	Policies	Devices	Objects	Intelligence

Context Explorer	Hosts
	Network Map
Connections	Hosts
Events	Indications of Compromise
Security Intelligence Events	Applications
	Application Details
Intrusions	Servers
Events	Host Attributes
Reviewed Events	Discovery Events
Clipboard	Vulnerabilities
Incidents	Third-Party Vulnerabilities

5a.
Check SID rule number

On the events page, you'll see all the IPS and PreProcessor events that occurred on your network. Check out each event, focusing on the snort ID (SID). We see the SID 42944 on top here:

	Message	↓ Priority	Classification	Cou
▼ ☐	OS-WINDOWS Microsoft Windows SMB remote code execution attempt (1:42944:2)	high	Attempted Administrator Privilege Gain	5
▼ ☐	EXPLOIT-KIT Magnitude exploit kit Internet Explorer exploit attempt (1:37918:2)	high	Attempted Administrator Privilege Gain	2
▼ ☐	MALWARE-CNC Win.Trojan.CryptoWall variant outbound connection (1:34318:5)	high	A Network Trojan was Detected	20
▼ ☐	MALWARE-CNC DNS suspicious .bit tcp dns query (1:42841:6)	high	A Network Trojan was Detected	15
▼ ☐	MALWARE-CNC Win.Trojan.HawkEye keylogger variant outbound connection (1:33886:3)	high	A Network Trojan was Detected	6
▼ ☐	MALWARE-OTHER Double HTTP Server declared (1:26369:2)	high	A Network Trojan was Detected	6

The higher the SID number is, the newer the rule is. A higher value also indicates how seriously you should take the event, but that's only a rule of thumb, all active rules could be serious.

5b. Determine the action

It's key to know what the Snort process did with the packets that generated an event. In the screen shown below, click on the box on the left side of an event to view the inline result of these packets as shown in this next screen.

	↓ Time ✕	Priority ✕	Impact ✕	Inline Result ✕	Source IP ✕	Sc Cc
▼ ☐	2021-04-06 22:53:27	high	①	↓ dropped	🖵 10.1.51.15	
▼ ☐	2021-04-06 18:56:46	high	①	↓	🖵 10.1.101.205	
▼ ☐	2021-04-06 17:59:41	high	①	↓	🖵 10.1.108.1	
▼ ☐	2021-04-06 15:18:06	high	①	↓	🖵 10.1.29.8	
▼ ☐	2021-04-06 15:01:38	high	①	↓	🖵 10.1.18.7	

Notice these are dropping so the IPS policy is in Prevention instead of Detection, so by hovering over the inline result here you'll see "Dropped" (this means Snort wants to drop these packets and the rule that triggered this event is set to be a drop rule), and in Detection mode, you'd see "would have dropped" instead.

5c. Possible user education about DNS sites

The goal here is to look for sites that were triggered by user action and decide if there's an opportunity to educate the user doing the triggering. First, make sure the packets were dropped and will continue to be, then inform the proper powers that be about what they should tell the problem user to make them less of a threat.

5d. Documentation

Open the packets in the Snort event. From Rule Actions, right click and then choose Rule Documentation to find out about the false positive reliability, plus intel on the possible attack. Remember, before you blacklist an IP because of an event, check the WHOIS to identify it first:

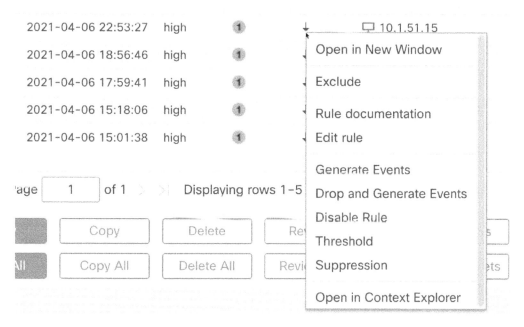

5e. Decide on action

You've got to do something here, even if it's just to verify that the rule is dropping and will continue to.

You might decide to blacklist a host, change the rule by disabling it, changing it to Generate events, or just have a little heart-to-heart with the pesky user.

Next, mark the event as reviewed by clicking on Review:

Step 6: Malware Analysis

To verify the file policy and file events, go to **Analysis>Files>Malware Events**:

Analysis	Policies	Devices	Objects	Intelligence

Context Explorer	Hosts
	Network Map
Connections	Hosts
Events	Indications of Compromise
Security Intelligence Events	Applications
	Application Details
Intrusions	Servers
Events	Host Attributes
Reviewed Events	Discovery Events
Clipboard	Vulnerabilities
Incidents	Third-Party Vulnerabilities
Files	Users
Malware Events	Active Sessions
File Events	Users
Captured Files	User Activity
Network File Trajectory	Indications of Compromise

6a. Verify SHAs

From the Malware Events page, you can verify the SHAs found. You can also right-click and white- or blacklist these files using the custom detecting lists in Objects.

On the right, there's a red circle with a dot in the middle that means the file has been download to the FMC:

Click on the file to gather more information like the trajectory the file has taken through your network.

	Detection Name	File Name	File SHA256	File Type	♦ Count
▼	Swf.Exploit.Rigek::malicious.tht.talos		○ b3669ec8...e2839b5f	SWF	8
▼	Win.Dropper.Tiny::1201	b69502174f6cdbc410f3c99556224b60	○ 2a311ea2...a8b07537	MSEXE	4
▼	W32.3EC3AECBE8-100.SBX.TG	d311d9a21d67a8ee05edeed17275d583	○ 3ec3aecb...c77088ca	MSEXE	4
▼	Win.Trojan.Nuclear::in01	qxrWmriaPVb2cRI.wxw1uR_EEnOuZR9mgVr3ReB3-1yiVm9H15-VbU3vyIDw4RGW3	○ 951b961f...d4a84184	ZIP	2
▼	Win.Exploit.Genericgb::95.sbx.tg	55fdd7ebca026cab5447075f560c545b0706555f5055555900015e525705575b	○ 9a59f2e4...04795fed	JAR	2
▼	Win.Exploit.Generic::malicious.tht.talos	xPF_HAXN7TK9bMAgBjZDwQzO1-Wf5GvrN5_IIRelhbrhqHAIWyTDbaOBMPWitjnX	○ 5624d9b8...fcbd86e0	ZIP	2
▼	Win.Exploit.Generic::in01	767aa23042721a9b5644565a530901020e01075a5550030b0203065057515607	○ 1697a5a0...0152c1ff	JAR	2
▼	Win.Dropper.Kovter::1201		○ 1ecc891e...af60cc69	MSEXE	2
▼	Win.Dropper.Generic::222355.in02	form.msi	○ 11f877eb...11d09286	MSOLE2	2

6b. Verify files

Head over to **Analysis>Files>File Events** and verify the file types being monitored. You're going to use this vital information to help you create your file policy and modify it later on.

Zero in on the categories, types, and dispositions as well as the action of each file monitored on your FMC:

Jump to...

	Category	Type	♦ Disposition	Action
▼	Executables	MSEXE	Clean	Malware Cloud Lookup
▼	Archive	7Z	Clean	Malware Cloud Lookup
▼	Graphics	BMP	Clean	Malware Cloud Lookup

Analysis>Files>Captured Files will reveal the current disposition of a known SHA256:

Jump to...

	♦ Threat Score	Type	Category
▼	●●●● Very High	MSEXE	Executables
▼	●●●● Very High	SWF	Multimedia
▼	●●●● Very High	MSOLE2	Office Documents
▼	●●●● Very High	PDF	PDF files
▼	●●●● Very High	JAR	Archive

6c. Send to Talos if needed

Click on an SHA to open up the file information and get the next screen. Select the cloud icon to send the actual file to Talos to run in their sandbox. You can send up to 100 files a day, per FTD device. The blue cloud resends the file to Talos to run again.

Finally, look at the bottom of the Trajectory section to find out where the file went in your network:

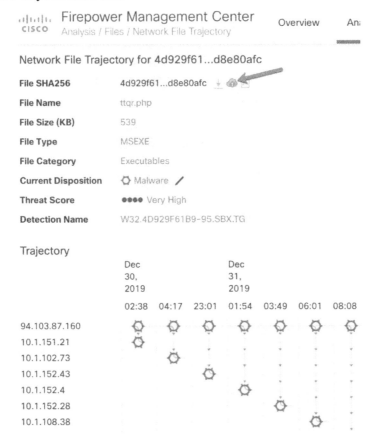

6d. Or run it in your own sandbox

Hit the down arrow icon on the top to download the file and move it onto your network for a run in your own sandbox.

It will show up as a zip file with a default password of "infected". You can change that if you want to in your User Preferences.

Optionally: Verify the FMC Updates and Cisco Known Bugs

Every few weeks, navigate over to **Overview>Dashboards** and then to the **Status** tab where you'll:

- Verify the product updates and inform anyone that needs to know about any new updates that show up and what's recommended for the current Cisco Firepower products. Also, the appliance information on the FMC and Devices.

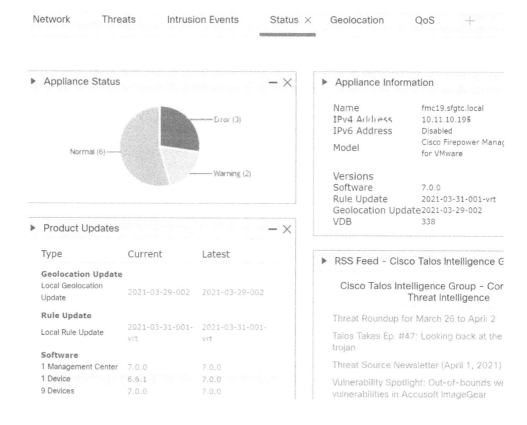

447

TODD LAMMLE
Advanced Cisco Security Services